Kinship and Gender

An Introduction

Linda Stone

Washington State University

WestviewPress

A Division of HarperCollins*Publishers*

Copyright © 1997 by Westview Press, A Division of HarperCollins Publishers, Inc.

Published in 1997 in the United States of America by Westview Press, 5500 Central Avenue, Boulder, Colorado 80301-2877, and in the United Kingdom by Westview Press, 12 Hid's Copse Road, Cumnor Hill, Oxford OX2 9JJ

Library of Congress Cataloging-in-Publication Data
Stone, Linda, 1947–
    Kinship and gender : an introduction / Linda Stone.
        p.   cm.
    Includes bibliographical references (p.   ) and index.
    ISBN 0-8133-2858-6 (hc)—ISBN 0-8133-2859-4 (pbk.)
    1. Kinship.   2. Sex role.   3. Gender identity.   I. Title.
GN487.S76   1997
305.3—dc21   96-52968
                                                                                        CIP

The paper used in this publication meets the requirements of the American National Standard for Permanence of Paper for Printed Library Materials Z39.48-1984.

10   9   8   7   6   5   4   3   2   1

Dedicated to the memory of
Margaret Ruth Stone

Contents

Illustrations

Tables

Photos

Preface

This book has come about through my teaching an undergraduate anthropology course, "Kinship and Gender," over a ten-year-period. I learned in this course that kinship, often a difficult topic to teach and painful to students, came alive for students in a new way when focused on issues of gender. I also found that students easily understood that a cross-cultural study of gender benefits from a knowledge of kinship.

The book is designed for undergraduate courses in kinship, gender, or, as with my course, the two combined. Except for the topic of kinship terminology, which is not treated here, it provides a basic introduction to anthropological kinship. It also includes nine in-depth ethnographic case studies to give students a better sense of the intricate interconnections between kinship and gender among a variety of cultural groups.

The book may be used as a supplementary text in courses that focus on gender cross-culturally but do not otherwise deal with kinship. However, in these courses, instructors might wish to skip over Chapter 5 ("Double and Cognatic Descent") since the material there on kinship is more technical and complex than that in other chapters.

In some respects I could not have chosen a more difficult time to write an introductory text on kinship and gender. Research and publication on gender are exploding, with new paths of study rapidly emerging and critiques of all previous concepts causing many to wonder where the field can find its bearings. Meanwhile, kinship, possibly the most tortured topic in anthropology, nearly slipped off the edge of professional interest. Yet, particularly when linked with gender, kinship is now seeing a revival; but if so, it will be a revival that reshapes kinship studies through new feminist and postmodernist challenges. In this introductory text I could not delve into current theoretical issues and debates of interest to professional readers. However, I have tried to give students a sense of the directions that contemporary investigations of kinship and gender are taking.

For their helpful comments on earlier versions of the manuscript I thank Lillian A. Ackerman, Barry S. Hewlett, Diane E. King, Jeannette Mageo, and Nancy P. McKee. A special thanks also goes to Karen Sinclair for her comments on the manuscript and for her inspiration and encouragement throughout this project. For their assistance with particular case studies, I am grateful to Nancy E. Levine, Kathryn Meyer, and Miranda Warburton. In addition, I thank James Rotholz for his assistance with the library research. For his considerable help and support during the preparation of the book, I am deeply grateful to my husband, Paul F. Lurquin. Finally, I thank Karen Sinclair's undergraduate students at Eastern Michigan University and my undergraduate students at Washington State University, who gave me valuable feedback on particular chapters.

Linda Stone

1

Gender, Reproduction, and Kinship

Women and men today are raising new questions about gender identity and the status of the sexes. In the process of forming new questions, we have seen a growth of interest in approaching the subject both cross-culturally and historically. This approach has been essential in that it allows us to address some of the larger concerns, such as whether and to what extent women have been universally subjugated to men or treated as "second-class citizens." In addition, many students have sought to look beyond the confines of their own cultures and times in order to gain a broader perspective on particular gender issues in their own societies.

As a field of study, gender refers not only to people's understandings of the categories "male" and "female" but also to the ways in which these understandings are interwoven with other dimensions of social and cultural life. The latter include the social roles that women and men play, the values surrounding male and female activities, and people's particular conceptions of the nature and meaning of sexual differences.[1] All of these aspects of gender vary widely from culture to culture.

In this book I explore gender cross-culturally through the framework of kinship. Specifically, I seek to introduce new ways in which some cross-cultural variations in gender can be understood. Kinship is an old, established specialization in anthropology, noted more for its difficult jargon and tortuous diagrams than for the light it sheds on gender. Indeed, A. F. Robertson (1991: 3) accuses anthropologists of having "punished generations of students with the complexities of 'kinship and marriage' in tribal

---

[1] It was once common to distinguish "gender," understood as a cultural construct that varied from culture to culture, from "sex," or the biological facts of life, presumed to be the same everywhere (Oakley 1972). But some scholars have more recently suggested that different cultures have different ways of constructing sex as well as gender (Laqueur 1990) and that this variation must be taken into account in the study of gender. For this reason, Yanagisako and Collier (1990) suggest that the distinction between sex and gender should not be maintained.

and peasant communities." Of course, my intention is not to punish yet another generation of students but, instead, to show that kinship, when stripped of certain of its more advanced "complexities" and focused on the subject of gender, can be both interesting and illuminating.

There are many areas in which the study of kinship and the study of gender easily intersect, but the one I emphasize in this book is reproduction. In all societies, human offspring are a vital concern; in fact, the very survival of any society depends on successful reproduction. And in all societies human reproduction is regulated. Laws, norms, and cultural ideologies define where, when, and in what contexts heterosexual intercourse is permitted or prohibited, encouraged or discouraged. When intercourse results in reproduction, a whole host of laws, norms, and values come into play to define this situation, especially as it relates to the allocation of children to particular individuals or groups. The meanings of "marriage" and "divorce," even the idea of "legitimacy," are all a part of how different human groups handle reproduction. Kinship is everywhere a part of the social and cultural management of reproduction and, as such, is intimately interlinked with gender. A primary concern of the book, then, is the sexual and reproductive roles of women and men. We will see how kinship shapes these roles and, in the process, affects gender.

Both ambivalence and controversy have surrounded the discussion of reproductive roles in relation to gender status. We know that, biologically speaking, women play a special role in reproduction—that they, and not men, undergo pregnancy and childbirth. Some scholars hold that gender is rooted in these biological facts of life, or that gender is rooted in sex differences. Consider Alice Rossi's (1977, 1985) work, which focuses on uncovering the influences of biological factors on women's behavior. She writes, for example, about how pregnancy stimulates certain maternal responses in women. But most social scientists feel that studies of biology do not go very far in accounting for differences in gender, as these differences vary considerably across cultures and, in their view, are largely learned. Barbara Miller (1993: 22) summarizes this view: "A simple rule of science is that variables (sex and gender hierarchies) cannot be explained by constants (genitals and chromosomes)." Some writers have shied away from discussion of reproduction, not wishing to fuel the notion that "biology is destiny." They are concerned that Rossi's approach can be used to justify the subordination of women as "natural," inevitable, and unchangeable. By contrast, their approach minimizes the difference in men's and women's reproductive roles (Rothman 1987) and stresses that, just because women get pregnant and give birth, it does not necessarily follow that they must be the primary caretakers of children, remain confined to the home, or be excluded from important political and economic pursuits. In particular, these writers argue that a subordinate status of women is not biologically rooted but socially imposed (or imposed by men).

Still other writers reject the idea that biology determines gender but nevertheless hold that women's reproductive roles *do* work as an instrument of their oppression or subordination to men. Some, most notably Michele Rosaldo (1974), claimed that women's reproductive roles confine them to the home and to domestic tasks. They argued that this domestic, "private sphere" of women is everywhere less valued than the "public sphere" of men, or the broader male world of politics and extra-domestic authority. The idea was that the male public sphere is superior because it encompasses the female domestic realm and involves economic and political activities of concern to larger social groups. However, critics countered that not all societies exhibit such a sharp division between private and public "spheres," that women in some societies do have public roles, and that female domestic activities are not necessarily everywhere devalued. Rosaldo (1980) came to agree with many of these criticisms; in particular, she concurred that gender conflicts in relation to a private/public dichotomy may be a characteristic of Euro-American society rather than a human universal.

Since that time, many have come to question not only whether a subordination of women was universal but also along what criteria such a claim could ever be made. How should we define the "status" of women, especially cross-culturally? Women in a particular society might be seen as "oppressed" by outsiders and yet have a very different view of their own situation and "status." In addition, it has become clear that women, even within one society, can differ widely not only in class or ethnicity but also in their perceptions of gender. For that matter, any woman's "status" will vary according to the different roles she plays within her society and the different situations she encounters. Faced with these kinds of considerations, studies of gender subsequently moved away from the issue of whether and in what sense there is a universal subordination of women, focusing instead on the different interests and strategies of women and men, as well as on gender in relation to other social divisions such as race, ethnicity, class, and age (di Leonardo 1991: 18; Lamphere 1993: 72).

In contrast to Rosaldo, others (e.g., Moen 1979) have argued that women are oppressed, not because their reproductive and domestic roles are devalued but precisely because their reproduction is everywhere highly valued socially and thus controlled by men. Men have power over women because men are in greater control of the political and economic forces that control human reproduction; or, men seek to control women in order to control reproduction (Robertson 1991: 41). Faye Ginsburg and Rayna Rapp (1995) have also looked at human reproduction in terms of the forces regulating it and the effects of this control on individuals and groups. But they go far beyond a simple statement of male dominance over women to suggest many ways in which global and international processes influence reproduction, affecting not only relations of gender but also relations of class and race. Indeed, the contributors to their book demonstrate numerous ways in which social inequalities are perpetrated through the politics of reproduction.

Human reproduction is clearly important to social life, yet its connections to gender remain controversial. We will encounter some additional debates in subsequent chapters. For now, however, I offer my own position: Although biology is not destiny, a male/female difference in reproduction is universal and everywhere affects gender. But the way in which this difference is related to gender is not everywhere the same. Local conceptions of and interests in reproduction, and the meaning it has to and for men, women, and social relations generally, do show considerable variation across time and place.

Although I thus agree with most other anthropologists that both kinship and gender are culturally constructed, I stop short of Jane Collier and Sylvia Yanagisako (1987), who argue that the study of kinship and gender should not be positioned with reference to biological "facts" of reproduction. These authors hold that biological "facts of life" are themselves culturally constructed and therefore cannot be taken for granted in a study of kinship or gender in any society.[2] They emphasize that different cultures may have different ideas about what counts as sexual differences between males and females, as well as different notions about the nature of human reproduction itself, and hence that each culture must be approached on its own terms in the study of kinship and gender. Their points are valuable and they raise fundamental issues that must be considered seriously. But my view is that a male/female difference in reproduction is universal (however varied the cultural constructions of this difference might be) and that on the basis of this "fact" we can begin to make meaningful cross-cultural comparisons.

In drawing out the connections between kinship and gender in the chapters ahead, I focus on two dimensions of reproduction with regard to women. One is women's sexuality and the other is women's fertility, or reproductive capacity. My aim is not only to show how various human groups perceive, evaluate, or argue over these two dimensions of womanhood but also, more specifically, to consider how cultural ideas about female sexuality and reproductive capacity are related in different societies. In some, female sexuality appears to be in the service of fertility, whereas in others a woman's sexual behavior can devalue her reproduction. For example, in Euro-American culture, female sexuality and fertility historically

---

[2] Collier and Yanagisako (1987) built upon the earlier work of David Schneider (1984) in kinship. Schneider argued that anthropologists influenced by Western culture perceive kinship in terms of biological or biogenetic relationships, but that such relationships cannot be assumed to apply to other cultures in the same way or to the same extent. Collier and Yanagisako directed a similar critique against the concept of gender. For a critique of their position, see Scheffler (1991).

seem to have been at odds with one another (see Chapter 7). Meanwhile, new reproductive technologies have resulted in further divisions and conflicts (see Chapter 8).

It is this particular relationship between female sexuality and reproduction, defined largely by the concerns of kin relationships and kin groups, that reveals a great deal about gender across cultures. The remainder of this chapter presents some basic terms and concepts in the study of kinship that I use as a foundation for exploring gender.

What Is Kinship?

Kinship is the recognition of a relationship between persons based on descent or marriage. If the relationship between one person and another is considered by them to involve descent, the two are **consanguineal** ("blood") relatives. If the relationship has been established through marriage, it is **affinal**. Thus, in American society, relatives such as one's mother, father, brother, sister, cousin, grandparent, and grandchild are consanguineal relatives, whereas one's father-in-law, sister-in-law, and so on are affinal relatives. In America one's uncle is a consanguineal relative if he is one's father's brother or mother's brother; but if the uncle is a father's sister's husband or mother's sister's husband, he is an affinal relative.

Societies vary in the extent to which kinship connections form the basis of their social, economic, and political structure. In some, kin groups *are* political groups, and economic relationships between people *are* kinship relationships. The whole fabric of such societies is woven with strands of kinship. In others, the major groups in the society are formed on other bases, and socioeconomic or political institutions are, at least technically speaking, separated from kinship. Yet even in these latter cases, kinship may play a powerful (if unofficial) role in economic and political life. It may be that a person lands a job or gets into a school because he or she is qualified "on paper," but in fact nearly everything valuable in society is distributed through links of kin. American society in particular seems intolerant of the use of kinship to achieve extra-domestic positions in public or professional life, but we are all aware of cases of this sort.

Although the official and other roles played by kinship vary considerably across societies, kinship relations *in general* entail the idea of rights and obligations. Some of these are codified in law, as when legal rules specify the order of succession to property when a person dies without a will. In other cases, persons may disagree about what constitutes their kin-based rights and obligations to one another. For example, my father's largely estranged half-brother thought he had a perpetual right to borrow money from any of his siblings, although they, to varying degrees, felt otherwise.

Still, the idea that links of kinship define rights and obligations between people is important: It is this aspect of kinship that gives it social force.

Kinship involves much more, however, than relations through descent and marriage, social structure, and rights and obligations between kin. Indeed, kinship is also an ideology of human relationships; it involves cultural ideas about how humans are created and the nature and meaning of their biological and moral connections with others. This dimension of kinship, its cross-cultural variations, and the implications for gender are reflected in different people's ideas about human procreation. For example, in her study of a group of people in Malaysia, Carol Laderman (1983, 1991) encountered the local belief that a baby begins not in the mother's womb but in the father's brain, where it exists in liquid form. She writes: "When I asked my midwife-teacher what that meant, she was equally startled. Imagine a grown, highly educated woman not knowing that a baby develops within its father's brain for forty days before its mother takes over! She pointed to her husband as an example, reminiscing about the time he carried their youngest child, and how he had craved sour foods during his pregnancy" (1991: ix).

The liquid fetus is thought to pass through the father's body and into the mother through sexual intercourse, a belief that has an important connection with gender. These people consider that in the process of their creation as humans, they acquire a rationality that distinguishes them from animals; and, furthermore, that men have more rationality than women. "It makes sense, therefore, for a baby to begin life within its father's brain . . . where it acquires rationality from a developed source" (Laderman 1991: 92). This example is but one of many illustrating the considerable variation among cultural beliefs about the nature and extent of male and female contributions to conception and fetal development.

Connections between gender and ideas about procreation can also be seen in Euro-American societies, despite the popular notion that Euro-Americans think about procreation only in a modern, scientific way. For instance, Carol Delaney (1991: 8) writes about the procreative metaphor of active, generative, male "seed" implanted in a passive, nurturing, female "soil" emphasized by the Western Christian tradition and other monotheistic traditions that portray a male God as creator of the world. This metaphor, which attributes a special life-giving force to males, continues to exist alongside our scientific understanding of human conception.

The ways in which a society defines and uses relations of kinship can collectively be called its kinship system. Along with ideas about reproduction, this system encompasses the rights and obligations recognized between kin or groups of kin, the categories into which kin are linguistically classified, and the rules, or norms, that specify modes of descent, patterns of residence, and forms of marriage. To understand these concepts, and to follow the discussions of kinship and gender throughout this book, the reader needs to become familiar with a basic tool of kinship studies: the Kinship Code.

The Kinship Code

Anthropologists use the elements of the Kinship Code to diagram kin relationships. The elements applicable to this book are presented in Figure 1.1. Note the term *ego* at the bottom of the figure. This term refers to the discrete individual upon whom a particular kinship diagram is centered. In this and other "egocentric" diagrams, it is conventional to shade in ego symbols.

Figure 1.2, which focuses on a female ego, shows how all the symbols of the Kinship Code can be used. Here, we see that Jennifer has two living parents. She has grandparents, too, but only one of them is still living. Her

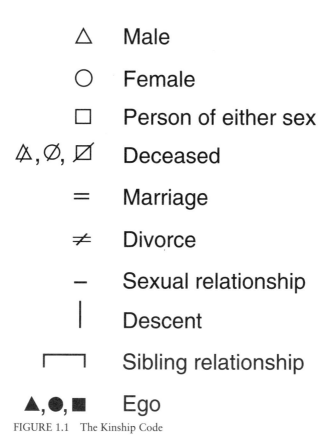

FIGURE 1.1   The Kinship Code

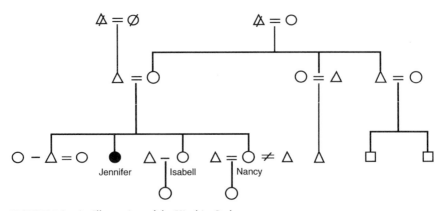

FIGURE 1.2   An Illustration of the Kinship Code

father was an only child, but her mother has a sister who has a son, Jennifer's cousin. Her mother also has a brother, who in turn has children. Jennifer herself is unmarried. She has two sisters, Isabell and Nancy. Nancy was married but then divorced and remarried. By her second marriage she has a daughter. The other sister, Isabell, is not officially married, but she has a "partner" and, through this union, a daughter. Jennifer's brother is married as well; and the diagram tells us that he is having some kind of affair on the side. (It does not specify whether others know of this affair; rather, it shows only that the person who constructed the diagram presumes to know.)

This egocentric diagram readily presents Jennifer's **kindred,** or a set of relatives traced to one particular ego. Although the diagram appears to suggest some biological relationships, it (and other diagrams) should not be understood as representing *actual* biological or genetic connections. On the contrary, it represents what these people are claiming to be the relationships between them or, more precisely, what the diagram drawer understood and wanted to show about these people in terms of their kinship. Based on the diagram, then, we cannot say, for example, that Jennifer's father is or is not her actual biological father. Possibly her father himself believes he is but in fact is not. The point is that kinship diagrams show kinship relationships that may or may not also involve biological relationships.

There are some things this diagram does not show. For example, it does not show whether any of Jennifer's siblings are older or younger than she. Nor does it show whether Jennifer was adopted. But if we wanted to represent such details, it would be easy to do, so long as we specified what is meant by the new notations we are using. For example, Figure 1.3 shows us that a particular female ego was adopted and that she has one younger sister and two younger brothers.

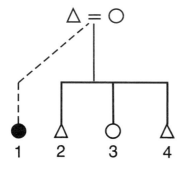

```
¦ = adoption
1,2,3,4 = sibling order
```

FIGURE 1.3   One Way to Show Adoption and Sibling Order
on a Kinship Diagram

Another convention in kinship notation involves a very simple set of
symbols, as follows:

M = mother
F = father
B = brother
Z = sister
W = wife
H = husband
D = daughter
S = son
P = parent
C = child

These letters can be used as a shorthand system for designating relationships. They also can be strung together to indicate the paths of a relationship. For example, we can indicate that a particular male ego has a relative
who is his MFBSD. This connection could be diagrammed as shown in
Figure 1.4.

Kinship diagrams can, and should, be tailored to show only what the diagram drawer feels is necessary in order to make his or her key points. For
example, Figure 1.4, showing an ego's MFBSD, could be more simply and
efficiently presented as shown in Figure 1.5.

If our only objective is to trace the connection between an ego and his
MFBSD, we need not indicate that ego has a father as well as a mother or

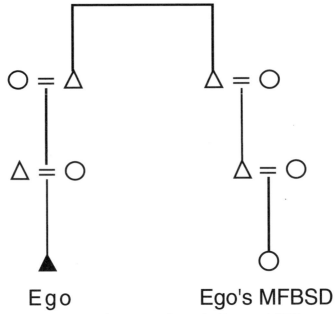

Ego   **Ego's MFBSD**

FIGURE 1.4   A Kinship Diagram Connecting Ego to an MFBSD

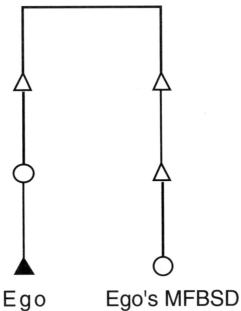

Ego   **Ego's MFBSD**

FIGURE 1.5   A Simplified Diagram Connecting Ego to an MFBSD

that his MF and MFB have spouses, even if all of these relationships also exist.

Not all kinship diagrams are egocentric. They can be used simply to show relationships between sets of people or groups. In Figure 1.6, for example, there is no ego as a reference point; nor is an individual's kindred depicted. The diagram merely indicates that two sisters have married two brothers.

I will continue using these triangles, circles, letters, and other symbols throughout the book, beginning with the following section, which introduces some of the key concepts involved in the study of kinship.

Key Concepts

Descent

Humans live in groups. To survive, they must be able to construct and maintain more or less cohesive groups. One reason kinship became and remains important in human societies is that it serves as a means of group formation. Indeed, kinship can be used efficiently to form discrete, stable groups that persist over time, beyond the lives and deaths of the people of a single generation. In Chapter 2 we will examine the evolution of human kinship more fully. But for now, to appreciate how kinship can be used to form groups, let us picture a hypothetical early human population. Imagine that this group is large, has settled in a densely populated area, and is trying to exploit resources that are less than abundant. There is no central government, and no mechanism to regulate who gets to use which resources when. Nor are there rules regulating who gets to live where, so these humans are engaged in a constant free-for-all struggle to establish occupancy of land and use of resources. They do, however, recognize the presence of kinship links among themselves; many are related to one another in some way, and many others are not. Figure 1.7 shows a fraction of this population of humans, along with the kinship relations (or lack of relations) that they believe exist.

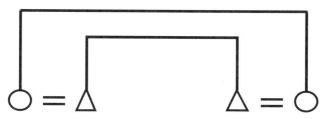

FIGURE 1.6   Two Sisters Married to Two Brothers

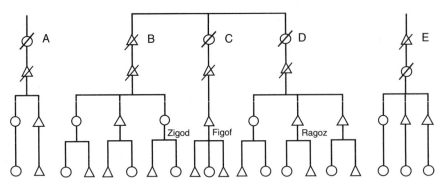

FIGURE 1.7   Kinship Connections in a Hypothetical Early Human Population

These people have kinship but, as yet, no groups based on kinship or on anything else, for that matter. Now let's assume that one woman, Zigod, is tired of this chaotic state of affairs and decides to form an exclusive group, with herself as its point of reference. Her plan is to stake a claim to a section of land and a set of resources and to establish the right of members of her group to occupy the land and use the resources. She calls together all of the people related to her by any connection (her siblings, cousins, nephews, nieces, and so on) and announces her plan. At first, some people go along with her; but soon a man, Ragoz, decides that he wants to implement the same plan, so he calls together all of his relatives. A problem immediately arises, since there is no mechanism to regulate who can or should be the central node of a group; and even if only a few people try to set themselves up as central nodes, many others will eventually find that they are potential members of two or more groups. Which group, for example, should the man Figof join, that of Ragoz or that of Zigod, given that he is equally related to both? In fact, this early human population could never form discrete groups on the basis of ego-centered kin groups, or kindreds, since membership in these groups would always be overlapping. And even if, say, Zigod managed to pull together a group for a while, it would collapse upon her death and the next generation would have to start all over again.

Realizing the inadequacy of her original procedure, Zigod comes up with a new idea: Why not form groups on the basis of *ancestors* rather than living persons? She picks her grandfather, B, and announces that a group will be formed consisting of all the descendants of B. This way *will* work. The idea catches on, and the population now has stable, discrete groups based on descent, as illustrated in Figure 1.8.

Everybody knows to which group he or she belongs, and the groups themselves can persist through generations yet unborn. Even Figod knows with which group to affiliate; he is a member of the group that traces descent from the ancestor C. In short, these humans now have stable, ongoing

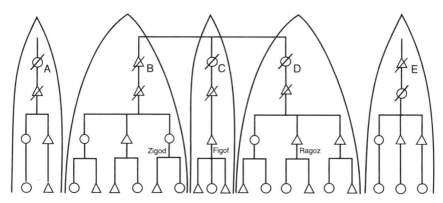

FIGURE 1.8   The Formation of Descent Groups from Common Ancestors

descent groups.[3] Order has come to the population. The descent groups are finally able to stake territorial and other claims, and to transmit these claims or rights to their descendants. This hypothetical example is admittedly a bit fanciful, but it does demonstrate how the notion of *descent from a common ancestor* can be used to form stable human groups (Keesing 1975: 17). In fact, most of the societies we will be examining in this book use descent as the basis for forming important groups.

The tracing of descent from a common ancestor is found in many though not all human societies. And among societies that do trace this descent, not all base the formation of groups on descent from a common ancestor. Still, all societies reckon descent in some way or another, whether or not they make use of common ancestors or the kin groups traced from them. Basically, there are three known modes of descent in human societies.

1. **Cognatic descent,** which is based on links through both men and women.
2. **Patrilineal descent** (also called *agnatic descent*), which is based on links through males only.
3. **Matrilineal descent** (also called *uterine descent*), which is based on links through females only.

Cognatic descent is the mode that Zigod used to form her descent group, and that the other groups of the population later adopted. Euro-Americans

---

[3] Strictly speaking, this way of forming descent groups would not necessarily produce discrete, nonoverlapping groups. For example, if members of any of these descent groups intermarried, their children would be members of two groups at once. This matter will be taken up in Chapter 5.

also tend to conceptualize descent as traceable through males and females; however, the term *cognatic* is best reserved for societies that actually use this mode of descent to form groups. Most Euro-American societies do not use descent to form groups. In America, for example, people are not divided up or organized according to their membership in descent groups, although many Americans individually recognize their ancestors and consider that they are descended from them. In this book the term **bilateral society** refers to a society that traces kin connections over the generations through both males and females, *but without the formation of descent groups.*

Cognatic societies are further discussed in Chapter 5, and the Euro-American system and its history are covered in Chapter 7. Patrilineal and matrilineal descent are cases of **unilineal descent,** traced through only one sex. Examples of both are provided in Chapters 3 and 4. There is also a fourth mode, called "double descent." This is a very rare form and will be covered in Chapter 5.

Labeling two or more societies patrilineal or matrilineal does not indicate that they necessarily have much in common aside from mode of descent. Indeed, these modes are employed in different ways and to different ends by the groups that use them. In later chapters we will see how modes of descent are interwoven with gender in different ways. Chapters 3 and 4 reveal specifically how patrilineal and matrilineal descent work and how discrete groups are formed using a rule of unilineal descent. But here we need to discuss the idea of descent groups a bit further.

With reference to kinship, Roger Keesing (1975: 9–11) drew attention to the distinctions among category, group, and corporate group. The term *category* refers to things that are classed together. All the items included in a particular category have something in common. Thus "opera lovers in America" refers to all those people who share (1) a love of opera and (2) residence in America. This is a category of people, but it is not a group. Those included in the category may never meet; they need not even know of one another's existence. But suppose there is a real organization, called Opera Lovers of America, that consists of actual members who meet every year or so to discuss and celebrate opera. This organization *would* be considered a group. A social group refers to human beings who not only have something in common but regularly interact with one another. Now suppose that the people in this group decided to collect dues from members, set up a common treasury, and use the money to provide fellowships for young, gifted people to study opera. The people of this group now *own* something in common, the money in their treasury. We would consider them a corporate group; their organization is a corporation. Should the organization then purchase property—say, an opera house—it becomes even more strongly corporate. When the organization must pay taxes or when it is sued by an individual, its members become very aware of their corporate existence. A **corporate group,** then, is a group of persons who collectively share rights (usually rights to some property or resource), privileges, and liabilities.

In the context of the societies discussed in this book, we will encounter kinship categories, kinship groups, and kinship corporations, so it is important to keep these distinctions among category, group, and corporation in mind. Societies have a way of reckoning descent; hence they can construct descent categories, such as "all the descendants of ancestor X." But not all societies form real groups on this basis. And within those that do, the groups so formed may or may not be actual corporate groups.

In many societies, corporate groups are formed on the basis of descent. Corporate descent groups operate very much like businesses or other kinds of corporations in society, and they may be very powerful in terms of their regulation of the lives of members. They may not only hold corporate property or assets but may also function as political units and as religious cults. Like all corporations they are, legally speaking, single entities and can persist despite the loss of individual members.

I mentioned earlier that American society is not organized on the basis of descent groups. Yet it would be possible for a particular set of kin to establish themselves as a descent group within this society. For example, if one set of kin decides that all the descendants of some common ancestor will regularly meet once a year to honor this person, we would have to say that *this* is a descent group. We could even say that some prominent American families, such as the Rockefellers, whose members collectively own some property or share some rights on the basis of descent, are corporate descent groups. But apart from these exceptions, descent groups are not relevant to American social organization.

Residence

In any society, descent needs to be considered in conjunction with residence patterns, since the physical closeness of people related by descent has a lot to do with the strength of the ties between them. There are many different possibilities. For example, the people of one descent group may all live in the same area. And if this is the case, they are likely to be quite a solid group. Alternatively, the descent group may have grown quite large, so some subgroups may have hived off and gone elsewhere. Over time, migrations of this sort sometimes result in descent groups that are highly dispersed. Two possible outcomes are shown in Figure 1.9. (For additional variations, see Keesing 1975: 39–43.) The two descent groups at the top of the figure are localized. As they grow and expand over time, their members continue to reside adjacent to one another. By contrast, the three descent groups at the bottom are dispersed. As time passes, the various branches of

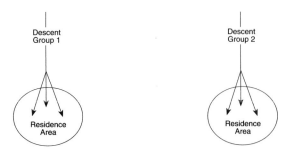

Localized Descent Groups

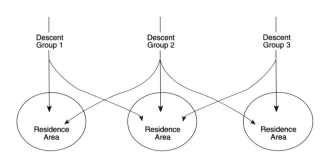

Dispersed Descent Groups

FIGURE 1.9   Localized and Dispersed Descent Groups

each group split up geographically, such that each residence area eventually contains members of different descent groups.

Whatever the outcome, the combination of descent and residence patterns affects the texture of life in communities. In many cases, people's ties to and identification with a locality may be as strong and as important as their ties of descent. For example, among the Nuer people (see Case 1 in Chapter 3), villages consisted of members of different descent groups. Each village was itself a corporate group, owning common rights to the use of certain resources. Among these people, loyalty to one's descent group was strong, but so was loyalty to one's village.

Residence is also important in terms of how it affects the structure of a **domestic group,** which consists of people who live together and share resources for their subsistence. Here we need to consider types of **postmarital**

residence. All societies have conventions or norms specifying where or with whom couples should live after marriage. The standard postmarital residence patterns are as follows:

1. **Patrilocal** (also called *virilocal*), whereby a married couple lives with or near the groom's kin.
2. **Matrilocal** (also called *uxorilocal*), whereby a married couple lives with or near the bride's kin.
3. **Ambilocal,** whereby a married couple can choose to live with or near the kin of either the groom or the bride.
4. **Neolocal,** whereby a married couple moves to a new household or location, living with kin of neither the groom nor the bride.
5. **Natolocal,** whereby a wife and husband remain with their own natal kin and do not live together.
6. **Avunculocal,** whereby a married couple moves to or near the residence of the groom's mother's brother(s).

A given society may have one dominant mode of postmarital residence but will at the same time show exceptions to it. For example, a society may be largely patrilocal, but some couples may live matrilocally or neolocally under certain circumstances at different times in their lives. In American society different types of postmarital residence are possible; but the norm, and the ideal, is neolocal residence. Avunculocal residence may seem a bit curious, but its significance will become clear in Chapter 4 when we examine matrilineal descent.

Marriage

Aside from relations based on descent, kinship concerns *affinal* relationships, or relationships established through marriage. Marriage is found in some form or other in all societies, and it is widely (though not universally) associated with the legitimization and allocation of children. Yet there is great diversity among institutions of marriage, and among the ways in which marriage both reflects and influences gender. Marriage is discussed more thoroughly in Chapter 6. For now, however, consider these basic terms referring to marriage forms: (1) **monogamy,** or marriage between two persons, generally a man and a woman; (2) **polygyny,** or marriage of a man to two or more women at the same time; and (3) **polyandry,** or marriage of a woman to two or more men at the same time. On a world scale, monogamy is the most common form of marriage. Even within societies that permit polygyny, most marital unions are monogamous. Polyandry is the rarest form.

With regard to marriage two other important terms are **exogamy** and **endogamy.** Exogamy refers to the rule whereby persons must marry *outside* a certain social category or group. In many societies descent groups are exogamous. Another example would be a society that imposed a rule of village exogamy. In this case, all persons of one village would be prohibited from marrying within it and would have to find spouses from other villages. Conversely, endogamy refers to the rule whereby persons must marry *within* a certain social category or group. For example, societies that are stratified by caste usually have rules prescribing caste endogamy, or marriage within the caste. In the United States there are no exogamy or endogamy rules as such. But some states prohibit marriages within a certain range of kin (e.g., between first cousins), thus imposing a kind of kindred exogamy. And although there is no rule, we do see a norm of class and ethnic group endogamy in the United States.

Kinship and Gender

With this brief introduction to kinship we have covered the distinction between consanguineal and affinal kin, the idea of an individual's kindred, and the concept of descent from ancestors as a basis for forming groups. We have also noted the importance of residence, as well as the various forms of postmarital residence and marriage. All of these dimensions of kinship combine in different ways in different societies and influence social structure to varying degrees. The same dimensions of kinship are also interwoven with gender relationships. But before delving into the subject of human societies and cultures, we must address some more basic questions: How did the recognition of kinship come about? When, where, and with what consequences did humans first come to think of one another as kin or nonkin? To what extent do our primate cousins "recognize" one another as kin or nonkin? When and why did human groups first begin to use kinship to form groups, or first begin to "invent" marriage and specify residence rules? And what can the study of the evolution of human kinship tell us about human gender? Not all of these questions can be precisely answered, but the next chapter discloses what we know so far.

References

Collier, Jane Fishburne, and Sylvia Junko Yanagisako. 1987. Toward a Unified Analysis of Gender and Kinship. In Jane Fishburne Collier and Sylvia Junko Yanagisako, eds., *Gender and Kinship*, pp. 14–50. Stanford: Stanford University Press.

Delaney, Carol. 1991. *The Seed and the Soil: Gender and Cosmology in Turkish Village Society*. Berkeley: University of California Press.

di Leonardo, Micaela. 1991. Gender, Culture and Political Economy: Feminist Anthropology in Historical Perspective. In Micaela di Leonardo, ed., *Gender at the*

Crossroads of Knowledge: Feminist Anthropology in the Postmodern Era, pp. 1–48. Berkeley: University of California Press.

Ginsburg, Faye D., and Rayna Rapp. 1995. Introduction: Conceiving the New World Order. In Faye D. Ginsburg and Rayna Rapp, eds., *Conceiving the New World Order: The Global Politics of Reproduction*, pp. 1–17. Berkeley: University of California Press.

Keesing, Roger M. 1975. *Kin Groups and Social Structure*. Fort Worth: Holt, Rinehart and Winston.

Laderman, Carol. 1983. *Wives and Midwives: Childbirth and Nutrition in Rural Malaysia*. Berkeley: University of California Press.

———. 1991. *Taming the Wind of Desire: Psychology, Medicine, and Aesthetics in Malay Shamanistic Performance*. Berkeley: University of California Press.

Lamphere, Louise. 1993. The Domestic Sphere of Women and the Public World of Men: The Strengths and Limitations of an Anthropological Dichotomy. In Caroline B. Brettell and Carolyn F. Sargent, eds., *Gender in Cross-Cultural Perspective*, pp. 67–77. Englewood Cliffs, N.J.: Prentice-Hall.

Laqueur, Thomas. 1990. *Making Sex: Body and Gender from the Greeks to Freud*. Cambridge: Harvard University Press.

Miller, Barbara Diane. 1993. The Anthropology of Sex and Gender Hierarchies. In Barbara Diane Miller, ed., *Sex and Gender Hierarchies*, pp. 3–31. Cambridge: Cambridge University Press.

Moen, Elizabeth W. 1979. What Does "Control over Our Bodies" Really Mean? *International Journal of Women Studies* 2(2): 129–143.

Oakley, Ann. 1972. *Sex, Gender and Society*. New York: Harper and Row.

Robertson, A. F. 1991. *Beyond the Family: The Social Organization of Human Reproduction*. Berkeley: University of California Press.

Rosaldo, Michele Z. 1974. Woman, Culture and Society: A Theoretical Overview. In Michell Z. Rosaldo and Louise Lamphere, eds., *Woman, Culture and Society*, pp. 17–42. Stanford: Stanford University Press.

———. 1980. The Use and Abuse of Anthropology: Reflections of Feminism and Cross-Cultural Understanding. *Signs: Journal of Women in Culture and Society* 5(3): 389–417.

Rossi, Alice. 1977. Biosocial Aspects of Parenting. *Daedalus* 106: 1–32.

Rossi, Alice, ed. 1985. *Gender and the Life Course*. New York: Aldine.

Rothman, Barbara Katz. 1987. Reproduction. In Beth B. Hess and Myra Marx Ferree, eds., *Analyzing Gender: A Handbook of Social Science Research*, pp. 154–170. Newbury Park, Calif.: Sage Publications.

Scheffler, Harold. 1991. Sexism and Naturalism in the Study of Kinship. In Micaela di Leonardo, ed., *Gender at the Crossroads of Knowledge: Feminist Anthropology in the Postmodern Era*, pp. 361–382. Berkeley: University of California Press.

Schneider, David M. 1968. *American Kinship: A Cultural Account*. Englewood Cliffs, N.J.: Prentice-Hall.

———. 1984. *A Critique of the Study of Kinship*. Ann Arbor: University of Michigan Press.

Yanagisako, Sylvia J., and Jane F. Collier. 1990. The Mode of Reproduction in Anthropology. In Deborah L. Rhode, ed., *Theoretical Perspectives on Sexual Difference*, pp. 131–141. New Haven: Yale University Press.

2

The Evolution of Kinship and Gender

In this chapter we briefly depart from human society to enter the world of the nonhuman primates. How much of what we see in human kinship systems is really unique to our species? After exploring kinship and gender among nonhuman primates, we will consider some speculations on the evolution of kinship, and the implications for gender, in our own species.

Primates are a natural grouping (an order) of mammals that includes prosimians (i.e., tree-dwelling animals such as lemurs and tarsiers), monkeys, apes, and humans. Some of the physical characteristics that distinguish primates from other mammals are binocular vision and the grasping hand with mobile digits and flat nails. Evolutionary trends characteristic of the Primate Order and most pronounced in humans also include prolongation of gestation of the fetus, prolongation of the period of infant care, and expansion and elaboration of the brain (Clark 1971).

Some primates, such as gibbons and many prosimians, live in "monogamous" pair bonds. Others, notably hamadryas baboons, live and mate "polygynously" in **one-male units** consisting of one adult male and several females. Still others, including chimpanzees, live in **multimale, multifemale units** where mating is largely promiscuous. There are even cases of "polyandrous" primates, such as the saddle-backed tamarins in South America (Goldizen 1987), whereby two to four males stay and copulate with one female, and all males help with the care of offspring.

An important feature in the social life of many nonhuman primates is dominance and the formation of "dominance hierarchies." Primatologists consider a "dominant" animal to be the one who usually wins in an aggressive encounter with another (Silk 1993). Very often (but not always) the dominant animal will have greater access to resources such as food, water, or sexual partners. In some cases the outcomes of aggressive encounters are linked so that "if A defeats B, and B defeats C, A can also defeat C" (Silk 1993: 214), resulting in the formation of a linear hierarchy. In other cases two or three animals are dominant over another set, which is dominant over yet another. In some primate groups the dominance hierarchy is fairly clear-cut; in others it is difficult to discern or varies considerably by context. And, of course, at any one time dominance relationships may be in flux. As we shall see later in the chapter, the concepts of dominance and aggression in primates are quite controversial.

Nonhuman primates are fascinating in their own right, but many researchers study them primarily to gain perspectives on human behavior and evolution. In this quest the two most favored primates have been baboons and chimpanzees (Strum and Mitchell 1987). In the past, some types of baboons (e.g., hamadryas baboons and Savannah baboons) were chosen for study because, like our ancestors, they left the trees during their evolution and made adaptations to open country. They were thus seen as a primate line that faced ecological challenges somewhat similar to those we experienced. But then different types of baboons proved to be very diverse. Research later focused on chimpanzees in comparison with humans, since analyses of chromosomes, blood proteins, and DNA confirm that chimps are our closest evolutionary "cousins." By these measures, humans and chimps are evolutionarily more related than chimps and gorillas. It is now thought that humans and chimpanzees diverged from one another about 5 million years ago. Although comparisons between chimpanzees and humans are still popular, human behavior is currently often analyzed in relation to the whole spectrum of primate behavior and social organization.

Certain trends in our study of primates are important to bear in mind as we examine primate kinship and gender. First, research has shown that nonhuman primates are far more intelligent and skilled, and live in vastly more complicated social orders, than was previously supposed. Not so long ago, particular adaptations among primates, such as tool manufacture and use, food sharing, and hunting, were believed to be uniquely human. Then came Jane Goodall's (1971) reports of chimps in Tanzania's Gombe National Park who were modifying and using twigs to extract termites and using leaves as sponges to soak up water for drinking. Other reports from the Tai forest (Ivory Coast) showed chimps using wooden clogs and stone hammers to crack open nuts (Boesch and Boesch 1990). Goodall also observed food sharing among Gombe chimps: Not only do mothers share food with infants, but adults share meat with one another, especially males with males (Goodall 1986: 374). Moreover, forms of cooperative hunting have been observed among chimps of Gombe, where a few females hunt along with the males (Goodall 1986: 286). Year-round sexual receptivity was long thought to be unique to human females, but research now reveals that certain nonhuman female primates can and do mate outside their estrous periods and that young female pygmy chimpanzees are almost continually receptive (Kano 1992: 154). In addition to these findings came the startling discoveries about the vocal communicative abilities of wild chimps and the learning of human sign language among captive chimps.

A second trend in recent decades has been the recognition of a far greater behavioral diversity between and within primate species than was previously known or presumed. As mentioned earlier, it was the discovery of such diversity among different types of baboons that led to the decline of a "baboon model" for human behavior and to the rise of the "chimpanzee model" in its place (Strum and Mitchell 1987). But now we find that there is diversity among chimpanzees as well. For example, studies of the Bonobo (pygmy) chimpanzees of Zaire show important contrasts with common chimpanzees, such as those of Gombe National Park in Tanzania. In terms of mating behaviors, wild pygmy chimpanzees not only copulate more frequently but also engage in ventro-ventral copulation, in contrast to the ventro-dorsal copulation seen among common chimpanzees (Kano 1992: 140); and among captive pygmies, mutual eye gazing during copulation has been documented (Savage-Rumbaugh and Wilkerson 1978). These mating behaviors may create stronger male-female bonds among pygmy chimpanzees. Grooming between male and female pygmies is also more frequent (Nishida and Hiraiwa-Hasegawa 1987). Among common chimpanzees, by contrast, male-male grooming is more frequent and bonds between adult males are stronger than those between adult males and females. Male dominance over females is not expressed among pygmy chimpanzees. For instance, a group of male pygmies will not attack a female, whereas a group of females will cooperate to attack a bothersome male (Kano 1992: 188).

Kinship and Evolutionary Theory

Some ideas about the evolution of kinship involve the notion of natural selection, first proposed by Darwin in 1859 and later refined through developments in genetics. Natural selection refers to differential reproduction, or the tendency of certain individuals in a particular environment to be more likely to produce more fertile offspring than other individuals. Those who reproduce the most have the highest **fitness** (defined as reproductive success), such that their genes are passed on to the next generation with the greatest frequency. Those traits (or, on another level, those genes) that favor fitness in a certain environment will be positively selected. Over time, then, natural selection operates on the basis of genetic variation (brought about by mutation and recombination), ultimately bringing about evolutionary change.

In 1964 W. D. Hamilton considered the problem of **altruistic acts** among animals in relation to natural selection. If we say that natural selection favors fitness, or reproductive success, then how do we explain individual behavior that enhances others' fitness while simultaneously reducing one's own? Why, for example, do some ground squirrels place themselves in considerable risk to predators by sounding alarm calls so that others can escape? And why do some castes of female wasps forsake reproduction altogether in order to labor for the wasp colony? An even more poignant example from the primate world is Dian Fossey's (1983) description of Digit, a male gorilla who altruistically gave his life to poachers in order that the other members of his troop could survive (discussed in Fausto-Sterling 1985: 175). To account for these altruistic behaviors, Hamilton came up with the concept of **inclusive fitness** whereby an individual can promote the transmission of his or her genes to the next generation not just through the children of that individual but also through altruistic acts that favor the survival (and eventual reproduction) of others who share at least some of the same genes—namely, close relatives such as brothers, sisters, nephews, and nieces. Thus Hamilton argued that the concept of fitness should be *inclusive* of the capacity for altruistic behaviors that favor kin. Later researchers have used the term **kin selection** to refer to the process by which natural selection acts on inclusive fitness. In essence, kin selection theory proposes a biological base for kin-favoring behavior.

Recent genetic data from a study performed in Gombe, the site of Goodall's and others' extensive studies of chimpanzees, bear upon primate kinship and kin selection theory (Morin et al. 1994). This study devised a handy technique for discovering genetic connections within chimpanzee groups. Previously it was hard to tell, beyond mother-child and maternal sibling connections, who was related to whom and in what ways. But by collecting hair samples for DNA analysis from the abandoned sleeping nests of chimps, the Gombe researchers were able to produce a genetic characterization of the community. In particular, they could now confirm and quantify a pattern of chimpanzee female dispersion. Evidently, the females of one group tend to migrate out at adolescence and mate with males of other groups. They may join these other groups, sometimes returning later to their natal community. Or they may go back and forth between groups. Males, by contrast, nearly always stay in their natal community for life. Thus Gombe chimps have developed a kind of "patrilocal" residence pattern. Figure 2.1 shows what happens as a result.

In short, the male chimps who stay put will, over the generations, be related to one another patrilineally (i.e., through males). One such hypothetical male "patriline" is shown in the diagram. We can presume that the chimps do not "know" about their patrilineal connections, but the pattern is there. In any case, the males who stay together will have close kin connections among themselves; and since these males associate closely with one another and cooperate to defend a territory as well as access to females of their group, this pattern may support kin selection theory. But among primates, the chimpanzee pattern of female dispersal is the exception. In most multimale primate species it is the males who disperse at adolescence.

In relation to fitness, researchers also use the concepts of **sexual selection** and **parental investment** in discussions of primate behavior. Sexual selec-

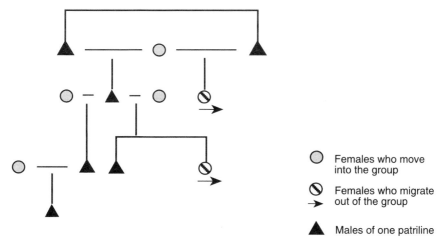

FIGURE 2.1 A Hypothetical Male "Patriline" Among Chimpanzees

tion refers to the process by which one sex (usually male) competes for sexual access to the other sex. And parental investment (Trivers 1972) refers to the contributions that parents make to the fitness of their offspring (the offspring's fitness by definition benefits their own fitness). Among most primates (and, indeed, most mammals), the female investment is much higher than that of the male. But there is considerable scientific interest in the conditions under which male investment beyond mating is favored, particularly among human beings. Some researchers suggest, following Trivers (1972), that sexual selection and parental investment are related: Whichever sex invests the most in offspring becomes the relatively scarcer resource for reproduction, so members of the other sex will compete with one another for access to this sex. Thus, for example, where the parental investment of females is very high relative to males, males will be in competition for the reproductive resources of females. By extension, sex differences in parental investment may be a function of reproductive strategy. Since infant primates require a relatively great amount of care if they are to survive to reproduce, female primates enhance their own fitness not by getting pregnant and giving birth as often as possible but, rather, by raising fewer offspring with better care. By contrast, males, whose parental investment is low, enhance their fitness by impregnating as many females as possible.

When researchers applied these concepts of fitness, kin selection, parental investment, and mating strategies to the study of the biological bases of behavior in insects and mammals, and even nonhuman primates, public reaction was neutral; but a storm of controversy was spurred over their application to human beings. This controversy began with the publication of *Sociobiology: The New Synthesis*, in which the author, E. O. Wilson

(1975), asserted that much human behavior is under genetic control. Many critics accused Wilson and other sociobiologists of being "biological determinists" who sought to "justify" human aggression, territoriality, and all sorts of social inequality by saying, in effect, that "it's in our genes" (Lewontin, Rose, and Kamin 1984; Sociobiology Study Group of Science for the People 1978). Others protested that sociobiologists ignored the fact that so much of human behavior is learned rather than genetically "wired in," or that they disregarded the force of human culture. These outcries fueled the "nature versus nurture" debate in the study of human behavior.

Sociobiology became a feminist issue in the 1970s when, for one thing, some sociobiologists argued that rape among humans, though undesirable, is really quite understandable because, after all, the males perpetuating it are merely trying (however unconsciously) to spread their genes (Barash 1979; Symons 1979; Thornhill and Thornhill 1983). For example, in comparing human males with male "rapist" mallard ducks, Barash (1979: 55) wrote that "perhaps human rapists, in their own criminally misguided way, are doing the best they can to maximize their fitness." A few years later, Anne Fausto-Sterling (1985: 5), a biologist who criticized sociobiology on many fronts, noted what a short step it would be from this line of thinking to the legal defense of a male rapist on the grounds that "his genes made him do it." Other sociobiologists (Alexander and Noonan 1979; Irons 1979; Trivers 1972) have contrasted human male and female "reproductive strategies," claiming that (to maximize their fitness) human males are naturally polygynous whereas females (who seek to promote their fitness by nurturing a smaller number of offspring than would be biologically possible to produce) are naturally monogamous. Moreover, they say, because women want to improve their children's fitness by increasing the parental investment of their mate, they devise ways of keeping a man around as provider and protector; and in trying to hold on to the man, they become "coy" and "clinging" females. Understandably, this line of argument drove many women to distraction.

Criticism of this form of sociobiology has come from within the field as well as from outside it. A female sociobiologist, Sarah Hrdy (1981), complained that previous sociobiologists had either ignored or misinterpreted females and female sexuality in their study of primate behavior and evolution. We will examine some of Hrdy's ideas in a later section; but for now note that she essentially asserted that female primates, far from being sexually passive, could be active, competitive, and aggressive and that their roles in human evolution were important. More recently, Susan Sperling (1991) has claimed that, although Hrdy's vision of primates may be more acceptable to feminists, it is still based on unwarranted assumptions about primate behavior and its meaning in human evolution. Sperling questions the larger idea of interpreting all primate behaviors as end points in evolutionary adaptation. She also points out that many primate behaviors are far more complex, varied, and context-dependent than sociobiological theory suggests.

The concepts of fitness and kin selection are central tenets of evolutionary ecology, a field devoted to the study of how evolutionary processes influence social behavior. Evolutionary ecologists maintain that social behavior, including that in humans, is influenced by natural selection. However, most of them veer away from the hard-line genetic determinism of earlier sociobiologists and discount the earlier sociobiological statements regarding human gender patterns. Along these lines, Barbara Smuts (1995) has recently advanced some very interesting ideas on the evolutionary origins of patriarchy, or male dominance. Smuts begins with some of the same assumptions as those held by sociobiologists—namely, that nonhuman and human primates seek to maximize their fitness and that males and females have different reproductive strategies. In short, males go for "mate quantity" whereas females pursue "mate quality" (1995: 5). But beyond these assumptions there ceases to be any similarity between Smuts' work and that of the earlier sociobiologists. For one thing, Smuts is quite explicit about not seeing human behavior as "genetically programmed"; rather, she argues that "natural selection has favored in humans the potential to develop and express any one of a wide range of reproductive strategies, depending on environmental conditions" (1995: 21). Thus, human social conditions such as patriarchy are not inevitable and can be changed. In addition, Smuts considers herself to be a feminist and attempts to show that a study of the biological or evolutionary roots of patriarchy is not incompatible with a feminist perspective.

Smuts focuses her attention on a behavior pattern she considers to be pervasive among most primate species: male aggression against females and female resistance to this aggression. She points out that males are aggressive against females in order to mate with them, to pursue "mate quantity"; but females, following their own reproductive interests, can and do resist. At the same time, there is variation in the extent to which females can successfully resist male aggression. Consideration of the numerous factors that may be involved in this variation has led Smuts to propose a set of hypotheses. One hypothesis concerns females' ability to resist male aggression by forming alliances with other females against males. Among the many primate species in which females bond together, this strategy works quite well. Among others, such as the common chimpanzees, females disperse at maturity to join new groups where they do not have female relatives to protect them. It is interesting, Smuts points out, that among the Bonobo chimpanzees (a species closely related to the common chimpanzee), females disperse out but are also able to form alliances with unrelated females in the new groups. These female bonds are developed through and supported by frequent homosexual relations between females. Thus, among common chimpanzees we see relatively high levels of male aggression against females, whereas among Bonobos male aggression is successfully resisted and males do not sexually coerce females. Applying the same logic to human evolution, Smuts proposes that the prevalence of patrilocal residence in human societies means that women are often deprived of the support of female kin and allies, leaving them more vulnerable to male aggression.

Another intriguing, if depressing, hypothesis proposed by Smuts is the following: "In pursuing their material and reproductive interests, women often engage in behaviors that promote male resource control and male control over female sexuality. Thus women, as well as men, contribute to the perpetuation of patriarchy" (1995: 18). Here Smuts suggests that in some circumstances women can facilitate their own reproductive success not so much by allying with other females as by allying with males who command more resources and by complying with customs that increase paternity certainty. Their behavior then promotes patriarchy.

Smuts' work is a refreshing change from the often blatant sexism of the earlier sociobiologists. From her feminist perspective, she offers concrete suggestions for reducing gender inequality that follow from her hypotheses on patriarchy's evolutionary origins. For example, on the basis of her first hypothesis discussed here, Smuts suggests that it is important for women to form political solidarities to protect themselves from male violence and domination. And in the context of her hypothesis concerning female complicity in male dominance, she emphasizes the need to identify and then change those female behaviors.

It is important to bear in mind that the assumptions on which Smuts bases her conclusions—the concepts of fitness, male and female reproductive strategies, and male interest in paternity certainty—remain highly controversial, especially where human behavior is concerned. Still, her work goes a long way toward showing, as Hrdy (1981: 14) pointed out earlier, that it would be a mistake to assume there is anything inherently sexist about exploring the biological bases of human behavior.

Kin Recognition

Kin recognition is known to be widespread among insects, birds, and mammals. In many species, behavior toward kin is markedly different from that toward nonkin. Thus, for example, mole rat aunts will care for nieces and nephews but not for nonrelated young, and Japanese quails show a clear preference for mating with first cousins (Wilson 1987). And in the case of the desert isopod, a burrowing insect who lives in burrows in nuclear family units but wanders about outside for food, any family member will drive out a nonfamily stranger who comes to the burrow embankment; and whenever and wherever family members meet, they show tolerance for one another but either aggression toward or avoidance of nonfamily strangers (Linsenmair 1987).

Nonhuman primates, too, are known to be able to recognize one another individually and to retain recognition over long periods. That kin recognition is a feature of nonhuman primate social life has also been well documented. Some researchers investigating this phenomenon have looked closely at primate behaviors such as grooming, spatial proximity (Who regularly hangs out with whom?), alliance formation (Who regularly comes to the defense of whom?), play, and co-feeding tolerance (Which animals feed peacefully side by side?). In the context of these (and other) behaviors, innumerable studies have shown that among primate species there is a strong bias in favor of kin as opposed to nonkin (Walters 1987; Bernstein 1991).[1]

In species such as rhesus monkeys, in which males emigrate to join other groups, related males sometimes leave together, joining the same new group; males also tend to transfer to new groups into which a male relative has previously immigrated (Gouzoules and Gouzoules 1987: 302). And among Gombe chimps, as noted above, related males form close, cooperative groups. Thus kinship may be an important factor in male alliance formation as well. For example, D. C. Riss and Jane Goodall (1977) have traced how the rise to top-rank (alpha-male) status on the part of a male chimp called Figan was accomplished through an alliance with his (maternally related) brother, Faben.

Indeed, there have been many observations of cooperative behavior among kin. From Gombe, Goodall (1986: 376–377) reported the following:

> Goblin once ran 200 meters when he heard the loud screams of his mother, Melissa, who was being attacked by another female. When he arrived, he displayed toward and attacked his mother's aggressor. Adult males often support their younger siblings, especially brothers, during aggressive incidents: thus Faben and Jomeo frequently hurried to help Figan and Sherry, respectively. Evered was very supportive of his grown sister, Gilka, and almost always intervened on her behalf.

However, the study of primate kin behavior is in most cases necessarily restricted to maternally related kin. In species such as chimpanzees in which mating is promiscuous, neither the human observers nor the animals can know who the father is or who is related to whom through the father. Of

---

[1] Studies indicate that not only cooperative acts but also aggressive acts are more frequent among nonhuman primate kin (Walters 1987; Bernstein 1991: 10). This finding might be considered evidence against kin selection theory, but opinions vary. Some researchers suggest that certain kinds of aggression between kin are carried out to reinforce learning of adaptive behaviors (Bernstein and Ehardt 1986).

course, this situation may change as use of the technique of extracting DNA from animal hairs spreads throughout primate research sites.

What we do know at present is that in certain species—for example, Indian langurs—a male will sometimes kill infants he has not sired. Indian langurs live in one-male polygynous units. A new male will sometimes enter such a unit, kill the current polygynous male, mate with the females himself, and kill off infants the females already have (Hrdy 1977, 1981). Infanticide, which has also been observed in other one-male primate species, is widely interpreted as a male strategy to promote individual fitness, or reproductive success, given that the female quickly resumes estrous after losing a nursing infant and the new male avoids wasting energy by protecting infants not his own (Goodall 1986: 522). However, the proposed link between this type of infanticide and male interest in maximizing fitness remains controversial (Zihlman 1995).

Researchers have expressed considerable interest in the question of whether male care of infants increases among primates with high levels of "paternity certainty." (The question has obvious implications for humans, though we do not need to assume that the male primates consciously "know" that males can be parents.)

Patricia Wright (1993) has shown how male care of infants varies widely among different primates. In her work, the category of "care" includes defense and protection, food sharing, and carrying. The conclusion she applies to all nonhuman primates is that "if male aid is not necessary for the survival of the infant, then the male does not invest in parental care" (1993: 136). In the particular ecological setting of the polyandrous tamarins of South America, male aid is essential to infant survival, and here all the males mating with a female will jointly assist in infant care to a high degree. Wright connects this pattern with the issue of "paternity certainty" by suggesting that "even with only the possibility of paternity, these males are willing to invest heavily in infant care" (1993: 139). But among langurs and other species in which males kill other males' infants, male care of their own infants is nonexistent beyond general defense of the herd of females and their young. In this case, paternity is more or less "assured" but, according to Wright, male assistance in infant care is not needed for infant survival.

Among multimale, multifemale species, males participate somewhat in infant care—a finding that some researchers have interpreted not as parental investment but as a means of gaining sexual access to the mother (Smuts 1985). Indeed, Smuts and David Gubernick (1992) suggest that, among primates generally, male care of infants is better understood as a mating strategy than as a parental investment strategy linked to "paternity certainty." According to this view, a male cares for a female's infants in order to befriend the mother and increase his chances of mating with her. If this hypothesis can be extrapolated to human evolution, male care of infants may have emerged from male-female "friendships" rather than from conditions of greater "paternity certainty." Hewlett (1991) concurs with this view and suggests by extension that, in human evolution, greater male care of offspring came about as a result of stronger social bonds between males and females.

Other behaviors in primates suggest the existence of additional forms of kin recognition. One is incest avoidance, which will be discussed later. Another is the adoption of orphaned infants by older female siblings, as has been observed among Gombe chimps (Goodall 1986: 101). Adoption of orphans by maternal kin has been reported in other species as well (Walters 1987).

There are many cases of strong attachments to younger siblings among chimpanzees and other primates. Consider the following account from Takayoshi Kano's study of pygmy chimpanzees in Zaire concerning an adolescent male, Tawashi, and his year-old little sister, Kameko: "Tawashi often approached his mother, peered into her face, and after looking awhile carried Kameko and took her for a walk. Once he made a nest 10 m from Kame [his mother] and, lying on his back played with Kameko on top of his stomach. He tickled her, held her up by the arms, embraced, and kissed her (open-mouth kiss), pressing his large open mouth everywhere on her body."

Kameko later died. Kano's account continues:

When we found Kameko dead, her small body was being held and carried around by Tawashi. He carried his little sister's body with all four limbs hanging down lifelessly; one of his arms pressed her against his chest; and he walked slowly in the tree apparently in deep thought. . . . The following morning, the first to leave his nest and approach the corpse was Tawashi. He lightly touched the corpse. . . . [The] mother, Kame, came later. She lingered near the corpse and stared at it. As the sun rose, flies started to swarm around the corpse. Several times Kame grabbed quickly at the air with her hand as she shooed them. . . . For a while, Kame's family seemed, in general, to live separate from the others. Then the family left together and did not come back to the feeding site. Six days later when we found Kame, she did not have the corpse.

This account suggests an emotional side to chimpanzee relationships, and one can clearly detect an emotional compassion on the part of the human observer. The observer in this case admits to a bit of "anthropomorphizing this situation" but wishes to make the point that, "in chimpanzees, we may have to admit that feelings exist that are similar to those of human beings" (Kano 1992: 174).

There is evidence that some primates are able to recognize not only their own kin but that of others as well. This trait has been observed among baboons, for example (Smuts 1985). And among pigtailed macaques, nonrelated individuals in aggressive encounters later "reconciled" not just with each other but also with each other's close kin (Judge 1983).

Nonhuman primates recognize their kin, but *how* exactly do they do so? Regrettably, this is not known, and as yet we have no way to probe into their consciousness. But with primates we feel that something more than the innate mechanisms of mole rats and desert isopods is involved. Some research suggests the existence of a recognition mechanism such as phenotype matching, or visual recognition of physical "family resemblances." But there is little consistent evidence that nonhuman primates use this mechanism. Another, more likely possibility (Walters 1987; Bernstein 1991) is an association mechanism whereby an infant primate simply grows up forming a close bond with and certain recognition of the mother, and gradually learns to distinguish, or classify, others on the basis of their interaction with the mother and him- or herself. The implication is that what exists inside the minds of primates are not "categories of kinship" but various learned "categories of association." Still, when we consider primates' recognition of one another's kin, it is tempting to speculate that something more complex is going on. As we will discover in the next section, things do get more complex.

Primate Kinship

We have seen that primates recognize some kin and behave differentially (usually favorably) toward them. We do not know precisely what this finding "means" for primates, but what should it mean for us? To what extent and in what ways can we catch a spark, if not a flame, of human kinship systems among primate groups? Or, conversely, are fully human forms of kinship unique to our species?

In the last chapter kinship was defined as the recognition of relationships based on (1) descent or (2) marriage. Robin Fox (1975, 1980) focused on these two fundamental aspects of human kinship, probing the extent to which either has any basis, however rudimentary, in primate life. His ingenious suggestion was that some types of primates have adopted a rudimentary sort of "marriage" pattern (which he terms "alliance") whereas other types have adopted a rudimentary "descent" pattern, but that no primate species exhibits both alliance and descent. His suggestion was that the two building blocks of human kinship *already exist among nonhuman primates;* the uniquely human development was merely to put the two elements, alliance and descent, together in one system. Let's consider each of these elements as they affect nonhuman primates.

Looking at Old World monkeys and apes, Fox contrasted those who live in one-male groups[2] with those who live in multimale, multifemale groups.

---

[2] Fox (1975: 12) includes monogamous primates in the category of one-male groups.

Hamadryas baboons are a good example of the former. These baboons live in wooded or steppe areas of countries such as Ethiopia and Sudan. They are organized into polygynous units consisting of one adult male and several females, usually about four, with their young infants. The male mates with these females and "herds" them, keeping them together in a unit and making sure that they don't stray. If a female does wander away, the male chases her back, sometimes biting her on the neck. If another male ventures into the group and attempts to copulate with the females, the herding male will fight him off. The young female daughters of this unit are allowed to stay with the group, but the young sons are driven off by the adult male.

Several such polygynous units of hamadryas baboons are loosely organized into larger units called "troops." Members of a troop move about an area together, and the adult males occasionally come together for defense (e.g., to fight off village dogs). But otherwise the adult males have little to do with one another, and there is no dominance hierarchy among them. When the young sons are driven away from the polygynous units, they become peripheralized, hanging out on the fringe of baboon society but staying within their troops.

Now, as the young peripheralized males mature, how do they find mates? Two mechanisms are involved. The first, called "apprenticeship," involves the efforts of a young male to attach himself to a polygynous breeding unit. He does not attempt to copulate with the females, as he would be forced away, but rather tries to gain acceptance from the older male by helping to herd the females and chase off any other males who come around. Eventually his presence becomes tolerated. Later, when the older male becomes too old, the younger one takes over as polygynous male of the herd and mates exclusively with the females. The second mechanism, called "kidnap," comes into play when a peripheralized male snatches away a female infant, raises and cares for her himself, and, when she is mature, mates with her. After several such successful kidnappings, he has his own group of females.

In Fox's view, the polygynous units of hamadryas baboons are cases of alliance. These are distinct breeding units, and the social mechanisms of the baboons result in long-term assignment of mates. Interestingly, the baboons have a breeding season; but rather than coming together to mate during this season, the males and females stay together year-round in relatively stable units (Fox 1980: 102). How long do such mating "alliances" last? One study (Abegglen 1984, cited in Stammbach 1987: 114–115) found that the polygynous males herded their one-male units for at least three years; but 70 percent of the females in these units changed their one-male units within three years. Thus females can transfer between units in spite of male herding and neck bites. The same study reported that females change their one-male units two to three times during their lifetimes. It also found that females tend to transfer into new units that contain females with whom they have previously lived. J. J. Abegglen (1984) has suggested that it is not just male herding but female bonding within these units that keeps the group together.

These relatively stable polygynous arrangements among the hamadryas baboons are not, of course, cases of "marriage" in any human sense, but Fox proposed that because of their relative stability and exclusivity they are getting close to being categorized as such. Now, what about "descent"? To see a kind of rudimentary descent pattern at work, Fox looked at multimale, multifemale Old World Monkeys such as common baboons (not to be confused with the hamadryas baboons described above), rhesus monkeys, vervet monkeys, and Japanese Macaques.

All four species live in groups consisting of a subunit of females with their young and a subunit of adult males. The males are arranged in a dominance hierarchy among themselves. At the same time, all adult males are dominant over all females. In contrast to chimpanzees, females of these species remain in their natal group and males usually disperse to join new groups at adolescence, although in some cases they remain for a time as adults in their natal group. The female core groups contain mothers with their young, and in some cases these units extend over several generations, producing "matrilines." Thus, for example, a subunit may contain an old mother, her daughters, and her daughters' infants.

Young males start to grow up in these units but then leave and spend time as peripheral males on the fringe. During this later period they may emigrate to another group, joining in with the adult males and establishing their position within the male hierarchy there.

Mating in these groups is brief and nonexclusive, although a male will sometimes form a "consort relationship" with one of the females in estrous. In this case, the male and female go off together for a few days or weeks and may copulate many times.

In these multimale, multifemale groups there is a dominance hierarchy not only among the adult males but also among the females.[3] In addition, the female hierarchy is established by maternal kinship. In fact, the different matrilines within the female core group are themselves ranked. For example, all the members of line A are higher than those of line B, who in turn are higher than those of line C, and so on. Every female of line A will thus be dominant over any female of line B. Rankings occur within each

---

[3] Fox (1975, 1980) also discusses the multimale, multifemale chimpanzees, who share many features of social organization with these Old World Monkeys. However, in the case of female chimps, who disperse out, a local female hierarchy is not well defined (Nishida and Hiraiwa-Hasegawa 1987).

matriline as well. A mother is dominant over her offspring, and the offspring assume a rank order based on birth. That is, the most recently born infant ranks highest, and the oldest one ranks lowest. Exactly why this rank ordering occurs is not known (Walters and Seyfarth 1987: 312), but there is some indication that the mother gives the youngest daughter assistance during her rise in dominance over her older sisters (Hrdy 1981: 111).

The males of these species have a linear hierarchy that they partly work out themselves based on relative strength, aggressive contests, and so on. But to some extent the position of a male in the male group is also determined by the position of his natal matriline in the female group, both in cases where he stays for a time in the adult male unit of his natal group and in cases where he transfers to another group. Thus a son of the highest matriline of the female group is very likely to become a high-ranking male in the male group that he joins. An example of this arrangement is shown in Figure 2.2.

Here we see three hypothetical matrilines, with line A highest in rank, followed by line B and then line C. The male offspring of these units then assume ranks (1, 2, 3, and so on, with 1 the highest in rank) within the new group to which they migrate.

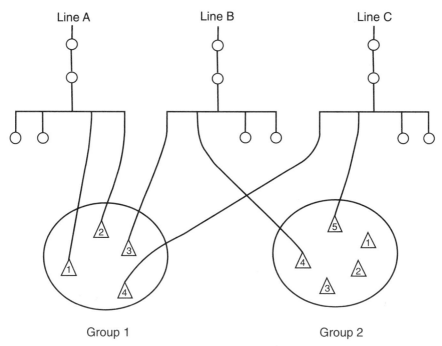

FIGURE 2.2   Male Rank Determined by Rank of Natal Matriline Among Some Multimale, Multifemale Monkey Groups

In an early study of rhesus monkeys, one researcher (Loy 1972, cited in Fox 1975: 16) found that 95.6 percent of the time he could successfully predict the dominance relationships that juvenile males would assume in the male linear hierarchy based on the matriline rank of their mothers. In many of these species the influence of the natal matriline on the rank of the male decreases as the male grows older, and attributes such as size and strength become more important (Walters and Seyfarth 1987: 312).

In this type of multimale, multifemale system there is clearly no "alliance" in Fox's sense of the term. In contrast to one-male groups, the multimale, multifemale primates do not engage in long-term association of mates. Instead, most of their mating involves a brief encounter between male and female. And unlike one-male groups, these multimale, multifemale primates exhibit what Fox calls "descent." To a considerable extent they behave differentially toward one another based not only on their immediate kinship connections (mother-child and sibling bonds) but also on their positions within *lines of matrikin* (i.e., on relationships based on descent over the generations).

In short, Fox saw among primates the rudimentary elements of true human kinship systems. Some primates exhibit "alliance," others "descent"; but the two patterns never occur together in the same primate system. If we were to take the alliance pattern of the hamadryas baboons and somehow combine it with the descent pattern of the multimale groups, we would have the full basis of human kinship. This, according to Fox, is exactly what our hominid ancestors did at some point.

Lars Rodseth and his colleagues (1991) take a somewhat different view. After comparing the social organization of a wide range of primates, including humans, in terms of the distribution in groups of males and females, kin and nonkin, they have concluded that humans are distinctive among primates in that both sexes maintain lifelong relationships with consanguineal kin—regardless of which sex leaves its natal group or whether both sexes do so. Among other primates, by contrast, only one sex (the one that stays put and does not disperse) maintains these lifelong ties with kin. According to Rodseth et al., it was this unique development among humans that allowed humans to link up and ally with other groups of nonkin. By maintaining ties with a dispersed son or daughter, humans could forge ties with the group to which the child moved. Thus a uniquely human trait, and one significant to our social organization, is the ability to maintain social relationships with others even when they are absent from us for prolonged periods.

Using data on hamadryas baboons (e.g., from Abegglen 1984), Rodseth et al. also make a case for Fox's "alliance" and "descent" already combined in one system. Not only do these baboons in their one-male units exhibit "alliance," just as Fox described, but the males of these units are loosely organized into troops or "clans" and, above those, into bands. There is evidence that hamadryas male baboons organize into clans and bands on the basis of common kinship through males. Hence we see an arrangement whereby the overall social organization (clans, bands) follows a "descent" pattern, yet within the structure there are distinct breeding units that follow an "alliance" pattern. Fox (1991) later agreed that if this is the case, the hamadryas baboons are an exception to his earlier generalization about primates.

Primate Gender

We will return to some of these ideas about primate kinship in the next section; but, first, let's consider primate "gender." Are there important or consistent behavioral differences between females and males (i.e., beyond the obvious differences in reproduction and infant care)? One interesting study of chimpanzees of the Ivory Coast's Tai forest showed that females are considerably more efficient than males at nut cracking, using stone and wooden hammers (Boesch and Boesch 1981, 1990): Females work with persistence, whereas males are easily distracted by social interactions. A similar sex difference in persistence has been found among chimpanzees of Tanzania, where females engage in termite fishing to a greater extent than males do. One factor that may account for this latter difference is the females' greater need for protein, given that adult female chimpanzees are often pregnant or lactating (Zihlman 1993: 36).

Male primates were previously thought to be more aggressive than females, but this assumption is not supported by current evidence, at least as far as frequency of aggressive acts is concerned. According to Smuts (1987: 401), there are sex differences in both style and context of aggression. In terms of style, the males of many species are more likely to precede aggression with "ritualized threats" (e.g., charging displays), whereas females often simply attack without warning. And an example of difference in context is that females are often highly aggressive when offspring protection is at stake, whereas males are highly aggressive when sexual access to females is threatened. However, as Hrdy (1981: 55) points out, female primates also compete with one another over males. Among many monogamous species, females aggressively drive out any female intruder.

With regard to primate gender, another widespread assumption has been that males are typically dominant over females. This idea still holds up in many cases, but our understanding of the overall picture is changing. Until recently both the popular imagination and the media fixed upon a rather extreme version of male dominance in the primate "wild," possibly involving the projection of a masculinity fantasy onto our primate "roots." King Kong, after all, not only scaled the Empire State Building with a scantily dressed and vulnerable woman in his grip but also demanded and extracted a virgin every year from his human population back home. Thanks to better field studies, this image has given way to the documentation of greater gender diversity. Seeing male dominance as a social system where males "have feeding priority, spatial priority, and often decide on travel routes," Patricia Wright (1993: 135) has concluded that male dominance is a feature of the societies of most Old World Monkeys and apes. At the same time she points out that "there are approximately 200 species of primates, and in about 40 percent of them females are dominant or equal in status" (1993: 127). Examples of female dominant species include squirrel monkeys and some lemurs. Among these species, females lead groups in travel, assume feeding priority over males, and can displace males from a location. In all the female dominant groups, breeding is strictly seasonal. Examples of species in which neither sex is dominant are monogamous species, such as gibbons and tarsiers. And among still other species (e.g., some capuchin monkeys), a male is always first in a local linear hierarchy whereas a female can be second, third, or fourth (Wright 1993: 135).

In another review, Joan Silk (1993: 216) makes the very interesting comment that, despite male dominance in some cases, "in all non-human primate species, females maintain considerable autonomy over their own lives." Indeed, although females in male-dominant species may encounter male aggression as well as displacement from males, they actually spend much of their lives on their own with their young or with other females. They exercise considerable choice in mating, they may form coalitions with other females against males, and through either friendly or nonfriendly behavior they can influence the male membership of their groups (Smuts 1987: 407). This issue of female autonomy is crucial in any discussion of human gender. In fact, a key question raised by primate studies is How, when, where, and under what circumstances did some human female primates lose their autonomy?

In primates, variations in male dominance normally correlate with **sexual dimorphism,** or the external physical differences between males and females. Sexual dimorphism concerns differences in size and weight, and in features such as larger or sharper canine teeth. For example, among male-dominant species (e.g., gorillas), males are considerably larger and weigh more. Among female-dominant species (e.g., lemurs), females are slightly larger. And among monogamous species where neither sex is dominant, the sexes tend to be equal in size. Although humans are more sexually dimorphic than these monogamous species, Silk (1993: 230) maintains that human societies generally exhibit a greater degree of male dominance than primatologists would predict on the basis of sexual dimorphism and mating practices.

Humans' interpretations of other primates' behavior not only change over time (Haraway 1989) but often, at any one time, are controversial. For example, researchers have not yet reached full agreement regarding the nature of those most-studied human cousins, the chimpanzees, even in terms of such basics as male dominance hierarchies and male dominance over females. As noted earlier, chimpanzees have been extensively studied at Gombe National Park in Tanzania, the site of Jane Goodall's and others' research, over three decades. In her first reports during the early 1960s, Goodall described the chimps as quite peaceful, harmonious, and egalitarian. But in the mid-1970s and continuing to the present, a "darker" side of chimp society emerged in reports of aggression, dominance struggles, infanticide, murder, rape, even cannibalism. Goodall's (1986: 313) own conclusion was that only long-term and sustained field studies could bring out the full picture. In the final analysis, Goodall (1986: 356) said, it is the interplay between the peaceful relationships and the aggression and dominance that shapes chimpanzee society.

Margaret Power (1991) countered by arguing that what Goodall and others observed at Gombe was *social change* among the chimps, who were not only increasingly surrounded by human settlement but also provisioned (fed) by the researchers themselves. Power points out that at Gombe and other research sites, feeding stations are indeed set up to habituate chimps to the presence of humans and to facilitate observations. And perhaps years of artificial feeding produced stress among the chimps that was increasingly played out in aggressive acts and dominance struggles. Thus, according to Power, Goodall's long-term data on chimps are not inaccurate as such but need to be interpreted in the context of induced stress over time.

Goodall did report that provisioning of chimps affected their behavior and made them much more aggressive (1971: 143, cited in Power 1991: 28). She also acknowledged that chimps were competing with local baboons for access to the provisioned food (in this case, bananas). But Goodall did not connect provisioning with the chimpanzee violence at Gombe in the 1970s. At this time there occurred a gradual killing off of all the males (and some of the females) of one chimp community by those of another (Goodall 1986: 503–514). These two chimp groups had previously been in friendly and peaceful contact; in fact, in the early (pre-feeding) days, they were not even considered separate groups. Members of both came to the feeding station; then, members of what became a separate group gradually stopped coming and members of the other group started to patrol "their" territory, which now included the feeding station. Goodall described the vicious attacks on one group by the males of the other. The following account details how a group of males (which included chimps named Faben, Satan, and Jomeo) continued to torture another male, Goliath, after a series of brutal attacks on him:

> The other males continued to beat up their victim without pause, using fists and feet. Goliath . . . soon gave up and lay quite still. Faben took one of his arms and dragged him about 8 meters over the ground. Satan dragged him

back again. Faben leaped onto Goliath and repeatedly stamped on him as he lay stretched out, face down. . . . With very rapid movements Jomeo began to drum with his hands on Goliath's shoulder blades while Faben sat on the old male's back, took one of his legs and, with his one good arm, tried to twist it around and around. (Goodall 1986: 508–509)

Eventually all of the males in the loser group were dead, along with some of the females; other females joined the winning group. Goodall and others interpreted this process by saying that it was a case of one subgroup splitting off from a larger group, that aggression and territoriality emerged as part of the process, and that chimpanzees are normally territorial and aggressively hostile to outsiders.

Based on studies of nonprovisioned chimps, Power (1991) gives a picture of chimp society that radically differs from that of Goodall's (1986) Gombe research. Power suggests that, unlike provisioned Gombe chimps, nonprovisioned chimps do not exhibit a structured male dominance hierarchy. Instead, they engage in "mutual dependence" relationships. For certain purposes and at certain times a "follower" will defer to a "leader," but in other circumstances this relationship can be reversed. Sometimes, for example, a charismatic individual emerges as a "leader" and takes on many followers. In contrast to the provisioned Gombe chimps, nonprovisioned males do not dominate females, and females can function as "leaders" too. The males do not defend a territory; rather, the groups live in undefended overlapping ranges. Individuals in one group (male or female) may also freely change membership and join other groups. According to Power, the whole arrangement closely resembles the egalitarian social organization of relatively undisturbed human foragers, such as the well-known !Kung people of the Kalahari Desert. Much has been written about the !Kung's egalitarian society (at least as it existed in the 1950s and early 1960s), which stressed informal leadership, a sharing ethic, near gender equality, and low levels of aggression (Lee 1979). Power suggests that both nonprovisioned chimps and relatively undisturbed human foragers like the !Kung of earlier times developed an egalitarian society as an adaptation to a foraging mode of subsistence.

Thus, even when the "facts" of chimpanzee behavior are agreed upon, the interpretation of them differs. The debate over chimp (and other primate) aggression is a long-standing one. Authors such as Richard Ardrey (1967) were accused of exaggerating primate aggression in an attempt to justify human aggression and territoriality. But those who, in the 1960s, argued against natural aggression and dominance among chimpanzees were later accused by Fox (1980: 89) of needing "the chimp to prove that our ancestors were promiscuous, egalitarian happy-go-lucky hippies."

"Reading into" primates (or, for that matter, human ancestors or the "earliest" human societies) what we want to see is all too tempting. It

should be remembered that chimpanzees, though the closest species to ourselves, are nevertheless chimpanzees, not human ancestors. We can learn a
great deal about humans, as primates, by examining the range of primate
variation; but as Robert Hinde (1987: 33) warns, "Attempting to draw
direct parallels between human and nonhuman species is a dangerous
pastime."

Kinship, Gender, and Human Evolution

The term **hominoid** refers to a classification of primates (Superfamily
Hominoidea) that includes apes and humans. Within this class is the category **hominid** (Family Hominidae), which includes modern humans and
their extinct ancestors. As noted earlier, hominids diverged from the rest of
the hominoid line about 5 million years ago. Remains of the earliest known
hominids, the Australopithecines, have been found in fossils dating from
about 2–4 million years ago or possibly earlier, unearthed at such sites as
Laetoli in Tanzania and Hardar, Ethiopia. According to some researchers
(e.g., Johnson and White 1979), these hominids constitute a single species,
Australopithecus *afarensis* (of which the famous Lucy, discovered at
Hardar, was one). Analysis of skeletal material, plus amazing footprints
preserved in volcanic ash at Laetoli, shows that A. *afarensis* walked
bipedally but likely were tree climbers as well. Except for their bipedal gait
these Australopithecines probably looked a lot like modern chimps.

It now appears that several different species of Australopithecines
spanned a period of 2 million years or more in east and southern Africa.
Experts do not agree on their evolutionary connections; nor do they agree
as to which kind of Australopithecine was the ancestor of the next important fossil hominid, Homo *habilis* (of the genus Homo and the species
habilis). The latter appeared around 2 million years ago in east and southern Africa and lived at the same time as some Australopithecines. The brain
of H. *habilis* showed a definite increase in size over Australopithecus. In addition, H. *habilis* (and possibly also some Australopithecines) constructed
stone tools, some of which were undoubtedly used to butcher meat. Both
most likely subsisted on plant food and meat, which they either hunted or
scavenged, or both. What proportion of their diet consisted of meat, and
how and to what extent they hunted, is not known.

H. *habilis* is considered ancestral to H. *erectus*, who appeared in Africa
about 1.5 million years ago and then spread to Asia and Europe. H. *erectus*
showed a further increase in brain size and left evidence of more advanced
tools, hunting of large animals, and use of fire. H. *erectus* lived for about 1
million years, possibly overlapping with archaic H. *sapiens*, who in turn
was ancestral to modern H. *sapiens*. H. *sapiens* first appeared 70,000–
100,000 years ago.

The fossil record tells us a great deal about human evolution, but we do not now (and may not ever) know some fairly major details such as when human language first developed or what sort of mating systems any of these creatures practiced. Yet research has advanced some interesting speculations as to what may have happened, and some of these carry implications for the development of human kinship and gender.

As noted earlier with regard to kinship, Fox maintained that a uniquely human innovation was to combine "alliance" with "descent" in one system. How could this process have come about? Fox's own answer points to one major adaptation: hominid hunting. The idea that hominid hunting played a pivotal role in making us human has an interesting history of its own. Known as the "hunting hypothesis," this line of thinking was in vogue in the 1960s and 1970s, supported by anthropologists such as Sherwood Washburn and Chet Lancaster (1968) and popularized by Robert Ardrey (1976). It held that the earliest hominids (Australopithecines), upon coming out of the trees, adapted to open country where, to survive, they took up hunting of large prey. Hunting changed everything. This new "killer ape" developed tools for hunting. In turn, tool making and use encouraged an increase in the size and complexity of the brain. Meanwhile, since it was easier to have one's hands and arms free to use hunting tools, bipedalism was further encouraged. In essence, then, it was early hominid big-game hunting that turned us into upright, large-brained, intelligent, tool-using creatures with potential for language and culture. And it was the males, not the females, who hunted. Males brought back the precious meat to females with their young. The implication of this scenario is that males were the prime movers in human evolution, but also that women *became provisioned by and dependent upon men.*

This early form of the hunting hypothesis was itself killed off by a number of findings. One was the discovery that chimpanzees make and use tools; hence tools could no longer be considered a distinctive hominid invention. In addition, there was insufficient evidence to support the contention that early hominids hunted with tools. Indeed, it soon became clear from examination of Australopithecine bones and skulls that these creatures were more likely prey (e.g., of hyenas) than predators (Brain 1981). And examination of early Australopithecine (*afarensis*) skeletons suggested that these creatures were still at least semi-arboreal. Australopithecus, no longer the mighty "killer ape" on the road to becoming "man," was now depicted as a small biped who still spent time in trees and was hunted successfully by carnivores.

At this point, some revisions of the hunting hypothesis may yet have been possible, but then another blow was dealt to it—namely, the rise of the "gathering hypothesis." According to this hypothesis, put forth by female researchers (e.g., Slocum 1974; Tanner, 1981, 1987), the diet of the hominids probably consisted largely of gathered plant foods. The same is true of modern hunting and gathering humans. For example, gathered plant food constitutes 60 to 80 percent of the diet (in calories) of the !Kung (Lee 1968). Among modern hunter-gatherers, gathering is primarily a female activity; thus it is likely that female hominids did the gathering. Researchers have also noted that, among chimpanzees, females use tools for foraging more frequently and more efficiently than males do. In short, the gathering hypothesis suggests that in hominid evolution, the earliest tools were those that women developed to make gathering more efficient. In addition, women devised containers to facilitate the transportation of gathered food and for hauling infants during gathering.

The gathering hypothesis made a lot of sense; it also fit the evidence better than the hunting hypothesis. But perhaps even more important, it revealed the male bias of previous studies of human evolution, in which women and women's contributions had been ignored.

As the gathering hypothesis took hold, tantalizing speculations about other human developments emerged. For example, Nancy Tanner claimed that females and males developed bipedalism for different reasons. In females, natural selection favored bipedalism for such activities as tool use and carrying babies; but in males, it was female sexual selection that favored bipedalism. As males stood up straight, their penises became more visible to females. And "an erect, unclothed male with an erect and quite visible penis might have proven noticeable and attractive" (Tanner 1987: 14). Though untestable for hominid evolution, this proposition is thought provoking and clearly places females in an active evolutionary role. Likewise, regarding the evolutionary reduction of large canine teeth, Tanner (1987: 14) proposed that "females may have come to prefer to mate more often with males who kissed then effectively than with those who growled at them and displayed large canines." Certainly these ideas are as reasonable as the ones we hear from male researchers about why human females developed large breasts and buttocks.

Although these counterarguments did not quite spell the end of the hunting hypothesis, they ensured that only cleaned-up and gender-inclusive versions of it would be available in the future. Nevertheless, John Tooby and Irven DeVore (1987) criticized the gathering hypothesis for ignoring the impact of hunting altogether, claiming that hunting might still have been important in hominid evolution, though at a later time than was earlier supposed.

This brings us back to Robin Fox and his ideas about how alliance was combined with descent to form human kinship systems. Fox's theory can indeed be considered a cleaned-up version of the hunting hypothesis. It is also set within evolutionary theory. His ideas are important to consider because, although he doesn't state them in quite this way himself, they suggest that the birth of fully human kinship is simultaneously the birth of female subordination.

Going back to hominid evolution, Fox places the "hunting transition" at around the time that Australopithecus was becoming H. *habilis;* certainly it was well under way by early H. *erectus* (Fox 1980: 143). By "hunting transition" Fox meant not just that hominids began to hunt in earnest with tools but that they began to *develop a division of labor by sex.* Each sex specialized in what it was physically best able to do: Men went for hunting, women for gathering. Before this time, presumably everyone foraged for him- or herself and there was occasional hunting of small mammals and some food sharing, as among chimps now. But the transition to sex-specialized hunting and gathering capitalized upon and intensified an arrangement that was already present in the hominid social repertoire (and exists among nonhuman primates today)—namely, coalitions of kin. This new order required heightened cooperation, which was provided by groups of kin. Indeed, cooperation was especially and increasingly important in male cooperative hunting, but also important in female gathering. Recall the male patriline groups of the chimps or the female matrilines of other multimale, multifemale groups: They exemplify the "descent" half of the picture, retained and intensified in hominid evolution.

Now for the "alliance" half. With the new sexual division of labor came a trade in food between male and female, and this trade changed their relations with each other. Before this time there were all-male associations (as among chimps and some multimale, multifemale monkeys) and all-female (with young) associations (as among multimale groups with matrilines), but adult males and females had little to do with one another except for interactions involving sex and male protection of females.

With the sexual division of labor, however, men and women needed one another in a new way: for food, for the trade of vegetables and meat. This trade, according to Fox (1980: 143), "is probably at the root of a truly human society." Males now needed females not just for sex but also for food—and later for food processing and cooking (i.e., for domestic labor). So there arose a new male motivation for intensifying and lengthening the association of males with females (and their young). Early human females, too, would probably have been interested in strengthening alliances with males because they wanted a regular supply of meat for themselves and their children. Meanwhile, of course, women were out there not just foraging but also gathering plant food that they would *bring back* to swap for meat. Thus they were headed toward *domestic units* that would eventually bring adult males together with adult females and their young.

Many physiological changes are occurring by this time (e.g., the brain is growing in size and complexity, and the period of infant dependency is lengthening), but one thing stays the same: Males are still competing for females. In fact, the competition is even more intense now that females are valued for their vegetables as well as for sex. Older dominant males (we still have a male hierarchy here) seek to acquire many females; they are more or less headed for polygyny, or perhaps some groups were polygynously mating before anyway. This situation induces not only competition among the older males but a shortage of females for the younger males. Tensions mount. But males can't just fight it out anymore; they need each other too much for the cooperative hunt and, later, for the exchange of other specialized services. Some way of regulating mating and access to the women (with their vegetables) has to emerge. And it does: Older males get to be in charge of *allocating females* as mates. Younger males eventually get women, but only by obeying a set of rules (which become marriage rules) that place the power of allocation of women in the hands of the older males. According to Fox, this is a distinctively human rule-bound way of doing what many nonhuman primate males do—peripheralizing young males in order to maintain (at least for a time) a monopoly over access to the females. Young male primates must later work their way back into the male hierarchy in order to mate. Among humans, young males become dependent on older males for mates (now brides). As we will soon see, in many human societies young males (and young females, for that matter) are dependent on their elders for spouses.

But why, meanwhile, did female hominids come to "agree" with this arrangement? Why did they not allocate themselves, or make up rules by which male mates could be allocated? Fox's answer (which not everyone is going to like) is that it was probably the female kin coalitions that initiated male monopoly of mate allocation in the first place. Here's what he says: "The impulse was more likely to have come from the female kin coalitions. The need of the female coalitions for male provisioning—meat for the children—was undoubtedly the push. The females could easily trade on the male's tendency to want to monopolize (or at least think he was monopolizing) the females for mating purposes, and say, in effect, 'okay, you get the monopoly—or the appearance of it anyway—and we get the meat'" (Fox 1980: 147). This account calls to mind the "coy" female portrayed by earlier sociobiologists. But in Fox's view, the males are just continuing an old primate pattern of mating dominance by older males. Under the new order, each sex is finding its place and getting what it wants:

> As with the control of sex among non-human primates, the control of mate allocation in *Homo* is in the hands of the dominant males (at least overtly), and again, they either monopolize or share on their own terms with initiated juniors. But the primary aim by now is not monopoly of intercourse necessarily, although this is expected to correspond roughly with power[;] it is *the economic and political control of women* (and for women *the domestic exploitation of men*). (Fox 1980: 152; original emphasis)

Domestic exploitation of *men?* If women in this system end up process-ing food, cooking, and taking on the considerably larger share of child care, it would seem that they, not the men, are being domestically exploited. Is Fox suggesting that, to maintain the vegetable/sex/meat trade, men were "forced" to hang around more in domestic units (as opposed to spending more time in male-bonded hunting groups)? Or does he mean that men were conned into "investing" more heavily in children? (This is a point to which we will later return.)

In the final analysis, according to Fox's theory, it is female need (or fe-male perception of children's need) for protein from the hunt that lies at the root of the new social system. Thus females clearly participated in hominid evolution, and their gathering was important; but it was ultimately male hunting that gave men the edge, leading to economic and political control over women. One might say that women sold themselves out for protein; or, as Fox claimed, perhaps women, seeing a golden opportunity for pro-tein, cleverly pretended to give males a monopoly over mate allocation.

But a few more things were going on in this new hominid system. In a sense, women became even more valuable to males. As though their sex and veggies were not enough, they were now valued as items of exchange. Control over women (as potential wives for others) became a source of male political power. In addition (and let's assume that human-style mar-riage was in place by this time), by doling out females, males acquired valu-able new kin, such as brothers-in-law and sons-in law. Indeed, with the combination of alliance (now marriage) and descent, we find a truly unique element in human kinship: The "contribution [of the human primate] is not the invention of kinship, but the invention of in-laws, affines, 'relatives by marriage'" (Fox 1980: 147–148).

Finally, although Fox seems to gloss over this part of the human kinship equation, he claims that females became valuable as producers of offspring. His theory does not address how males become interested in their *own* off-spring, though he does mention greater male parental investment as some-thing sought by the evolving females (1980: 139), a claim that is consistent with earlier sociobiologists' accounts. Fox also notes that a man's recruit-ment of other males was an advantage in many respects, but that such re-cruitment could be accomplished through arranged marriages (in which male in-laws would be gained) as well as through reproduction. He does not mention the production of daughters as a source of new items for ex-change, though this observation would be in keeping with his other points.

Fox's theory can be criticized on two other fronts. First, does it really make sense that women gave men monopoly over mate allocation (real or putative) in exchange for meat when they had so much else to bargain with—namely, vegetables, sex, domestic labor, and offspring? Of course, fe-males were receiving male protection and male parental investment, too.

But the question is, How do we go from male and female exchange of mutually valued products and services to male political and economic control over women? Was meat *that* important? Advocates of the gathering hypothesis have made a strong case that gathered food was probably just as important as hunted meat. Add to this the fact that women in modern hunting-gathering societies do hunt some small animals and the case for females' desperate need for male-hunted protein becomes a little weaker.

Second, what about sex? Fox claims that the evolving hominid males, much like male nonhuman primates, wanted sexual access to females; but nowhere does he mention sex, in and of itself, as a motive for females.

An entirely different picture is presented by Sarah Hrdy (1981), who sees female primates as sexually motivated and assertive and female strategies for sex and reproduction as important in human evolution. In her view, females evolved an interest in promiscuous sex so that many males would "presume" that they could have "fathered" a female's child. Multiple male care for, or at least lack of harm to, her offspring would result, thus enhancing the fitness of both her offspring and herself. Hrdy and others have also seen the human female's loss of physical signs of ovulation in this light: Concealed ovulation was naturally selected since it helped to decrease paternity certainty. Hrdy argues that paternity uncertainty was an advantage for evolving hominid women, but that as human society developed, males devised ways to increase paternity certainty (through seclusion of women, chastity belts, and so on). Thus women lost their autonomy, otherwise at a high level among primate females, as a result of male success in increasing paternity certainty. But Hrdy does not discuss the transition: How and why did the male strategy come to supersede the female strategy?

Each of these two theories connects human kinship with male ascendancy over females. For Fox, it is the marriage tie that became important since males acquired a monopoly over allocation of females in marital alliances. But for Hrdy, it was descent, specifically the father-child bond, that became important since males, to increase their fitness, had to figure out ways to promote paternity certainty as they increased their parental investment. Fox claims that male parental investment was something females wanted and got, whereas Hrdy insists that this investment was in the males' own interest. Interestingly, both theories suggest that females emerged as slightly cunning and deceitful. According to Fox's theory, the females likely gave males only the "appearance" of monopoly over mate allocation while presumably playing some role in this allocation themselves. It is almost as though the women discussed it all beforehand and decided to keep their little secret to themselves. According to Hrdy's theory, however, females were far from consciously deceitful; natural selection merely hid their ovulation for them. But still they emerged with a secret that worked to their advantage over males, and their success hinged on the males being fooled.

Before leaving this topic, we should note yet another way in which human hunting has been linked to the origins of human gender inequality. Marvin Harris (1993) argues that male hunting of large game gave men the edge over women not because they brought back valued protein from the hunt but because men thereby gained familiarity with and monopoly over the manufacture and use of weapons. Males became the specialized hunters because of the superior strength of their arms, chests, and shoulders, enabling them to better master the use of spears, heavy clubs, and bows and arrows. Then, of course, males became even more specialized as warriors fighting against other human groups. But the original impetus for male dominance proceeded from the fact that males were not only stronger than females but more skilled in weapon use, which in turn gave them more authority and more power in public decision making. Harris then goes on to trace how different kinds, or stages, of human warfare affected gender in very different ways. He explains that, as state systems and social classes developed, warfare was eventually taken over by professionals, and inequalities between men and women become a matter of their relative contributions to economic production.

Incest and Exogamy

In the last section we saw that nonhuman primates engage in regular patterns of mating, whereas humans have institutionalized marriages. From a certain point of view we could say that the basic difference between nonhuman and human primates is not so much behavioral as related to the fact that humans have invented rules and institutions within which to set and regulate their behavior. We can carry this point further by noting two other distinctive features of human kinship. First, whereas nonhuman primates exhibit "incest avoidance," most human societies have an "incest taboo." And, second, many nonhuman primates engage in "dispersal" of one sex at adolescence, whereas humans invented "exogamy," the rule whereby one must marry outside a certain group. We will consider each of these concepts in turn.

The human incest taboo is a ban on sexual relations between primary kin: mother-son, father-daughter, and brother-sister (Fox 1989: 31). Some societies include other relatives in their own category of "incestuous union," but what we find common to nearly all societies is the ban on sex between primary kin. The incest taboo is not, however, universal among humans. It is well known that royal families of ancient Egypt, Peru (Inca), and Hawaii allowed or encouraged brother-sister marriages (and thus mating), and that in Egypt some royal father-daughter marriages occurred as well.

For decades, anthropologists have been interested in explaining why human societies have an incest taboo, why it is nearly universal, and why people in so many societies regard incest with horror and disgust. Claude Lévi-Strauss (1969) saw the taboo as a key to what it meant to be human rather than "animal." With this taboo humans marked themselves off as being part of human "culture" as opposed to animal "nature." And in terms of kinship systems the taboo is important because if it did not exist (and if people regularly practiced incest), we wouldn't need even kinship systems to regulate human reproduction. Instead, as Fox (1989: 54) put it, a "mother-children group could settle down to a cosy little inbreeding arrangement and be totally self-sufficient for purposes of reproduction." In short, we would not need kinship rules by which to recruit new members to groups; each group would just incestuously "grow its own."

Although the incest taboo is a central element of human kinship systems, Fox (1989, 1980) and others have convincingly shown that many previous theorists were mistaken when they tried to locate the origin of human kinship systems in the emergence of nonincestuous human mating. The idea was that, having banned incest and so having separated themselves from the animals, humans then had to define other rules of mating and of allocating children to social groups. But it is now known that most mammals in the wild exhibit patterns of incest avoidance (Brown 1991). Studies of primates, for instance, show that although some incestuous matings take place, these are very rare. Indeed, among many primates and other wild mammals, patterns of dispersal of the young ensure that most breeding will not occur between close genetic kin. Thus, rules aside, and specifically in terms of behavior, humans are not unique in incest avoidance.

Over the past century, many theories sprang up to explain the human incest taboo. Most were not very satisfactory, and even today debates continue over the issue (Brown 1991: 128). The two most popular theories were those originally proposed by Edward Westermarck (1891) and Sigmund Freud (1918). Westermarck proposed that persons raised together, or persons living closely together from early childhood, develop a natural aversion to having sexual relations with one another. He had brother-sister relations in mind, but the same line of thinking applied to parent-child relations as well, accounting for the aversion to sexual relations between child-rearers and children. Since it is usually the case that parents raise children, and siblings live together in childhood, an incest avoidance results between primary kin. In Westermarck's view, this natural incest aversion was a human instinct that evolved or was naturally selected to prevent the harmful effects of close inbreeding. Only later was a taboo developed to discourage any aberrant tendencies.

According to Freud (who focused more on parent-child incest), humans unconsciously do wish to commit incest, but this desire is repressed. His idea was that repression is triggered by guilt. Ridiculous as it might seem today, what Freud proposed was that at some time in the remote past there existed a human "primal horde" headed by a father who kept, all to himself, a group of women with whom he mated. His sons, wanting access to the females, killed him (not unlike Indian langurs); but then, since they had been raised to respect and obey their father, they felt guilty and so "tabooed" their own access to the women (their mothers and sisters). Humans since then have somehow inherited all this trauma and continue to "live it out." Of course, later Freudians found it necessary to dispense with this idea of the "primal horde" as a prehistorical event, but they retained the notions of unconscious desire, guilt, and repression to account for an incest taboo.

These two theories of Westermarck and Freud were at odds. One maintained that humans normally do not want to commit incest, so we need a taboo for the few misfits who do. The other held that humans really do want to commit incest, but that this impulse immediately triggers guilt and repression, leading to a taboo that expresses and confirms that very human psycho-familial process.

Both theories have been criticized, but of the two, Westermarck's has perhaps held up a little better. The idea of an aversion to sex between children raised together received support from studies of the Israeli *kibbutzim* (communal villages), where male and female infants are detached from their parents and raised together through adolescence. According to these studies, children raised together showed no sexual interest in one another upon reaching adulthood and, though free to do so, did not marry one another (Shepher 1983). Additional support for Westermarck has come from studies of a Chinese custom called "minor marriages," whereby parents adopt a female child to raise as the future bride of their son. The girl and boy are raised together and, later, are forced to marry. These marriages were found to be considerably less fertile, less happy, and far more prone to divorce than regular, or "major," Chinese marriages (Wolf 1970; Wolf and Huang 1980).

A lot of the theorizing about the incest taboo entails the implicit or explicit assumption that close inbreeding is biologically or genetically disadvantageous. But just how detrimental would inbreeding be? On the one hand, within a small group whose gene pool contains largely "good" genes, close inbreeding over time would not be harmful and might even be advantageous. On the other hand, close inbreeding would be disadvantageous to sexually reproducing organisms who live in a changing environment, since loss of genetic variation, and thus loss of flexibility in adaptation, would result. A biological "motive" for either incest avoidance or the incest taboo is still being debated.

Now, what about exogamy? How and why did humans develop exogamous rules? These rules are common in many kinds of societies and are presumed to have been very important in the development of human culture; yet kin group exogamy is not considered a human universal (see Chapter 6). Another important point, and one that has been stressed repeatedly (Fox 1980, 1989; Brown 1991), is that exogamy and the incest taboo are different, though related. The incest taboo has to do with restrictions on *sexual relations,* whereas exogamy has to do with restrictions on *marriage.* Fox (1989: 54) was quite right when he wrote: "While every teenager knows these [sex and marriage] are different, many anthropologists get them confused." Some anthropologists tried to explain exogamy by calling it an "extension of the incest taboo"; others tried to explain the incest taboo by saying that it forced people to "marry out." But these attempts only muddled the problem further.

The incest taboo and exogamy are related in the sense that if a society bans sex between two people, it would be rather stupid to allow them to marry. The reverse, however, does not hold. A society can forbid people to marry one another but still allow them to have sexual relations. Indeed, some societies specify categories of people whom one is forbidden to marry but with whom one may have sex.

Exogamy, unlike the incest taboo, is rather easy to explain: It helps foster peaceable relationships between groups. We saw earlier that, according to Fox's theory, evolving hominids (or, rather, male hominids) found that power over mate allocation was politically advantageous, in that by allocating mates one could acquire useful in-law relatives. It is but a small step from this arrangement to a rule of exogamy, which guaranteed that a group of people would use marriage to make connections with other groups.

If a group forbids marriage within itself, it is forced to acquire spouses from other groups; and when that happens, harmonious relationships between the groups are promoted by the fact of their interdependency for spouses. This interdependency was undoubtedly important to early humans, who were now armed with lethal weapons, as groups expanded, moved about, and bumped into one another, possibly competing for resources. An anthropologist of the last century, Sir Edward B. Tylor (1889: 267), put it succinctly: "Again and again in the world's history, savage tribes must have had before them the simple practical alternative between marrying out or being killed-out." Recall the chimpanzees at Gombe, who (regardless of what *really* caused their problem) were unable to capitalize on this uniquely human invention when faced with territorial dispute. Or, for a human example, consider the bitter war between Muslims and Serbs in the former Yugoslavia. Outsiders have been unable to end this conflict. But it might stop if the Muslims and Serbs merely instituted one simple rule: All Muslim males could marry only Serbian women, and all Muslim women could take only Serbian husbands. We could combine this with, say, a patrilocality measure ensuring that the women moved to the regions of their husbands. Conflict would likely cease, then, not just because young people of enemy groups would be forced to intermarry but also because, over time, all the people in the predominantly Serbian areas would have sisters, daughters, and grandchildren among the Muslims, and all the people in the Muslim areas would have sisters, daughters, and grandchildren among the Serbians. Unfortunately, these two groups are unlikely to adopt such a marriage rule, so deep is the discord between them; but the example certainly shows how a rule of intermarriage could help deter intergroup conflict.

The rule of exogamy prescribes marriage outside a certain group. But there may be many groups *into* which marriage is permitted; or, as in the hypothetical Serbian-Muslim example above, it may be that two groups are directly exchanging spouses, so that the people of group A must not only marry outside group A but also marry *into* group B. The potentials for deterring conflict or for forming strong alliances are of course greater in cases where groups systematically exchange spouses.

Marriages can be used, then, to deter hostilities or, more positively, to form and cement alliances between groups. Western European history is full of examples of political alliances formed through marriages between royal families. Of course, peace or long-lasting political alliance through intermarriage is not always guaranteed (as European history also shows), but the rule of exogamy can increase its likelihood.[4]

Human Kinship

From the world of primates we have seen that humans are not unique in terms of either avoiding incest or making kinship connections a core feature of their social behavior. Kinship among primates goes far beyond a strong and enduring mother-child bond. The social life of many primate species entails the structure (if not the concept) of descent. In other species we see a rudimentary kind of mate assignment that results in relatively long-term and stable associations between adult males and females. But the special human development, according to Fox (1975, 1980), was to combine "descent" with adult male-female "alliances" in one system. This sys-

---

[4] Rodseth et al. (1991) have added insights to the anthropological discussions of exogamy. They rightfully argue that a simple rule of exogamy does not necessarily lead to intergroup alliances. They also point out that an "exogamous" mating pattern is not unique to humans, given evidence that adult female hamadryas baboons also transfer out to new "clans" and "bands." What *is* unique to humans, they emphasize (along with Fox 1989), is a system where membership in one descent group determines the other group or groups into which one may or may not marry, and where a systematic exchange of spouses may be used to form long-term intergroup alliances. In their view, this system was made possible by the uniquely human ability to maintain ties with dispersing children.

tem of mate allocation resulted in a new category of kin: in-laws. We presume that, at some point, descent group exogamy became significant and served as a mechanism by which groups could relate to one another in potentially nonhostile ways. We have also seen that male dominance over females is evident in some, though by no means all, primate groups. Finally, we have noted that female nonhuman primates exhibit an autonomy over their own lives beyond that found in many, if not most, human societies.

What happened next? The answer is not clear, as we do not know what kinds of kinship organization were experienced by early human hunting-gathering groups. Various authors have tried to show that the original human mode was monogamy or polygyny, or that the first human societies were matriarchal, patriarchal, or egalitarian; but all such theories run up against the same problem that we saw before with chimps—namely, that of "reading into" human origins what one wants to see. Studies of modern hunter-gatherers show variation in kinship systems. What we do know is that human kinship became extremely important as a framework of social structure and that it became tightly interwoven with economic relationships, politics, and religion. With the advent of pastoralism (livestock herding) and food production, kinship likely became even more complex, since it would have been used to define rights over new kinds of productive property and to transmit these rights to subsequent generations (Keesing 1975). It was at this stage that the "kinship corporations" discussed in the last chapter became so important. In the next three chapters, we shall examine interrelationships between human kinship systems and gender in societies with patrilineal, matrilineal, and cognatic descent.

References

Abegglen, J. J. 1984. *On Socialization in Hamadryas Baboons*. Cranbury, N.J.: Associated University Press.

Alexander, Richard D., and Katherine M. Noonan. 1979. Concealment of Ovulation, Parental Care, and Human Social Evolution. In Napoleon A. Chagnon and William Irons, eds., *Evolutionary Biology and Human Social Behavior: An Anthropological Perspective*, pp. 436–453. North Scituate, Mass.: Duxbury Press.

Ardrey, Robert. 1967. *The Territorial Imperative*. London: Anthony Blond.

_____. 1976. *The Hunting Hypothesis*. New York: Bantam Books.

Barash, David. 1979. *The Whisperings Within: Evolution and the Origin of Human Nature*. New York: Harper and Row.

Bernstein, Irwin S. 1991. The Correlation Between Kinship and Behavior in Non-Human Primates. In Peter G. Hepper, ed., *Kin Recognition*, pp. 6–29. Cambridge: Cambridge University Press.

Bernstein, Irwin S., and C. L. Ehardt. 1986. The Influence of Kinship and Socialization on Aggressive Behavior in Rhesus Monkeys (*Macaca mulatta*). *Animal Behavior* 34: 739–747.

Boesch, Christophe, and Helwige Boesch. 1981. Sex Differences in the Use of Natural Hammers by Wild Chimpanzees: A Preliminary Report. *Journal of Human Evolution* 10: 585–593.

_____. 1990. Tool Use and Tool Making in Wild Chimpanzees. *Folia Primatologica* 54: 86–99.

Brain, C. K. 1981. *The Hunters or the Hunted? An Introduction to African Cave Taphonomy.* Chicago: University of Chicago Press.

Brown, Donald E. 1991. *Human Universals.* New York: McGraw-Hill.

Clark, W. E. Le Gros. 1971. *The Antecedents of Man*, 3rd ed. Edinburgh: Edinburgh University Press.

Fausto-Sterling, Anne. 1985. *Myths of Gender: Biological Theories About Women and Men.* New York: Basic Books.

Fedigan, Linda Marie. 1982. *Primate Paradigms: Sex Roles and Social Bonds.* Montréal: Eden Press.

Fossey, Dian. 1983. *Gorillas in the Mist.* Boston: Houghton Mifflin.

Fox, Robin. 1975. Primate Kin and Human Kinship. In Robin Fox, ed., *Biosocial Anthropology*, pp. 9–35. New York: John Wiley and Sons.

_____. 1980. *The Red Lamp of Incest.* New York: E. P. Dutton.

_____. 1989 [orig. 1967]. *Kinship and Marriage: An Anthropological Perspective.* Cambridge: Cambridge University Press.

_____. 1991. Reply to Rodseth et al., "The Human Community as a Primate Society." *Current Anthropology* 32(3): 242–243.

Freud, Sigmund. 1918. *Totem and Taboo.* New York: A. A. Brill.

Goldizen, Anne Wilson. 1987. Tamarins and Marmosets: Communal Care of Offspring. In Barbara B. Smuts, Dorothy L. Cheney, Robert M. Seyfarth, Richard W. Wrangham, and Thomas T. Struhsaker, eds., *Primate Societies*, pp. 34–43. Chicago: University of Chicago Press.

Goodall, Jane. 1971. *In the Shadow of Man.* London: Collins.

_____. 1986. *The Chimpanzees of Gombe: Patterns of Behavior.* Cambridge: Harvard University Press.

Gouzoules, Sarah, and Harold Gouzoules. 1987. Kinship. In Barbara B. Smuts, Dorothy L. Cheney, Robert M. Seyfarth, Richard W. Wrangham, and Thomas T. Struhsaker, eds., *Primate Societies*, pp. 299–305. Chicago: University of Chicago Press.

Hamilton, W. D. 1964. The Genetic Evolution of Social Behavior. *Journal of Theoretical Biology* 7: 1–51.

Haraway, Donna. 1989. *Primate Visions: Gender, Race and Nature in the World of Modern Science.* New York: Routledge.

Harris, Marvin. 1993. The Evolution of Human Gender Hierarchies: A Trial Formulation. In Barbara Diane Miller, ed., *Sex and Gender Hierarchies*, pp. 57–79. Cambridge: Cambridge University Press.

Hewlett, Barry S. 1992. *Intimate Fathers: The Nature and Context of Aka Pygmy Paternal Infant Care.* Ann Arbor: University of Michigan Press.

Hinde, Robert A. 1987. Can Nonhuman Primates Help Us Understand Human Behavior? In Barbara B. Smuts, Dorothy L. Cheney, Robert M. Seyfarth, Richard W. Wrangham, and Thomas T. Struhsaker, eds., *Primate Societies,* pp. 413–420. Chicago: University of Chicago Press.

Hrdy, Sarah Blaffer. 1977. *The Langurs of Abu*. Cambridge: Harvard University Press.

_____. 1981. *The Woman That Never Evolved*. Harvard: Harvard University Press.

Irons, William. 1979. Natural Selection, Adaptation, and Human Social Behavior. In Napoleon A. Chagnon and William Irons, eds., *Evolutionary Biology and Human Social Behavior: An Anthropological Perspective*, pp. 4–39. North Scituate, Mass.: Duxbury Press.

Johnson, Donald, and T. D. White. 1979. A Systematic Assessment of Early African Hominids. *Science* 203: 321–330.

Judge, P. 1983. Reconciliation Based on Kinship in a Captive Group of Pigtail Macaques. Abstract. *American Journal of Primatology* 4: 346.

Kano, Takayoshi. 1992. *The Last Ape: Pygmy Chimpanzee Behavior and Ecology*. Stanford: Stanford University Press.

Keesing, Roger M. 1975. *Kin Groups and Social Structure*. Fort Worth, Tex.: Holt, Rinehart and Winston.

Lee, Richard B. 1968. What Hunters Do for a Living: Or, How to Make Out on Scarce Resources. In Richard B. Lee and Irven DeVore, eds., *Man the Hunter*, pp. 30–48. Chicago: Aldine.

_____. 1979. *The !Kung San: Men, Women and Work in a Foraging Society*. New York: Cambridge University Press.

Lévi-Strauss, Claude. 1969 [orig. 1949]. *The Elementary Structures of Kinship*. Translated by James Harle Bell, John Richard von Strummer, and Rodney Needham. Boston: Beacon Press.

Lewontin, R. C., Steven Rose, and Leon J. Kamin. 1984. *Not in Our Genes: Biology, Ideology and Human Nature*. New York: Pantheon Books.

Linsenmair, K. E. 1987. Kin Recognition in Subsocial Arthropods, in Particular in the Desert Isopod *Hemilepistus reaumuri*. In David J. C. Fletcher and Charles D. Michener, eds., *Kin Recognition in Animals*, pp. 121–208. Chichester: John Wiley and Sons.

Loy, James. 1972. The Effects of Matrilineal Relationships on the Behavior of Juvenile Rhesus Monkeys. Abstracts of the 71st Annual Meeting of the American Anthropological Association.

Morin, P. A., J. J. Moore, R. Chakraborty, L. Jin, J. Goodall, and D. S. Woodruff. 1994. Kin Selection, Social Structure, Gene Flow, and the Evolution of Chimpanzees. *Science* 265: 1193–1201.

Nishida, Toshisada, and Mariko Hiraiwa-Hasegawa. 1987. Chimpanzees and Bonobos: Comparative Relationships Among Males. In Barbara B. Smuts, Dorothy L. Cheney, Robert M. Seyfarth, Richard W. Wrangham, and Thomas T. Struhsaker, eds., *Primate Societies*, pp. 165–177. Chicago: University of Chicago Press.

Power, Margaret. 1991. *The Egalitarians—Human and Chimpanzee: An Anthropological View of Social Organization*. Cambridge: Cambridge University Press.

Riss, D. C., and J. Goodall. 1977. The Rise to Alpha-Rank in a Population of Free-Living Chimpanzees. *Folia Primatologica* 27: 134–151.

Rodseth, Lars, Richard W. Wrangham, Alisa M. Harrigan, and Barbara B. Smuts. 1991. The Human Community As a Primate Society. *Current Anthropology* 32(3): 221–241.

Savage-Rumbaugh, E. S., and B. J. Wilkerson. 1978. Socio-Sexual Behavior in *Pan paniscus* and *Pan troglodytes*: A Comparative Study. *Journal of Human Evolution* 7: 327–44.

Shepher, Joseph. 1983. *Incest: A Biosocial View*. New York: Academic Press.

Silk, Joan B. 1993. Primatological Perspectives on Gender Hierarchies. In Barbara Diane Miller, ed., *Sex and Gender Hierarchies*, pp. 212–235. Cambridge: Cambridge University Press.

Slocum, Sally. 1974. Woman the Gatherer. In Rayna Reiter, ed., *Toward an Anthropology of Women*, pp. 36–50. New York: Monthly Review Press.

Smuts, Barbara B. 1985. *Sex and Friendship in Baboons*. New York: Aldine.

_____. 1987. Gender, Aggression and Influence. In Barbara B. Smuts, Dorothy L. Cheney, Robert M. Seyfarth, Richard W. Wrangham, and Thomas T. Struhsaker, eds., *Primate Societies*, pp. 400–412. Chicago: University of Chicago Press.

_____. 1995. The Evolutionary Origins of Patriarchy. *Human Nature* 6(1): 1–32.

Smuts, Barbara B., and David J. Gubernick. 1992. Male-Infant Relationships in Nonhuman Primates: Parental Investment of Mating Effort? In Barry S. Hewlett, ed., *Father-Child Relations: Cultural and Biosocial Contexts*, pp. 1–30. New York: Aldine de Gruyer.

Sociobiology Study Group of Science for the People. 1978. Sociobiology—Another Biological Determinism. In A. L. Caplan, ed., *The Sociobiology Debate*, pp. 280–290. New York: Harper and Row.

Sperling, Susan. 1991. Baboons with Briefcases Vs. Langurs in Lipstick. In Micaela di Leonardo, ed., *Gender at the Crossroads of Knowledge: Feminist Anthropology in the Postmodern Era*, pp. 204–234. Berkeley: University of California Press.

Stammbach, Eduard. 1987. Desert, Forest and Montane Baboons: Multilevel Societies. In Barbara B. Smuts, Dorothy L. Cheney, Robert M. Seyfarth, Richard W. Wrangham, and Thomas T. Struhsaker, eds., *Primate Societies*, pp. 112–120. Chicago: University of Chicago Press.

Strum, Shirley C., and William Mitchell. 1987. Baboons: Baboon Models and Muddles. In Warren G. Kinzey, ed., *The Evolution of Human Behavior: Primate Models*, pp. 87–104. Albany: State University of New York Press.

Symons, Donald. 1979. *The Evolution of Human Sexuality*. New York: Oxford University Press.

Tanner, Nancy. 1981. *On Becoming Human*. Cambridge: Cambridge University Press.

_____. 1987. The Chimpanzee Model Revisited and the Gathering Hypothesis. In Warren G. Kinzey, ed., *The Evolution of Human Behavior: Primate Models*, pp. 3–27. Albany: State University of New York Press.

Thornhill, Randy, and N. Thornhill. 1983. Human Rape: An Evolutionary Analysis. *Ethnology and Sociobiology* 4: 137.

Tooby, John, and Irven DeVore. 1987. The Reconstruction of Hominid Behavioral Evolution Through Strategic Modeling. In Warren G. Kinzey, ed., *The Evolution of Human Behavior: Primate Models*, pp. 183–237. Albany: State University of New York Press.

Trivers, Robert L. 1972. Parental Investment and Sexual Selection. In B. Campbell, ed., *Sexual Selection and the Descent of Man*, pp. 136–179. Chicago: Aldine.

Tylor, Edward B. 1889. On a Method of Investigating the Development of Institutions: Applied to Laws of Marriage and Descent. *Journal of the Royal Anthropological Institute* 18: 245–269.

Walters, Jeffrey R. 1987. Kin Recognition in Non-Human Primates. In David J. C. Fletcher and Charles D. Michener, eds., *Kin Recognition in Animals*, pp. 359–393. Chichester: John Wiley and Sons.

Walters, Jeffrey R., and Robert M. Seyfarth. 1987. Conflict and Cooperation. In Barbara B. Smuts, Dorothy L. Cheney, Robert M. Seyfarth, Richard Wrangham, and Thomas T. Struhsaker, eds., *Primate Societies*, pp. 306–317. Chicago: University of Chicago Press.

Washburn, Sherwood L., and Lancaster, C. 1968. The Evolution of Hunting. In Richard B. Lee, ed., *Man the Hunter*, pp. 293–303. Chicago: Aldine.

Westermarck, Edward A. 1891. *The History of Human Marriage*. London: Macmillan.

Wilson, E. O. 1975. *Sociobiology: The New Synthesis*. Cambridge: Harvard University Press.

_____. 1987. Kin Recognition: An Introductory Synopsis. In David J. C. Fletcher and Charles D. Michener, eds., *Kin Recognition in Animals*, pp. 7–18. Chichester, England: John Wiley and Sons.

Wolf, Arthur P. 1970. Childhood Association and Sexual Attraction: A Further Test of the Westermarck Hypothesis. *American Anthropologist* 72: 503–511.

Wolf, Arthur, and C. S. Huang. 1980. *Marriage and Adoption in China, 1845–1945*. Stanford: Stanford University Press.

Wright, Patricia Chapple. 1993. Variations in Male-Female Dominance and Offspring Care in Non-Human Primates. In Barbara Diane Miller, ed., *Sex and Gender Hierarchies*, pp. 127–145. Cambridge: Cambridge University Press.

Zihlman, Adrienne L. 1993. Sex Differences and Gender Differences Among Primates: An Evolutionary Perspective. In Barbara Diane Miller, ed., *Sex and Gender Hierarchies,* pp. 32–56. Cambridge: Cambridge University Press.

_____. 1995. Misreading Darwin on Reproduction: Reductionism in Evolutionary Theory. In Faye D. Ginsburg and Rayna Rapp, eds., *Conceiving the New World Order: The Global Politics of Reproduction*, pp. 425–443. Berkeley: University of California Press.

3

The Power of Patrilines

In Chapter 1 we saw that one advantage of a mode of descent is that people can apply it to form groups within a society. Here, we will see how this works with patrilineal descent, or descent through the male line only. At the top of Figure 3.1, the dead man, A, is a founding ancestor of a patrilineal group. The shaded symbols represent his patrilineal descendants; together they form a patrilineal descent group.

As shown in this diagram, both males and females are born into the group, but only males can pass on membership. All persons inherit membership in a patriline through their father; but only sons can transmit it to their offspring. Notice that, when this principle is operating, it is always quite clear who is and who is not a member of the group; and this clarity persists over the generations.

What about women in this system? Obviously their position is different from that of men: Though born into a patriline like their brothers, they cannot pass on membership to their children. Thus the woman B in Figure 3.1 is a member of the shaded group, but her children belong to the patrilineal group of the man C, who is her husband and their father.

This diagram also shows that males and females are members of patrilineal descent groups; but societies vary in terms of the extent to which women are considered full members of their natal patrilines, and in terms of what happens to them when they marry. In some societies, such as the Tallensi of Ghana, women hold full membership in their natal patrilines throughout life and retain specific rights and duties vis à vis their natal patrilineal group. In others, such as that traditionally found in southern China, a woman at marriage is more fully identified with her husband's patriline and retains fewer rights in her natal group. Another example concerns a type of marriage that was practiced in ancient Rome, as we will see later in the chapter.

Figure 3.1 illustrates the core definition of *patrilineal*. This construct is important because, for one thing, most of the people of the world follow a

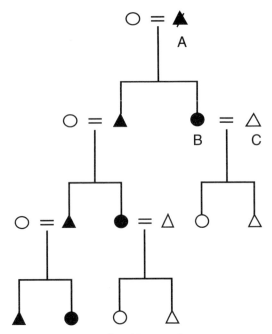

FIGURE 3.1   A Patrilineal Descent Construct.
Members sharing patrilineal descent are shaded.

mode of patrilineal descent. David Aberle (1961) once calculated that 44 percent of a representative sample of cultures in the world is patrilineal (with 36 percent bilateral or cognatic, 15 percent matrilineal, and 5 percent double). These percentages would look even more impressive if one were to calculate them by population. Patrilineal descent covers large and densely populated regions such as China and India. It is also prevalent in the Middle East and much of Africa. For those of us raised in European or Euro-American societies, then, it is important to grasp the concept of patrilineal descent if only to comprehend the basics of the social worlds around us.

So far we have seen what constitutes the patrilineal construct and how it can be used to form and perpetuate descent groups. Before proceeding further, however, we need to understand that the designation of *patrilineal* does not mean that the society in question recognizes only kinship on the male side, or through males, or that it ignores kinship to and through the mother. Indeed, virtually all societies exhibit **bilateral kinship,** whereby individuals consider that they are related to their mothers and fathers and, through them, to other people. Kinship is nearly everywhere recognized through both parents (but see Case 4 in Chapter 4). Kinship is thus normally bilateral, even in societies where descent is unilineal.

Why would a society adopt patrilineal descent? As we saw in Chapter 1, by adopting a mode of descent, whether patrilineal, matrilineal, or cognatic, a society has a handy means of forming descent groups, which in turn become fundamental to its social organization. But this fact alone does not explain why some, indeed most, societies adopted patrilineal as opposed to matrilineal or cognatic descent. Many anthropologists have argued that particular modes of descent probably arose out of different patterns of postmarital residence. If, for example, residence is patrilocal, then females born into a group move out at marriage, whereas the males stay put. These males would then be patrilineally related to one another. It thus makes sense that this group would adopt patrilineal descent, since each residential area would already consist of a core of patrilineally related males. As control over resources becomes an important consideration, these males could transmit rights over resources through patrilineal lines. Alternatively, groups with matrilocal residence, in which males leave at marriage to join wives' groups, would adopt matrilineal descent. (Cognatic descent is covered in Chapter 5.)

Some anthropologists have further suggested that different patterns of postmarital residence are, or at least were initially, related to different patterns in the sexual division of labor. Thus, if males make the major contributions to subsistence and if their subsistence activities require close cooperation (as in group hunting or plow agriculture), then it would be convenient to keep closely related males together in a local group. But if a society relies on cooperative groups of women (as in communities that practice hoe agriculture), then matrilocal residence might be a better option (Gough 1961).

It is true that most patrilineal societies are patrilocal. However, residence rules vary among matrilineal societies (Divale 1975). In addition, attempts to test whether matrilocal residence is found in societies with a predominance of females involved in subsistence have shown no significant correlation (Ember and Ember 1971; Divale 1975). But among patrilineal societies, the association with patrilocal residence is strong; and it is possible that whatever fostered patrilocality in human societies simultaneously set up a predominance of patrilineal descent.

In Chapter 2 we saw that chimpanzees display a pattern of female dispersal at maturity—a pattern that is the exception among nonhuman primates but is comparable to patrilocality among humans. Lars Rodseth and his colleagues (1991: 237) suggest that the human pattern may be "derived from a chimpanzee-like pattern." This idea is speculative, of course, but one implication is that a pattern of female dispersal may have been established among humans even before the institution of marriage developed.

Some studies (e.g., Otterbein 1968) have shown significant associations between patrilocality and other cultural characteristics such as polygyny, feuding, and internal warfare. William Divale (1975) even suggested that extensive polygyny was a cause of feuding and internal warfare because it deprived some men of wives, promoting adultery, wife stealing, and fights over women. If this is (or was) true, it carries implications for gender, linking patrilocality with aggressive, competitive males and making women important as sources of male conflict. Whatever the origin (male cooperation, male conflict, or something else), a pattern of patrilineal descent with patrilocality has persisted in many parts of the globe, surviving even changes in economic and political organization.

We now turn to the question of what patrilineal descent groups do, and why they are important to the societies that have them. In some patrilineal societies, clearly bounded descent groups may own property in common and transmit it through the generations, worship common deities or common ancestors, function as political units, take legal responsibility for the actions of all members, and engender in members a basic and primary identity with the descent group. From the point of view of the individual, the descent group (and not just "the family" in some unspecified sense) may determine how one survives economically as well as when one marries, whom one marries, and, in general, how one lives and what one does throughout his or her entire life. But the specific power a patrilineal descent group has, or the way it functions, must be considered for each society separately.

Lineage and Clan

A group of people who trace their descent to a common ancestor through known links are called a **lineage.** If the people do so patrilineally—that is, if they trace their descent to their common ancestor through male links—they are a **patrilineage.** To see how groups are formed with patrilineal descent, we can look at a hypothetical group of people who have used this principle to form descent groups. Figure 3.2 shows two distinct patrilineages in this hypothetical society.

Lineage A consists of all the living descendants of Sam who can trace themselves to him through male links. Lineage B consists of all the patrilineal descendants of Alfred.

Lineages A and B can be considered descent groups. We can presume that the members of each recognize their lineage identity and interact with one another in some way. Recalling a distinction made in Chapter 1, we can say that the lineages here are descent groups, but we do not yet know if they are also corporate descent groups. In some societies, lineages are corporate descent groups; in others, they are not. If the members of lineages A and B hold some property and/or have certain rights in common, then each of these lineages is a corporate descent group and, much like a business corporation, can be regarded as a single entity for some purposes.

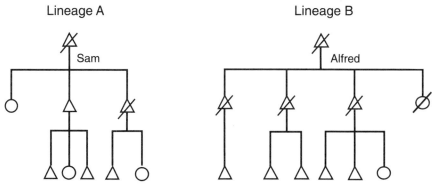

FIGURE 3.2   Two Patrilineages

Another kind of descent group (and one that also may or may not be a corporate group) is called a **clan.** A clan is like a lineage except that the members do not know all of the genealogical connections among themselves. In Figure 3.3 lineages A and B from our earlier example have been turned into subunits of one larger clan.

Here, the group members consider that they are of the same patrilineal clan because they are all descendants, through male links, of a common ancestor, Snake. They do not know exactly how their own founding lineage ancestors, Sam and Alfred, were related, but they believe that somewhere

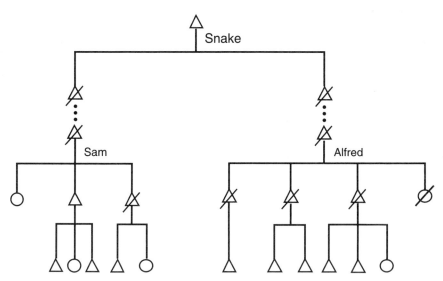

FIGURE 3.3   Two Lineages of One Clan

along the line they link up with two brothers, the sons of Snake. The dotted lines in the diagram indicate uncertainty about genealogical connection. The people of this society may say that since the ancestors' kinship links were formed so many generations ago, no one remembers just how the genealogy goes. But they all know they are of the same clan because they all have the same clan name, Snake, which has been inherited patrilineally. Children always take the clan name of the father. Clans are inevitably given names, and no matter how many generations have passed, everyone knows his or her clan by the patrilineal inheritance of the name.

Another difference between a clan and a lineage is that the founding ancestor of a clan is often (though not always) a mythological figure—that is, a god, a plant, an animal, or a special object, rather than an ordinary human being. Many clans have "origin myths" about themselves that involve creation from a mythological being. The clan may be named after this being, as in the case of the Snake clan above. The plant, animal, or whatever has sacred significance to the clan, so clan identity tends to be intermingled with the people's religion and mythology. This identification of a group with a plant, animal, or object is called **totemism,** the totem being the plant, animal, or object with which a group identifies.

It is often the case that a society has both clans and lineages, and, if so, the lineages will be subunits of the clan, as in the hypothetical example given here. In other cases, however, a society will have lineages but no clans (as in Case 2 of this chapter) or clans but no lineages. Either way, lineages and clans represent the descent groupings that people can form using a mode of descent. The difference between them is that lineages are perceived by the people themselves as grounded in known or presumed genealogical connections, whereas clans mark an identity of general relatedness and common descent (Murphy 1986: 107).

One example of patrilineal clan organization is the ancient Roman clan, or *gens.* This organization was discussed by Lewis Henry Morgan, a nineteenth-century American scholar who was himself a founder of the study of kinship. It was Morgan (1964, orig. 1887) who first noted organizational similarities among early Roman "tribes" and certain native American clans in the United States. In this respect he went far beyond previous scholars who had seen the Roman gens as merely a ceremonial institution and not a corporate kinship group based on patrilineal descent (White 1964: xxx–xxxi).

Morgan wrote that early on, before the founding of Rome (around 753 B.C.), there were a number of independent Latin tribes united in a loose confederacy. Tribes were subdivided into *gentes* (clans). The legendary Romulus was said to have united a number of these, and eventually gentes of other groups (e.g., the Sabines) were added. Over a century, three hundred gentes were united at Rome, and the chiefs of these gentes formed a governing council, which became the Roman Senate.

The gens was strictly patrilineal. Morgan (1964: 244) summarized the rights and obligations encompassed by the Roman gens as follows:

I.   Mutual rights of succession to the property of deceased gentiles.
II. The possession of a common burial place.
III. Common religious rites; sacra gentilica.
IV. The obligation not to marry in the gens.
V.   The possession of lands in common.
VI. Reciprocal obligations of help, defense, and redress of injuries.
VII. The right to bear the gentile name.
VIII. The right to adopt strangers into the gens.
IX. The right to elect and depose its chiefs.

Morgan elaborated each of these in detail, but even from this summary list it is clear that the gens was a named, exogamous, highly corporate group with land and property rights held in common, and with religious and political significance. Some of the characteristics of the gens influenced later Roman society. For example, regarding the "right to elect and depose its chiefs," Morgan (1964: 255–6) believed the fact that Roman senators were elected, and that the office was nonhereditary, was a direct continuation of the similar democratic element in the determination of the clan chiefs. Regarding item II—"possession of a common burial place"—elite Romans buried their dead in family tombs, as is still done today in parts of Italy.

The corporate nature of the gens faded away fairly early in ancient Rome. According to Morgan, this transition occurred as Roman society developed as a state and as land and other property came into the hands of individuals, ceasing to be communally held by the clan.[1] What eventually emerged among the upper classes in Rome were individual, largely nuclear family units, each in separate control of considerable property. A sense of clan identity continued (and was embodied in the patrilineal family name, or *nomen*), but the clan as such was no longer a corporate group. By this time each clan had come to be named after some illustrious human ancestor, in contrast to earlier clans that had likely taken names from totemic animals or objects (Morgan 1964: 252).

The early upper-class Roman family has been noted for the rather extraordinary powers vested in the male head, or *paterfamilias*. This man held full power over his family property and considerable authority over his

---

[1] It was this aspect of Morgan's work that caught the attention of Karl Marx and Friedrich Engels. They believed that it helped confirm a stage of "primitive communism" in human cultural evolution, an egalitarian stage that ended with the emergence of private property (Engels 1942 [orig. 1884]).

children, slaves, and any other dependents attached to his household, often including his wife. Indeed, he wielded the power of life and death over his own children. The authority of the paterfamilias lasted until his death. Thus at the pinnacle of each family unit was the eldest surviving male. A male grew up under the power (*potestas*) of his father (or grandfather or great grandfather, if still alive) and became legally independent only at this man's death. If at this time he was still a minor, a guardian (usually a father's brother, if available) would be appointed over him until he came of age.

Women, by contrast, were in a sense perpetual minors. They had a legal male guardian at all times, regardless of their age (Pomeroy 1975). Legally, this arrangement lasted until the late third century A.D. If a woman married in a union called "free marriage," she remained under the control of her father (or guardian), who not only arranged her marriage but also had the authority to divorce her from her husband and marry her to another man (Treggiari 1991). In "free marriage" a woman retained both her family name (rather than taking that of the husband) and the right to inherit from her father. In another type of marriage, called "marriage with *manus*," the authority over the bride was transferred from the bride's father to her husband; the woman took the name of her husband's gens and acquired the right to inherit a share of his family property. Marriage with manus in ancient Rome was an example of a system whereby a woman at marriage lost many rights in her natal patriline and was largely incorporated into her husband's kin group.

Whether a woman married "free" or "with manus" was up to her father or guardian. Early on, marriage with manus was considered more prestigious, but by the Late Republic (in the first century B.C.) "free" marriage had become the more common form (Corbier 1991).

We will revisit the ancient Romans later in this book. Their case is interesting, first, because ancient Rome provides good illustrations of the manipulation of marriage for the formation of political alliances (Chapter 6) and, second, because Roman patterns of kinship and gender show changes over a long time span, some of which are relevant to developments in Euro-American patterns (Chapter 7).

Patrilocality

At this point we must put patrilineal groups aside and consider once more the question of residence. As we saw in Chapter 1, descent rules and residence rules (or norms) should be considered together in our examination of a given society or culture. What we need to know, first of all, is whether a descent group is also a residence group, or, to put it another way, whether and to what extent descent and residence overlap. If they do overlap, we will know that the descent group is likely to exert a fairly strong influence on the lives of its resident members, or at least that it has the potential to do so. We can look at this phenomenon in terms of patrilineal societies. As noted earlier, most patrilineal societies in the world are also patrilocal, such that a couple, at marriage, moves in with or near the groom's kin. For now, let's consider the case of a couple moving right into the groom's parents' household, as this is what often happens in actuality. Figure 3.4 shows who would be living with whom in this patrilineal-patrilocal society, in an ideal state (which seldom occurs) where patrilocality continued over the generations and subgroups never split up or hived off from one another.

Here, two different patrilineal groups are illustrated. The members of descent group 1 are darkly shaded and those of descent group 2 are lightly shaded. Notice that a woman from the former group married a man from the latter. The individuals left unshaded are people who belong to assorted other patrilineal groups and who have married members of descent group 1 or 2. Loops are drawn around those individuals who all live together in one house. The diagram makes clear that in domestic units the *male patrilineal relatives stay together*. For men, the patrilineal group is literally grounded in residence; these men will inevitably have a lot to do with and be within easy access of one another. If they have to get together to discuss some issue or make some important decision, they're all right there. United by both "blood" and residence, the potentials for male solidarity are high. So are the potentials for conflict and jealousy, of course. But if these men recognize some lines of authority (e.g., that the eldest male acts as "head" and/or that elder males in general have authority over younger ones), an organized social life is possible. By adding another factor such as some valuable property held in common by these men, we can easily see how an important social unit might emerge.

For the moment we must assume that the patrilineal kin groups shown in Figure 3.4 are exogamous; that is, marriage within the patrilineal group is

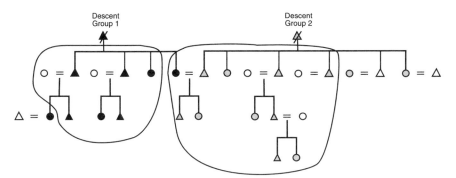

FIGURE 3.4 Patrilocal Residence. Members of Descent Group 1 are darkly shaded and members of Descent Group 2 are lightly shaded. The loops surround the people who, following patrilocal residence, will live together.

not permitted. Now, the women inside each loop are either unmarried individuals (and bound to leave when they do marry) or married-in "outsiders" coming in from other patrilines. In contrast to the men, their solidarity is likely to be weak. In addition, husbands begin marriage on their own "turf." Thus the burden is on wives rather than husbands to make the major adaptations and adjustments to married life, at least initially.

This diagram depicts an ideal type. In reality, patrilineal-patrilocal groups eventually split up. Residential groups worldwide tend to undergo their own "cycles" of expansion, contraction, and hiving off as marriages, births, and deaths take place and as resources fluctuate (Fortes 1958; Robertson 1991: 6–25). At times other factors also come into play. It may be that in a given society (see, for example, Case 2 in this chapter) the notion of patrilineal males staying together over the generations is a cultural ideal, yet brothers usually split up upon the death of the father and live in separate households. It may be that some of the women marrying into such a group are themselves related, or come from the same community, and so are not initially strangers to one another. Or it may be that, within a given "patrilocal" group, a couple is residing in the town or village of the groom's kin, but not in his parental household. The point is that, whatever its configuration, a patrilineal-patrilocal pattern suggests important, built-in differences in the marital and domestic situations of men and women.

Patrilineal societies tend to be patrilocal, but there are exceptions. For example, the Mundurucú Indians, a tribal group settled on a tributary of the Amazon River in Brazil, are patrilineal with matrilocal residence (Murphy 1986: 78). In this case, men at marriage move to the villages of their wives. Here, they reside not in their wives' dwellings but in a central men's house along with other married-in men and adult but unmarried sons of the village women. In the dwellings surrounding the men's house, sisters live together with their mothers and raise their young children. But these children belong to the descent groups of their fathers. Another example of a patrilineal-matrilocal society is the Yupik Eskimo of Southwestern Alaska, whose social organization is very similar to that of the Mundurucú (Ackerman 1992).

Patrilineal Procreation

To sum up thus far: Societies may employ a rule of patrilineal descent to form groups. These may be highly corporate, and if so, they become important and powerful units in the community. In addition, patrilineal groups are usually patrilocal, and patrilocality carries some implications for domestic and marital relationships.

Patrilineal groups tend to share another feature as well—namely, the fact that relationships traced patrilineally are important and close but are also tinged with a sense of formality and duty. In patrilineal societies this formality is often offset by informal, warm, and affectionate relationships traced through the mother—especially those between a male and his mother's brother. These relationships, which were common in ancient Rome (Bettini 1991: 39–66), will be examined more fully in the case studies in this chapter.

Yet another feature is shared by patrilineal groups, and this one is crucial to gender: To survive, the patriline must acquire male children. Only sons can transmit membership. If only daughters are born, the patrilineal group dies out. Not surprisingly, therefore, patrilineal groups have built within them a whole host of cultural mechanisms that express a "favoring" of male over female children.

An immediate word of caution is in order here: I do not mean to suggest that all patrilineal societies go so far as to disparage the birth of daughters. In fact, as we will see in Case 1, a patrilineal society may have reasons for desiring the birth of daughters as well as sons. What I do mean, however, is that in patrilineal societies the acquisition of sons is a *primary* concern. This fact has implications for both men and women, for the institution of marriage, and for children.

Parents in strongly patrilineal societies often say that sons are necessary to "continue the line" (by which they mean the patriline, of course); to serve as heirs; to provide labor or income to a household; to care for parents in old age; and, often, to assist parents in a spiritual way after death. In these societies, the association between sons and the spiritual welfare of parents and other ancestors is cross-culturally strong. Thus ideas and practices regulating fertility and aiming at the production of sons may be deeply interwoven with religion.

Although practices vary across societies (and this is an important point to remember), children generally belong to the patrilineal units. In other words, the patrilineal units tend to have a kind of instant and permanent "custody" of children. In the case of dissolution of a marriage, young children may remain with the mother for a time, but ultimately their fate is in the hands of the patrilineal units to which they belong. Among most patrilineal peoples, children belong not to individuals exclusively but to groups; and in the event of divorce, their fate is decided not through a legal battle between individual mothers and fathers but within the principle of patrilineal descent.

Patrilineal descent carries implications for men and women in their roles as husbands, wives, and parents. Let us now see how this arrangement works inside two very different societies.

CASE 1: THE NUER

The Nuer were until very recently a pastoral, cattle-herding people who inhabited the swamp and savannah areas of Southern Sudan. They were studied in the 1930s by British anthropologist, Sir E. E. Evans-Pritchard (1990, orig. 1951). In the area on which his work focused, there were about

200,000 Nuer. Although many Nuer cultural traditions survived into modern times, much changed as the Nuer were brought under British colonial rule and, later, into the Sudanese state with its devastating civil wars (James 1990: xxi). The description of the Nuer given here refers to their way of life at the time of Evans-Pritchard's now-classic study.

Shortly before Evans-Pritchard embarked on his research, the Nuer were involved both in internal warfare (with some Nuer groups displacing others) and in conquest and displacement of a closely related group, the Dinka (Kelly 1985). The warfare and territorial expansion of the Nuer, halted by British colonial intervention, were important because they undoubtedly influenced some features of Nuer kinship that Evans-Pritchard described as stable, timeless aspects of Nuer culture. In particular, some of the Nuer marriage forms discussed in this chapter may have been promoted, or intensified, as conquering Nuer sought to recruit followings of captive Dinka or other conquered Nuer. The importance of this historical context to Nuer kinship was pointed out by later researchers—most notably, Kathleen Gough (1971). Gough also suggested that much of Evans-Pritchard's discussion of Nuer kinship characterized only a minority "aristocratic" segment of the population. These points should be kept in mind as we explore Nuer kinship based on Evans-Pritchard's early work.

The largest Nuer political units were what Evans-Pritchard called "tribes," headed by Leopard-Skin chiefs who were sacred persons but had no effective political authority. The real political life of the Nuer was interwoven with their patrilineal kinship structure, organized into lineages and clans. These units regulated blood feuds, warfare, and the settling of disputes (Evans-Pritchard 1940).

The pastoral life of the Nuer moved them every year between wet-season villages and larger dry-season camps that consisted of two or more such villages. Their smallest political units were the wet-season villages, which were headed by informal leaders called "bulls."

Nuer clans were exogamous (i.e., marriages were not permitted within them) and subdivided into lineages. The lineages, in turn, were subdivided into segments, the smallest of which were about three to five generations deep. In addition, the lineages were residentially dispersed, so that each village contained homesteads representing different lineages and each such homestead had lineage kin in other villages. Villages were themselves corporate groups, holding the grazing grounds, fishing pools, and plots of land in common. But each village was associated with a main lineage and often called after the name of this lineage.

The Nuer were patrilocal in that wives generally moved into the villages and homesteads of husbands, but various other arrangements were also possible. A woman married into another village might have left her husband and returned to her home village with her children, or a man might have decided, for any number of reasons, that he wanted to live and raise a family in the village of his mother's brother rather than that of his own father. In short, along with or in spite of a general pattern of patrilocality, actual residence patterns indicated a great deal of flexibility and individual choice among the Nuer.

In many respects, Nuer males and females led contrasting, and often quite separate, lives. For instance, the sexes moved into adulthood in very different ways. For females the transition was gradual; and the first ceremonial attention a female received took place during her wedding. But for males, approaching adulthood meant that their identities would be bound up with warriorhood and strong associations with other males. Between the ages of fourteen and sixteen, young males were initiated into adulthood and warrior status through a painful ritual that involved the incising of six permanent lines (called *gar*) across their foreheads. The gar were seen as the marks of manhood; and, indeed, the Nuer did not view foreign males, lacking gar, as "men," whatever their ages (Evans-Pritchard 1990: 255). Males who underwent this initiation ritual together formed an **age-set,** a sort of lifelong "club" within which members closely associated with one another in a spirit of equality. Upon initiation, a boy received a spear and an ox from his father, became a warrior, and was henceforth forbidden to milk cows, a task permitted only to women and uninitiated males. Only after initiation (and after serving a warrior stage) was a man permitted to marry. For a boy's male elders this was the real meaning of the initiation: Since the boy's marriage and reproduction were now real possibilities, they saw in his initiation the potential for their lineage to continue.

Males and Females in the Web of Kinship

Within villages were homesteads, consisting minimally of a man and his wife (or wives) grouped around a cattle byre, where cattle were sheltered. Wives had separate huts around the byre; the common husband could spend the night in one of the huts, or he could sleep in the byre. Commonly a married man along with his married brothers, and, if alive, their father, would live together, with their byres and huts huddled around a common cattle corral in a kind of hamlet.

The byre, considered the heart of a homestead, was seen as a male space primarily (though women could freely enter it): "Very early in life small boys are driven by their father or elder brothers away from their mothers' huts to the byre, the place of the menfolk of the family, where they eat, sleep, and spend the leisure hours of the day. When they are about seven or eight years of age they sleep there instead of in their mothers' huts, where the women and girls eat and sleep and near which they spend most of the day" (Evans-Pritchard 1990: 125).

Thus, whereas men were associated with byres, women were associated with huts, around which their activities of cooking and gardening took place. Male economic activities centered on hunting, fishing, and the herding and tending of cattle (except for milking, which, as noted, was limited to females and uninitiated males).

The cattle byre, representing male space and serving as a kind of "men's club," was also associated with the patrilineage itself. When a new byre was built, a man would "make a libation of beer to the guardian spirits and ancestral ghosts of the lineage before its central support is planted, so that they may give peace and prosperity to all who dwell therein" (Evans-Pritchard 1990: 125). An ancestral shrine was also kept in a byre.

Cattle, the economic mainstay of Nuer life, were owned by men. Wives were "given" certain cows to milk by husbands, but they did not really own them and had no rights to dispose of them. Males owned cattle corporately; in fact, the cattle were ultimately considered to be the corporate property of the lineage (Evans-Pritchard 1990: 128). In actuality, of course, the cattle were divided among the different byres of individual married men. But if a man died, his brothers and eventually his sons would inherit them; and if there were no brothers or sons, other patrilineally related males would assume the rights to the cattle.

Although they did not own cattle, women were considered to be economically crucial and central to the home because only they (and, technically speaking, young males not yet initiated into adulthood) could milk the cows. Thus, in a sense, men were dependent on women:

> However many cattle a man may possess, he is helpless without a wife or mother or sister to milk the cows. It is only through marriage that a man can have a home of his own, and one of the most serious consequences of divorce is that it compels him to attach himself to the home of a kinsman whose womenfolk can milk and cook for him" (Evans-Pritchard 1990: 130). Indeed, Evans-Pritchard underlined the Nuer cultural view of women as central, as a node drawing men together, when he remarked that "Nuer group themselves around a herd, and the rule prohibiting men from milking means that in grouping themselves around a herd they also group themselves around the milkmaid who serves the herd (1990: 131).

Lineages and lineage identity were important among the Nuer; but equally important, though sometimes at odds with lineage solidarity, were other kinship relationships. Recall that earlier in this chapter I distinguished between descent and kinship, observing that in nearly all societies kinship is *bilateral* (i.e., traced through both parents) and may be considered to include affinal relationships as well. In Nuer social life the relationships of kinship were as important as those based on descent; there was a balance between the value and importance of relatives traced through the mother and those traced through the father (Evans-Pritchard 1990: 6). This point is important not only because it provides an insight into Nuer social life but also because it allows us to understand that among the Nuer, as with many other patrilineal societies, there was some tension or conflict between lineage-based interests and loyalties on the one hand and kinship-based sentiments on the other.

Women had very particular roles to play in the system of which these relationships were a part. First, a married woman reproduced for her husband's lineage, and her children became members of it. But look at the case of the polygynous household illustrated in Figure 3.5. Here, the males of groups A and B are all equal members of lineage X and are patrilineal kin to one another. But those of group A feel a kind of special cohesiveness and a separateness from group B because their mothers are different persons. After writing that fathers drove young boys from their huts to the byre, Evans-Pritchard further noted: "As boys grow up they attach themselves more and more to the byre, but each remains, both in sentiment and by social alignment, also a member of his mother's hut" (1990: 127).

The Nuer called all the people of either group (A or B) "brothers of the hut" (*kwi dwiel*). But when referring to paternal half-brothers (from A and B together), they called them "brothers of the byre" (*kwi luak*). Brothers of the hut were inevitably closer than half-brothers who only shared a byre:

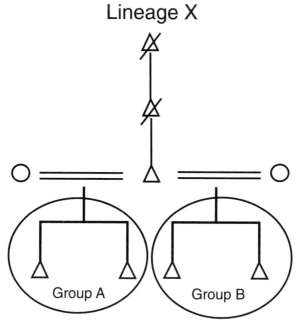

FIGURE 3.5 Nuer Brothers from a Polygynous Marriage. The full brothers of Groups A and B are cohesive, but units A and B feel a distance from one another because their mothers are different persons.

"[The Nuer] recognize that whereas full brothers pool their resources, helping each other even to the point of forging their rights, paternal half-brothers insist on their rights and try to avoid their obligations, doing for each other what their self-interest demands of them. Nuer are not surprised at—they expect—coldness between half brothers, and disagreements and disputes between them" (Evans-Pritchard 1990: 142).

When a polygynous father died, the various sets of half-brothers would likely split into separate groups. Thus there was always potential *fission* in the group due to the separate loyalties engendered by the *separate mothers* reproducing the lineage. This idea of the difference that separate mothers can make also seems to have affected relationships over the generations; for instance, the Nuer spoke of one's father's paternal half-brother as a kind of "wicked uncle," as someone not to be trusted (Evans-Pritchard 1990: 158).

A second role played by women in this system was to link their children to nonlineage kin (i.e., to the children's maternal kin). These latter relationships were quite different in character from those based on common patrilineal descent. Relationships with one's maternal kin were regarded as more close, affective, and tender than relationships with one's paternal kin. As mentioned earlier, this dichotomy is a common feature of patrilineal societies. Among the Nuer, as with other patrilineal groups, there was a special relationship between a male and his mother's brother, but the sentiment extended to other kin on the mother's side as well.

At the same time, relationships among close patrilineally related males were rather strained in a way that contrasted with relationships traced through the mother. Evans-Pritchard elaborated the Nuer case as follows:

> In Nuer family life there is always a pull on the children in both directions: a pull of legal and religious norms and of the whole pattern of the politico-social structure towards the father's kin and lineage, and a pull of personal affection towards the mother's people. Rights in the herd, duties of blood revenge, and status in the community hold a man to his father's kin, but with these go jealousy about cattle, resentment against authority, and personal rivalries. . . . The paternal ties are stronger, if there is a touch of hardness in them. The maternal ties are weaker and for this reason are tenderer. (1990: 139–140)

Later he described the situation even more bluntly: "The privileges of agnatic [patrilineal] kinship cannot be divorced from authority, discipline and a strong sense of moral obligation, all of which are irksome to Nuer" (1990: 162).

The texture of Nuer family life, as discussed so far, can be summarized in terms of the three different kinds of relationships that a male ego would have with three different types of uncle, as illustrated in Figure 3.6. There is a continuum here. With the man A ("wicked uncle"), ego's relationship is tense and problematical. With the man B, the relationship is close and co-

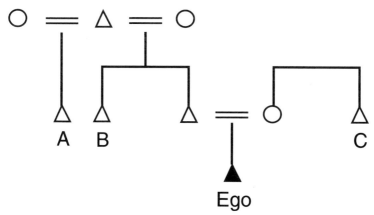

FIGURE 3.6   A Nuer Male's Relationships with Different Types of Uncle. Ego has a close, affective relationship with the Man C, a more distant relationship with B, and he is likely to mistrust the man A.

operative, but it has that "touch of hardness." With the man C, the relationship is close and highly affective. Notice that the quality of each of these relationships is very much determined by the position of the women in this diagram. Ego has a closer, more relaxed relationship with MB than with FB. But at least with FB, the "linking woman" is fairly close to ego; she is his own FM. With the man A, by contrast, the woman in question (A's M, ego's FFW) is distant from ego.

Looking at the system as a whole, and also remembering women's domestic roles, especially the central role of milking cows, we see that women are affecting the system in three ways: They are continuing the patriline, they are pulling some men together, and as sources of fission they are pulling other men apart. In their role as reproducing wives, at least, they both create and destroy. Thus women's roles within the structure of Nuer kinship and descent are related, at least in my view, to a certain ambivalence toward women expressed by Nuer males as well as to what Evans-Pritchard called a "latent hostility between the sexes" (1990: 133). In Nuer mythology, one story tells how women have brought mosquitoes to the world; in another, they are bringers of death. Even more telling is the following:

> Nuer men also say that women have bad mouths and that evil comes out of them, and they account for this by a story which relates that the mouths of women used to be, before God changed their position, where their vaginas are now; and they say that women are sensual and fickle, God having at their request, as another story relates, cut their hearts in two so that one half might be added to the male organ to give them greater pleasure in coitus. There are other stories which suggest a deep-lying hostility toward women. (Evans-Pritchard 1950, cited in Biedelman 1966: 457)

This account is interesting in its phrasing of the hostility toward women in such graphic, sexual terms and in the imputation of female sexual greed. But the point I especially wish to stress is that it is within the framework of Nuer *kinship* that we most clearly see the forces of male ambivalence and hostility toward women. This having been said, let us now consider women's and men's roles as they affect reproduction and its consequences.

Marriage and Children

We already know a few things about marriage among the Nuer—for example, that they practiced polygyny. How common it was is not known. Evans-Pritchard mentioned that "monogamous marriage was much commoner," but he adds that polygyny was "frequent enough to have set its stamp, through its association with wealth and social influence, on the lineage system" (1990: 140). Evans-Pritchard also claimed that the Nuer regarded polygyny as the ideal form of family. But we can assume that by this he meant it was ideal in the eyes of men, since elsewhere we learn that the Nuer word for co-wife, *nyak*, in its verb form also means "to be jealous" and that jealousy between co-wives was likely (1990: 134–135).

Evans-Pritchard is also ambivalent on the subject of the husband-wife relationship. On the one hand, he mentioned (1990: 133) that husbands had unquestioned authority over wives. But, as Micaela di Leonardo (1991: 6) points out, he elsewhere referred to wives insulting husbands or, in a quarrel, knocking out a husband's tooth, an act for which the woman's father had to compensate the husband with a cattle payment.

Along with polygyny, the Nuer practiced a form of the **levirate,** whereby a widow is "inherited" by her dead husband's brother. Among the Nuer the levirate was optional for the woman, and even if she joined the brother he was considered a "pro-husband" and the woman remained the legal wife of the dead husband. The **sororate,** whereby a man marries the sister of his dead wife, was also practiced; but among the Nuer this could happen only if the dead wife had been childless.

In all forms of marriage, a core concern of the Nuer was the acquisition of male heirs for patrilines. Nuer notions of immortality, for men at least, were tied to the siring of sons: "A man's memorial is not in some monument but in his sons. . . . Every man likes to feel that his name will never be forgotten so long as his lineage endures and that in that sense he will always be a part of the lineage" (Evans-Pritchard 1974 [orig. 1956]: 162).

But where sons were concerned, the Nuer went further than most other patrilineal societies that merely encourage or reward the production of sons; indeed, the Nuer claimed that all males *must* have at least one son. One may wonder how this was possible in cases of male sterility or impotence; but, as we shall soon see, the Nuer arranged matters in such a way that any man could, eventually, have a son.

First, however, we need to delve into Nuer ideas about marriage and paternity. These ideas and their related practices were intimately bound up with cattle, which the Nuer used to pay **bridewealth.** A legal marriage among the Nuer was a marriage cemented with bridewealth, or the transfer of wealth from the kin of the groom to the kin of the bride. Bridewealth cattle were ultimately dispersed among the bride's kin in a standard way. Thus, for example, if forty head of cattle (a figure given as a standard by Evans-Pritchard 1990: 74) were transferred in a marriage, twenty of them would be distributed among the bride's father and his kin and twenty among the bride's mother and her patrilineal kin. (These cattle, which were received by women but not actually "owned" by them, joined the herds belonging to the husbands.) In short, the bridewealth went to both sides of the bride's family, and it did so in equal amounts, reflecting the balance between the maternal and paternal kin that I discussed earlier. In turn, it was not just the patrilineal kin of the groom but also some maternal kin who contributed bridewealth cattle for him, although the main portion was the responsibility of his close patrilineal kin who held a herd in common and shared rights in it. For both families, however, a marriage and the movement of cattle it entailed were the concern not just of two patrilines but also of two bilateral networks of kin.

This bridewealth was seen not as a "payment" for the bride but, rather, as a transfer of wealth that guaranteed the *rights of the husband's patriline to the future children* of this woman. Thus the bridewealth at once legalized the marriage, legitimized the children, and guaranteed the allocation of the children to the husband's patrilineal units.

The practice of bridewealth marriage had an important consequence. In order to bring in a bride, a Nuer group needed to amass a lot of cattle for bridewealth. Normally the only way this could be done was to first acquire cattle from marrying off a daughter. Thus, among the Nuer, *daughters as well as sons* were necessary and valued. Unlike some other patrilineal groups, the Nuer did not regard the birth of a daughter as unfortunate or sorrowful, for a daughter was a bringer of cattle, a provider of bridewealth for her brothers.

Bridewealth cattle were not handed over all at once in a marriage. Rather, they were given in stages, and at each stage the two groups of kin would argue about the exact numbers and kinds of cows. As with the delivery of cattle, so marriage itself was seen by Nuer as a kind of continuum. There was no one-time signing of papers, no single "I now pronounce you man and wife" formula that made the marriage real; indeed, if all went well, one simply became more and more married.

Marriages were usually initiated by the young couple and then approved by the two sets of kin. Females married at about seventeen or eighteen to older males of varied ages (Evans-Pritchard 1990: 57). Before marriage, both males and females were expected to be sexually active. Young unmarried persons met and conducted their affairs at various nighttime "dances," often held at a wedding party for someone else. As Evans-Pritchard (1990: 51) reported: "Girls witness serious love-making and courtship earlier than boys. At dances small girls follow their more experienced sisters and cousins, imitating their movements during the dancing and afterwards sitting with them while the young men pay them compliments and try to persuade them to retire with them into the long grass." The point of this romance and courtship, which occupied a great deal of time and energy among Nuer youth, was marriage and reproduction: "Even in childhood it is clear to Nuer that marriage and the birth of children are the ultimate purpose of the sexual functions to which all earlier activities of a sexual kind—play, lovemaking, and courtship—are a prelude, a preparation, and a means" (Evans-Pritchard 1990: 49–50).

Once a proposal was accepted by all concerned, the establishment of the marriage proceeded by stages, and at each stage more cattle were transferred from the groom's kin to those of the bride. During the first stage, called *larcieng* (betrothal), a dance, feast, and sacrifice of an ox were performed at the bride's home with the groom and his people as guests. Though not an obligatory stage, the larcieng signified that both sets of kin provisionally agreed to the union. The next stage, *ngut* ("wedding"), was held a few weeks later, entailing generally the same activities as the betrothal, and also held at the bride's home. In one wedding ceremony, the groom's kin and the bride's kin called out the respective clan "spear-names" of the bride and groom. This procedure served as a public affirmation that since the clans were *different*, the marriage was proper (recall that clans were exogamous). That night there was a dance, and the next day the bride's father sacrificed an ox, the meat of which was distributed to the groom's kin. At the wedding itself the ghosts of lineage ancestors were ritually invoked to witness the union. There was also a ritual acknowledgment of the importance of lineage continuity. In one rite, a male relative of the bride, acting as "master of ceremonies," called out that the bride would bear her husband a male child (Evans-Pritchard 1990: 66).

By this stage, many cattle would have been given over to the bride's kin. If any of these cattle died after the transfer, they had to be replaced by the groom's kin. But after the next marriage stage, *mut* (consummation), this requirement was no longer the case. With mut, the marriage was starting to get quite serious. During this stage, the bride was taken to the groom's home and put inside a hut. The groom joined her there and the marriage was consummated. In this connection Evans-Pritchard gave a curious report: "[The groom] enters the hut and gives his bride a cut with a switch and seizes her thigh, she refusing his advances and crouching by the wall of the hut. He strikes her with a tethering-cord, snatches the cap off her head, breaks her girdle, and consummates the marriage. Reluctance is imposed on her by custom and she pretends to resist even when she has known her husband often before in the gardens" (1990: 70).

Beyond the obvious allusion to husband dominance, this scene is difficult to interpret.[2] In any event, on the day after consummation, another rite was held paralleling the earlier one in the bride's home during the wedding. Here, a male kin of the groom (the master of ceremonies on his side) sacrificed an ox. Before spearing it, he "speaks of the beast and the bride, telling the spirits and ghosts of his lineage to witness the union and to bless it with sons so that the lineage may continue" (Evans-Pritchard 1990: 70).

The completion of mut signaled the growing strength of the marriage in ways other than the fact that dead bridewealth cattle no longer had to be replaced. First, after mut, the groom could claim compensation from a man who committed adultery with his wife. The usual fee for this was six cows. Second, after mut, the wife (but not the husband) was no longer permitted to attend nightly dances. Finally, after mut, the wife's head was shaved, symbolizing her new status as a married woman.

Even then, the couple had farther to go along the marriage continuum. After mut the whole marriage could still be called off, by the bride or groom or a kin group, in which case all the bridewealth cattle would have to be returned to the groom's kin. And at this stage, the husband and wife were still not living together. The next stage, which completed the marriage, was the birth of the first child. Between the mut and the birth, the wife remained in her father's home, where she was given her own hut. Here her husband would visit her at night, leaving early in the morning. Later, when the first child was weaned, the wife moved to the husband's home and was given a hut there. Only then would the wife's father begin to disperse the bridewealth cattle among the bride's kin. At this point a divorce could take place, and in this event (or in the event of the wife's death) the bridewealth cattle would be returned to the groom's kin except for six cows that would remain with the bride's group as a guarantee that the one child was the legal child of the husband and a member of the husband's patrilineal groups.

With the birth of a child and the movement of the bride to her husband's home, the marriage was considered complete. Nevertheless, there was one

---

[2] Evans-Pritchard himself seemed to interpret this ritual as symbolic of a woman's virginity at marriage (1990: 70), but his conclusion is hard to accept given Nuer attitudes toward premarital sex. Biedelman (1968: 118) interpreted the same ritual as an expression of hostility between affines—the different kin groups of the bride and groom—but this conclusion, too, is unsupported by any further evidence.

last stage to undergo: the birth of a second child. With only one child present, the marriage could be ended by divorce. But once a second child was born, divorce was no longer possible, because after this point bridewealth cattle could never be returned. Now, at this stage, a woman *could* leave her husband (what we would call separation). She could even take up with another man and live with him. What the finality of her marriage meant was that (1) she could not remarry, and (2) should she bear other children in the future, begotten by whomever, they were automatically her legal husband's children and members of his lineage/clan. This is the reason all the cattle were given. After two children had been born, the patriline had permanent rights over whatever issued from the woman's womb. The Nuer referred to a woman's bearing children by other men after leaving her husband as "giving birth in the bush."

From the foregoing we can see that the production of children for the husband's patriline was a fundamental, core purpose of marriage, and that bridewealth cattle not only established formal marriage but also served as a statement of and guarantee for rights over children of the woman. The whole system of gradual marriage and gradual bridewealth made it easy to break off negotiations or cancel the marriage in the beginning; but once the couple's fertility was verified, this became harder to do, and eventually it was impossible to sever the tie between the husband's patriline and the woman's reproduction. Needless to say, one reason for canceling a marriage would have been the couple's failure to have children. But with easy termination at this stage, both the man and the woman were free to enter other marriage unions and test their fertility through them.

In addition, as noted earlier, not all domestic unions were formal marriages, since it was possible for a woman, even with two children, to leave her husband and take up with another man, living in his home. Evans-Pritchard referred to the latter type of union, which he said occurred frequently, as "concubinage" and distinguished three kinds—widow, wife, and unmarried. In the first case, a widow takes up with some new man, refusing the option of the levirate; in the second, a wife (some time after bearing two children) leaves her husband and lives with another man; in the third, a never-married woman lives with a man without getting married to him. In the first two cases, moreover, any forthcoming children would be allocated to the woman's legal husband. And in the third case, the couple could have married, with bridewealth, after having a child. Or the man could simply give four to six cows to the woman's parents in order to claim this one child but not marry the woman. But as Evans-Pritchard (1990: 118) points out, "This fee (*ruok*) is not bridewealth. It gives him no rights in the woman nor in any future children she may bear to him or to other men. Children born of a concubine by different men become in consequence members of different lineages."

Evidently widow and wife concubines and their children were not seen as inferior in any way to regular wives and children. As for unmarried concubines, although Evans-Pritchard described them as "women of strong character who valued their independence and did not desire matrimony," he also noted that "they are not so highly esteemed as wives and in a quarrel their children may suffer the reproach of bastardy" (1990: 118).

The Nuer engaged in a number of other interesting marital practices that would seem bewildering if we did not already understand the importance to them of acquiring children (especially sons) as future members of patrilineal groups. We will take a look at these practices and eventually discover how it is possible that *all* Nuer men could have sons. One clue has already been given. We have seen that if a fully married woman left her husband and "gave birth in the bush," the children would legally be her husband's, even though he and everyone else knew that he was not the biological father. Anthropologists use the term **genitor** for the biological father and **pater** for the legal father. For the Nuer, paterhood was primary; it was what the system had been organized to achieve for all men. The "real" father was a pater who might have been but was not necessarily the genitor. We in American society have other ideas about "fatherhood" and a great concern over who the genitor is. However, we may fast approach the Nuer's view with the advent of the New Reproductive Technologies (see Chapter 8).

I do not mean to imply that the Nuer were unconcerned or uncaring about the role of genitor. Nuer males preferred to beget their own children and, for that matter, acknowledged "social and mystical links" between a child and its genitor (Evans-Pritchard 1990: 120). In addition, in cases where the genitor and the pater of a daughter were different men, the genitor would, upon the marriage of this daughter, receive a "cow of the begetting" from the bridewealth paid for her (Evans-Pritchard 1990: 121).

Still, the pater was primary. Let us now look at male strategies for becoming paters. The first step a man, in collaboration with his kin, could take to have legal children was to get married. His doing so resulted in a simple monogamous union. If the union were fertile, the man, seeking more children and/or possibly having other motives, could add wives to his home. The addition of wives was likely to increase the number of his children. Whatever other benefits it brought to individuals, polygyny was a strategy to increase the number of a man's children and the number of members of the patriline.

What happened if the original union was infertile? In this case, polygyny, the taking of another wife or wives, would have been essential and the first wife might or might not have been divorced. Let's say the first wife was not divorced and the man eventually took two more wives but none of the three wives ever became pregnant. We would consider it likely that the man was the one with the fertility problem, and so would the Nuer. At this point there would still have been other options available to him. One is what I call "blind-eye adultery," whereby the man turns a "blind-eye" to an adulterous affair on the part of one or more wives in the hope that someone will get pregnant. He will be the pater of whatever child is produced. Evans-Pritchard reported (1945: 23) that older sonless Nuer men exercised this option, but younger men were still too concerned with their sexual rights and their wives to consider it. A slight variation on this theme, involving the use of a "surrogate genitor," has been reported in other African societies (Barnes 1951: 4; Brain 1972: 162; Gluckman 1965: 188). In this case, a man asks a friend or kinsman to sleep with his wife in the hope that she will conceive.

Sooner or later one of these measures is likely to work. Still, it could happen that a married man dies before any of them have a chance to do so. Indeed, a man could die before getting married at all; and yet it has been said that all Nuer men (barring those who die before puberty) *must* have a male heir. As it turns out, the Nuer system had prepared for even this possibility with the very distinctive option of **ghost marriage.** In this case, a patrilineal kinsman, such as a brother or cousin, would take a wife *in the name of* a deceased, childless man, and have children by her in the dead man's name, as illustrated in Figure 3.7.

Here, the man A, though considered unmarried in his own right, has ghost-married the woman B to his childless dead brother, C. The woman B refers to C as her dead husband and addresses A as "brother-in-law." The children of this union refer to the man A as the Nuer equivalent of "uncle." Now, why would the man A go to all this trouble? There are two reasons. First, it was his patrilineal duty to do so. The Nuer believed that if a man had a close patrilineal kinsman who died childless, or even sonless, it was his duty to take a wife in the name of the dead man before taking a wife in his own name. Second, the Nuer believed that the soul of a dead childless man hovers about in discontent, eventually attacking its own patrilineal kin and causing illness in one of them or some other misfortune in the group.

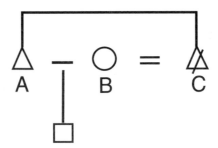

FIGURE 3.7   A Nuer Ghost Marriage. The man A "ghost married" the woman B to his dead brother, C. The children belong to the dead man.

Arranging a ghost marriage then became a part of the cure for the illness or misfortune (Evans-Pritchard 1990: 109).

Nuer women, like men, were eager to have children, and their identity as women was very much dependent on their fertility (Hutchinson 1980). We have seen that the Nuer system abounds with options and strategies by which males and their patrilines can acquire sons. Some of the same options could of course help women, too. If a married woman failed to have children, "blind-eye adultery" might have alleviated her childless state. But what if the woman herself was barren? In many societies around the world, barrenness is a monumental tragedy for a woman, who may suffer pity and ostracism. The Nuer, however, instituted yet another ingenious marriage form that transformed female barrenness into a kind of reproductive potential. This is the famous institution of **woman-woman marriage.** In this case, a woman presumed to be barren could elect to divorce her husband and remain in her father's home. (Since she had not born children, she would not have moved to her husband's home.) Then, because of her barrenness, she could "count as a man" among her natal patrilineal kin. A marriage to another woman would have been arranged for her, and bridewealth paid, turning the barren woman into a husband. Next, the barren woman would have arranged for a man (the choice of the man was hers) to sleep with her wife as a type of "surrogate genitor." Children of this union were considered members of the woman's natal patrilineal groups, and the woman herself was considered their pater, or legal father. In Figure 3.8 ego is a barren woman who, after divorcing her husband, has entered woman-woman marriage. The shaded symbols represent people who belong to the same patrilineal descent group.

The children of ego's wife would now refer to ego as "father." Woman-woman marriage was not a lesbian relationship, but the barren woman did take on the social role of husband/father. For example, she had a great deal

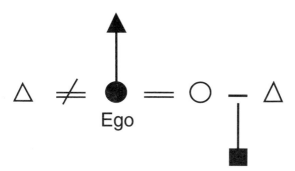

FIGURE 3.8   A Nuer Woman-Woman Marriage. Ego is a barren woman who "counts as a man." After divorcing her husband, she married another woman and arranged for a man to have children with this woman. Ego is the legal father of the children and the children are members of Ego's natal patrilineage.

of authority over her wife, just as a male husband would have had. And if the wife independently took a lover (i.e., not the genitor chosen by the barren woman) and was discovered to have done so, the barren woman was entitled to claim a fee from the lover as adultery compensation.

As far as her natal patriline was concerned, this barren woman "counted as a man" in every respect and was able to reproduce the patriline, just as would a son. Thus the patriline was able to transform a barren daughter into a mechanism for its own reproduction. Rather then being pitied or scorned, the individual woman became an "honorary male" and was given a socially meaningful role to play. Woman-woman marriage has been reported in other African societies (Brain 1972: 60; Gluckman 1965: 184; Herskovits 1937). Among these societies there is a great deal of variation in the extent to which female husbands adopted male roles; but in all such cases, including the Nuer, female husbands could use their "honorary male" status to secure political and social advantages (Sacks 1979: 77).

These forms of marital and nonmarital, but quite acceptable, unions among the Nuer—simple legal marriage (monogamous and polygynous), ghost marriage, woman-woman marriage, and various form of concubinage—are striking for their sheer variety. But one prominent feature of Nuer marriage forms is the ease with which both men and women could circulate through legitimate sexual and marital unions. Another is the precision and clarity with which children were allocated to husbands/lineages, and the fact that these arrangements were set through cattle payments. These different marriage forms can also be seen, at least in part, as available strategies whereby individual Nuer and their lineages could acquire children/sons, even in cases of male or female infertility. But here the roles of men and women were quite different. Men (whether or not they were genitors) acquired legal children through the payment of bridewealth. If the bridewealth was not paid, the children were not theirs. In a sense, then, it was not really the men who "passed on" patrilineal descent but, rather, the women whose bridewealth men paid:

> The person in whose name she was married with cattle is the pater of her children whether he begat them or not, was dead or alive at the time of her marriage and the birth of her children, or is a man or a woman. Hence it follows that agnatic [patrilineal] descent is, by a kind of paradox, traced though the mother, for . . . [her children] may count as children of a man their mother has never even seen. They may have been begotten by several fathers, but they all have the same pater. It is the fertility of the womb which the lineage receives by payment of bridewealth. (Evans-Pritchard 1990: 122)

Several important consequences followed from this system in which children were allocated according to bridewealth payments: Women had rather autonomous control over their own sexuality (Gough 1971: 111). Premarital sex was not discouraged or punished. Women had a lot to say about who (or even if) they married. After marriage they were free to leave their husbands (though they would lose whatever children had been born to them). And even adultery was not so serious. Evans-Pritchard (1990: 120) commented that among the Nuer adultery was illegal but not immoral, adding that he was "struck among the Nuer both by the frequency of adultery and the infrequency of quarrels or even talk about it." A fee was collected from the male offender; but unless the adultery became a persistent problem, in which case a man might divorce a wife (1990: 134), women were not punished for it.

To conclude this section on the Nuer: We have seen that patrilineal descent was used to form very important groups, the clans and lineages. Primary rights and obligations were defined by membership in these groups, yet relationships of kinship, as opposed to descent, were equally important in Nuer social life. Close but often tense patrilineal ties were balanced by affective relationships traced through the mother. Ambivalence and hostility toward women were expressed in connection with their roles as mothers of sets of sons and milkmaids for a homestead: They were seen to draw males together, but within the lineage structure they were also blamed for pulling males apart. Women also reproduced patrilineages, even though cattle payments actually determined allocation of children. Through such payments, a woman's children were allocated to a patriline regardless of who fathered the children. Women exercised rather autonomous control over their own sexuality, and their sexual behavior had no impact on the way in which their children were legitimized and allocated to legal fathers and to lineages. Reproduction was of great concern to both men and women, but in cases of fertility failure, Nuer society abounded in other options by which men and women could acquire legal children. Even barren women could acquire children for their father's patrilines through woman-woman marriage. In Case 2, we will see both striking similarities and contrasts with the Nuer.

CASE 2: NEPALESE BRAHMANS

Our second case concerns the Brahman peoples of Nepal. Nepal is a small country in the Himalayas, with a population of around 20 million. It lies between India to the south and China (Tibet) to the north. Its numerous ethnic groups speak different languages. Many of these groups, especially those classified as Indo-Nepalese speakers, are Hindu. Others follow Buddhist traditions, often mixed with Hindu practices. The Brahmans are an Indo-Nepalese group. Their ancestors came north from India, beginning as early as the twelfth century A.D., when people in India were fleeing Moslem invasions. In most areas of Nepal, the Indo-Nepalese people became economically and politically dominant.

The term *Brahman* is actually a caste designation. Indeed, a few words must be said about the Nepalese caste system, since some of the ideas on which it rests are important to kinship and gender. Castes in Nepal are ranked status groups,[3] with the ranking sanctioned by religion. The whole system is expressed through Hindu religious ideas concerning purity and pollution: Higher castes are considered more pure than lower castes. Brahmans are at the very top of the caste hierarchy. And only Brahman males, on account of their higher caste purity, may become Hindu priests. Their decision to do so is a matter of individual choice, but it is a choice restricted to the Brahman caste. Beneath the Brahmans are a number of other high-ranking castes whose male members, like Brahman males, wear the "sacred thread." This is an actual thread stretched over a shoulder and under an arm, made sacred by the action of Hindu priests and bestowed upon males at the time of their initiation into adulthood and simultaneously into their castes and lineages. Next are a number of mid-ranking castes collectively classed as *matwali*, or "liquor-drinking." This term refers to the fact that it is acceptable for such people to drink liquor, not that they go about drinking excessively. The higher thread-wearing groups, by contrast, are not supposed to consume liquor. Finally, at the bottom are the low untouchable castes, somewhat similar to the untouchables of India. Although other castes interact with them regularly, they are considered impure and physical contact with them is thought to be polluting. If a person accidentally makes physical contact with an untouchable, a ritual of purification is necessary to restore his or her caste purity.

All of these castes have rules covering members' diet and other behavior. In addition, there are rules governing interactions between different castes. The most important one is that higher castes cannot consume boiled rice (*bhat*, the mainstay of Nepalese meals) cooked by lower-caste persons. Conversely, lower castes can and do consume boiled rice prepared by groups they recognize as higher. Thus, for instance, Brahmans may cook boiled rice and serve it to all other groups but can consume only that which has been prepared by fellow Brahmans.

Caste endogamy is both an ideal and a norm in Nepal, and this is especially true for Brahmans. Indeed, the only way Brahman men and women can have caste-pure Brahman children is through a religiously sanctioned caste endogamous marriage,[4] a matter that I will elaborate later.

---

[3] Caste continues to be important in Nepal, especially in the rural areas of the country. There is some regional variation among caste categories and caste rankings. But many Nepalese individuals, including Brahmans, have denounced the caste system altogether. And in Nepal, as in India, caste is now "illegal" in the sense that the government does not recognize discriminations according to caste.

[4] In Nepal some castes may marry women upward (i.e., into higher castes) in religiously sanctioned unions. However, if Brahman men enter these unions, their children will be of a caste rank lower than Brahman.

The notions of purity and pollution, so important in the caste system, are also fundamental to kinship and gender among Brahmans. Just as higher castes are considered more pure than lower castes, males as a category are considered more pure than females. The reason: Women menstruate, and menstrual blood is considered an extremely polluting substance. During their menstrual periods, women must segregate themselves; they become, like the lowest of castes, untouchable, though in their case this is a temporary state. Contact with them is thought to be highly polluting for all initiated males. Brahman women themselves say they have a lower status than males because they menstruate (Bennett 1983: 216).

The opposition between purity and pollution defines the relative status of groups according to caste and to sex. But within this permanent group ranking, Nepalese Hindus also perceive fluctuating states of individual purity/pollution. In daily life and throughout the course of one's life, one will inevitably and necessarily encounter "pollution," or enter a state of personal pollution, after which purificatory acts must be performed. For instance, because women are inevitably polluted when they menstruate, they must take a ritual bath afterward in order to restore a state of relative purity. In Brahman culture nearly everything having to do with the body and its functions is considered to be a polluting act or a source of pollution. Thus ingestion of food, bodily eliminations, and sexual activity (however essential they may be to the survival of individuals and groups) are all deemed impure activities that need to be followed by purificatory acts such as washing.

For Brahman men, sexual activity is considered to be not only polluting but physically draining and spiritually distracting (Bennett 1983: 126, 220). Not surprisingly, they claim that women need sex more than men and blame women for causing carnal lapses among men that draw them away from more lofty pursuits.

With this background information in mind, we can now take a close, intimate look at Brahman kinship and gender. This group has been studied with greater attention to women's roles and women's own ideas than was the case with Evans-Pritchard's studies of the Nuer. For material on Brahman kinship and family relationships, readers can consult my own work (Stone, 1978, 1989); and for information on high-caste (Brahman and Chetri) women, they can refer to the major study conducted by Lynn Bennett (1983). Drawing from these sources, I describe the system as it applies to rural Brahman peoples in the hill areas of Nepal, thereby covering a somewhat more orthodox set of beliefs and practices than one would find in Nepalese towns and cities.

In these rural areas Brahmans live in small villages, usually mixed with other caste groups. Households are organized around farming, although some family members may have off-farm jobs that bring cash income. At lower elevations, in the hilly regions of Nepal, the Brahmans' most important crop is wet rice, but other grains are grown as well. Livestock (especially goats and water buffalo) are also kept. Both men and women work the fields (e.g., women plant and men plow), but women are primarily responsible for domestic tasks such as carrying water, washing clothes, processing food, cooking, caring for children, cleaning the house, and so on.

Like the Nuer, Brahmans are both patrilineal and patrilocal. But as the reader has probably anticipated, there are striking contrasts between Nepalese Brahmans and the Nuer in the areas of marriage and sex. In particular, the sexual behavior of Brahman women is very strictly controlled. A Brahman woman must be a virgin at marriage; if she were known not to be, a religiously sanctioned wedding would not take place. In the village of my studies, the virginity of brides was safeguarded by arranging the marriages of females early (to males a few years older), often before they started menstruating. The age of marriage is rising in rural Nepal, however (Acharya and Bennett 1981: 65). In her husband's home, where she is probably a stranger, a bride is expected to be shy, demure, and obedient and her behavior is carefully supervised by her in-laws, especially her mother-in-law. Marriages are arranged by parents. A great deal of time, energy, and expense goes into the search for a groom or a bride and the arranging, negotiating, and carrying out of a marriage union. For a female, marriage is also an initiation into adulthood and into her caste; without marriage a woman

PHOTO 3.1   A wedding in Nepal. Photo courtesy of Linda Stone.

is not considered an adult or even a full-caste person. Males experience a separate initiation (at around age eight), through which they assume adulthood and caste membership.

In rural areas Brahman groups seek brides for the labor they can provide as well as for their fertility. Polygyny is permitted, but it is rare and socially approved only if the first wife remains childless. For a man, marriage is an important life transition; but it is a relatively smooth one since he remains home on his "turf" surrounded by his people, all of whom believe that he and his parents have unquestionable authority over the bride. For females, by contrast, marriage is traumatic, and the adaptations a woman must make are likely to be difficult for a number of years. At the end of a wedding, a particular ceremony (*mukh herne*, or "seeing the face") emphatically underlines the low position of the bride in her new home:

> The bride is seated, always slumped over with downcast eyes, while the women of the family, starting with the groom's mother, lift her veil to look at her face. They must place some money in her lap, and for that they buy the privilege of being as critical as they like in their comments about her. After her mother-in-law has seen her face, the bride must touch her mother-in-law's feet with her forehead (*dhok dine*). The other women of the family also have their feet touched by the bride. And then it is time for the neighbor women to come and see the bride and evaluate the new member of their village. (Bennett 1983: 90)

Following a period of "boot camp" existence, during which the bride is given heavy chores, watched, and criticized openly, she begins her rise in the household hierarchy through a demonstration of successful fertility. With the birth of each child, especially sons, she becomes a more trusted family member and is treated more leniently. Eventually her senior in-laws die off, her husband (generally) sets up his own home, and she becomes the most senior woman in the household, where her sons will bring in new brides for her to put through the whole experience again.

The Patriline

Every Brahman belongs to two patrilineal categories: the *thar* and the *gotra*. Males assume the thar and gotra affiliations of their fathers, and women at marriage take the thar and gotra names of their husbands. The thar name is one's last name. Both the thar and the gotra are ideally exogamous. The gotra name, though rarely used or heard in everyday life, is invoked during certain religious rituals and is seen as a kind of religious or spiritual category (Bennett 1983: 17). Thus the thar and the gotra are patrilineal kinship *categories*, but not actual kinship groups. That is, members of a thar or gotra do not come together for any purpose, own any property in common, or share rights and obligations with one another. Though both are sometimes translated as "clan," neither is a clan in the sense referred to earlier in the chapter. Rather, the thar and gotra are important for personal identification and for specifying those people whom one cannot, or at least should not, marry.

The kinship unit that *is* a group and has significance in ordinary life is the *kul*, or patrilineage. Women are born into the kuls of their fathers and later join the kuls of their husbands. But they are only peripheral members of their husbands' kuls and do not participate in certain kul activities (Bennett 1983: 129). Kuls may be quite large (five to six generations deep), but they can also be limited to a single family; the size depends on the particular history of the kul in question. If they are large, they are likely to be residentially dispersed over different villages. Over time, of course, they may shrink or grow, die out completely, or break up into two or more sections whose members eventually see themselves as belonging to distinct kuls.

The essence of the kul is that the members all worship the same set of lineage gods (*kul devta*). Worshiping occurs both separately by individual households and communally in a gathering of the whole kul. In addition, kul members must observe so-called death pollution for one another. When one kul member dies, the others must conduct a number of rituals and maintain a number of restrictions on food, clothing, and behavior. The length of time for death pollution observance varies according to how closely a person is patrilineally related to the deceased kul member (Bennett 1983: 19).

Beneath the level of the kul is another group, the *pariwar*, or household—the most important patrilineal unit in Brahman society. People of this group live together, work together, and conduct a number of rituals together; in addition, the male members own property jointly. The pariwar is the major unit of both production and consumption throughout Nepal (Bennett 1983: 22). The eldest male of this unit serves as head and exercises considerable authority over the others.

Figure 3.9 illustrates the relationships that exist among the thar, gotra, kul, and pariwar, all by reference to an individual ego (adapted from Bennett 1983: 20). Using the terms developed earlier, we find that the thar and gotra are descent *categories*, the kul is a descent *group*, and the pariwar is a *corporate* descent group. As we can see from the diagram, the thar and gotra are separate categories, but they overlap at the level of the kul. In addition, although ego's kul members share his or her thar and gotra affiliations, other people in ego's thar or gotra are not necessarily relatives of ego.

Nepalese Brahmans believe that, ideally, the pariwar should cover several generations, with sons of one family bringing in their wives to this unit, reproducing children, and staying together until the death of their father or even longer. In actual practice, however, married sons of one family usually

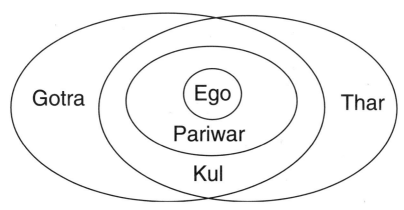

FIGURE 3.9 Ego in Relation to Kinship Categories and Groups Among Nepalese Brahmans

split up and separate their property before the common father dies. Even so, most couples start out married life within the husband's household and are well into raising their own children before the group splits.

When this split does occur, the brothers divide the family land and property equally. Women do not normally inherit in this system, though a widow can hold land or other property in trust for her sons. Women at marriage are given a dowry of clothing, jewelry, and household utensils.

Using this basic patrilineal framework, we will examine the nature of the Brahman patriline and the ways in which gender relationships are interwoven with it—indeed, inseparable from it. Toward this end we will consider three aspects of the patriline, or, more specifically, three core concerns of Brahman society with respect to the patriline: (1) The males of a patriline should maintain solidarity; (2) the line should continue (i.e., sons should be produced); and (3) the line of descent should be kept "pure." As we will see, *wives,* or affinal women, are a threat to all three of these core Brahmanical concerns. Following the study by Bennett (1983), we will also see that other dimensions of Brahman kinship affect relations between women and men. But, first, let's take a look at the three central dimensions of patrilineal kinship.

Male Patrilineal Solidarity.   During my stay in a village of Nepal, a woman with whom I was quite close spoke against her young daughter-in-law, Devi. "She is not shy, that one. When you were photographing the other day, she tried to get into all of the pictures!" She went on in agitation, accusing Devi (who by my own daily observation was quite modest, unobtrusive, and spent most of her time performing the most grueling of household chores) of flirting with village men.

Elsewhere in Nepal, another woman made the following accusation against her sister-in-law: "My elder sister-in-law used *tuna* (black magic) against my brother so that he would separate from mother and father. He had said he wouldn't separate from them until the day he died. So sister-in-law said some spells over some food and gave it to him to eat" (cited in Bennett 1983: 182).

These accusations are typical; over and over again I heard them directed against young women married into a household. The accusations against Devi concerned her presumably immodest behavior, a clear allusion to flagrant sexuality that would bring shame to her husband's house. In the second case, which concerned the presumed use of "black magic," a woman was accused of trying to pull her husband away from his household.

In these and other cases, married-in, or affinal, women are seen as a threat. At stake here is the idea of *male patrilineal solidarity*. We are already familiar with this idea, having encountered it in relation to the Nuer (see Case 1). As was true of the Nuer, close patrilineal kin among Nepalese Brahmans in rural areas have a great deal to do with one another. They live with or near one another, stand to inherit each other's land, and in innumerable ways are dependent upon one another's cooperation and assistance. The lineage (kul) embodies the cultural idea of the importance of male patrilineal solidarity. As Bennett (1983: 136) reported:

> When asked why they thought that large kuls were better, informants invariably mentioned that this provided them with more "brothers" [patrilineal male kin in general] to back them up in quarrels or help their sons enter government service. However . . . it is evident that size and extension of the kul is equally important for symbolic reasons: the larger the kul, the more perfectly it embodies the deeply held value of agnatic [patrilineal] solidarity.

One ritual, *devali*, expresses this idea well (Bennett 1983: 131–136). Devali is the communal worship of the lineage gods. Nepalese Brahmans believe that worship of these gods, among other things, ensures that the gods will help the kul to prosper and promote its continuity though human fertility. How often the devali is carried out, and exactly when, depends on the particular traditions of each individual kul. On the occasion of the worship, male kul members gather at the house of the eldest among them. Inside this house are kept the lineage gods, represented by stones; for the devali itself they are carried in procession to a special shrine where male kul members sacrifice animals (goats and chickens) to them. This part of the ceremony is considered very sacred, but of special significance for our purposes is the fact that *women are excluded* from it. Though married into the kul, women must not witness this central sacrifice; they are forbidden to enter the shrine at this time, and the stone representations of the gods are hidden from their view during the procession to the shrine. Women do attend the devali celebrations, coming along to the house of the eldest male with their husbands; they also prepare some special foods that, along with the blood sacrifice, are offered to the lineage gods. But their place on the sidelines is clear; indeed, it symbolizes that although they have married into a kul, they are only peripheral members of it.

The devali celebration and reinforcement of male patrilineal solidarity entail the exclusion of women in part because women, in their role as wives, are considered to be a threat to that solidarity. As Bennett wrote of the devali, "The oft-repeated sentiment that brothers would get along if only their wives did not set them against each other is here enacted" (1983: 135–136).

Why are wives seen as a threat to male patrilineal solidarity? In this respect the Nepalese Brahmans are somewhat different from the patrilineal Nuer, who see women in polygynous marriages as the focus of splits between half-brothers and their descendants. Among Brahmans (for whom polygyny is rare) the idea is not that women will pull half-brothers or their own separate sets of sons apart but, rather, that they will pull apart full brothers, their separate husbands. According to Bennett (1983: 169–170), wives are seen by men, and by other women, too (as we saw in the examples cited earlier), as manifesting this dangerous tendency out of crass self-interest. Recall that a woman enters her husband's household at marriage as a low-status outsider and, usually, as a stranger to all the people among whom she will now live. To promote her own interests, then, she supposedly seeks to lure her husband to her side, encouraging him to split off from his brothers and divide up the property. As Bennett (1983: 169–170) has observed, the suspicion with which the husband's household regards the new bride is

> greatest in the first months and years after marriage, before she has children that give her common interests with the patriline. It is at this stage that she may be held responsible for any misfortunes that befall her in-laws. . . . [S]he will very likely be accused of taking pieces of her wedding jewelry back to her *maita* [natal home] and pretending that it is lost. . . . A more serious common accusation is that the daughter-in-law has stolen something—such as a brass vessel or some grain—that is clearly family property.

At this stage, the one person in the household whom the bride might possibly secure as a buffer between herself and her demanding in-laws is her husband. One informant told Bennett (1983: 176) that "if the husband doesn't love you, no one in the household loves you." Yet by trying to pull her husband to her side she is seen by others, and by the society generally, as "pulling him away" from the patrilineal group.

And it gets worse. Bennett reports that "women told me frankly that sex, as the means to have children and as the means to influence their husband in their favor, was the most effective weapon in the battle for security and respect in their husband's house" (1983: 177). But then, the wife's very success in this respect constitutes the image of her as a threat: "A young man's attraction to his wife may be interpreted by his family as a betrayal of them" (1983: 177). Clearly this appears to be a no-win situation for the bride.

One can imagine all sorts of family tensions centering on this very fundamental aspect of Brahman kinship. Perhaps the relationship affected most is that between a woman and her mother-in-law as these two compete over the loyalty of the husband/son. To her mother-in-law a new bride is expected to show great deference and servitude. In the village studied by Bennett, "daughters-in-law are, even now, expected to greet their *sasu* [mother-in-law] by touching their foreheads to her feet. They must also drink the water from washing their *sasu*'s feet before each meal, ask if they may wash her clothes, and rub oil on her feet at night" (1983: 180). Despite these public displays, the mother-in-law feels privately that the daughter-in-law is attempting to seduce her own son away from her.

The most effective way out of the lowly status of outsider-bride is, of course, reproduction—especially reproduction of sons who will continue the husband's patriline. Thus sex serves as a "weapon" in women's battle for status and respect in the household, not only because it may win the affection of husbands but, even more important, because it may result in pregnancy and birth, the subjects of the next section.

Patriline Continuity.   I believed one older women in a village of Nepal to be particularly religious, as she was forever performing *puja* (worship) to the gods. When I commented upon her religiosity to one of her kin, her husband's brother's son, he said, "Yes she does that, but the gods will not accept her offerings." "Why?" I asked, surprised. "Because she is *aputri*" (a woman beyond childbearing age who has never conceived).

Among Nepalese Brahmans there is great concern to have sons: to continue the patriline, to provide heirs, to provide household labor (or income), and to provide parents with caretakers in old age and after their deaths. The role of sons in the funerals of parents, and in their spiritual welfare in the afterlife, entails deeply felt religious beliefs. When a parent dies, a son must observe a number of austerities and conduct crucial rituals to ensure the safe passage of the parent's soul from this world to the next. In addition, a son must perform the annual *sraddha*—a commemorative ceremony in which the deceased is ritually fed and thus sustained—not only for his parents but also for his patrilineal ancestors ascending three generations. Brahmans profess that any failure or negligence in the performance of these ceremonies places the departed soul in peril. In particular, if the funeral rituals were performed improperly, or not at all, the departed would become a "ghost" (*bhut* or *pret*) rather than a proper ancestor. Such ghosts are believed to wander about in painful hunger and inflict harm on the living (Stone 1989: 13). If a person simply has no son at the time of his or her

PHOTO 3.2   The author with members of her host family in Nepal. Photo courtesy of Linda Stone.

death, another patrilineal male relative can be called in to perform the rituals; but this idea is disturbing, "almost as if the rituals lose some of their efficacy" (Bennett 1983: 130).

Thus, both Brahman men and women are very concerned about producing sons. Daughters may be welcome, too, although their birth is generally met with less joy; and if a couple already has daughters, another one may be disappointing.

The pressure to bear children, especially sons, falls more heavily upon women than men. For one thing, it is the wife and not the husband who is blamed if a married couple fails to reproduce. This blame is phrased more in spiritual than in physiological terms; it is simply the woman's moral fault, probably on account of sins she committed in her previous lives (Hindus believe in reincarnation). Also, it is older childless women (rather than older childless men) who are pitied and ostracized in the rural community and likely to be suspected of being witches. Finally, if a woman does remain childless, her husband may well take another wife.

In the village of my studies (Stone 1978), Brahmans not only emphasized the importance of reproduction for women but actually made several distinctions that, as illustrated in Figure 3.10, reveal a rather striking hierarchy of values concerning female fertility. Spanning the left side of this diagram are negative categories or conditions. The first three mark categories of women who are considered to be inauspicious as well as unfortunate. A

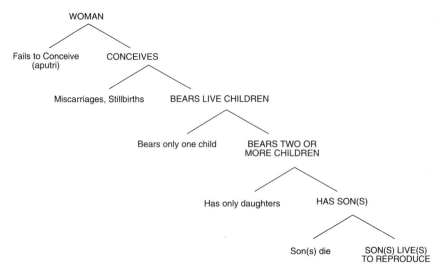

FIGURE 3.10   Nepalese Brahman Distinctions Concerning Female Fertility

woman who has never even conceived (aputri) is, as we have seen, considered so unworthy that the gods will not accept her offerings. At the next
level, among women who have conceived, is a separation between those
who have born live children and those who have experienced only miscarriages or stillbirths. The latter are less inauspicious than the aputri, but they
suffer mild ostracism nevertheless. As some female Brahmans explained to
me, this ostracism was a means of avoiding the contagion of these women's
condition. In particular, they stressed that repeated miscarriages may be
caused by a disease that can be passed through physical contact from one
woman to another (Stone 1978: 8–9).

Regarding women who have given birth, another distinction is drawn between those who bear two or more children and those who bear only one
(male or female). An older one-child woman is called a *kaga bandhya*, a
word that comes from the name of a crow that, it is said, gives birth to only
one offspring in its lifetime. For Hindus this crow, like the lowest of castes,
is very impure. The one-child woman does not suffer severe scorn or ostracism, but I was told that orthodox Brahman males should immediately
bathe themselves for purification if they spot such a woman upon waking
in the morning.

At the positive points of this hierarchy (spanning the right side of Figure
3.10) are women with successful fertility. Of course, the luckiest women of
all are those whose sons live to reproduce.

Despite all this very real pressure on women and men to bear children,
Nepalese Brahmans, in contrast to the Nuer, have very few options by

which to acquire children in case of fertility failure. Polygyny, which is allowed, might benefit childless or sonless men, but it does not help a barren woman. If a woman is fertile but her husband is sterile, she is not free to divorce him and remarry. Brahman society also does not allow for "surrogate genitors," "ghost marriages," or "woman-woman marriages." (Indeed, my village friends in Nepal found my description of Nuer marriage forms and reproductive strategies to be disgusting and bizarre.) Nor is adoption a realistic possibility for Brahman couples, especially those in rural areas, unless it involved a close patrilineal orphan (Stone 1978).

As we will see in the next section, the complicating issue in rural Nepal is the pressure on couples not only to reproduce children/sons for their lineages and for themselves but also to reproduce *pure* children. When a Brahman family takes in a bride, they seek from her not just children but Brahman children.

Purity of Descent.   In order for a couple to produce caste-pure Brahman children, two things (beyond biological parenthood) are necessary: first, the man and woman must both themselves be Brahman; and second, they must be united in a religiously sanctioned marriage (called *bihaite*) performed by Hindu priests. This type of marriage is also, significantly, called "gift of the virgin" (*kanyadan*) marriage. We will discuss these requirements to see how purity of descent is tied to the sexual behavior of women and, by implication, how women are seen as an ever-present threat to purity of descent.

The first requirement concerns the maintaining of Brahman status by individuals. One is, of course, born into the Brahman caste, with membership officialized later through initiation. However, one can lose one's Brahman status, or be effectively excommunicated from the caste. This would happen if a man or woman publicly violated an important rule of caste behavior. For example, if a Brahman publicly consumed rice cooked by a lower-caste person, he or she would no longer be Brahman and would assume the caste rank of the person whose boiled rice was eaten. Another way caste status can be lost is through sexual behavior, but this differs significantly for men and women. For men, the situation is straightforward and simple: A Brahman man loses his Brahman status only if he has sexual relations with a woman of an untouchable caste. In this case he, too, would become untouchable. But he may have premarital or extramarital relations with any nonuntouchable woman without losing his Brahman rank or his ability to reproduce Brahman children through a Brahman wife.

For women, the situation is very different. A Brahman woman becomes a full-caste person only through bihaite marriage to a Brahman male. In terms of sexual behavior, she then maintains this Brahman status if, and only if, her sexual relations are exclusively with this one male, her husband, throughout her entire life, even if her husband should die. Any deviation from these restrictions results in the loss of her Brahman status and her inability thereafter to produce Brahman children. Sex outside the bihaite marriage effectively "pollutes" the woman's womb.

If an unmarried female were known not to be virgin, she would lose her Brahman status and be completely unmarriageable in bihaite, or "gift of the virgin" marriage. Once properly married in bihaite, a Brahman woman would likewise cease to be Brahman through any adulterous affair, and any children of the union would be lower caste as well. If the adultery is known up front, the woman can be sent away; but the problem, of course, is that it may *not* be known (except to the woman and her lover, who are not telling). This, according to Bennett's analysis, makes Brahman women, in their roles as wives, dangerous. Through any lapse in their sexual behavior, they become a threat to the purity of descent of the patriline: "It is obvious that if a woman's sexuality is not guarded, the offspring of other men, from other lineages and even other castes, may be mistakenly incorporated" (1983: 125).

A Brahman woman may only have one bihaite, "gift of the virgin" marriage union in her lifetime. Widow remarriage in bihaite is not possible. Although a Brahman widow could enter into *lyaite*, a type of elopement marriage, this option is not sanctioned by Hindu religious ritual. And a Brahman widow who enters such a union can no longer be Brahman, so there is this price to pay.

One case from the village of my studies, though it involves the disappearance rather than the death of a husband, illustrates how some women talk about the option of elopement. A Brahman woman was married in bihaite to a Brahman man when she was eight years old. She moved in with his family and began her life as a low-status daughter-in-law, performing all the hardest household chores under the supervision of what she described as a particularly harsh mother-in-law. Then a few years after marriage her husband ran away to India and has not been heard from since. When I met this woman and heard her story she was eighteen. Throughout all those ten years she had remained in her husband's household in her low status, with little hope of any change. I asked her why she didn't run off with some other man in elopement. She reacted as though I had suggested she jump off a bridge, explaining that to do this would mean the loss of her Brahman status and the bringing of shame upon her family. It occurred to me that with this decision, if she stuck to it, the woman was forever forsaking something I had been taught was crucial to all Brahman women. I said, "But then you can never have children," upon which she burst into tears. The decision she made was caste purity over reproduction and motherhood; in her case she could not have both.

Whatever individual choices are made in such circumstances, among Brahmans the idea of a widow is quite negative. For one thing, a widow is seen as somehow morally responsible for her husband's death (Bennett

1983: 244). For another, her husband's patriline can make no further use of her fertility (Bennett 1983: 244). Yet at the same time a widow might be young and therefore potentially sexual. Having no legitimate basis in a marriage, her sexuality can only be seen as a threat to a community's morality. Indeed, the colloquial word for widow—*randi*—also means prostitute (Bennett 1983: 219).

Brahman men may form elopement unions without losing their Brahman status (unless, of course, they take up with an untouchable woman). Still, there is a price to pay for men, too. In these cases of elopement, the man remains Brahman but he can neither consume boiled rice cooked by his eloped wife nor produce Brahman children through her. Children of these unions would become members of his lineage, but since they are beneath the purity of his caste, they would be excluded from certain religious rituals regarding his lineage. For example, like all women, they could not participate fully in the man's lineage rituals (devali) described earlier. And a son born of such an elopement union, since he would not be a Brahman male, could not perform the crucial funeral rituals for the father.

Elopement unions among Brahmans are uncommon, but they do occur. The existence in Nepal of a caste called Jaisi testifies to this, for the children of an elopement union between a Brahman man and a Brahman woman become Jaisi in caste. Jaisi is a high, thread-wearing caste, but still, of course, below Brahman. In the village I studied, a multicaste village, 15 percent of all marriage unions were by elopement. Of these (a total of thirty-five), ten involved Brahman individuals.

The Inferiority of Wives

By now it is clear that within the Brahman kinship system affinal women occupy a decidedly inferior status (Bennett 1983: 142). We have covered three central concerns of the patrilineal system—male patrilineal solidarity, patriline continuity, and purity of descent. In terms of male patrilineal solidarity, affinal women are seen as divisive and threatening. In terms of patriline continuity, they are crucial. But in terms of the third concern, purity of descent, these women are dangerous. Affinal women become a sort of necessary evil.

We have also seen that in terms of patrilineal solidarity, continuity, and purity, it is the *sexual* aspect of affinal women that is of concern. Thus, in Bennett's account, affinal women are "dangerous" because of their potential as seducers of husbands and polluters of lineages through their illicit sexuality. And as we saw earlier, women are categorically less pure than men because they menstruate.

This concern with female sexuality and its dangers is most vividly represented in the *tij–rishi panchami*, an annual women's festival that spans three days. It comes in two parts. The first, *tij*, is intended to help prolong the life of one's husband. As noted, there is a strong belief among Brahmans that women are responsible for the length of their husband's life. The idea of dangerous female sexuality is clear in this context, since a husband's longevity is considered to depend especially upon his wife's virtue and chastity, or her sexual fidelity to him. During tij, married women endure a one-day fast and later conduct other rituals.

The purpose of the second part of the festival, *rishi panchami*, is to purify women from the sin of having unknowingly or inadvertently touched a man while menstruating during the previous year. As mentioned, during menstruation women are thought to be highly impure and untouchable. If a woman accidentally touches a man during a menstrual period, the contact is polluting to the man and sin accrues to the woman. For rishi panchami, women get together in large groups, go to a river, and undergo purificatory bathing rituals. These rituals are quite rigorous: "First . . . [a woman] must rub red mud . . . on her genitals 360 times [symbolic of each day in a year] and then splash river water to wash away the mud. . . . She continues rubbing mud and sprinkling water 360 times each on her feet, knees, elbows, mouth, shoulders (or armpits) and forehead. The whole process is then repeated with "white" mud, . . . oil seed husk . . . and cowdung" (Bennett 1983: 225–226). And all this is just the beginning of a longer process of washing and other purificatory rituals!

At the very end of the festival, women gather in household groups to worship the mythological founders (*rishi*) of their husbands' (and thus, by marriage, their own) gotras (the patrilineal categories that, as noted earlier, are important in religious ritual). The mythology of the rishi is itself very telling of the Brahman cultural view of affinal women. The rishi were legendary wise men who lived in the forest and spent their time in spiritual pursuits. However, they had wives, and their wives' sexuality distracted them from these higher pursuits. In one myth the wives are unfaithful to their rishi husbands, causing them further harm. But one wife, Arundhati, remains faithful. Along with the rishi themselves she becomes a focus of women's worship during the final part of the tij–rishi panchami festival.

Thus we see how one religious ritual expresses both the concerns of patrilineal kin groups and the inferiority of women. But the inferior status of affinal women is also expressed in many ways during everyday life. These often have to do with a woman's relationship to her husband, whom she is expected to see as her "lord" and to whom she must show great deference. Before her daily rice meals, a Brahman woman should bow her forehead down to his feet and, in a quest for her own religious merit, pour water over his feet and drink it. As we saw earlier, a similar act shows deference to her mother-in-law. In both cases, the woman does not gulp down the water, but merely plops a drop or two into her mouth. Still, the symbolic significance of the act is clear.

Publicly, a woman addresses her husband with the high respectful form of the pronoun "you" (*tapai*), whereas he addresses her with the lower form of the pronoun (*timi*) or, if he is angry or displeased, with an even lower form (*ta*). In the household the woman takes her meals after her husband and, rather than eating off a clean plate, is given the used (and thus "polluted") plate of her husband as an expression of her lower status and subservience (Bennett 1983: 91).

The Superiority of Daughters

From this description of Brahman life so far, the inferior, and apparently unenviable, position of women is clear. In so many ways the social and religious strength of the patriline and its concerns with solidarity, continuity, and purity restrict the lives of women and make them subservient to men. However, a major contribution of Bennett's work was to show that this description is "emphatically not the whole picture" (1983: 124). In all of the foregoing, the impact on women has concerned women in their role as wives—that is, affinal women. But Brahman women, like women in all societies, play more than just this role. To bring out the other dimensions of

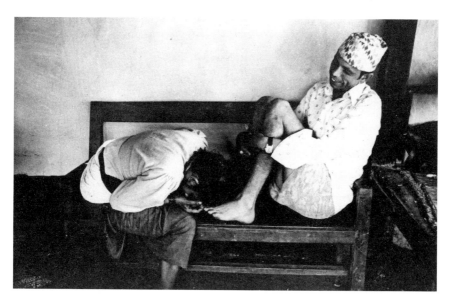

PHOTO 3.3   A Nepalese Brahman woman conveying a gesture of respect (*dhok dine*) to her husband. Photo courtesy of Linda Stone.

gender in this society, Bennett distinguished between the dominant *patrifo-cal* model of Brahman kinship and the submerged, less visible, but still im-portant *filiafocal* model. By patrifocal ("focused on the father") Bennett meant the system as seen from the angle of the patriline itself, covering all the ideas, values, and practices discussed in this chapter. In this connection, affinal women are important in their roles as reproducers of the lineage, yet they are threatening, dangerous, and inferior to men. But in the same sys-tem there is also a filiafocal ("focused on the daughter") undercurrent: Women are important, not in their roles as wives but in their roles as daughters or sisters. In contrast to affinal women, these consanguineal women are considered *sacred* to their fathers and brothers (as well as to their mothers and some other kin), and they are literally worshipped by fa-thers/brothers on certain religious occasions. At these times the males bow down and touch the feet of the daughter/sister. Since a daughter is sacred and religiously superior to her father, he receives religious merit by giving her in marriage to another family. Filiafocal relationships concern not only relations between males and their daughters/sisters but also relatives traced through the daughters/sisters. For example, just as a daughter is sacred and "high" to her father, so too is the man she marries, her father's son-in-law. Thus filiafocal relationships are central to the whole kinship system, a part of the social fabric of Brahman life.

Aside from being religiously sacred, daughters/sisters are generally re-garded and treated with affection by fathers/brothers and other consan-guineal kin. These relationships are important in a woman's life. Even though a woman is under the ultimate authority of her husband and his family, her relationships with her consanguineal kin in her natal home re-main strong and serve as "crucial sources of emotional, legal, and some-times even monetary support" (Bennett 1983: 251).

In childhood and during periodic return visits after marriage, females are indulged by their natal kin. At marriage, they move to a low, decidedly in-ferior position within the husband's house. But eventually most women, through successful fertility, move away from the position of bride/daughter-in-law to become mothers and, later, mothers-in-law themselves. In con-trast to the category "wife," "mother" is associated with purity and re-garded with reverence. Bennett (1983: 254–256) shows how motherhood transforms a woman from a low-status and "dangerous" affine into a highly respected and powerful domestic figure that transcends both the pa-trifocal and filiafocal dimensions of Brahman kinship. In a way, then, motherhood purifies female sexuality.

The case of Nepalese Brahmans shows that patrilineal descent, even in a society that we can characterize as very strongly patrilineal with powerful patrilines, has a more complex relationship with gender than one might at first suppose. It is not simply that patrilineal descent favors males over females. In this case, there are two sides to one system: a dominant one that defines affinal women as dangerous, and a submerged one that defines consanguineal women as sacred. Motherhood, a highly esteemed role, connects and transcends the two and ultimately gives women their most powerful and fulfilling roles. To be sure, the filiafocal dimension of Brahman kinship may not give women much power in the society overall, but it does affect how women and men see themselves and each other, and how gender is dynamically defined and played out over the course of life.

Contrasts and Concerns

We have taken a close look at two very different societies that trace descent patrilineally. In both societies, patrilineages are important social units, and the cultural ideology that surrounds the solidarity and continuity of these units exerts a powerful influence on men and women. Also in both societies, the power of patrilines is reinforced with religious beliefs and rituals. In this section we will consider two similarities among the Nuer and the Nepalese Brahmans in terms of the ways that kinship is related to gender, followed by a look at some important contrasts.

One of the strongest similarities between the two groups is that, from the perspective of patrilineal interests, women as wives are seen as divisive. In both societies they are blamed for pulling patrilineally related men apart and for threatening the solidarity of the patriline. Since the Nuer and the Brahman patrilines are strictly exogamous, women from outside are crucial to lineage continuity; yet as outsiders with interests of their own, they are mistrusted and readily accused of causing trouble between men. In the Nuer case, an ambivalence surrounds women because they are seen as both divisive and as unifying (with respect to sets of sons) and, through their exclusive roles as milkers of cows, as central, nurturant nodes in a homestead. Among Brahmans, however, women are not seen as domestically central or unifying. Yet there is an ambivalence surrounding Brahman women, too: From a patrifocal standpoint, they are dangerous to the patriline but absolutely necessary for its continuity. Although Nuer women are also necessary to patrilineal continuity, they and their sexuality are not seen as dangerous.

Another similarity between Nuer and Brahmans is that, although patrilineal descent is used in both societies to form important groups, in each case there are also other important sets of relationships based on linkages through women. In both cases, patrilines and a supporting kind of "patrilineal ideology" may be dominant, but in neither case does patrilineal descent and its ramifications provide the complete picture of kinship for the society. In short, among both the Nuer and the Brahmans, linkages through women provide significant countercurrents to the dominant patrilineal structure; and knowledge of these is crucial to an understanding of kinship as well as gender.

Recall that among the Nuer we have seen the formation of *matrifocal subunits* within patrilines. In this society, where polygynous unions are more common than among the Brahmans, sons of one mother develop their own special solidarity in opposition to their half-brothers, or the sons of the mother's co-wife. This matrifocal subunit is important, first, because it is usually along these breakages between half-brothers that patrilineages eventually split. Second, as we have seen, the tensions between sets of half brothers passes over the generations, so that a man's father's half-brother is seen, culturally, as a likely "wicked uncle" and the sons of this man are also mistrusted. Among Nepalese Brahmans it is not matrifocal subunits but rather *filiafocal ties* that bring about what Bennett referred to as the "submerged" aspect of the kinship structure. Filiafocal relationships are those traced to a daughter/sister and, through her, to other relatives as well. In this context we examined some important relationships of affection that could be used by married women as valuable and much-needed sources of emotional and material support. We also saw that a man's consanguineal sister and daughter are sacred to him, and religiously superior to him, so they are worshipped by him in religious ritual. In a sense, then, father/daughter and brother/sister relationships are the reverse of that between husband and wife.

Finally we come to an area of sharp differences between the Nuer and the Nepalese Brahmans. For one thing, although both societies value female fertility highly and regard the production of sons as necessary, the two groups differ dramatically in terms of the options they provide for acquiring children. Among the Brahmans the options are few. If a couple fails to have children, or sons, they may resort to polygyny, an option that may alleviate the state of childlessness or sonlessness for the man. But that's it. Polygyny does nothing to alleviate the problem for the childless/sonless woman, who will then be stigmatized in the society. At times, polygyny does not work for the man either, in which case he is stuck with his situation and can do nothing more. To acquire children, Brahmans essentially have to "grow their own" and, failing that, must suffer the consequences. Nuer society, by contrast, abounds with options for acquiring children. Aside from polygyny, Nuer society offers strategies ranging from "surrogate genitor" to "blind-eye adultery," and if all else fails there is always "ghost marriage" to ensure that all males will ultimately have sons. Perhaps the most striking contrast with the Brahmans is the Nuer option of "woman-woman" marriage, whereby a barren woman can "count as a man" and, through marriage to another woman and use of a surrogate genitor, acquire children for her father's lineage.

This contrast between the two groups is related to yet another factor: female sexuality. Among the Nuer, as we saw, a woman has rather autonomous control over her own sexuality. Virginity at marriage is not expected, let alone insisted upon. Extramarital affairs might temporarily anger a husband, but the wife is not held to be morally at fault, is unlikely to be divorced, and is certainly not rendered incapable of producing further legitimate children for the husband's lineage. A woman is also relatively free to divorce her husband and to form any number of additional legitimate unions with other men over her lifetime. Among Brahmans, by contrast, there is deep concern with female virginity at marriage and confinement of her sexuality to her husband for her entire life. Any deviation from this restriction results not only in loss of her caste status but also inability to thereafter produce Brahman children.

Thus we can say that among Brahmans the value that a patriline places on a wife's fertility is encompassed by and secondary to the value placed on her sexual "purity." Only if she is a virgin at marriage and sexually faithful to her husband can she produce Brahman children for her husband's patriline. Any case of known adultery would excommunicate the woman from her caste, dispel her from the marriage, and disqualify her from further caste-pure reproduction. But among the Nuer, the rules by which children are allocated to husbands and lineages remain independent from the mother's sexual behavior. In other words, a woman's sexual behavior cannot devalue her fertility. The contrast between Nuer and Brahmans becomes especially clear when we look at the consequences of adultery. To put it somewhat crudely, among Brahmans adultery "pollutes" the woman's fertility; from the patriline's point of view, it is akin to destruction of property. But among the Nuer, again from the standpoint of the patriline, adultery is mere theft, punishable by a fee of six cows.

Many Euro-American readers will conclude that the sexual restrictions on Brahman women and the consequences to women for violation of society's rules are a bit harsh. Yet the Brahman case is in some ways more familiar to Euro-Americans, or closer to their own traditions, than that of the Nuer. Certainly the concept of female sexual "purity" is far from alien to the Western world. We are all familiar with the idea of a woman's "reputation" being contingent on her sexual behavior. And despite the 1960s "sexual revolution" most people would agree that a sexual double standard for men and women still obtains in Euro-American societies. These societies have never gone so far as to categorically devalue a woman's future fertility on account of her past sexuality, but they have very much devalued those women whose sexual "virtue" has supposedly lapsed. Rather, I think, what Euro-Americans would find new and unfamiliar are Nuer arrangements. Nothing in Euro-American traditions compares to woman-woman marriage, for example. And the idea of a married woman's adultery being handled simply by her lover's payment of a fee to the husband goes against Euro-American sentiments.

Why is it that some societies develop a concern with female sexual purity, and why has this concern become a part of Euro-American traditions? We will consider some ideas related to this question in a later chapter. But first, let's take a look at societies with another mode of descent altogether: societies without patrilineages, societies that trace descent directly through women.

References

Aberle, David F. 1961. Matrilineal Descent in Cross-Cultural Perspective. In David M. Schneider and Kathleen Gough, eds., *Matrilineal Kinship*, pp. 655–727. Berkeley: University of California Press.

Acharya, Meena, and Lynn Bennett. 1981. *The Rural Women of Nepal: An Aggregate Analysis and Summary of 8 Village Studies*. Kathmandu: Centre for Economic Development and Administration, Tribhuvan University.

Ackerman, Lillian A. 1992. Yupik Eskimo Residence and Descent in Southwestern Alaska. *Inter-Nord* 19: 253–263.

Barnes, J. A. 1951. *Marriage in a Changing Society* (Rhodes Livingstone Papers, No. 20). London: Oxford University Press.

_____. 1968. Some Nuer Notions of Nakedness, Nudity and Sexuality. *Africa* 38 (2): 1–131.

Bennett, Lynn. 1976. Sex and Motherhood among the Brahmans and Chetris of East Central Nepal. *Contributions to Nepalese Studies* 3: 1–52.

_____. 1983. *Dangerous Wives and Sacred Sisters: Social and Symbolic Roles of High Caste Women in Nepal*. New York: Columbia University Press.

Bettini, Maurizio. 1991. *Anthropology and Roman Culture: Kinship, Time, Images of the Soul*. Translated by John van Sickle. Baltimore: The Johns Hopkins University Press.

Biedelman, T. O. 1966. The Ox and Nuer Sacrifice: Some Freudian Hypotheses About Nuer Symbolism. *Man* 1: 453–467.

Brain, Robert. 1972. *Bangwa Kinship and Marriage*. Cambridge: Cambridge University Press.

Corbier, Mireille. 1991. Constructing Kinship in Ancient Rome: Marriage and Divorce, Filiation and Adoption. In David I. Kertzer and Richard P. Sallers, eds., *The Family in Italy: From Antiquity to the Present*, pp. 127–144. New Haven: Yale University Press.

di Leonardo, Micaela. 1991. Gender, Culture and Political Economy: Feminist Anthropology in Historical Perspective. In Micaela di Leonardo, ed., *Gender at the Crossroads of Knowledge: Feminist Anthropology in the Postmodern Era*, pp. 1–48. Berkeley: University of California Press.

Divale, William Tulio. 1975. An Explanation for Matrilocal Residence. In Dana Raphael, ed., *Being Female: Reproduction, Power and Change*, pp. 99–108. The Hague: Mouton Publishers.

Ember, Melvin, and Carol Ember. 1971. The Conditions Favoring Matrilocal Versus Patrilocal Residence. *American Anthropologist* 73: 571–594.

Engels, Friedrich. 1942 [orig. 1884]. *The Origin of the Family, Private Property and the State*. New York: International Publishers.

Evans-Pritchard, E. E. 1940. *The Nuer: A Description of the Modes of Livelihood and Political Institutions of a Nilotic People*. Oxford: Clarendon Press.

_____. 1945. Some Aspects of Marriage and the Family Among the Nuer (Rhodes-Livingstone Papers, No. 11). London: Royal Anthropological Institute of Great Britain and Ireland.

_____. 1950. The Nuer Family. *Sudan Notes and Records* 31(1): 21–42.

_____. 1974 [orig. 1956]. *Nuer Religion*. New York: Oxford University Press.

_____. 1990 [orig. 1951]. *Kinship and Marriage Among the Nuer*. New York: Oxford University Press.

Fortes, Meyer. 1958. Introduction. In Jack Goody, ed., *The Developmental Cycle in Domestic Groups*, pp. 1–14. Cambridge: Cambridge University Press.

Gluckman, Max. 1965. Kinship and Marriage Among the Lozi of Northern Rhodesia and the Zulu of Natal. In A. R. Radcliffe-Brown and Daryll Forde, eds., *African Systems of Kinship and Marriage*, pp. 166–206. Oxford: Oxford University Press.

Gough, Kathleen. 1961. Variation in Matrilineal Systems: Variation in Residence. In David M. Schneider and Kathleen Gough, eds., *Matrilineal Kinship,* pp. 545–576. Berkeley: University of California Press.

_____. 1971. Nuer Kinship: A Reexamination. In T. O. Beidelman, ed., *The Translation of Culture: Essays to E. E. Evans-Pritchard*, pp. 79–121. London: Tavistock Publications.

Herskovits, M. J. 1937. A Note on "Woman Marriage" in Dahomey. *Africa* 10: 335–341.

Hutchinson, Sharon. 1980. Relations Between the Sexes Among the Nuer: 1930. *Africa* 50(4): 371–387.

James, Wendy. 1990. Introduction. In E. E. Evans-Pritchard, ed., *Kinship and Marriage Among the Nuer*, pp. ix–xxii. New York: Oxford University Press.

Kelly, Raymond. 1985. *The Nuer Conquest: The Structure and Development of an Expansionist System*. Ann Arbor: University of Michigan Press.

Morgan, Lewis H. 1964 [orig. 1887]. *Ancient Society*. Cambridge, Mass.: Harvard University Press.

Murphy, Robert F. 1986. *Cultural and Social Anthropology: An Overture*, 2nd ed. Englewood Cliffs, N.J.: Prentice-Hall.

Otterbein, Keith. 1968. Internal War: A Cross-Cultural Study. *American Anthropologist* 70: 277–289.

Pomeroy, Sarah B. 1975. *Goddesses, Whores, Wives and Slaves: Women in Classical Antiquity*. New York: Schocken Books.

Robertson, A. F. 1991. *Beyond the Family: The Social Organization of Reproduction*. Berkeley: University of California Press.

Rodseth, Lars, Richard W. Wrangham, Alisa M. Harrigan, and Barbara B. Smuts. 1991. The Human Community As a Primate Society. *Current Anthropology* 32(3): 221–241.

Sacks, Karen. 1979. *Sisters and Wives: The Past and Future of Sexual Equality*. Westport, Conn.: Greenwood Press.

Shelton, Jo-Ann. 1988. *As the Romans Did: A Source Book in Roman Social History*. New York: Oxford University Press.

Stone, Linda. 1978. Cultural Repercussions of Childlessness and Low Fertility in Nepal. *Contributions to Nepalese Studies* 5(2): 7–36.

———. 1989. *Illness Beliefs and Feeding the Dead in Hindu Nepal*. Lewiston, N.Y.: Edwin Mellen Press.

Treggiari, Susan. 1991. Ideals and Practicalities in Matchmaking in Ancient Rome. In David I. Kertzer and Richard P. Saller, eds., *The Family in Italy: From Antiquity to the Present*, pp. 91–108. New Haven: Yale University Press.

White, Leslie A. 1964. Introduction. In Lewis H. Morgan, *Ancient Society*. Cambridge, Mass.: Harvard University Press.

4

Through the Mother

This chapter explores matrilineal societies, those in which descent is traced through females. Figure 4.1 shows the tracing of matrilineal kin from a common ancestor, with shaded symbols representing persons who share matrilineal kinship. Here, females and males are members of their mother's matriline by birth; but, in direct opposition to the case of patrilineal descent, only women can transmit this membership to offspring over the generations. The matrilineal principle, like its patrilineal counterpart, can be used to construct corporate kinship groups such as lineages and clans.

How do matrilineal societies work? Does descent traced through women give females special positions or power in these societies? Do we find cases where the corporate matrilineal property (e.g., land or livestock) is owned and controlled by women, or cases where women act as heads of the descent groups? When the group is matrilineal and matrilocal, do we find cases where affinal males enter new households as low-status grooms, subservient to their wives and at the beck and call of their fathers-in-law?

As it turns out, matrilineal societies show a great deal of variation. There are indeed cases of female ownership of property. But there are also cases of matrilineal societies in which property is owned by males, with ownership passing to their sisters' sons. In still other cases, descent group property is owned by women but *controlled* by their matrilineal male kin. And in matrilocal situations, affinal males may indeed enter their wives' households as newcomers with little authority over their wives, though, to my knowledge, there are no cases where husbands show subservience to wives and in-laws in any way comparable to the patrilocal-patrilineal example of the Nepalese Brahmans discussed in the last chapter. Most commonly, males are heads of matrilineal kinship units, but there are some societies, such as the Ashanti of West Africa, in which females act as heads along with males.

What sorts of gender relationships occur in societies with matrilineal descent? To address this question, we will first look at how earlier generations

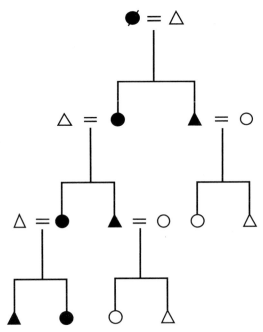

FIGURE 4.1   A Matrilineal Descent Construct. Persons sharing matrilineal descent are shaded.

of anthropologists viewed matrilineal societies, an analysis that leads directly to the core issue of "male dominance."

In the nineteenth century there was some confusion between matrilineal descent and the concept of "matriarchy," or "rule by women." Some scholars such as Johan Bachofen (1891) believed that the earliest human societies were matriarchal, and that matriarchy was an early, and clearly inferior, stage of human cultural evolution. These societies were thought to have been thoroughly controlled by fearsome Amazon-like women. Later, according to this line of thought, a shift to patriarchy occurred as human society became more "civilized." Matrilineal descent was seen as but a part of a larger matriarchal social organization; and the few cases of living matrilineal societies were interpreted as curious "remnants" of our species' matriarchal past. Other scholars argued against this view at the time, some holding that the earliest human societies were already patriarchal; but eventually the whole idea of distinct "stages" of human cultural evolution fell out of favor. Still, the association between "matrilineal" and "matriarchal" lingered on in the popular imagination.

Today anthropologists generally agree that cases of true matriarchy do not exist in human society, and that they most probably never have. It's easy enough to find societies in which women play prominent social, religious, or even political roles, in which they are clearly influential or power-ful in numerous spheres of life. And an argument can be made for the existence of gender equality (Ackerman 1982; Lepowsky 1993) or near equality (Shostak 1981) in some societies. But convincing cases of "female-dominant" societies, or societies in which women and not men (or men only rarely or exceptionally) hold the major positions of official authority, have not (yet) been found.

Matrilineal societies, however, do exist. But it is important to remember that *matrilineal* means simply "descent through females." It is not synony-mous with *matriarchy*.

Once this confusion was cleared up, another problem developed. Believ-ing there were no true matriarchies, anthropologists possibly went too far in the other direction and took male authority or general male dominance as a given. Indeed, a few decades ago there was little discussion about why male dominance might be universal or even whether, in what sense, or to what extent it is so. For example, David Schneider (1961: 5), who exam-ined this issue in relation to matrilineal kinship, simply stated that in all unilineal descent groups, whether patrilineal or matrilineal, "women are re-sponsible for the care of children" and "adult men have authority over women and children." In matrilineal systems, according to Schneider, de-scent is traced through women, but authority is still vested in men. Con-trasting the differences between patrilineal and matrilineal descent, Schnei-der (1961: 7) wrote:

> Perhaps the first and most profound [difference] is that in patrilineal descent groups the line of authority and the line of descent both run through men. That is, both authority and placement are male functions. In matrilineal de-scent groups, on the other hand, although the line of authority also runs through men, group placement runs through the line of women. The lines of authority and placement are thus coordinate in males in patrilineal descent groups, but separated between males and females in matrilineal descent groups.

At this point, matrilineal societies came to be seen, prototypically, as those in which women are primarily under the authority of their brothers and maternal uncles, and men are concerned with exercising control over their sisters and sisters' children. A child's real authority figure would be not his or her own father but his or her mother's brother. Property would be held by males and inherited by their sisters' sons. Seeing matrilineal males in control, some anthropologists, such as Meyer Fortes (1959), went so far as to urge that we see "descent" in matrilineal systems as proceeding not from a mother to her child but, rather, from the mother's brother to the sister's son. Although this argument had some merit (at the very least it moved away from confusing matrilineal descent with matriarchy), it ultimately pushed women too far into the background, where their own kinship roles, interests, strategies, and powers became all too easy to ignore.

Later, Roger Keesing (1975), though critical of the male bias evident in previous studies of kinship, invited students to see male members of a matrilineal group as a kind of "board of directors" of the kinship corporation. Putting it this way had the advantage of specifying that we are here talking about authority within descent groups, and not necessarily about structures of authority in the broader society or, for that matter, about "male dominance" in all spheres of social life.

The hypothetical matriline shown in Figure 4.2 illustrates this view of matrilineal male authority and its transmission. Here, the men A, B, C, and D are currently the senior males of the matriline. They collectively own and control the matriline's property, which passes collectively to their sisters' sons; in turn, these sons, along with other matrilineal kin of that generation, will be the next generation's "board of directors." Each of the individual men in this system may also pass other property to his respective sisters' son or sons. These senior males meet together to discuss and decide upon the matriline's affairs. Collectively they have authority over women and children who are members of the matriline. Individually they have authority over their respective sisters, nieces, and nephews.

Let's say that the man A is the most senior and, as such, is official head of the matriline. He has authority over all other matriline members. When he dies his authority passes to the man E, a sister's son. If he has many sisters and those sisters have many sons, there could be a rule stating that, say, his

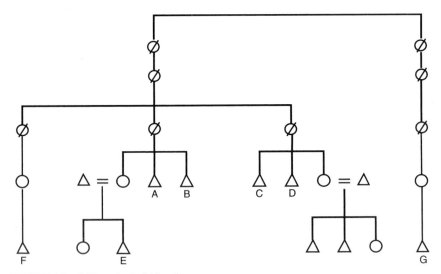

FIGURE 4.2   A Hypothetical Matriline

position goes to the eldest sister's eldest son. Yet even if he has no sister at all, succession could occur, since no doubt there would be someone (an MZDS or MMMZDDDS such as the man F or the man G in the diagram) who would then be head.

The Matrilineal Puzzle

The earlier anthropologists were rather intrigued by this combination of descent through females with authority vested in males, since it was believed to account for the special "tensions" in matrilineal societies that were not found in patrilineal ones. Audrey Richards (1950) was the first to coin a phrase for these tensions: "the matrilineal puzzle." This "puzzle" referred to what Richards saw in matrilineal societies as built-in strains in the relationship between a woman's husband and her brother. Both would want to control her. Also, both would want to control her children, the one man as their father, and the other as their maternal uncle. Naturally this situation would produce some conflict. Schneider (1961:22) later generalized the brother's control as extending to the "children's matrilineal descent group," since this group as a whole has interests in the woman's children that might run counter to the desires of the husband. The idea of a matrilineal puzzle, then, was based not only on the assumption of male authority over sisters and sisters' children within a matriline but also on the assumption that males, in any society, would naturally want to exert some control over their own wives and children. In a sense, male authority would come into conflict with itself.

This image of a "puzzle" focused attention on the question as to how matrilineal societies cope with the combination of authority through men and descent through women. On the basis of this question, anthropologists interpreted certain features of the social structure of matrilineal societies as attempted "solutions" to the matrilineal puzzle. Consider, for example, the case of a matrilineal society that is also matrilocal, as illustrated in Figure 4.3.

In this figure, the symbols representing members of one matriline are shaded. The arrows indicate males moving matrilocally into their wives' residential units at marriage. Loops enclose those people who will stay together. Note that the male members of the shaded matriline are split up upon their marriages, each going off to his own wife's group. In Keesing's (1975: 63) terms, the male "'board of directors' is scattered away from 'corporation headquarters.'" How are these men to run an efficient matriline when they are split up from one another? Not only that, but along with their departure, new men (nonmembers) are moving in with the sisters as their husbands. Wouldn't the affinal husbands be able to exert control over their own wives and children and thus threaten the position of the matriline's male authorities? Well, one partial "solution" here would be to have nucle-

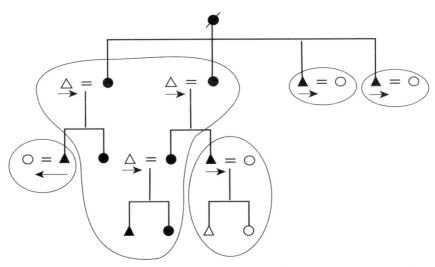

FIGURE 4.3 A Matrilineal, Matrilocal Group. Members of one matriline are shaded. The loops surround those persons who, following matrilocal residence, will live together. The arrows show men moving to the residences of their wives.

ated settlements, with everyone in the society living fairly close together. Then the brothers would leave upon marrying, but they wouldn't go very far. They would be close enough to come back together periodically to discuss important matters pertaining to the matriline and to keep an eye on their sisters and their sisters' children.

Another option would be to combine matrilineal descent with patrilocal residence. This arrangement would keep male matriline members together, but it would also eventually produce another problem, as Figure 4.4 illustrates. Here the males stay together, but this "solution" works for only one generation. Their sister leaves at marriage and moves in with her husband. So her children, the next generation's male matriline members, are away, growing up elsewhere. Again, this situation invites their own fathers to exercise more control over them. For their mothers' brothers, the problem is, as Keesing (1975: 64) put it, how do they "get back" the children? Nucleated settlements might help in this case, too; but yet another "solution" was thought to be *avunculocal residence*, or residence of a male at marriage with his mother's brother or brothers. This arrangement is illustrated in Figure 4.5, which shows a woman moving patrilocally at marriage. But then her sons, upon their marriages, move back to the place(s) of their mother's brother or brothers. In some societies it may be that a man in search of a wife must go to the place of his MBs, who would then find a local bride and arrange a marriage for him.

Anthropologists saw still another "solution" to the matrilineal puzzle in the arrangement of the "visiting husband." This arrangement is rare but

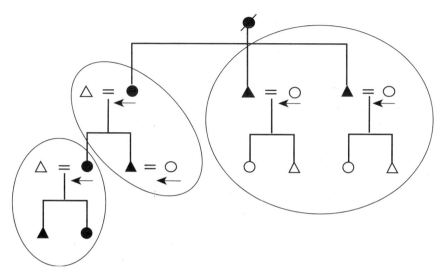

FIGURE 4.4 A Matrilineal, Patrilocal Group. Members of one matriline are shaded. Loops surround those persons who, following patrilocal residence, will live together. Arrows show women moving to the residences of their husbands.

quite interesting in its own right. Here, brothers and sisters remain together in one domestic unit for life. After marriage neither the wife nor her husband move at all; rather, the husband "visits" his wife from time to time for purposes of sex, companionship, and procreation. He may spend a night with her from time to time, but he lives with his sister. Meanwhile, the woman's brother or brothers live with her but go off to "visit" their own wives. Insofar as there really is a matrilineal puzzle, this would seem the

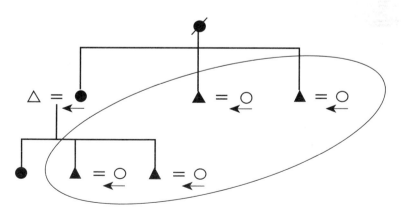

FIGURE 4.5 A Matrilineal, Avunculocal Group. Members of one matriline are shaded. The loop surrounds those persons who, following avunculocal residence, will live together. Arrows show women moving into the residences of their husbands.

ideal solution, since it keeps matrilineal males together over the generations. The "visiting husband" arrangement has been found in a few matrilineal societies such as the Nayar (see Case 4 in this chapter). In this case, the people also practiced polyandry and polygyny. Thus, for example, one woman could have many husbands, each of whom visited her on different nights; and a man could have more than one wife to visit. Children, of course, belonged to the matrilines of their mothers, and the issue of which husband was the biological father was not considered important. A child called all of his or her mother's husbands "father."

All of the so-called solutions to the matrilineal puzzle were seen by anthropologists as only partial. The fact remained that matrilineal societies, however residentially organized, were plagued by tensions. Males and females seemed to be pulled in conflicting directions. Consider the case of a married woman. She has a bond with her husband, who has some domestic authority over her and is, after all, generally the father of her children. But first and foremost she must respect the interests of her brother (or maternal uncles, etc.). If her ties to her husband become too strong, they will threaten the strength of the matrilineal kinship group. The woman also has to take her children into account. Her husband may be their father, but their position in society, their welfare, and most likely their inheritance of property are all bound up with her brother (or with male matrilineal kin in general). Now consider the case of a married man. He may want to have his own children but needs to be more concerned with the fertility of his sister than with that of his wife. If he does have children, he won't have much authority over them anyway, for higher authority will be held by their mother's male matrilineal kin. If his ties to his own wife and children become too strong, they, again, will threaten the strength of the matrilineal kinship group. In the end, it was considered that in matrilineal societies the ties between brothers and sisters must remain stronger than those between husbands and wives. Strong marriage ties would spell the doom of matrilineal descent. So would strong ties between husbands and children. Many matrilineal societies were studied in terms of the ways in which individuals, in their different roles, struggled through these built-in stresses and strains.

Anthropologists writing about the matrilineal puzzle felt that seeing matrilineal descent in this way helped to account for a number of features commonly associated with matrilineal descent. For example, matrilineal societies tend to have high rates of divorce. This finding would be expected since the marriage ties in these societies need to be weak, or at least weaker than brother-sister or niece-maternal uncle ties. If something has to break under the "strain" of matriliny, it should be the marriage. Through the matrilineal puzzle patterns of nucleated settlements or avunculocal residence were interpreted as partial "solutions." More generally it accounted for the observation that matrilineal societies are quite rare (see Chapter 1). And seeing matrilineal descent in this way was consistent with the observation that systems of matrilineal descent are "fragile." In the nineteenth and early twentieth centuries, under the impact of colonialism and the advance of world capitalism, most patrilineal societies remained patrilineal, but many matrilineal societies dropped their systems of descent and gradually became patrilineal or bilateral themselves.

Matrilineal systems were thus seen as beset by special strains, as fragile and rare, possibly even doomed to extinction. Early anthropologists became interested in questions such as How did these systems arise in the first place, and, what, precisely, are the conditions that break them down or, more rarely, keep them going?

These anthropologists were assuming that males would "naturally" be torn between themselves and each other, wishing to control both wives/children and sisters/nephews. They may have been right to say that clear cases of female-dominant societies or matriarchies do not exist, but were they right in assuming that all matrilineal societies would illustrate the strains and tensions of combining male authority with descent through females? Were they right in assuming, in the first place, that males always have authority over females within descent groups?

Later research on matrilineal societies challenged the monolithic image of male authority implied by the matrilineal puzzle. Without rejecting the premise of universal male authority as such, some anthropologists suggested that the status or power of women would tend to be higher in matrilineal societies than in most patrilineal ones, especially if the societies were also matrilocal. Alice Schlegel (1972: 141–142) phrased this idea in psychological terms: "In matrilineal societies there is a cognitive set toward the importance of women that has an effect in mitigating male dominance. . . . I hypothesize that the descent system, by emphasizing one parent, both parents equally, or each parent in a different way, conditions the attitude that the individual learns toward sexual differences and carries over in his behavior toward members of the two sexes."

Schlegel also drew attention to the variation in male authority among matrilineal societies by comparing different matrilineal groups in terms of male authority within the domestic sphere of the home. She granted that matrilineally related males would have authority over women within the larger descent group, but wanted to assess the extent to which a woman's husband or brother held authority over her in the domestic sphere in different matrilineal societies. She concluded that matrilineal societies could be categorized along a continuum ranging from those with strong husband authority and weak brother authority to those with strong brother authority and weak husband authority. Of special interest to her were those societies in the middle of the continuum, showing equal husband and brother authority over a woman. She found that women in matrilineal societies with equal husband and brother authority were more autonomous—in other words, that domestic authority over women was altogether *less* in these societies than in the other types of matrilineal societies.

Later anthropologists were even more critical of the concept of the matrilineal puzzle. They argued that matrilineal descent was a perfectly ordinary, reasonable way of forming and operating groups in a society and that it need not be seen as odd or peculiar (Poewe 1981). Why, they asked, should it be viewed as a "puzzle" at all? Without claiming to have found any matrilineal matriarchies, these critics nevertheless called for a reassessment of the whole issue of gender in relation to matrilineal descent. In the process, many of them challenged the idea of universal male dominance, claiming that in at least some matrilineal societies (and in some bilateral societies, too) a case could be made for a kind of gender balance or gender equality.

Meanwhile, the matrilineal puzzle should not be entirely discounted. It did, after all, point up the error of assuming that matrilineal descent is an indicator of matriarchy, or that matrilineal descent is just a "mirror image" of patrilineal descent. In fact, its main virtue is that it drew attention to *male* roles within matrilineal societies—and, clearly, these are important. (Better still, of course, would have been a simultaneous focus on the important *female* roles within patrilineal societies.)

The main limitation of the matrilineal puzzle was its blurry, unfocused vision of women and women's roles in matrilineal societies. In addition, during the "puzzle" era of matrilineal kinship studies, male authority was flatly assumed to be a given. Later researchers brought out the considerable variation that characterized authority, power, and influence among both males and females in societies with matrilineal descent. Here we will take a look at two very different cases.

CASE 3: THE NAVAJO

During the period from babyhood to adolescence there is little difference in ritualistic treatment of male and female children. At adolescence, however, there is a definite change. The girl . . . becomes a tribal symbol of fecundity at her adolescence ceremony, and from then on a symbol of the power of reproduction.

—*Gladys Reichard (1950)*

These people among whom a girl's first menstruation is a public rejoicing, and among whom women are powerful symbols of life, growth, and rejuvenation, are the Navajo. The largest Native American group, they now number around two hundred thousand persons.

The ancestors to the Navajo are thought by anthropologists to have been among the last migrants to enter North America from Asia across the

Bering Strait more than twelve thousand years ago. From homelands in Alaska and Western Canada, these people began a migration to the American Southwest. Navajo history places their new settlement in a region now mostly encompassed by northern New Mexico. According to anthropologists, they arrived in this region between A.D. 1000 and A.D. 1500; but Navajo tradition asserts that they have always lived in this area. Origins aside, the Navajo of the Southwest were originally hunter-gatherers. It is not clear how far back in time their matrilineal social organization goes.[1]

Early on, the Navajo traded and intermarried with other indigenous peoples, including Paiutes, Utes, and Pueblos in the Southwest; later, after 1540, Spanish settlements began to encroach on native land. From the Pueblos the Navajo adopted agricultural techniques and began to practice a mixed agriculture-hunting economy. They lived in small groups with informal leaders and had no overarching political structure. Navajo relationships with both the Pueblos and the Spanish varied from peaceful trade to mutual raiding and sporadic warfare. And from both of these groups, the Navajo acquired significant cultural elements that they wove into their own traditions.

From the Spaniards the Navajo acquired the horse in the 1600s, considerably increasing their mobility and their range of contacts with other peoples. Through raids on the Spanish they also acquired sheep and goats, and by the late 1700s sheep herding had become a central feature of their economy. Women's clothing, consisting of a blouse, velvet jacket, and flaring skirt, was also adopted from the Spanish.

With their herding and agriculture, the Navajo adapted to an arid desert region, a harsh land but also beautiful, with deep canyons, grand mountains, and mesas. Within small dispersed settlements they lived in "forked stick" hogans (houses) made of earth and wood. During raids, some took slaves and others were taken as slaves by outside groups. Compared with other Native American societies, however, the Navajo were relatively dispersed, a fact that spared them Spanish domination and decimation from epidemics.

But a far more serious threat lay just ahead. By the mid-1800s, American forces were in the region, determined to put a stop to Navajo raiding. In 1863, under Kit Carson, the U.S. military subdued the Navajo, largely by destroying their homes and crops and taking their livestock. Soon after, about eight thousand Navajo were imprisoned at Fort Sumner. This was a very dark period in Navajo history, often referred to as the "Long Walk"

---

[1] Some anthropologists believe that the Navajo adopted matrilineal descent from the Pueblo Indians; but others have suggested that the Navajo were already matrilineal when they entered the Southwest (see Levy, Henderson, and Andrews 1989).

because the Navajo were made to walk the three hundred miles to Fort Sumner from the point of their surrender at Fort Defiance. Many died or were killed along the way; and at Fort Sumner they endured deplorable conditions.

The Navajo remained incarcerated for four years. In 1868 they were allowed to return home, but "home" was now an Indian reservation, under legal control of the U.S. government. Here, after enduring initial hardships, and despite their pacification and loss of autonomy, the Navajo began to reconstruct their lives around sheep herding and farming, renewing many of their cultural traditions.

Another blow came to the Navajo in 1933 with the government's Stock Reduction Program. The Navajo livestock population had been expanding, creating a serious problem of erosion from overgrazing. Livestock permits issued to the Navajo forced them to get rid of livestock above a certain limit. The program was quickly invaded by corruption and misunderstandings on all sides. In the end, with half their livestock gone, the Navajo were left embittered, now forced to depend on seasonal wage work as well as herding and agriculture for their livelihood.

From this period to the present, the Navajo economy and culture changed dramatically. Wage work and craft production became major sources of income whereas herding and agriculture declined. Beginning in the 1880s, Anglo influences entered the reservation with the establishment of trading posts, schools, medical facilities, and Christian missions. Along with the loss of many Navajo traditions, recent years have seen a growth in self-government and a strong push for Navajo self-determination.

Since their entry into the Southwest, the Navajo experienced fairly rapid economic changes, and these undoubtedly had repercussions on gender relationships. As agriculture developed, reliance on male hunting declined. During the same period, male roles in raiding and warfare became important, but these activities were abruptly ended by the U.S. military action in 1863. In early reservation times, agriculture and herding had involved both men and women in important economic activities. But following the stock reduction, wage work was largely available only to males, and women became economically dependent on men. This situation is changing now as more women are becoming employed and pursuing educational opportunities (Shepardson 1982). In the same period since stock reduction, regional and class variations have occurred among male and female economic roles (Lamphere 1989).

Kinship Traditions

Descent. This description of Navajo kinship refers to these people's recent past, roughly the period from 1940 to the early 1970s. Many of the Navajo traditions have not continued, but in some respects the overall character of Navajo kinship and gender is still evident now. As we will see, one aspect of Navajo life that was important in the past, and persists today, is the centrality of women's social and symbolic roles.

Navajo clans (of which more than sixty still exist) were matrilineal, named, exogamous categories. Many of the clan names reflected their origin as place names—for example, Deer Spring, Water-Flows-Together, Coyote Pass, Narrow Gorge, and Yucca-Fruit-Strung-Out-In-a-Line. Navajo clans were not corporate groups in the sense that clan members did not hold property in common or come together for any economic, social, or religious purpose.

Both marriage and sexual relations were forbidden within the clan. Sexual relations between clan members were considered incestuous, and the Navajo believed that those who broke this taboo would become insane, die, or produce deformed children (Aberle 1961: 109). Aside from enforcement of these marriage and sex prohibitions, the main function of the clan was to oblige members to provide one another with hospitality and assistance— particularly assistance with religious, or curing, ceremonies. A Navajo man traveling to a distant area of the reservation would immediately seek out fellow clan members who, even if they were initially strangers to him, would provide food and shelter. For curing ceremonies the family of the ill person could rely on neighboring clanspeople not only to participate but also to help with the expenses of food and other costs of the ritual.

Some clans had special links to one another, forming what anthropologists call **phratries,** or groupings of clans together into larger units. Among the Navajo some members of linked clans considered themselves to be related. Because these phratries were exogamous units, marriages between members of linked clans were forbidden.

Clans were residentially dispersed, so that any one area encompassed members of different clans and the members of a specific clan were scattered over a wide region. Of course, members of a clan who happened to live in one area or in adjacent areas had more to do with one another in terms of providing hospitality and cooperation. Some anthropologists have viewed these localized portions of a clan as the constituents of a loosely defined matrilineal descent group. David Aberle (1961: 115) calls such a group a "Local Clan Element" and suggests that in the period before sheep herding became prominent, it may have been a corporate group that held land.[2] He also gives evidence supporting his contention that in the past the Local Clan Element

---

[2] Aberle (1981b) later preferred to call this kind of unit a "co-residential kin group." Many other anthropologists have also posited the existence of effective Navajo units (based at least partly on matrilineal kinship) that were localized and smaller than the clan. Most widely noted of these units was the Navajo *outfit,* a term first used by Clyde Kluckhohn and Dorothea Leighton (1946). Still other anthropologists, most notably Louise Lamphere (1970, 1977), deny that such units existed, pointing out, among other things, that there is no Navajo word for them. This controversy continues (for discussion, see Kelley 1982; Adams 1983).

was held responsible for the crimes committed or debts incurred by an individual member. And using sources supplied by early Catholic missions, he makes the interesting point that in cases of murder, the clan of the murderer had to pay compensation to the clan of the victim—three or four horses for a male victim, but five or more horses for a female victim (Aberle 1961: 116).

If a clan segment, or matrilineage, had these functions in the past, they were not maintained for long. By the reservation period, the Navajo were not living in highly organized descent groups. Neither clans nor subunits of clans had official leaders or transmitted property. Possibly this lack of highly organized clans helps account for the fact that the Navajo expressed little concern over clan continuity (Reichard 1928: 29).

Although each Navajo was born into his or her mother's clan, a relationship of descent to the father and the father's matriclan was also acknowledged. The Navajo expressed this distinction by saying that one is "born of" mother's clan but "born for" father's clan. Thus, when asked her identity, a woman might say, "I am Bitter-Water, born for Salt" (Kluckhohn and Leighton 1946: 64). In other words, she recognized a link of descent to and through the father, but it was a link to the father's *matrilineal* clan. Thus Navajo descent tied each person to two matriclans: the one in which the person was a member, through the mother, and the other that he or she was "born for," through the father.

One implication of the "born for" concept was that fatherhood was given importance and seen as complementary to motherhood (Lamphere 1977: 70). Being "born for" father's matriclan also affected other relationships. For example, those who were "born for" the same clan considered themselves to be like siblings and were forbidden to marry. Likewise, a person considered those "born for" one's own clan to be like one's own children and thus could not marry them. Today, in some of the more developed areas of the reservation, these marriage restrictions are breaking down (Miranda Warburton, personal communication).

Another implication of this Navajo concept of descent was that a father was regarded as both an affinal and a consanguineal relative, giving him a kind of dual kinship status (Witherspoon 1975: 31–36). On the one hand, a person's father was an affine because he had *married into* that person's clan. Accordingly, Navajo children sometimes addressed or referred to their fathers as in-laws. On the other hand, the father was seen as a consanguineal relative, a direct ascendant whose clan the person was "born for."[3]

---

[3] Witherspoon (1975: 45–46) used this idea of a father being both an affinal and a consanguineal relative to address a controversy in Navajo kinship studies over whether or not marriage into one's own father's clan was permitted. According to him, local attitudes toward marriage into the father's clan depended on whether individual Navajo wished to emphasize either the affinal aspect of the relationship to the father, in which case the marriage would be condoned, or the consanguineal aspect of the relationship, in which case the marriage would be disfavored.

This distinction between consanguineal and affinal relatives was important to the Navajo. Relationships in the former sphere, among matrilineally related kin, were felt to have a special kind of solidarity, based on ideas of giving and sharing (Witherspoon 1975: 56). The closest and most enduring bond of all was that between mother and child, but the sentiments of closeness, solidarity, giving, and sharing were extended to other consanguineal kin. In contrast to this were affinal relationships, based not on sharing and giving but on exchange and reciprocity. Among affinal relationships, the most important bond was that between husband and wife. Witherspoon (1975: 56–57) elaborates the difference, contrasting the mother-child and husband-wife relationships:

> Navajo mothers do not give life, food, and loving care to their children because they want the same in return. A mother loves and helps her child regardless of whether he is a king or a bum, a worker or an indolent, . . . a contributor or a parasite, moral or immoral. . . . [But] when a husband is a bum or an indolent, or immoral, the wife usually gets rid of him. . . . The relationship is supposed to be advantageous to both through mutual obligations of assistance. Where one party falters, the relationship loses its balance and disintegrates.

The Navajo universe of kin was divided into two categories: those with whom the solidarity was mother-child-like—intense, and based on giving and sharing in terms of sheer need—and those with whom the solidarity was husband-wife-like—based on agreement and exchange, with an emphasis on equity in the exchange rather than on another person's need.

As matrilineal descent among the Navajo did not engender tensions between a woman's brother (or other senior matrilineal kin) and her husband, it did not display this element of the matrilineal puzzle discussed in the previous section. Neither brothers nor husbands appear to have had strong authority over sisters or wives. Among siblings, older ones, regardless of sex, had some authority over younger ones. Nor did Navajo men appear to be pulled in different directions by their ties to their sisters' children and their own children. In general, fathers had more authority over their own children than did the children's mother's brothers. The mother's brothers were, however, important figures to children in that they provided instruction and discipline and played an important role in arranging their marriages.

The Navajo case does not show a strain between male authority and descent through women. Robin Fox (1989: 103) argues that this was the case because the matrilineal clans had few functions. But what Navajo matrilineal descent, combined with matrilocal residence, does show with respect to gender are a number of themes pervasive in Navajo culture. One is a complementarity between the sexes. This is expressed in Navajo mythology and religious ritual (Lamphere 1969). One student of Navajo religion has summarized as follows: "The ritual teachings stress male and female as a basic form of symbolism; the notion is that only by pairing can any entity be complete" (Reichard 1950: 29). Another theme is the social centrality of women that comes about through their reproductive roles. A third and related theme concerns the dual kinship position of men, as noted earlier, and the tensions that emerge as men move between their roles as sons and husbands of women.

Residence. The Navajo matrilineal clan was important for identity, marriage and sex prohibitions, hospitality, and cooperation. But the social unit of primary importance in everyday life was the group of people who lived together and placed their sheep into one herd. The camp, as this unit will be called here,[4] consisted of a few hogans, each usually containing a separate married couple, nuclear family, or small extended family group. A family usually had a winter house and one or more summer homes near good pasture. Camps were quite often far apart from one another and did not link together to form larger communities or villages.

The Navajo camp was not a corporate group since members did not collectively own property. However, members did pool their sheep into one herd and did manage many of their resources communally, so the camp functioned as a corporate enterprise (Witherspoon 1975: 73). Along with a sheep herd, members shared food, use of agricultural fields, and other assets and resources.

Residence was primarily matrilocal, although it was possible for a couple to move neolocally, branching off from one camp and establishing a new one. Alternatively, a couple could reside patrilocally, in the husband's natal camp, or move back and forth between the husband's and wife's natal camps.

In the case of matrilocal residence, the husband was the newcomer. He shared in the resources of his wife's camp, but was expected to contribute his share of the labor. Yet, especially in the early years of marriage, the husband retained important ties to his own mother's group, returning there to help with the work. Often the husband would keep his own sheep with his natal group, only gradually moving them over, a few at a time, to his wife's camp as the marriage stabilized.

In his new home, the husband was expected to maintain proper relationships with his wife's kin. Most important was the Navajo practice of **mother-in-law avoidance.** A respectful restraint in the interaction between a man and his wife's mother is common practice in many societies, but among the Navajo, the two were not to have physical or even eye contact (though this restriction is no longer strictly observed). One consequence was that the two could not share the same hogan. With his wife's married

---

[4] Other terms in the literature include "subsistence residential unit" (Witherspoon 1975: 71), "homestead group" (Downs 1972: 31), and "extended family" (Shepardson and Hammond 1970: 45).

sisters, the husband was also expected to keep his distance in order to avoid making their husbands jealous; and sexual relations with them would have constituted adultery. But there were no restrictions on his behavior with his wife's unmarried sisters, whom he later might marry, as we will see.

Camps were organized around women, who in turn played active and forceful roles within them. In his study of the Rough Rock–Black Mountain area, Witherspoon (1975) drew attention to what he called the "head mother," a senior woman around whom a camp would nucleate. All members could trace a tie to her, based upon two rules of residence: (1) Every Navajo had the right to reside with his or her mother, and (2) every Navajo had the right to live with his or her spouse. Individual married couples then worked out their own arrangements, based on factors such as the relative resources of the camps and personal preference. Matrilocal residence was generally adopted, and at any one time, most couples would be living matrilocally. Figure 4.6 (based on Witherspoon 1975: 72 –76) illustrates a typical camp.

Here, A is the head mother. Her husband, B, is important in the camp and participates in its management by virtue of being her husband, regardless of whether he is the father of her children. Two of A's children, a daughter C and a son D, have exercised the first right of every Navajo, to reside with his or her mother. An unmarried daughter, F, also lives with A. A second son, G, has exercised the second right of residence and lives

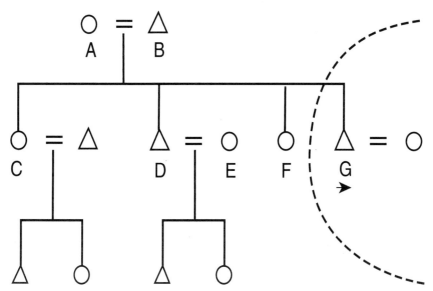

FIGURE 4.6 A Navajo Camp. The broken half-circle and the arrow show that the man G has left this camp to live matrilocally with his wife.

matrilocally with his spouse. The head mother's daughter-in-law, E, has exercised the same right and lives patrilocally with her husband.

If the woman C and her husband divorce, he will return to his mother's camp, whereas C and her children will remain where they are. If the woman C dies, the husband may remarry within this unit (he could marry C's sister, F), or he may leave; but either way, his children would normally remain in the camp and be raised by other women there.

If the man D and his wife E divorce (or if D dies), the wife and her children will return to her mother's camp. But if this wife dies, the situation becomes a little more complicated. Technically, the children, having neither a spouse nor a mother, have no clear residence rights. As Witherspoon (1975: 76, 128) reports, the children would normally remain in the husband's camp and be raised there. Still, the situation is a little awkward, and Witherspoon has suggested that this may have been one reason why patrilocal residence was not more common.

Both the husband and wife of the senior generation participate in the running of the camp and the management of its affairs. In this context the role of wife may be very significant. About her Witherspoon (1975: 82) has noted: "If one has lived a long time in one of these units, one soon becomes aware of who ultimately has the cards and directs the game."

Labor and Property. Within camps, the division of labor by sex was not sharply defined. Men tended to work more in house building, agriculture, and care of cattle and horses, whereas women worked more in care of sheep and goats, weaving, cleaning, cooking, and child rearing. But these divisions were flexible and variable (Lamphere 1989); indeed, it was common for women or men to perform any task, or for tasks to be carried out by women and men together. Most ceremonial practitioners were male, but women could also become practitioners. As for political roles, which became important on the reservation, they were once held predominantly by men but, recently, have been taken on by women as well. There are also indications that before the reservation period, some women went to war along with men and that those who were successful warriors became war chiefs (Reichard 1928: 53).

Land was not owned by any one person or group, but, instead, camps had use-rights to the land they occupied and all resident members shared these rights (Lamphere 1977: 83). Sheep, horses, and other livestock were individually owned, but, as noted, camp members jointly managed livestock and kept sheep in one herd. Sheep were the mainstay of the Navajo economy, and there are indications that women owned more sheep than men did, although men owned more of the cattle and horses (Aberle 1961: 142). Male and female children were given their own sheep by their parents.

At death a person's livestock and other personal property were divided in various ways among the members of the camp and other relatives and friends, distribution sometimes depending on who showed up at the funeral. Generally speaking, there was a matrilineal emphasis in this distribution of personal property, at least in earlier days. As Reichard (1928: 94) wrote during her study of Navajo culture in the 1920s: "Under ordinary circumstances a man's sister and brother, or his mother, if she is living, will inherit the bulk of his property. If they are not living his sister's children or their daughters' children are the next in succession."

As we have seen, among the Navajo both women and men played important economic roles, and property such as livestock was individually owned, such that neither sex had greater access or control. Economically the sexes were complementary and ran a cooperative enterprise in the camp. A complementarity between the sexes was also seen in terms of descent, which, though matrilineal, incorporated husbands/fathers through the notion that one was "born for" the father's matriclan as well as "born of" the mother's.

Marriage. In the past, Navajo marriages were usually arranged by parents. Both males and females were considered marriageable after puberty, and it was common to see arrangements for a girl's marriage being made shortly after her puberty ceremony. The bride and groom may not have known one another, but their consent was usually sought. Arranged marriages were customarily accompanied by the payment of bridewealth, consisting of horses and other livestock, from the groom's family to kin of the bride. This bridewealth was believed to ensure the husband's sexual rights to his wife (Aberle 1961: 125; Witherspoon 1975: 24).[5]

It was also possible for a couple to establish a marriage simply by living together, without any public ceremony, parental arrangement, or payment of bridewealth. These unions were somewhat like the elopement unions of the Nepalese Brahmans, discussed in the last chapter. Many remarriages were enacted in this way. Divorce was frequent and easy for either men or women to instigate: The couple simply split, and no bridewealth was returned.

Polygyny was once permitted among the Navajo, but it is now forbidden. Aberle (1961: 119) estimates that polygynous unions accounted for 5 to 10 percent of all marital unions in the 1930s, but they may have been more

---

[5] Witherspoon (1975: 24) further suggested that the bridewealth payment conferred the woman's reproductive rights to the husband, and that if a wife failed to bear children a husband could leave her and ask for the return of the bridewealth. But these arrangements seem unlikely. Shepardson and Hammond (1970: 173–4) wrote that bridewealth cannot be regarded as progeny price since with matrilineal descent the children would automatically have become members of the mother's clan. And Aberle (1961: 125) held that there was no evidence to suggest that bridewealth was paid in return for paternal rights.

common at an earlier time.[6] A 1960s study of a Navajo Mountain community reported six cases of polygyny out of ninety-two unions (Shepardson and Hammond 1970: 182).

By far the most common polygynous unions were cases of **sororal polygyny,** or the marriage of one man to two or more sisters. Obviously this type of polygyny was easier to carry out in a largely matrilocal context; otherwise, a man married matrilocally to two unrelated women, living in different camps, would have had to divide his residence and labor contributions among the different groups.

Of sororal polygyny at Navajo Mountain, Shepardson and Hammond (1970: 179–180) wrote:

> Propinquity breeds polygyny. A man and his wife's sister, living in the same camp, seeing each other daily, perhaps herding together, will sometimes feel a mutual attraction and start engaging in sexual intercourse without asking the consent of anyone. This relationship may continue and shade into an accepted polygynous marriage, if the first wife is amenable. When the affair becomes evident, frequently because the paramour is pregnant, the first wife may accept the situation with equanimity and the attitude that "This is the way things are; members of the same family should share with each other and live in harmony."

The authors of this study and others also reported cases of conflict and sexual jealousy between sisters.

Another common practice was the **levirate,** whereby a woman married her dead husband's brother. Such unions were not mandatory, however. Cases of "stepdaughter marriage," whereby a man is married to one woman and simultaneously to her daughter by a previous union, also occurred, as did unions of a man with a woman and her sister's daughter. Of the six cases of polygyny examined in the Navajo Mountain study, one involved a man married to a mother and daughter and another concerned a man married to two sisters plus the daughter of one of them. Of these unions, the authors reported: "On several occasions we were told, 'She became too old to be a wife to him, so she gave him her daughter'" (Shepardson and Hammond 1970: 181). In other cases, a man married a woman with the understanding between them that her young daughter would also become his wife when she matured (Aberle 1961: 122).

We have seen that the husband-wife relationship was the most important affinal bond, and that as this type of bond it was based on ideas of exchange and reciprocity. Ideally, a husband and wife were mutually coopera-

---

[6] Polygyny may have been more common earlier due to a shortage of men. In pre-reservation days, many men were killed in raiding and hunting (Shepardson and Hammond 1970: 179).

tive and helpful to one another. One woman from Copper Canyon spoke of the public speeches that relatives of the bride and groom gave at weddings: "'They tell the man to take care of the wife, to think of the home—how to build it—and to think about the food and getting wood and water. Later they say he should never take his hand to his wife (i.e., beat her). For the woman, she is told to cook, wash, iron, take care of the house, fix the bed, and keep care of the children'" (cited in Lamphere 1977: 71).

Although adultery occurred among the Navajo, as in all societies, sex was ideally supposed to be confined to marriage; and both husbands and wives expressed sexual jealousy (Leighton and Kluckhohn 1947: 86). Female premarital sex was apparently not considered a serious matter, though some reports indicate that brides were ideally expected to have been virgins (Aberle 1961: 125; Frisbie 1982: 20). Having a child before marriage was "regarded unfavorably" (Aberle 1961: 128), but children born outside of marriage, who would become members of their mother's clan without any problem, were not looked down upon. In addition, no reports indicate concern over premarital male sexual behavior, but "excessive" sexual behavior on the part of either sex was frowned upon and believed to cause illness (Leighton and Kluckhohn 1947: 89).

Women, Men, and Reproduction

According to Navajo religion, there are worlds below and above this one. In the past, Navajo deities, or Holy People, lived in worlds below. At various times, for different reasons, the Holy People climbed up from the lower worlds into higher worlds, reaching the fifth or current world. Once, escaping a flood, they reached the Earth Surface and here, in different ways according to different stories, the Earth Surface People, or Navajo, were brought into being.

By the time they reached this world, the Holy People had lost the power to reproduce, and destructive monsters also inhabited the world. But then one of the Holy People, First Man, discovered a baby girl and he and First Woman cared for her. She became Changing Woman, a very central and powerful being in Navajo religion. Changing Woman personifies life, reproduction, and motherhood and is considered the creator of the Navajo. She is associated with the Earth itself and is called Changing Woman because, like the Earth with its seasons, she has the power to continually return to her youth after reaching old age. In Navajo tradition, Changing Woman restored the power of generation and, through union with the male Sun, gave birth to two twins, Monster Slayer and Child-of-the-Water, who destroyed the monsters threatening the world.

When Changing Woman had her first menstrual period, a great ceremony was held for her. This is the religious referent for the Navajo Kinaaldá, or girl's puberty ceremony, held upon a girl's first menstruation. During her Kinaaldá, a girl becomes the symbol of Changing Woman and thus represents the power of reproduction (Frisbie 1967: 373).

The Kinaaldá is a four-day, four-night ceremony through which the young girl is blessed and protected, and during which she receives instruction in her life and duties as an adult woman. Her behavior during these four days and nights is closely monitored, since it is believed that anything she says or does during this time reflects what kind of person she will be as an adult. Among many other activities performed to enhance her beauty and her skills, she undergoes a physical "molding," whereby, while she is lying down, another woman "molds" her body into a proper and beautiful shape. Another central activity is the girl's grinding of corn that is used to make a large cake, baked in the earth.

The Kinaaldá is a highly public ceremony, attended by ceremonial specialists ("singers") who give songs and prayers. It is a sacred ceremony, a public announcement of the girl's adulthood and eligibility for marriage, and "a time for rejoicing" (Frisbie 1967: 7). There are no puberty rites for males.

During her Kinaaldá the young girl ritually "becomes" Changing Woman; and, according to tradition, it is Changing Woman who made human reproduction possible. As one Navajo man, Frank Mitchell, expressed it: "'The ceremony was started so women would be able to have children and the human race would be able to multiply. To do this, women had to have relations with men. The Kinaaldá was created to make it holy and effective, as the Holy People wanted it to be'" (cited in Frisbie 1967: 348). Thus the Kinaaldá ceremony dramatically illustrates the high value placed on human reproduction in Navajo culture, but also the central and overwhelmingly positive position of women as reproducers. Women are associated not just with human reproduction, and their own potential motherhood, but more generally, with life-giving forces, renewal, growth, and rejuvenation. As Witherspoon (1975: 16) wrote: "Essential parts, as well as the earth itself, are called mother. Agricultural fields are called mother, corn is called mother, and sheep are called mother. . . . These applications of the concept -*ma* [mother] certainly make it clear that motherhood is defined in terms of the source, sustenance, and reproduction of life."

Symbols of life, fertility, and motherhood include the earth, the color yellow, yellow corn, yellow corn pollen, red menstrual blood, and the color red. All of these come together in Kinaaldá. The cake, made of yellow corn, ground by the Kinaaldá girl at her first menstruation, also includes a red substance mixed with the corn, and is baked in the earth before being served to all participants of the ceremony.

This ritual focus on women as central symbols of life and reproduction is in striking contrast to Christian mythology in which female fertility is given quite a different role. Here a male God is creator and human reproduction follows from the sin of a woman, Eve. Later, Christ arrives through virgin birth. As different as can be from the female deity of Navajo lore, who continually ages and renews her youth to rejuvenate life, is the composite Christian Eve/Mary figure, an "Unchanging Woman" whose sexuality/ fertility are either considered sinful or denied (Moody 1991).

According to Navajo ideas of reproduction, males (symbolized by white corn) are important, too, though symbolically, ritually, and in terms of descent they are not as central. Recall what Frank Mitchell said of Kinaaldá: "To do this, women had to have relations with men." During the wedding ceremony, the couple eat white corn and yellow corn mixed together (Witherspoon 1975: 17), calling to mind traditional Navajo conceptions in which male semen (white) and female menstrual blood (red) combined to produce a child. But in one sense, women contributed more than clan identity to a child; indeed, it was believed that with her breast milk the mother passed on some of her own characteristics to her infant (Wright et al. 1993).

Although menstrual blood was clearly associated with fertility, traditionally it was also seen as dangerous, and there were several restrictions on women at the time of their menstruation. Menstruating women were not to enter ceremonial hogans, nor could they have a "sing" (curing ceremony) performed over them at this time. They were not to milk goats (or the milk would stop), enter crop fields (or the crops would die), carry water, or have contact with children or livestock (Wright 1982a, 1982b; Bailey 1950: 9–11). Contact with adult males was not restricted, but there were two very different ideas regarding sexual intercourse during menstruation. Some Navajo claimed that it would virtually guarantee conception; many others held that it would cripple the man (Bailey 1950: 11). But in sharp contrast to the Nepalese Brahmans described in the last chapter, the Navajo did not view menstrual blood as a source of impurity, nor did they connect it in any way with the religious *inferiority* of women. Wright (1982b) suggested that among the Navajo menstrual blood was considered dangerous because it signaled *temporary infertility*. As noted, there was the notion that a woman's menstrual blood helped to form a baby; as one Navajo woman said to Wright (1982b: 388), "When you get your period, you know you aren't pregnant. When you miss your period, it's because the blood is being made *into* the baby." Hence flowing menstrual blood symbolized conception failure or momentary infertility and so was considered threatening to things associated with fertility and creative potential, such as crops, livestock, and children. For example, Wright (1982b, following Bailey 1950: 9) notes that, according to Navajo belief, a menstruating woman was not dangerous to an old infertile horse, but she could harm a young, fertile horse by riding it.

In Navajo communities, children were, and are today, highly valued and desired by both women and men. In contrast to the societies discussed in

Chapter 3, the Navajo have no religious prescriptions necessitating the bearing of children for the well-being of one's soul after death. Rather, children are economically important and valued for their labor. At young ages they are active in sheep herding, hauling water, and bringing firewood. Parents also want children to take care of them in old age. And there is an idea, at least among women, that having children means one will not be lonely. As a Navajo woman commented: "'Being a mother is always good. If you don't have children there is no one to help you at all, and you are always lonely'" (Wright 1982b: 381). Navajo mythology also makes several references to women who are lonely without their children (Spencer 1947: 39–40). The identity of "woman," then, is in some respects inseparable from that of "mother" (Witherspoon 1975: 15).

The Navajo traditionally considered a couple's infertility to be due to sterility in either the man or the woman (Bailey 1950: 20). In cases of failure to have children, divorce would have been an option for both husband and wife. As one Navajo man from the area of Ramah put it: "'If two people don't have children they agree to separate and each try someone else. She will try four men before she decides it's her fault. He will try four women also. If they find one who has children for them they will live together. If not, one of the men will stay with the woman anyway, maybe'" (cited in Bailey 1950: 20).

In contrast to some matrilineal societies, the Navajo did not require the termination of an infertile union. In their Navajo Mountain study, Shepardson and Hammond (1970: 118) noted that "several marriages of many years' duration between couples who are childless indicate that sterility is not considered sufficient cause for divorce." As in the past, childless couples today are sometimes given children to raise by relatives who have many children or who are having difficulty caring for all their children. A woman unable to have children might see this inability as one of life's hardships; but no censure of childless women, nor social punishment such as ostracism, has been reported.[7]

Men and Kinship

This glimpse into Navajo kinship has thus far revealed a complementarity between the sexes and a centrality in the position of women, in terms of

---

[7] One possible exception was reported by Kluckhohn (1944: 15). He refers to a study of witchcraft in which "some informants insisted that only childless women could be witches." The same study found that, in general, accusations of witchcraft were far more commonly directed at men than at women. In addition, Ginsburg and Rapp (1991: 319), using material from Wright (1982b), argue that Navajo women's menstrual taboos "subtly point out and punish women who do not become pregnant." I, however, do not draw this conclusion from Wright's study.

both their symbolic roles as reproducers and their social roles as transmitters of descent and "head mothers" in camps. But what about men in this matrilineal-matrilocal system? As noted earlier, Navajo men had a kind of dual kinship status. For one thing, fathers could be seen as either consanguineal or affinal kin. We also saw that this distinction was important, in that consanguineal ties were associated with the strong mother-child bond and the sentiment of "unconditional love," whereas affinal ties were associated with the more fragile husband-wife bond of mutual obligation. Thus "father," in contrast to "mother," held a somewhat ambiguous status, as was reflected in attitudes toward the father: "The father was at best a helpful friend, good instructor, and strong disciplinarian, or at worst, an undependable friend, inconsistent helper, or unsure ally" (Witherspoon 1975: 35). In addition, the stability of the father's ties to his children was contingent on the stability and duration of his marriage to their mother. If the marriage broke up, children almost always remained with the mother and the father had very little to do with his children, particularly if they were young at the time of the divorce and he remarried.

Men had a dual kinship status in another respect, too. In matrilocal situations, it was the husband who bridged two intermarrying families and moved between them. Particularly in the early years of marriage, the husband would divide his time and loyalties between two camps, keeping sheep in both and only gradually becoming a permanent resident in his wife's camp as the marriage stabilized. In the last chapter we saw that affinal women in strongly patrilineal societies were considered divisive and threatening to male patrilineal solidarity. But in the matrilineal Navajo case, we find that matrilocal males, though sometimes blamed for inciting jealousy between sisters, were themselves seen as being pulled apart by women, by wives and mothers. As Witherspoon (1975: 27) wrote: "A Navajo man is virtually tossed between two women, and through them he gets his status and works out his role in the social system. His relationship to these two women involves two kinds of relationship to a womb. One is a kind of extrusion; the other is a kind of intrusion. One is symbolized by birth; the other, by sexual intercourse. One is described as the utmost in security; the other is considered to hold latent danger."

Another important dimension of male-female relationships can be seen by reference to a particular Navajo religious tale. There are many different versions of this story. One relates that, while in a lower world, before his emergence to this one, First Man discovers the adultery of his wife, First Woman, and hits her. First Woman complains of this to her mother, Woman Chief, who scolds First Man and then tells him that she, not he, is really master of all things. Soon after, First Man calls all the men together and they decide, in retaliation for this affront, to leave the women to themselves and to cross over the water to form their own community. As time goes by, the women fail at growing their crops and suffer great hardship. But the men are successful. Both sexes suffer from sexual desire and make inappropriate compensations, but for the women it is much worse. News of their horrible actions gets back to one man, who then tells the others: "The women, whom you left (for good) four years ago (in order) to cross (over here) are abusing themselves with any old thing. They are fornicating with tapering smooth rocks, fornicating with quills, fornicating with hooked cactus and straight spined cactus (and are) fornicating with the calves of animals. Blue foxes have intercourse with them, and Yellow foxes and badgers, they say" (Haile 1981: 30). The consequence of such unions is the birth of monsters who plague this lower world and later the Earth Surface, until they are killed off by Changing Woman's sons. But meanwhile, the men realize they must reunite with the women so that the group can procreate. They then do so.

Like all religious stories, this one can be interpreted in various ways. Karl Luckert (1981: 17, 23) suggested that it developed as the Navajo were switching from hunting and gathering to agriculture. Pointing out that agriculture was originally in the hands of women, Luckert argued that this shift in subsistence deprived males of their primary economic function. Men then took charge of agriculture, and the story represents men's attempt to regain their position as providers.

Many others see in this tale a theme we have encountered before: the complementarity of the sexes (Reichard 1950: 31; Farella 1984: 134–144). In the version given here, more blame is placed on women than on men for the separation of the sexes (indeed, female adultery is believed to have started all the trouble), and it is women who, with their "perverted" sexuality, bring forth the monsters. But both sexes suffer from the separation. The women fail completely, but the men realize that they cannot procreate without women. In the end the two sexes come back together, each realizing it needs the other.

In this story and other Navajo religious traditions, Farella (1984) sees the cultural recognition that sexual desire is basic to society and necessary for human continuity. The sexes must stay together; yet the Navajo acknowledge all the strains their union will engender, such as jealousy and adultery. Of this dimension of Navajo gender, he wrote: "There is, of course, the other side to all of this as well—the jealousy, the worry, the adultery. But, if sexuality is necessary, and it is, then these go with it. That which assures that people will come together and continue together also drives them apart. The basis for alliance and conflict are one and the same" (Farella 1984: 144).

CASE 4: THE NAYAR

The Nayar, now numbering more than two million people, live in the state of Kerala in southwest India. Their origin is uncertain, but they are presumed to have been a matrilineal hill tribe who moved to the plains and coastal regions of Kerala in the fourth century A.D., possibly fleeing "barbarian" invasions (Gough 1961b: 303). Here they became settled agriculturists, rulers, and warriors in a society based on plow agriculture and organized into kingdoms, such as the Kingdoms of Calicut and Cochin. This region was a part of South Asian Hindu civilization, with religious practices and a caste system somewhat similar to those of the Nepalese Brahmans described in the last chapter.

The very interesting kinship traditions of the Nayar take us back to a period ranging from the mid-1300s to the late 1700s, before the British conquests in India. These traditions were studied by anthropologist Kathleen Gough (1961b), who used historical records to supplement her own fieldwork among the modern Nayar in the 1940s. By this time many features of the earlier system had disappeared and matrilineal descent was disintegrating; yet some traditions persisted and many earlier practices were remembered, especially by older people.

In these centuries before the British conquests, the people of Kerala were stratified into numerous castes. At the top were Nambuduri Brahmans, themselves subdivided into higher and lower orders, who served as priests and religious leaders over a wide region, collectively operating somewhat like the Catholic Church in medieval Europe (Gough 1961b: 306). Below them were Nayar rulers, consisting of members of royal matrilineages that ruled kingdoms; and below these were chiefdoms controlled by chiefly Nayar matrilineages. Chiefdoms were divided into villages, and in some of these were Nayar village headmen whose matrilineages owned the village land through appointment by chiefs or kings. Below all these were commoner Nayar castes whose members lived in the rural areas, and it is the kinship traditions of this group that will be discussed here. Below commoner Nayars were assorted lower castes (Nayar and non-Nayar), some of them considered highly polluting to all higher groups and physically segregated from other castes. In several of these castes were serfs who worked the land for the commoner Nayars and other, higher castes.

The kingdoms of this period were engaged in a nearly constant state of war, and males of the commoner Nayar group served as soldiers. In earlier centuries this warfare entailed swords, shields, and bows and arrows; later, gunpowder and cannons were introduced and the wars became more destructive. For Nayar males, military training started early (at about age seven) in village gymnasiums, and for much of their young adult lives they were away from their homes and off at war.

Clan and Lineage

Commoner Nayars lived in villages along with people of many other castes. But within villages they lived in their own neighborhoods among fellow caste persons. They were divided into matrilineal clans, which in turn were named, exogamous categories. In the clans, which dispersed among different neighborhoods and villages, sexual relations were forbidden. Like the Navajo clans, these were not corporate groups, but members had rights of hospitality in each other's homes. There was one other obligation: All clan members had to be informed of the births or deaths within the clan. Upon receiving the news, all clan members observed a fifteen-day period of birth or death pollution, during which they maintained restrictions on their behavior and diet.

Clans were subdivided into matrilineages. Gough (1961b: 324) defined these matrilineage units in terms of both descent and residence, such that a lineage consisted of all those members of one clan who lived in one neighborhood of a village. In any one neighborhood there could be from six to ten different lineages representing different clans, but all shared the same caste. Neither clans nor lineages had official leaders.

The lineage was not an economic unit, and members did not own property in common. But in several senses it was corporate. For one thing, if a branch of a lineage died out, the other lineage members became heirs to the property. In addition, whereas clanspeople had only to observe birth and death pollution for all members, the people of a lineage were obliged to attend the funerals of dead members and to visit any house where the birth of a new lineage member had occurred. Lineage members also worshiped a common lineage goddess and felt a moral obligation to avenge the murder of a member or offenses to one another.

The different lineages of a neighborhood, each representing different clans, were linked together in special relationships known as *enangar*. These linkages ensured that an important ceremonial cooperation occurred between the lineages, as I will discuss shortly. The enangar links between lineages within a neighborhood took a "chain-like" form, so that, hypothetically, the lineages A–I in Figure 4.7 could all be connected as shown. Here, lineage A has an enangar relationship with B and C. For certain ceremonies, lineages B and C must perform functions for A. When B needs this kind of cooperation, lineages A, D, and E must provide the services, and so on down the chain.

Lineages were further subdivided into Property Groups, which in turn were fully corporate units. Each Property Group included people who were related within a depth of three to six generations, and there were as many as eight such units within one lineage. Members of a Property Group normally lived in one household. All members were matrilineally related and jointly owned property, consisting of land, buildings, and serfs.

Residence at marriage was **natolocal**, in that both husbands and wives stayed where they were, each in their own Property Group. Children stayed with the mother and her household throughout life. Thus each Property

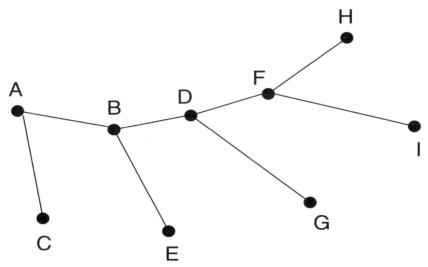

FIGURE 4.7   Nayar Linked Lineages. The circles labeled A-I are lineages.

Group consisted only of matrilineally related kin, and husbands and wives did not live together. Property Groups were headed by the oldest male member, called the *karanavan*. He managed the household and was the legal guardian of all members.

Each of these matrilineal kin categories and groups was named, and a Nayar person would take these names along with a personal name and the title of "Nayar." "A typical name might therefore be 'Thengiparambil Padikkil Kirakkut-Velappil Govindan Nayar'—Clan of the coconut garden, lineage of the gatehouse, household of the eastern garden, Govindan (personal name) Nayar'" (Gough 1961b: 325).

One other unit was important in the commoner Nayar social system: the neighborhood "caste assembly," a grouping of all the karanavans of one neighborhood. This unit met occasionally to manage neighborhood temples and to judge violations of religious law or caste law.

Marriage

The Nayar had one of the most intriguing marriage systems ever found in human societies. Already we have seen that they practiced natolocal residence, which is itself quite rare. But also note that their marriages could be both polygynous and polyandrous, and that each commoner Nayar female underwent two types of marriages, one known as *tali-tying* (the tali was a gold ornament) and the other known as *sambandam*, a "joining together" with one or more "visiting husbands."

Here's how it worked. Every ten years or so, each lineage gathered together all of its prepubescent females and on one day, in one grand ritual, married them to the males of its special enangar (linked) lineages. Evidently a village astrologer paired off grooms and young girls according to their horoscopes. The entire village witnessed the event. The marriage ceremony must have been fairly impressive: In some areas the bridegrooms arrived on elephants, accompanied by musicians (Gough 1955).

Before the marriage ceremony began, each girl, though she had not yet menstruated, underwent a mock first-menstruation ceremony during which she was secluded and other rituals were performed. Later, during the marriage ceremony itself, each groom tied a gold tali around the neck of his bride. With this tali, "a girl was regarded as having attained the status of a mature woman, ready to bear children and perpetuate her lineage" (Gough 1961b: 328). The tali was worn until death.

After the tali-tying, each couple was secluded in a room for three days and three nights. If a girl was nearing puberty, sexual intercourse might take place during the seclusion. On the fourth day the groom departed, and from this day forward, he and the bride did not need to have anything more to do with one another. A woman had to fulfill only one obligation to her tali-tying husband—namely, upon his death, to observe fifteen days of death pollution for him.

It was absolutely imperative that the tali-tying marriage be performed for a girl before her first menstruation. If a girl was known to have menstruated before this ceremony, she was excommunicated from her caste and the caste assembly forced her Property Group to send her away and perform her funeral rituals. Most likely she would have been sent off elsewhere to become a slave.

After the tali-tying marriage the woman was free to have sexual relations with any man she chose, provided that he was of her own caste or of a higher one. The men with whom she had these acceptable relationships were considered her husbands, even though no religious ceremonies marked the establishment of these "joining together" unions. The husbands were expected to give their wives some gifts on each of three major festivals during the year. If these gifts stopped coming, the end of the relationship was signaled. But either husbands or wives could easily terminate these unions at any time.

There was apparently no limit to the number of "joining together" husbands a woman could have. Based on information from historical sources, Gough (1961b: 358) wrote: "It seems probable that each woman had a small number of husbands from her local caste group who, while their relationship lasted, visited her regularly, but that women also received occasional fleeting visits from itinerant Nayars of appropriate rank, perhaps during military operations." Since a Nayar woman could have more than one visiting husband, the society was polyandrous; and since a Nayar man could have a number of separate wives, the society was also polygynous. Marriages were restricted by a rule of clan exogamy and by a rule that women could not marry men of lower castes. In addition, a woman could not have two or more husbands from the same lineage and a man could not have two or more wives from the same lineage. The man who performed the tali-tying marriage with a woman could, if he and she wanted, become one of her husbands, but this outcome was not necessary. Males could enter "joining together" unions at any time, whether or not they had ever served as tali-tiers at all.

A husband usually visited a wife at night after having dinner in his own household. It was considered impolite to his own mother for a man to visit a wife for many hours during the day, and too much time spent with a wife could arouse jealousy in the man's mother. After spending the night, the husband would leave before breakfast. If two men showed up on the same night to visit the same wife, there was a simple solution: The husband who arrived first would place his weapons outside his wife's door to let any other husbands know that they should come at some other time. Gough (1961b: 359) also noted that "usually a woman's regular husbands knew each other and informally agreed upon their turns." Likewise, co-wives apparently did not object to sharing visiting husbands (Fuller 1976: 4).

These arrangements should not be interpreted as reflecting sanctioned casual sex or promiscuity. As we have seen, there were rules forbidding sexual relations between certain people and rules governing who could form "joining together" unions with whom. It is true that husbands and wives did not form domestic units and that interactions between them were largely restricted to nighttime visiting, but there was one very crucial obligation that visiting husbands had to wives. When a woman became pregnant, all husbands who might be the father were obliged to acknowledge their possible paternity by giving gifts of cloth to the woman and, after the birth, paying the expenses of the delivery to the midwife. This was a very serious matter, for if no man made these payments, the father of the child was assumed to be a lower-caste male—in which case the woman's male matrilineal relatives could put her and her child to death. At a minimum the caste assembly would force her Property Group to drive her away and perform her funeral rites, and she would likely end up sold into slavery. If a woman was known to be having sexual relations with a lower-caste man, she and her lover could be executed. Even in recent times, a sexual union with a lower-caste man has brought punishment: "In an orthodox household today, a girl who becomes pregnant by a low caste man will be either expelled from the house by her male seniors or, at best, will be thrashed and will receive much subsequent harsh treatment" (Gough 1958: 455).

Both the tali-tying and the "joining together" marriages *legitimized* female reproduction. As Gough (1961b: 362) wrote, "I have called these institutions 'marriage' because they limited and regulated sexual relationships and because they served to legitimize children." The first tali-tying marriage fulfilled these objectives by transforming the female herself into a legitimate childbearer for her Property Group, lineage, and caste. As Gough's analysis makes clear, the tali-tier, who so briefly played a role in the girl's life, is really a symbol, or representative, of males of the whole caste—the caste with whose males the woman could legitimately procreate. Whether or not sexual intercourse actually took place during the ceremony was irrelevant; the seclusion with the male symbolized sex and symbolically conferred potential sexual rights in the woman to males of the caste who were outside the woman's lineage and clan, as all linked-lineage (engandar) males automatically would be. At the same time, according to Gough, the ceremony was a ritual statement indicating that males of the woman's matrilineal kin groups had relinquished their own sexual access to her while retaining their rights over her reproduction. After this rite was performed, a woman and her male matrilineal kin maintained a great deal of distance and formality in their relationship. Indeed, a man was forbidden to touch any junior woman of his Property Group once her tali-tying ceremony had occurred; after this rite, a man was not even allowed to be alone in a room with his sister's daughter.

Upon completion of the tali-tying ceremony, the girl received a new title of *amma*, or "mother" (Gough 1955: 65). Now that the woman was legitimized as a reproducer, her individual children were further legitimized through the visiting husbands' gifts to the woman and payment to the midwife at each child's birth.

Thus there were two occasions on which a woman could face a severe penalty of execution or excommunication, and on both such occasions her fertility and the legitimacy of her reproduction were the central issues: first, if she menstruated before her tali-tying ceremony (though she could hardly have exerted any control over this eventuality) and, second, if no legitimate husband showed up with a gift at the birth of her child.

Gough aptly (1961b: 357) described Nayar marriage as "the slenderest of ties." Neither children nor economic interests, nor common residence, united married couples. Each partner had primary, binding ties with his or her matrilineal kin. Recall from Chapter 2 that in many human societies of the past (as well as some current ones), marriages were enacted to form alliances between groups, and that these alliances were often socially and politically very important. It is clear that the Nayar were not using or benefiting from "joining together" marriages in this way. Yet their system of enangar linked lineages brought about the same end; indeed, their tali-tying ceremonies could be seen as affirming the intermarriageability of the linked lineages and, hence, as expressing their alliances with one another (Gough 1955: 49). That the tali-tying union had duration and meaning beyond the ceremony itself is suggested by the fact that the tali was worn until death and a woman (as well as her children, by whomsoever begotten) was required to observe death pollution for the tali-tier. She did not, however, observe death pollution for "visiting husbands."

In this system of marriage there was understandably little connection between fathers and children. Husbands neither had rights in a woman's children nor passed property or title to them and, for that matter, often didn't know which of a woman's children were their own. Yet the male role in reproduction was fully recognized, husbands were fond of children they thought might be their own, and children were thought to physically resemble their genitors. But if a husband's relationship to the mother ended, so did all connection with the children who might have been his.

In contrast to father-child and husband-wife ties, the bond between mothers and sons was close and strong. This relationship was based not only on important mutual obligations and expected loyalty but on love as well. Also strong and close, though somewhat less so than the mother-son bond, was that between mothers and daughters. As for authority, children of both sexes quickly learned that it would come not so much from the mother as from her brothers, clearly and directly. Females were to obey and revere mother's brothers; but, as noted, upon maturity a woman had little contact with senior male matrilineal kin. Relations between a male and his mother's brother were formal, distant, and often hostile. Males, who themselves sometimes assumed authority positions within the household, often resented the strong authority of the mother's brother.

Whereas the husband-wife bonds were weak, the brother-sister ties were strong, for which reason the Nayar case was readily used by anthropologists to illustrate the matrilineal puzzle. The Nayar were seen to represent one "solution" to the problem of how to combine descent through women with authority vested in men. In this case, the solution was to keep matrilineally related males together and the husband-wife bond weak so that brothers could rule over sisters without interference from husbands, who might grow attached to their wives and develop interests in their children. Indeed, Nayar society does seem to have been organized in such a way that the husband-wife bond was not allowed to flourish or threaten matrilineal solidarity. Aside from natolocal residence and lack of a man's rights in his children (even if he thought he knew which ones were his), a characteristic of this society was to allow a woman's mother's brother to dismiss any of her visiting husbands if he chose to do so. In addition, we can see in witchcraft or sorcery beliefs both a tension between affinal and consanguineal relatives and a resolution of this tension in favor of matrilineal solidarity. As Gough (1961b) reported, Nayar sorcery was believed to be powerless among lineage kin, and it was most often practiced by Property Group members against the wife of their leader, the karanavan. This man, of all the men in a matrilineal Property Group, was expected to show primary allegiance to the group. He also commanded the group's economic resources. Thus members of his Property Group did not wish to see him become too attached to a particular wife or to give her valuable gifts or cash that would otherwise be their joint property. If he did so, they might hire low-caste practitioners of sorcery to recite spells to bring illness to this woman or her kin. Whether or not it worked, word of the attempt would get around and hostilities would develop between the two groups. The usual consequence was termination of the "joining together" union.

In death, as in life, the attachment of a husband and wife to one another was discouraged: "After a man's death his current wives were permitted to come and view his corpse. They were then ceremonially conducted out. . . . They must not look back at the house of death and they might never visit it again" (Gough 1961b: 361).

Fertility

The Nayar were very concerned with human reproduction and the fertility of matrilineal women. New births, as we have seen, had to be announced to all clanspeople, and lineage kin were required to visit the houses where new births had occurred. Children may have been desired for any number of reasons, but, in contrast to the Navajo case, they were not needed for their labor. Hard agricultural labor was done by serfs. Young boys and girls (before the tali-tying rite) played and went to village schools. When older, the males would serve as warriors and, with distinctions earned in wars, would bring honor to their kin groups. Later in life some would become Property Group leaders (karanavan) and serve on the caste assembly. As in other Hindu areas, sons were also needed for religious reasons, since male descendants performed important funeral ceremonies for their departed kin and carried out periodic rituals to assist their well-being after death. In the case of the matrilineal Nayar, the crucial funeral rituals were performed for a woman by her eldest son or next-closest junior male relative; and for a man, they were conducted by whatever male was immediately junior to him within the Property Group, usually a younger brother or a sister's son.

Females, of course, reproduced the group, and concern was expressed for the continuity of the matriline. As Gough (1961b: 327) reported, if a Property Group had no childbearing women, it would adopt girls from another branch of its lineage. Still, women were blamed for infertility, and childless women were considered most unfortunate. Deborah Neff (1994: 477) writes that this attitude continues today: "Among some Nayars, she [an infertile woman] will be an inauspicious guest at weddings and sacred rituals. Social ostracism serves to increase her suffering and vulnerability, and as a barren woman she is often cut off from networks of sustenance and support."

What also continues today is the idea that a woman's infertility is associated with and brought about by the anger of deities and disharmony in the matrilineage. An infertile woman is a sign of loss of prestige and decreasing fortunes for the whole matrilineage. Women are considered powerful, in a religious sense, because of the greater possession of *sakti*, or divine energy, that accrues to them on account of their ability to reproduce. But in Nayar religion and ritual, this power is most clearly recognized in its negative manifestations. A fertile woman dissipates her sakti for the benefit of the group; but an infertile one accumulates the most sakti, which, upon her death, becomes a source of danger to her matrilineal kin, who in turn may suffer from her frustrated ghost (Neff 1994).

Female fertility was important to matrilineal kin groups, but, again in contrast to the Navajo case, the association between women and reproduction was not so much venerated as considered dangerous under conditions of fertility failure. Most of the ceremonial attention to female reproduction seems to have been connected either with promoting female fertility or with preventing or overcoming infertility. Before the tali-tying ceremony, and at a girl's later first menstruation, lineage members worshiped their lineage goddess, or *dharma devi*, whose propitiation could enhance the fertility of the young girl. In general, it was important to propitiate lineage goddesses since they could inflict miscarriages and sickness in childbirth (Gough 1961b: 342). Snake gods were also worshiped as they were believed to hold the power of fertility or infertility over women. Each Property Group household devoted a separate area of its garden to snake gods. If a woman seemed unable to conceive, a special ceremony was held during which the other women of her Property Group (after purifying themselves through fasting and sexual abstinence) became possessed by the snake gods and danced wildly, some going into trance. Gough (1961b: 342) suggested that snake gods were phallic symbols, representing the spirits of dead genitors of the matriline "who had been so essential to its perpetuation, yet so firmly excluded from its everyday affairs."

Female sexuality, though allowed rather free reign within certain rules, was also considered a source of social danger. A woman's sexual misconduct brought dishonor to her matrilineal kin groups. Males would sometimes fight duels to avenge the honor of a kinswoman against a charge of her having committed incest or of having committed adultery with a lower-caste man. Another danger was sexual desire between matrilineally related males and females in one household of a Property Group. We have already seen that, as a defense "against desire" (Gough 1961b: 351), interaction was restricted and touching forbidden between a woman and her senior matrilineal kin after her tali-tying ceremony. But beyond even that, the whole of the house of a Property Group was divided rather sharply into male and female spaces. Leading into the house were separate staircases for males and females; and in the front and back of a house were separate male and female verandahs. Women occupied much of a central courtyard during the day, carrying out such activities as cooking, rice pounding, and child care. At night, males could sleep in rooms off the courtyard, but women's bedrooms, in which they received their visiting husbands, were on a separate floor upstairs, an area hardly ever entered by males of the house.

Among the Nayar, women thus wielded a great deal of control over their own sexuality, at least within the parameters noted. And the men who slept with them, their visiting husbands, had no authority over them or their children whatsoever. Still, a woman was expected to show deference to a husband when he visited; and brothers, especially elder brothers, and mother's brothers, had authority over women of the Property Group. For example, a woman was to be obedient and devoted to her brother and to perform domestic services for him. With her mother's brother, she was to be even more deferential: "A woman must remain standing and remove her upper clothing [a sign of respect] when her mother's brother entered her presence. She must not speak first to him, must not laugh in his presence, and must respond with extreme submissiveness to his requests" (Gough 1961b: 351).

The authority of males in the Property Group, especially that of the karanavan, was ritually acknowledged in household worship of spirits of dead karanavan. Every household contained a separate room devoted to this worship, where the spirits of the dead karanavan were each represented by wooden stools, on which the spirits would come to sit. The living karanavan made offerings of cooked food to these spirits twice a year. The spirits themselves were punitive and were believed to bring illness or other misfortune to the Property Group or lineage if any members failed in their duties toward one another. On days of worship, women prepared food for the offerings but were otherwise excluded from participation. They were prohibited from entering the shrine room on the day of worship, but also whenever they were in a state of pollution (e.g., during menstruation). Thus they were excluded from ritual worship of the group's deceased male matrilineal kin. Gough (1958: 452) suggested that the worship of dead karanavan expressed the legal authority of males in the Property Group and that women were excluded from this cult of the dead because in life they were excluded from the sphere of legal authority. Gough (1958: 452) also held that women's reproduction gave them a kind of "moral authority" instead, and that their reproductive roles, though valued, were, to the Nayar, opposed to the legal and economic power of men.

All women, like children, were legal minors; they could not give evidence at trials and they could not serve on the caste assembly. The most important figure of authority over women was the karanavan, the legal and official head of the Property Group. This man had substantial authority over all members of the household, male and female, and held the power of life and death over the Property Group's serfs. He could inflict corporal punishment on women and children of the group. The karanavan rather tightly oversaw and managed all economic activities of the Property Group. In his household he was to be shown great respect. Like any woman's mother's brother, he could dismiss a visiting husband of a female member if he chose.

The eldest woman of the household directed the activities of the other women and had informal authority over other women and children; but no woman had legal authority over any other. In only one circumstance did a woman exercise much power within the Property Group, and that was when her own son or her own younger brother was the karanavan, in which case she may have functioned as the real, if unofficial, manager of the estate.

Most observers have been interested in the polyandrous aspect of Nayar marriage, partly because polyandry is so rare. Looking at it from the standpoint of a matriline, we can see that Nayar polyandry would have helped to maximize fertility for each matrilineal group, in the sense that no one woman, if herself fertile, would be kept childless because of her union with an infertile male. Along these lines Gough (1955: 53) commented: "A Nayar *taravad* [lineage] is perpetuated by its women. Hence the extraordinary value set by Nayar on obtaining a sufficiency of husbands and thus children for their lineage. The *tali*-rite dramatizes this need of the lineage for male sexual partners who ('like breeding bulls,' as a Calicut prince remarked) will fulfill the one role denied to men of the lineage in respect of their sisters and nieces."

In addition, Gough and many other observers have drawn a connection between Nayar polyandry and the fact that Nayar males, especially young virile ones, were specialized in military service and thus sporadically away from their villages for many months at a time. In the context of monogamy (or even polygyny, for that matter) this would have meant that an individual woman would be without a husband (impregnator) for long periods. With polyandry, however, we have a situation where if one husband is gone, so be it, as other husbands may be around. Later, in Chapter 6, we will again encounter the association between polyandry and the mobility of a young male population. Meanwhile, with respect to the Nayar, Gough (1955: 47) has noted that polyandry began to die out when Nayar soldiering was stopped, around 1810, even though the matrilineal lineage system was maintained for much longer.

Before leaving the Nayar we should consider one last, very interesting feature of their system of marriage: **hypergamy,** or the marriage of a woman upward into a higher-status group. The practice of hypergamy was widespread in this part of India. As we have seen, Nayar women could accept as visiting husbands men of their own caste or of higher castes, but not men of lower castes. They could take as husbands Nayar men of chiefly or royal lineages, thereby conferring prestige on their households. They could also take as husbands Nambuduri Brahmans, the highest caste. But here the situation was a little different. Nambuduri Brahmans were not only non-Nayar but were themselves patrilineal and patrilocal and had their own ideas and practices regarding marriage. Among the top-ranking Nambuduri Brahmans only the eldest son of a family could marry with full religious rites. (This arrangement kept the family estate intact and prevented the group living on one estate from becoming too large.) These eldest sons married Nambuduri Brahman women (of lower suborders) who lived patrilocally with them. The younger sons, though not permitted to marry in the way the eldest sons could, did become visiting husbands of Nayar women. To the Nayar these unions were regular marriages and worked just like other "joining together" marriages. But to the Nambuduri Brahmans they were not "marriages" but, rather, an accepted form of concubinage, since the Nayar women involved did not move in with or have any rights at all in the estate or the kin groups of the Nambuduri Brahman husbands. Thus the two groups carried on these unions, which to the Nayar woman meant having a husband (and a prestigious one at that, given his high caste rank) and to the Brahman man meant having a concubine.

Today, very little is left of the Nayar marriage system (Fuller 1976). The tali-tying rite is no longer performed, marriage is monogamous, and matrilineality has been shifting toward patrilineality (Menon 1996: 141). Husbands now have rights in and obligations to their children, and most couples live in nuclear family units. A shift to patrilineal descent may be a long-term trend, but even today matrilineal kin are considered ideally unified and responsible to one another. They continue to worship the family god of fertility and, as we have seen, to be concerned with the reproduction of matrilineal women.

The major changes that resulted in the termination of polyandry and visiting husbands came about with British conquests and, later, British rule (Gough 1961a: 646–647). As the British took over politically and militarily in the 1800s, Nayar armies were disbanded. With the development of a new capitalist economy, land became private property rather than remaining under the management of descent groups. Serfs became wage workers and many Nayar males, now left without a military role, eventually entered other occupations. The wealthier ones became doctors and lawyers or entered other professions. The Nayar now became more mobile, not temporarily for military service but more generally in search of work and other opportunities. It was easier, of course, for wage- or salary-earning males to move to another location with their wives and children than with members of a large Property Group. As males became more interested in their children and the children's economic welfare, pressures mounted to find legal means to disrupt matrilineal inheritance rights, and eventually the Nayar enacted various laws that broke up the property rights of matrilineal descent groups (Gough 1961b).

These changes came about over a long period of time. As late as the 1940s, during Gough's fieldwork, many older people could remember observing tali-tying ceremonies and the natolocal residence that was the rule among orthodox families. And as we have seen, a concern about unions of women with men of their own caste or higher castes was maintained. Gender relationships have tended to follow the pattern of the broader Indian society such that, along with arranged marriages, there have been trends toward social concern for female virginity at marriage, marital fidelity, and authority of husbands over wives. These trends led one observer to remark: "The autonomy of Nayar women has declined; their status and position has relatively worsened, although it remains, of course, considerably higher than that of the majority of Indian women" (Fuller 1976: 149).

Matrilineal Contrasts

In this chapter we have taken a look inside two very different matrilineal societies. One was a Native American group living on a reservation, with herding and, secondarily, agriculture as a subsistence base. The other was a South Asian Hindu caste group, also rural, but politically part of a kingdom and specialized in military service. Economic differences between the two groups had varying effects on the lives of women and men. Among the Navajo, both males and females played important economic roles and neither sex appears to have had greater access to or control over crucial resources. Among the Nayar, neither males nor females played direct roles in subsistence, for they had serfs who engaged in agricultural and other labor for them; but males controlled the matrilineal group's productive property and economically managed the group's estate.

In both of these societies, descent was traced through the mother and important descent categories were formed on this basis. But in the case of the Navajo, descent through the mother was not the sole means of determining descent identity, for the Navajo also identified each person with the father's matriclan and held that one was "born for" the father's clan. Somewhat like the patrilineal Nuer with their "matrifocal subunits" (see Chapter 3), the Navajo illustrate that a dominant unilineal mode of descent does not always provide the whole picture of kinship within one society. Fatherhood was important to individual Navajo and, in many respects, complementary to motherhood. Among the Nayar, by contrast, individual fatherhood was barely recognized and descent through the father was not used to identify a person with any kinship category or group.

Although both the Navajo and Nayar were matrilineal, this principle of descent through the mother was related to gender in different ways. Most striking is the contrast in the connection between matrilineal descent and authority within residence groups. For the natolocal Nayar, residence groups consisted exclusively of kin who were matrilineally related to one another. Among these groups, the eldest male was the official and legal head of the group, and no woman could assume this position. Succession was based on seniority within the matriline. Once born into a group through the mother, males assumed authority positions based on age. Within this group, mothers' brothers held clear authority over sisters' children. Older women had informal authority over younger ones, and over their own young children, but all women and children were considered legal minors.

For the Navajo, interpersonal authority seems to have been much weaker. Nothing comparable to the Nayar karanavan, or head of the Property Group, existed in the Navajo camp. Here, women exercised a great deal of power, and it was around "head women" that camps were organized. Nayar women, by contrast, could exercise power (and informal power at that) only when their own sons or younger brothers were karanavans.

Among the Nayar, females were excluded from the worship of deceased karanavan because of their reproductive roles (Gough 1958: 452). The Nayar saw female reproduction in opposition to the world of male leadership. But among the Navajo, men and women were seen as complementary in terms of both reproduction and leadership. According to one religious story about this society, the sexes reunite because they must do so in order for the people to procreate. Thus both males and females have a connection to reproduction.

Both Navajo and Nayar women had culturally valued status because of their reproductive and transmission-of-descent capabilities; but the two societies differed widely in terms of the nature and implications of this valuation. In both societies reproduction and children were considered very important. But here the similarity ends; and at this point, we must ask the question, Reproduction *for whom?* The Navajo apparently expressed no strong concern with "continuing the line." They also had no religious ideas about the necessity of bearing children. Ancestors were not worshiped, nor did people's fate in the afterlife depend on the ministrations of their descendants. Navajo women may have felt that to be mothers was "the only way to be," but there is no indication that they were under pressure to reproduce *for* their matriline. It should also be noted that Witherspoon (1975) wrote not about Navajo camps or kin groups having rights *to* children but, rather, about individuals having rights of residence and rights to camp resources based on ties to a mother or spouse. In the end, reproduction seems to have been largely a matter *for* the married couple—perhaps for women in particular, as they generally had a stronger bond with their children. All of these factors may be related to the fact that the Navajo, unlike the Nayar, did not use matrilineal descent to develop highly organized descent groups in control of transmittable property. At the same time, Navajo women were symbolically associated with reproduction and life itself, an association that was venerated and given public, religious expression at a girl's puberty ceremony. It is possible, then, that the positive symbolic role of women as life givers in this matrilineal society was connected to the absence of well-defined matrilineal descent groups with strong interests in the actual reproduction of real-life women. Significantly, Navajo women were not ostracized or socially punished for infertility.

A very different situation obtained among the Nayar. Here were well-defined descent groups with property, interests in a woman's reproduction, and concern for continuity. As we have seen, these descent groups were male-controlled Property Groups and lineages. A woman's reproduction, however personally rewarding it may have been, was also a matter *for* these groups. Female children were needed to continue them; male children were needed to lead them and to worship their departed members. Yet the Nayar religious rituals that linked women and reproduction largely expressed anxiety over real women's actual reproduction; hence their propitiation of lineage goddesses and snake gods who could enhance or hamper a woman's fertility. A lineage goddess was herself a manifestation of Bhagavadi, a major Nayar deity who was a goddess of war and "more concerned with men than with women" (Gough 1958: 456). This female image is certainly quite different from the life-giving, rejuvenating Changing Woman of the Navajo.

In terms of reproduction and its consequences, however, there are some basic similarities between these two matrilineal societies. In both cases, and in contrast to the patrilineal societies discussed in the last chapter, the placement of a woman's children in kin categories and groups was relatively easy and straightforward. Children belonged to their mothers' categories and groups. Paternity, whether social or biological, was less important than in the patrilineal cases. There was no need for, say, cattle payments to govern the allocation of a woman's children to individuals and groups, as among the Nuer; and there was no need to tie a woman permanently in marriage to a man, as among the Napalese Brahmans. As with matrilineal groups generally, Navajo and Nayar women were free to enter and leave marital unions. In terms of fertility, this arrangement meant that infertile unions could be terminated.

Among both the Navajo and Nayar, women had fairly autonomous control over their sexuality and its consequences—but with one major difference: Among Nayar women, sexual relations with a lower-caste man were forbidden. If discovered, the woman was subjected to severe punishment, her fertility was henceforth devalued, and she along with any presumed child of this union were expelled from the group. In addition, a Nayar woman had to have a tali-tying marriage before she was permitted any husbands; otherwise, she was expelled. These rules safeguarded the honor and caste standing of the group, in ways similar to the case of the Nepalese Brahmans described in Chapter 3.

Another contrast concerns the relationship between female sexuality and female fertility among these groups. Aside from the restrictions already noted, Nayar women were allowed any number of sexual partners. From the standpoint of the kin group, female sexuality was given free reign in the service of fertility, somewhat comparable to the situation among the Nuer, who had many options to maximize a kin group's reproduction. But among the Navajo, the sexuality of both males and females was ideally restricted to one partner in marriage (or more, in cases of polygyny), and it was within these individual marriages that reproduction assumed its greatest meaning. For the Navajo, then, as revealed in their religious stories, sexual desire (both male and female) was considered necessary for procreation in general, even though it was known to bring about friction (jealousy, adultery) between women and men. Thus sexuality and fertility, with all their attendant blessings and problems, were centered on the marital relationship.

Through these two cases we have seen that matrilineal descent does not produce matriarchies, and that different societies vary considerably in terms of the ways that matrilineal descent is related to gender. But perhaps one thing is true of almost all matrilineal societies, at least in contrast to many strongly patrilineal ones: The man who has the most authority over a woman (brothers and mothers' brothers among the Nayar; fathers, mothers' brothers, and elder brothers among the Navajo) tends not to be the one who has legitimate sexual access to her. By contrast, in the two patrilineal societies discussed in the last chapter it was husbands who had both authority over wives and sexual rights in them. Personally, I would have thought that women in matrilineal societies might feel more independent, or less constrained, when men with authority over them were not also their sexual partners. Interestingly, exactly the opposite idea was expressed by a contemporary Nayar woman in her conversation with anthropologist Shanti Menon (1996: 140): "It is easier to talk with and persuade a husband, rather than a brother. I think most women have some degree of power over men in a situation where they are sexually involved, and that is not the case with brothers. There is always a distance and it is impossible to talk with them beyond a point."

References

Aberle, David F. 1961. Navajo. In David M. Schneider and Kathleen Gough, eds., *Matrilineal Kinship*, pp. 96–201. Berkeley: University of California Press.

_____. 1981a. A Century of Navajo Kinship Change. *Canadian Journal of Anthropology* 2(2): 21–36.

_____. 1981b. Navajo Coresidential Kin Groups and Lineages. *Journal of Anthropological Research* 37(1): 1–7.

Ackerman, Lillian A. 1982. Sexual Equality in the Plateau Culture Area. Ph.D. dissertation, Washington State University, Pullman, Washington.

Adams, William Y. 1983. Once More to the Fray: Further Reflections on Navajo Kinship and Residence. *American Anthropologist* 79: 58–83.

Bachofen, Johan J. 1981. *Das Mutterrecht* (The Motherright). Basel: Benno Schwabe.

Bailey, Flora L. 1950. *Some Sex Beliefs and Practices in a Navajo Community*, vol. 40, no. 2. Papers of the Peabody Museum of American Archaeology and Ethnology, Harvard University.

Downs, James F. 1972. *The Navajo*. New York: Holt, Rinehart and Winston.

Farella, John R. 1984. *The Main Stalk: A Synthesis of Navajo Philosophy*. Tuscon: University of Arizona Press.

Fortes, M. 1959. Primitive Kinship. *Scientific American* 200(6): 146–157.

Fox, Robin. 1989 [orig. 1967]. *Kinship and Marriage*. Cambridge: Cambridge University Press.

Frisbie, Charlotte Johnson. 1967. *Kinaaldá: A Study of the Navajo Girl's Puberty Ceremony*. Middletown, Conn.: Wesleyan University Press.

_____. 1982 Traditional Navajo Women: Ethnographic and Life History Portrayals. *American Indian Quarterly* 6(1, 2): 11–33.

Fuller, C. J. 1976. *The Nayars Today*. Cambridge: Cambridge University Press.

Ginsburg, Faye, and Rayna Rapp. 1991. The Politics of Reproduction. *Annual Review of Anthropology* 20: 311–324.

Gough, Kathleen. 1955. Female Initiation Rites on the Malabar Coast. *Journal of the Royal Anthropological Institute* 85: 45–80.

_____. 1958. Cults of the Dead Among the Nayars. *Journal of American Folklore* 71(281): 447–478.

_____. 1961a. The Modern Disintegration of Matrilineal Descent Groups. In David M. Schneider and Kathleen Gough, eds., *Matrilineal Kinship*, pp. 631–652. Berkeley: University of California Press.

_____. 1961b. Nayar: Central Kerala. In David M. Schneider and Kathleen Gough, eds., *Matrilineal Kinship*, pp. 298–384. Berkeley: University of California Press.

Haile, Father Berard, O.F.M. 1981. *Women Versus Men: A Conflict of Navajo Emergence* (The Curly Tó Aheedlíinii Version). Edited by Karl W. Luckert. Lincoln: University of Nebraska Press.

Keesing, Roger M. 1975. *Kin Groups and Social Structure*. Fort Worth: Holt, Rinehart and Winston.

Kelley, Klara B. 1982. Yet Another Analysis of the Navajo Outfit: New Evidence from Historical Documents. *Journal of Anthropological Research* 38(4): 363–381.

Kluckhohn, Clyde. 1944. *Navajo Witchcraft*, vol. 22, no. 2. Papers of the Peabody Museum of American Archaeology and Ethnology, Harvard University.

Kluckhohn, Clyde, and Dorothea Leighton. 1946. *The Navajo*. Cambridge: Harvard University Press.

Lamphere, Louise. 1969. Symbolic Elements in Navajo Ritual. *Southwestern Journal of Anthropology* 25: 279–305.

_____. 1970. Ceremonial Cooperation and Networks: A Reanalysis of the Navajo Outfit. *Man* 5: 39–59.

_____. 1977. *To Run After Them: Cultural and Social Bases of Cooperation in a Navajo Community.* Tuscon: University of Arizona Press.

_____. 1989. Historical and Regional Variability in Navajo Women's Roles. *Journal of Anthropological Research* 45(4): 431–456.

Leighton, Dorothea, and Clyde Kluckhohn. 1947. *Children of the People.* Cambridge: Harvard University Press.

Lepowsky, Maria. 1993. *Fruit of the Motherland: Gender in an Egalitarian Society.* New York: Columbia University Press.

Levy, Jerrold E., Eric B. Henderson, and Tracy J. Andrews. 1989. The Effects of Regional Variation and Temporal Change on Matrilineal Elements of Navajo Social Organization. *Journal of Anthropological Research* 45(4): 351–377.

Luckert, Karl W. 1981. Editor's note, paragraphs 20 and 31. In Father Berard Haile, O.F.M., *Women Versus Men: A Conflict of Navajo Emergence* (The Curly Tó Aheedlíinii Version). Edited by Karl W. Luckert. Lincoln: University of Nebraska Press.

Neff, Deborah L. 1994. The Social Construction of Infertility: The Case of the Matrilineal Nayars in South India. *Social Science and Medicine* 39(4): 475–485.

Menon, Shanti. 1996. Male Authority and Female Autonomy: A Study of the Matrilineal Nayars of Kerala, South India. In Mary Jo Maynes, Ann Waltner, Birgitte Soland, and Ulrike Strasser, eds., *Gender, Kinship, Power: A Comparative Interdisciplinary History,* pp. 131–146. New York: Routledge.

Moody, Gail. 1991. Mythological and Kinship Roles of Women in Navajo and Euro-American Cultures. Unpublished manuscript.

Poewe, Karla O. 1981. *Matrilineal Ideology: Male-Female Dynamics in Luapula, Zambia.* London: Academic Press.

Reichard, Gladys A. 1928. *Social Life of the Navajo Indians.* New York: Columbia University Press.

_____. 1950. *Navajo Religion: A Study of Symbolism,* vol. 1. New York: Pantheon Books.

Richards, A. I. 1950. Some Types of Family Structure Amongst the Central Bantu. In A. R. Radcliffe-Brown and D. Forde, eds., *African Systems of Kinship and Marriage,* pp. 207–251. Oxford: Oxford University Press.

Schlegel, Alice. 1972. *Male Dominance and Female Autonomy: Domestic Authority in Matrilineal Societies.* Human Relations Area Files Press.

Schneider, David M. 1961. The Distinctive Features of Matrilineal Descent Groups. In David M. Schneider and Kathleen Gough, eds., *Matrilineal Kinship,* pp. 1–29. Berkeley: University of California Press.

Shepardson, Mary. 1982. The Status of Navajo Women. *American Indian Quarterly* 6(1, 2): 149–169.

Shepardson, Mary, and Blodwen Hammond. 1970. *The Navajo Mountain Community: Social Organization and Kinship Terminology.* Berkeley: University of California Press.

Shostak, Marjorie. 1981. *Nisa: The Life and Words of a !Kung Woman*. New York: Random House.

Spencer, Katherine. 1947. *Reflection of Social Life in the Navajo Origin Myth*. University of New Mexico Publications in Anthropology No. 3. Albuquerque: University of New Mexico Press.

Witherspoon, Gary. 1975. *Navajo Kinship and Marriage*. Chicago: University of Chicago Press.

Wright, Anne. 1982a. An Ethnography of the Navajo Reproductive Cycle. *American Indian Quarterly* 6(1, 2): 52–70.

_____. 1982b. Attitudes Toward Childbearing and Menstruation Among the Navajo. In Margarita Artschwager Kay, ed., *Anthropology of Human Birth*, pp. 377–394. Philadelphia: F. A. Davis Company.

Wright, Anne, Mark Bauer, Clarina Clark, Frank Morgan, and Kenneth Begishe. 1993. Cultural Interpretations and Intracultural Variability in Navajo Beliefs About Breastfeeding. *American Ethnologist* 20(4): 781–796.

5

Double and Cognatic Descent

This chapter introduces two other types of descent and shows the different ways in which they interrelate with systems of gender. In the last two chapters we saw that patrilineal and matrilineal systems of descent are quite distinct from one another in terms of structure. But in this chapter, after going through the remaining modes of descent, we will see that there is sometimes only a fine line between forms of descent that are called by different names. The first one we will examine is the rare form known as **double descent.**

Double Descent

A society whose kinship patterns are traced on the basis of double descent contains both matrilineal and patrilineal groups at the same time. Accordingly, each person in that society simultaneously belongs to two groups, one traced through the mother and one traced through the father. Figure 5.1 shows the structure of double descent.

Here, we see two groups, one traced by matrilineal descent and the other by patrilineal descent. Ego belongs to both—that is, to both his or her mother's *matri*lineage and his or her father's *patri*lineage. Both descent groups are corporate groups. The key to double descent systems is that the two descent groups always have quite different functions, or are important in very different contexts. Otherwise there would be clashes. For example, if matrilineal groups sought to transmit land or houses matrilineally while patrilineal groups were seeking to transmit them patrilineally, then each man's own sons and sister's sons would be at odds with one another over the inheritance of the man's land and house. The following case study shows how in one society matrilineal and patrilineal groups coexist yet are kept distinct, and why maintaining a distinction between them is seen as important to the people themselves.

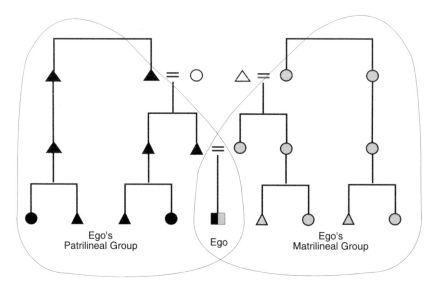

FIGURE 5.1 A Double Descent Construct. Ego belongs to two descent groups, one patrilineal (the members of this one are darkly shaded) and one matrilineal (members of this one are
lightly shaded).

CASE 5: THE BENG

The Beng are an African group living in Côte d'Ivoire (formerly known as
the Ivory Coast). At the time that anthropologist Alma Gottlieb lived with
the Beng in the late 1970s and early 1980s, they numbered around ten
thousand persons. Before the colonial era and French domination of this region, Beng subsistence had been based on hunting, gathering, and horticulture. The Beng also carried out extensive trade with neighboring groups,
largely through their production of valued kola nuts. When the French introduced cash cropping, especially of coffee and cocoa, male hunting declined and male labor became important in agriculture. Today women also
work in agriculture and continue to gather.

Politically, the Beng are divided into two regions, each with its own king
and queen. (These regional leaders are, of course, under the higher authority of the Republic of Côte d'Ivoire.) The kings are publicly more prominent than the queens, but the queens are powerful and the kings consult
them on major matters (Gottlieb 1989b: 247). In both regions there are
several villages, each of which is presided over by a male and a female chief.
These chiefs are seen as co-rulers and must come from the same matriclan,
as do the king and queen of each region.

By now, many Beng have converted to Islam and a few are Catholic. Still,
an older, traditional religion co-exists with the new religions. Traditional
Beng religion focuses on a cult of the Earth, a major (male) deity. Each vil-

lage has shrines to the Earth, with priests (called "Masters of the Earth") who offer sacrifices to these shrines. The Earth is believed to have great powers, including control over human fertility and fertility of crops (Gottlieb 1988: 66).

The Beng recognize double descent, with both matriclans and patriclans. Both the matriclans and the patriclans are corporate groups, and both subdivide into lineages. The patriclans are strictly exogamous. Aside from this marriage restriction, patriclans are important in a number of ways (Gottlieb 1992: 62–69). It is from one's patriclan that one inherits a number of food taboos, or a list of particular foods that one is forbidden to eat. The Beng believe that if a person violates a patriclan food taboo, he or she will become ill and must seek a healer who is a patriclan member. Each patriclan has rights to its own local medical knowledge concerning the treatment of food taboo violations. This is regarded as secret clan knowledge. One's patriclan also becomes important at death. Patriclans carry out ritual treatment of the corpse of a dead member and determine the burial spot of the deceased. Finally, patriclan members are believed to inherit certain talents and personality types.

In some ways the matriclans are more prominent than the patriclans in Beng society and culture. For one thing, agricultural land is inherited matrilineally, from mothers' brothers to sisters' sons. Second, as noted, political leaders must be members of specific matriclans. Third, and perhaps most important, one's personal identity is enmeshed in the matriclan. The Beng say that the soul is inherited from the mother, and, "when asked to characterize matrikin, Beng typically explain, '*ã se do*' ('we are all one')" (Gottlieb 1986: 700). Matrikin, who are seen as "close" and "caring," provide one another with cooperation and emotional support. Yet in another sense Beng matrikin see themselves as "too close," saying, for example, that they are too close to be friends, whereas patrikin can be friends (Gottlieb 1989a: 70).

Much more negatively speaking, witchcraft power is believed to be inherited matrilineally and witchcraft is believed to be effective only against a witch's matrikin. Thus the relationships among matrikin, though "close" in one respect, are also tinged with mistrust. Interestingly, one may not only inherit witchcraft power but also "buy" it from other witches, either by paying with money or by giving up a part of oneself—say, the use of an arm. For women, another means of "buying" witchcraft is by "selling" one's menstrual cycle and breasts (Gottlieb 1989b: 253). In this case, the woman who is "purchasing" witchcraft power never develops breasts or menstruates and is, of course, infertile. Harm to the matriclan is in decided opposition to the function of reproducing it; and, as a parallel to many other societies, an infertile Beng woman is likely to be suspected of witchcraft.

Unlike the patriclans, the matriclans are not exogamous. Indeed, a preferred form of marriage is one in which a man marries a matrilateral "second cousin"—say, a MMZDD. The Beng say an advantage of this form of marriage is that, should a couple quarrel, the matriclan members will intervene to put pressure on the couple to resolve their differences. But if the husband and wife come from different matriclans, their respective matrikin will not be so interested in keeping the marriage together (Gottlieb 1986: 700).

Marriages are arranged by parents, with both bride and groom having little say in the matter (Gottlieb 1986: 699). Residence is patrilocal. Polygyny is permitted and considered an ideal by men. Particular co-wives may get along, but Beng women generally disfavor polygyny (Gottlieb 1988: 57). Females, but not males, are supposed to be virgins until their engagement or marriage. Many years ago, a child born to a woman before her engagement or marriage was killed (Gottlieb 1989a: 67).

Gottlieb (1989a) provides an interesting analysis of how double descent among the Beng is interwoven with relationships between the sexes as well as with major religious beliefs and practices concerning men, women, and sexuality. She points out that the Beng see their two types of descent groupings as complementary and jointly responsible for the social structure. But the Beng say that these two types of descent, these two different types of clans, should be kept distinct; they should have complementary but different spheres of activity. As we have seen, this division of the functions of matrilineal and patrilineal descent groups is the key to understanding how double descent systems work. For the Beng, the sex act, which intimately joins male and female, becomes a symbol of the mixing together of types of clans. Since this mixing is seen as dangerous, the sex act itself is regarded as a potential threat and must be subjected to certain controls: "The sex act is a symbolic means of 'straddling a fence,' separating two discrete realms. To (metaphorically) straddle this fence through sex is to combine metaphorically the two types of clans, which should not be combined; hence the sex act, as metaphor, must be strictly regulated in order to control and contain the meaning for which the . . . act stands" (Gottlieb 1989a: 72).

One way in which the sex act is regulated concerns an important Beng religious taboo: Sexual intercourse should not, under any circumstances, take place in the forest or fields. These natural areas (in contrast to the village, where sexual intercourse is permitted) are the special province of Earth, the aforementioned Beng male deity who is regularly worshiped by elders of the various matriclans. The Beng go to some trouble to mark off the boundary between things of the village and things of the forest and fields—specifically, by ritually planting a kapok tree in each village, "which serves to make sexual activity in that village acceptable" (Gottlieb 1988: 62). Human copulation in the areas of the Earth is believed to pollute Earth. The seriousness with which Beng regard the taboo against copulation in the forest is evident from the punishment meted out for its violation:

As punishment, the couple are led to the spot where they committed their act. They are accompanied by old and middle-aged men of their own and some surrounding villages. A Master of the Earth (a ritual leader who offers sacrifices to the Earth) oversees the ritual punishment: the couple is made to repeat the sex act while jeered on by the angry crowd, who beat them and burn them with switches and firebrands. . . . The punishment over, a cow is sacrificed to the Earth by way of apology for having been polluted (Gottlieb 1989a: 70).

One suspects that a Beng, once caught, is unlikely to try copulating in the forest again. Under the circumstances, it seems unlikely that a couple would try it even one time, but Gottlieb (1988: 63) reports that, "in fact, such illicit acts seem to be common: an informant of about thirty-three years recalled at least five cases as having occurred within her recent memory for three Beng villages." She also reports that this punishment was given to an errant couple during her stay among the Beng. Some cases of forest sex are cases of rape, and these may be blamed on madness caused by witchcraft: "In one case I recorded a well-known healer was bewitched and attempted to rape his wife in the forest. She escaped, and when he 'came out of it' within a few hours, he hanged himself in the forest for shame" (Gottlieb 1988: 63).

Even after undergoing public punishment for their act, a man and woman who have had sex in the forest or fields are considered to be permanently polluted, or "dirty," and to bring bad luck to others. For this reason, if unmarried, this man or woman will have difficulty finding a spouse or will have to marry someone else who is permanently "polluted" (Gottlieb 1989a: 71).

There are other punishments for sex in the forest. Perhaps the anger of the Earth will bring a difficult childbirth to the woman offender, or stop the rains and so harm the crops. The latter outcome is one from which everyone suffers; thus a couple violating this taboo "jeopardize the lives of the entire Beng people: a general drought will ensue that, if the Earth is not properly propitiated in time, will result in the ruin of the entire year's crop and, ultimately, the starvation of all the Beng" (Gottlieb 1988: 62).

Significantly, both punishments—difficult childbirth and drought—represent "aborted fertility in, respectively, the village (human) and the farm (crop) spheres" (Gottlieb 1989a: 70). Gottlieb argues that in Beng thought, human and forest/field fertility are related and seen as parallel, but that the point is to keep these fertility realms separate. Human sex in the forest violates the boundaries between things of the village and things of the forest, angers the Earth, and brings destruction to both human and crop fertility. But if these realms are kept properly separated, the Earth can enhance both crop and human fertility. A ritual connection between Earth and human fertility can be seen in the following rite: "During his wife's pregnancy a husband should contribute an egg to the Master of the Earth to ask that his wife's childbirth go well and she deliver the baby successfully. After the delivery the husband will sacrifice a chicken with which to thank the Earth" (Gottlieb 1988: 66).

A number of other Beng rules deal with human sexuality out of its proper place, seen as offensive to the Earth and thus harmful to fertility. One is that all Beng adults are to bathe in the morning to "wash off sex" before going to the fields or entering the forest. In fact, they must do so regardless of whether they actually had sex the previous night. Another Beng rule is that a menstruating married woman (a symbol of human fertility) must not go into the forest or fields. If she violates this rule, her next childbirth will be difficult and the crops in the field will die. Gottlieb (1988: 60–61) provides an example:

> About a year ago a menstruating woman was in the forest to work in her husband's yam field. Two days later, all the leaves of the yam plants in that part of the field fell off and the yams died. In addition, she herself developed bad stomach cramps. She consulted a diviner to discover the cause of her stomach cramps and he accused her of having been in the forest while menstruating. She confessed but explained that her period had come while she was in the fields and she didn't want to return to the village right away. However, as a result of her misjudgment the whole year's yam crop ... in that field was destroyed and the Earth was polluted. . . . To rectify the latter condition, the woman's husband was required to sacrifice a female hairy goat.

There are other menstrual taboos among the Beng, but, significantly, these are all means of keeping human fertility in its place or ways to protect the woman herself from danger. Thus, Gottlieb (1989a: 72–73) points out that among the Beng, and in contrast to many patrilineal societies, menstruating women are not seen as polluting in and of themselves or as dangerous to men; rather, menstruation is seen as a symbol of human fertility, so to protect successful fertility in both humans and crops, menstruating women must be kept from the realm of the forest and fields. She also points out that punishments for violating the taboo on human sex in the forest are equal for men and women. In the case of this illicit sex act, a metaphorical and dangerous mixing of the types of clans, both males and females are held responsible.

Other examples of equivalent status for males and females in Beng society can be seen in the marriage relationship. First, when it comes to arranging the marriage of a daughter, the Beng follow a principle whereby all of a couple's odd-numbered daughters (by birth order) are considered to "belong" to the father, who can marry them off as he likes; but all of the even-numbered daughters belong to the mother, for her to marry off at will (Gottlieb 1986: 712). Second, husbands and wives are expected to show respect to each other, and the social judgment that results from failure to do so is equal for men and women. For the Beng, the gravest insult to a spouse is to throw a chicken at him or her during the heat of an argument. When either the husband or the wife commits this act, the marriage is considered irreparably ended. But Gottlieb (1986: 702) also points out one slight advantage of women over men in marriage: "Women's hearts are said to be 'hard' . . . in contrast to men's hearts, which are seen as 'soft' . . . [thus] women are quicker than men to anger, and after an argument, women remain bitter but men forget quickly. Because of this constellation of perceived gender-linked differences, in case of any conjugal dispute, it is the duty of the husband to apologize to his wife, regardless of whether he thought himself in the wrong."

Why some societies develop double descent is not precisely known. The most popular explanation has been that double descent societies are transitional, inasmuch as they represent societies that were once matrilineal but later incorporated patrilineal descent principles as well (Fox 1989: 132). Most, if not all, double descent societies are patrilocal, whereby patrilineally related men stay together and bring their wives into the group.

Cognatic Descent

A descent group can be formed through the tracing of an ancestor's descendants through both male and female links. This is a case of cognatic descent, whereby both males and females may reproduce the group. Figure 5.2 shows a cognatic descent construct. All of the people in this diagram

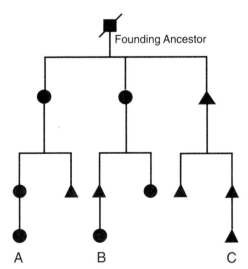

FIGURE 5.2   A Cognatic Descent Construct. All descendants of the founding ancestor can be included in the descent group.

are the cognatic descendants of the founding ancestor. Notice that person A is connected to the ancestor through two female links; person B is connected through a male and a female; and person C is connected through two males. Indeed, purely "matrilineal" or "patrilineal" links between an individual and the founding ancestor are possible, as is any combination of male and female linkages.

It may be helpful at this point to emphasize the difference between cognatic descent and double descent. In Figure 5.3, double descent is illustrated by the diagram on the left, and cognatic descent, by the diagram on the right. In the case of double descent, two loops enclose ego along with his or her separate matrilineal and patrilineal groups. Notice that ego does not share any group membership with two of the four grandparents (i.e., his or her FM and MF). But in the right-hand diagram, loops enclose ego with all of his or her ancestors. Ego can trace descent equally from all ancestors through any male and/or female links.

The cognatic descent construct reflects the way that most Euro-Americans perceive their connections to their ancestors and descendants. However, most Euro-American societies are not cognatic. As mentioned in Chapter 1, a cognatic society is one that uses descent to form corporate groups. By this definition most Euro-American societies are not cognatic because they do not form corporate groups based on descent. There have been some exceptions; for example, the Scottish clan was a true cognatic descent group (Fox 1989). To see how cognatic descent works, recall our encounter in Chapter 1 with a hypothetical woman, Zigod, who formed groups in her society based on descent from a common ancestor. Also recall Figof, who became a member of a descent group separate from that of Zigod. Figure 5.4 illustrates these two descent groups in this hypothetical society. Thus far, Zigod's group, A, and Figof's group, B, are discrete groups. If we apply the concept of "descent from a common ancestor," there is no question of which individuals belong to which group. But look what happens in Figure 5.5 when a

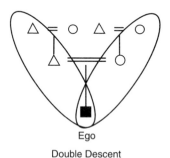

Double Descent

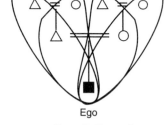

Cognatic Descent

FIGURE 5.3 The Difference Between Double Descent and Cognatic Descent. In the double descent diagram two loops enclose Ego with his/her separate patrilineal and matrilineal groups. In the cognatic descent diagram loops enclose Ego with all of his/her ancestors.

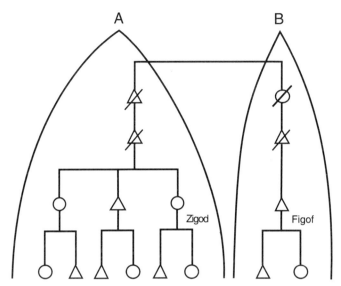

FIGURE 5.4   Descent Groups A and B in Zigod's Society. Ogives enclose the separate descent groups.

member of group A marries a member of group B. Here, using a cognatic principle, we see that the children of this union, the individuals X and Y, belong to *both* descent groups. The same would be true for the children,

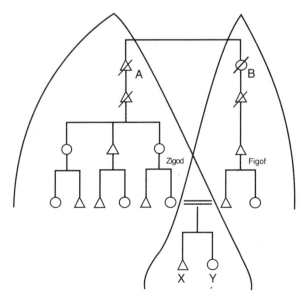

FIGURE 5.5   Overlapping Cognatic Descent Group Membership. Persons X and Y can belong to both of the decent groups A and B.

grandchildren, and so on, of any persons who married with members of other groups; and, by extension, the number of groups to which individuals could belong would increase over the generations. Thus, in the case of inter-marriage between groups, cognatic descent results in descent groups with *overlapping membership*. These are quite different from the neat, discrete unilineal descent groups formed through matrilineal or patrilineal descent.

This overlap is not a problem in and of itself. It is possible for people in this system to belong to a plurality of groups at the same time. After all, in cases of double descent, a person belongs to two descent groups simultaneously. But as with double descent, cognatic descent requires that the groups have different functions, or at least that they call upon their members to participate in activities in different places and/or at different times.

In fact, cognatic societies do form discrete groups; and they do so simply by using some mechanism other than descent to pare down the large group of all possible members to a smaller group of "real" or "active" members. One mechanism often employed is parental residence (Keesing 1975: 92). For example, a cognatic society could have a rule that all the descendants of an ancestor are potentially members of a group. But in that event, whenever two people from two different descent groups marry, they must decide with which group they will live. Their children will then become "real" members of that group. Thus the children, potentially members of two descent groups, become active members of one through their parents' residence choice. In Figure 5.6, we can see that the children of the husband (X)

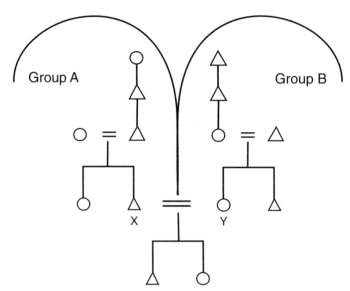

FIGURE 5.6 Residence Choice and Descent Group Membership in a Cognatic System. The children of X and Y will belong to the group (A or B) in which X and Y decide to live.

and wife (Y) will become members of group A should the couple reside with the husband's people, or members of group B should the couple reside with the wife's people.

This is not to say that once the parental choice is made the children necessarily lose all rights in the other group; rather, the point is that, for now, their primary affiliations (or "primary rights," as Keesing [1975: 92] terms them) are set with one group. In some cases the situation may be quite fluid, with people switching memberships through life, becoming a part of one group now and affiliating, through residence, with another group later.

In light of such factors as membership in descent groups based on parental residence and the possibilities for shifting memberships, many anthropologists came to view cognatic descent systems as simply more "flexible" than unilineal ones and speculated that these systems might be found in areas characterized by a precarious relationship between resources (e.g., land) and people. Thus, for example, if the territory of one descent group became too crowded, individuals could use their cognatic ties to join other groups (Fox 1989: 153). Or in cases where postmarital residence was an open choice, couples could go to whichever group had more resources to offer at the moment. Some ecological forces may be at work behind the formation of descent systems, but there are also many exceptions to the outcomes that these ecological considerations would predict (Keesing 1975: 139).

Another way in which a cognatic society can get around, or at least reduce, overlaps among memberships in descent groups would be to follow descent group endogamy, or to encourage marriage within the group (e.g., between cousins). Whenever two people born into the same group marry, their children will, through both parents, belong to one group. Of course, they could be linked by descent to yet other groups through their grandparents, who were not cousins, and so on; but each case of descent group inmarriage will cut down on the number of possibilities.

A feature common to many, though not all, groups with cognatic descent is that they have a built-in "patrilineal bias." In other words, the group members may express a strong preference to reside patrilocally, or patrilineal descendants might be given preference to a group's land and resources. Regarding the latter case, Keesing (1975: 92) argues that both a principle of cognatic descent and a principle of patrilineal descent would be at work in the society: Patrilineal descendants would be given preference for residence and land rights, but if there were enough land to go around, other, cognatically related kin could also come in, though it would take their descendants a few generations to become accepted as full members of the group. When a cognatic society exhibits a "patrilineal bias," there is really very little difference between such a cognatic society and an ordinary patrilineal society such as the Nuer (Case 1), who, though strongly patrilineal and basically patrilocal, also allow nonpatrilineal kin to join their residence groups. Over time, the descendants of these people come to be considered real patrilineal members and are treated accordingly. There is no point in quibbling over whether a particular society is best described as "cognatic with a patrilineal bias," "cognatic but also with a patrilineal principle," or "patrilineal and patrilocal but with allowance for some cognatic kin to move in." If a terminological distinction needs to be made, the best course is to follow what the people themselves say about their own system. If they say that all the descendants of an ancestor have rights to membership in the group, they can be considered cognatic.

Cognatic descent interrelates with gender in some important ways. One way applies to societies in which affiliation with a descent group depends on postmarital residence choices. In these cases each descent group will have somewhat uncertain control over female fertility, or its own reproduction. Thus, if a woman is born into descent group A, and if she and her husband decide to affiliate with A, her fertility belongs to that group and through her fertility the group is perpetuated. But if the couple decides to affiliate with her husband's descent group, B, then A loses this opportunity. Similarly, a son of descent group A may bring in a wife patrilocally and through her fertility the group is perpetuated; or the couple may decide otherwise and A loses this opportunity for reproduction.

An example of how this type of descent interrelates with gender comes from the cognatic Maori of New Zealand. Before British colonial rule, the Maori were a highly stratified society organized into chiefdoms. In this society one's social rank was very important and could supersede considerations of gender. Thus, although women were inferior to men of their own rank, a higher-ranking woman was superior to a lower-ranking male. Traditionally the Maori were organized into cognatic descent groups called *hapu*. These in turn were internally stratified into three broad classes: those of high rank, those of middle rank, and commoners. The highest-ranking member of a hapu was the chief, and normally this was a man who descended through a pure line of patrilineal descent and primogeniture (succession of eldest sons) from the founding ancestor. Within the hapu, all senior lines of descent (those genealogically closer to the main, chiefly line) were superior to junior lines. Within families, the sons were ranked by age, with elder brothers superior to younger; and the descendants of elder brothers were also superior to the descendants of younger brothers. Most males affiliated with the father's hapu and lived patrilocally. But in some cases, a man would have more to gain if he affiliated with the descent group of his mother or his wife (e.g., that line might be more senior in another hapu than his father's line in the father's hapu). Or, a man who was a younger brother might want to leave his hapu to avoid the older brother's domination and superiority. The hapus were exogamous at the upper levels of society but endogamous at the lower levels. Patrilineal affiliation and patrilocality were considered ideals; but since some individuals had more to gain by affiliating with a wife's or mother's hapu, these ideals were not always achieved.

Officially, older brothers were superior to younger ones; but in many cases the younger brothers, through sheer creativity and ability, managed to wrest power and prestige away from older ones. This happened frequently enough that younger brothers constituted a threat to the system and were viewed, in some aspects of Maori culture, with fear and mistrust. Karen Sinclair (1986) suggests that among the upper levels of society, the position of women was similar to that of younger brothers. Though officially not very powerful, they, too, challenged the system with their "creativity" (in this case, their fertility): The children that a woman produced *could* be destined for her husband's hapu, and such was the ideal. But given the element of choice and flexibility in this system, they could wind up in her hapu instead. Thus, unlike patrilineal-patrilocal groups, the upper-ranking Maori hapu lacked control over female fertility. Sinclair (1986) shows how Maori mythology depicts both younger brothers and women as threatening entities and how women in particular are seen as both givers and takers of life.

Another way in which cognatic descent may carry implications for gender concerns those societies in which cognatic descent and options for

PHOTO 5.1   Melanesian women in Irian Jaya (Indonesia), Dani tribe. Photo courtesy of Linda Stone.

residence result in groups with fluid and shifting membership. To see how this system ties in with the roles of men and women, we will briefly look at two cases from Melanesia, an island group in the southwest Pacific.

CASE 6: THE KWAIO

The Kwaio, who number around seven thousand people, live on Malaita Island of the Solomon Islands in Melanesia. Their kinship traditions were studied by Roger Keesing (1970, 1982, 1987). Along with other groups of the region, the Kwaio have been subjected to Christian missionary activity, colonization, and westernization. Keesing (1987: 34) writes that despite these influences, in the central mountains of Malaita some three thousand Kwaio speakers remain "defiantly committed to their ancestral religion and customs. These traditionalists preserve a numerically thinned but substantially intact social structure."

Like many other Melanesian groups, the Kwaio subsist on pig raising and horticulture. Traditionally, they had informal leaders and engaged in blood feuds and wars. The informal leaders were characteristic of a type of political leaders found throughout Melanesia called "big men." Melanesian "big men" had no formal authority but led factions and competed with one another for power and dominance. Their success depended on their ability to enhance their prestige by operating as central points in the exchanges of goods between local groups.

The Kwaio region is divided into territories controlled by different descent groups. Each territory is associated with a set of founding ancestors. To follow the Kwaio system, Keesing (1970) distinguishes between the "primary" and "secondary" rights that one could obtain in these territories. By secondary rights Keesing means the rights to live in the ancestors' territory, garden the land, and participate in some of the descent group's religious rituals. Primary rights are a little stronger: A person exercising them participates more extensively in the affairs of the descent group, takes a larger role in its rituals, and becomes similar to a "voting member with full rights" in the landowning corporation of the descent group (Keesing 1975: 93). Primary rights in the descent group territories, called *fanua*, are transmitted to the groups' patrilineal descendants. Each fanua consists primarily of scattered settlements of male patrilineal kin, along with their in-marrying wives from other groups.

So far the Kwaio may seem to be a standard patrilineal-patrilocal group; but in addition to this structure, any person has secondary rights to other fanua—not fanua to which his descent link is purely patrilineal but, rather, those to which he traces a link through female ancestors or through a combination of male and female ancestors. Thus a man has primary rights to the fanua of his father, but he may, for whatever reason, decide to suspend these rights and reside, say, in the fanua of his mother's father, activating his secondary rights in this fanua. There he brings his wife and raises his children, and after a prolonged residence he acquires full primary rights in this fanua. As noted, however, this system is quite fluid: Over the course of his life, a man may live in and activate secondary rights in several different fanua to which he has cognatic links. But since most men stay in their father's fanua, and since postmarital residence is usually patrilocal, it turns out that these cognatic descent groups consist mostly of patrilineally related males and their wives, and basically look very much like a patrilineal-patrilocal society. This feature, along with the fact that the strongest rights (i.e., the primary rights) are transmitted patrilineally, gives the Kwaio system a definite "patrilineal" twist. At the same time, the Kwaio themselves emphasize that *all* descendants of a founding ancestor (i.e., descendants traced through both male and female links) have rights to live and garden in the ancestor's fanua.

Each fanua is associated with ancestral shrines, and ritual worship of the ancestors is the major focus of Kwaio religion. Indeed, the ancestors are so important to the Kwaio that they are considered "unseen members of the community." As Keesing (1982: 112–113) notes: "A substantial portion of the conversations that take place in a Kwaio settlement are not between living humans but between the living and the dead. . . . Almost every day . . . [a particular woman] . . . will converse silently with her mother and father, long dead, and her grandfather; and through them to more remote ancestors. . . . [The ancestors] . . . are part of the daily social life of Kwaio communities." Ancestors, like humans, desire pork, and so are offered pigs as sacrifice. Sacrifices are made to please the ancestors, who, if pleased, may protect their descendants or, if displeased, may harm them. Nearly every illness or misfortune is attributed to the wrath of ancestors. In this way the ancestors serve as powerful sanctions on human behavior; fear of their anger discourages disobedience to the many rules governing proper behavior in Kwaio culture.

Although any given fanua may appear to be largely patrilineal-patrilocal based on its composition, the relationship between the Kwaio and their ancestors is fully cognatic. Ancestors are worshiped by their cognatic descendants. When a woman marries and lives in her husband's fanua, she raises pigs to be sacrificed to her own ancestors along with the pigs she raises for her husband and his ancestors. It is thus from both of their parents that children "inherit" ancestors to worship. In addition, each descent group has a priest who propitiates ancestors, and when this priest dies, the group holds a great ritual that draws in his cognatic descendants and includes them all in a temporary ritual seclusion.

Women and men play very different roles and have very different relationships to the Kwaio cult of the ancestors. For one thing, direct propitiation of the ancestors is a strictly male affair. And, as is the case throughout Melanesia generally, women are considered sources of "menstrual pollution," which is seen as dangerous to men and to sacred phenomena.

The different roles of men and women are best seen in relation to male/female spaces in a Kwaio settlement. At the center of this settlement is a dwelling. Both men and women may occupy it, though there are separate male and female spaces within. In addition to occupying this space, the males of a household may sleep or eat in a separate men's house located above. Beside that is a sacred area where ancestral shrines are kept and worshiped. No woman may ever go to either the men's house or to the sacred area. But below the central dwelling are exclusive women's spaces—menstrual huts and, below these, a separate area for giving birth. During menstruation, a woman must go to a menstrual hut for seclusion. Any vegetables she eats can be taken only from special "menstrual gardens" located there. Her very young children can accompany her in menstrual seclusion, but at about the age of one and a half, a male child can no longer do so. To give birth, a woman goes lower still, to a place where she has built a "childbirth hut." Here she will remain for fifteen days after the birth, out of the sight of men.

Aside from these sharp spatial divisions, there are innumerable behavioral restrictions ensuring that the world of men and ancestors is kept apart from the world of women and reproduction. Keesing (1982) points out that in Kwaio cosmological thought, women with their reproductive powers are indeed opposed to men and the power of the ancestors. He describes how the rituals surrounding a woman giving birth are the mirror opposite of the rituals of a man "creating an ancestor" at the death of a priest. Yet in the end the two realms connect, since women, by giving birth, are producing future ancestors. And senior or respected women, though never allowed near sacred ancestral shrines during their lifetimes, may be buried there in death.

From this standpoint we see that women's reproductive powers define their religious roles, that their reproduction separates them from the male realm of ancestral powers, and that their menstruation and childbirth are "polluting" to men and to the ancestors. Yet Kwaio women themselves do not view their menstrual seclusion as oppressive. As Keesing (1982: 221–222) notes, "In addition to giving women dangerous weapons, it [menstrual pollution] establishes a separate base for women's power. Women in the menstrual hut or clustered in support of a mother in childbirth have a solidarity . . . which they do not have in everyday domestic life. . . . [T]hey are free from both male domination and from the heavy work burdens of everyday life." This example reminds us that menstrual taboos, as such, cannot always be interpreted cross-culturally as indications of female oppression (Buckley and Gottlieb 1988). Among the Beng, too, as we saw in the previous section, menstruation is a powerful symbol of fertility, and the restrictions on menstruating women are aimed at protecting human and crop fertility.

Keesing (1987) reports that although Kwaio women do not challenge men's right and claims, they have their own distinctive visions of themselves in relation to Kwaio culture. They see themselves not only as important agents in maintaining virtue and order in society but also as primarily responsible for cultural transmission and continuity over the generations. Moreover, whereas men view women as sexually passive and vulnerable, and thus in need of male control, women view themselves as in control over their own sexuality.

Keesing also points out that Kwaio women play important ritual and religious roles, even though the sphere of their activity is kept separate from male/ancestor religious spaces. In addition, he notes that in Kwaio culture, emissions from men (e.g., vomit, urine) are deemed polluting and that Kwaio women, though potentially polluting on account of their menstruation, are not themselves considered polluted (Keesing 1982: 70).

These cultural ideas about the pollution of female menstruation, and about the danger of women generally, are widespread throughout Melanesia. In Keesing's assessment, however, the situation among the Kwaio is far milder than what has been reported from nearby highland New Guinea, where most of the groups are patrilineal. Many attempts have been made to explain these Melanesian expressions of the dangers of sexual contact with women, and especially the dangers of menstrual pollution. Before returning to this issue, let's take a brief look at one of these New Guinea groups—in this case, a group, like the Kwaio, with cognatic descent.

CASE 7: THE HULI

The Huli live in the southern highlands of New Guinea. Early studies by Robert Glasse (1965, 1968) were undertaken in the 1950s, at which time the Huli numbered about thirty thousand people. Like the Kwaio they raised pigs, practiced horticulture, had "big men" informal leaders, and were involved in constant internal warfare. Also like the Kwaio they had a system of cognatic descent, holding that all descendants of a founding ancestor were eligible for membership in the group that controlled that ancestor's territory. The rights of the patrilineal descendants of the ancestor were regarded as superior to the rights of other cognatic descendants. In contrast to Kwaio residence, however, Huli residence was extremely fluid, and it was not the case that most of the males in one local area were patrilineally related to one another.

Glasse called the Huli local group a "parish." Parish members owned territory in common, and rights to membership could be acquired through cognatic descent. But membership in the parish was not based on residence. Instead, for males, membership was activated and maintained by fulfilling obligations to the group. There were basically three such obligations: (1) defense of the group in war, (2) contributions to the group's war debts, and (3) participation in certain of the group's religious rituals (many of these were fertility rites). Any cognatic descendant of a founder who kept up these obligations was a parish member, whether or not he also lived in the parish. Failure to keep them up resulted in suspension or termination of membership.

Not just cognatic descendants of founders but also affinal relatives and even friends of members could come to reside in a parish; and if they fulfilled the three obligations mentioned above, they could acquire membership. In addition, many males had multiple memberships and multiple residences in the various parishes to whose founding ancestors they were cognatically related. Some men kept two or more households in different parishes and rotated between them. And, finally, people could change residences, abandoning old ones and taking up residence in new parishes. In short, although the parish was a geographically bounded and named unit, its resident membership was in constant flux.

Warfare was a central preoccupation among the Huli. Wars arose out of interpersonal grievances, which were as likely to start within one parish as between two parishes. Conflicts spread, men took sides, and the whole thing could easily be perpetuated since people needed to avenge the deaths of those killed in battle. Peace could be made by one party's payment of compensation for a death to another. Glasse (1968: 107) maintained that Huli cognatic descent fostered conflict precisely because membership in Huli groups was "nonexclusive." Members of groups had divided loyalties. At the same time, the Huli system offered outlets: To escape conflict one could always leave and join another parish.

Women (although they did not participate in warfare obligations) also had memberships, based on cognatic linkages, in different parishes. It was possible for them to have multiple residences as well—in part, because husbands and wives (as among the Nayar) did not live together in the same household. At marriage a woman usually moved to a parish in which her husband was a resident member, but there she would live in a separate house, perhaps with her mother-in-law, while her husband lived in another house. The houses of a husband and a wife could be a few yards or a couple of miles apart. A woman, at a later stage in her life, might reside part of the year elsewhere, with other relatives. Meanwhile, since polygyny was practiced, a man might have different wives in different parishes.

The Huli had some beliefs about sex and about relations between women and men that were roughly similar to those of many other highland New Guinea groups. Young males were taught that contact with women, especially sexual contact, was dangerous. They were taught that sex would hamper their health and bring premature aging. Menstruating women were considered especially dangerous: "If a man should be seen by one his skin will shrivel and his hair will turn gray. Copulating with an unclean woman injures a man internally, even fatally. To avoid these hazards men restrict contact with women" (Glasse 1965: 29). In fact, menstruating women were believed to emit a kind of poison. There were several menstrual taboos that women were to follow in order not to harm men, and among men a leading reason for divorce was that a wife had failed to observe these taboos.

To help avoid contact with women, young males, after initiation at about age seven or eight, left their mothers' houses and joined those of their fathers. From about age thirteen, boys were forbidden to eat food cooked or handled by women. Thus married men not only lived apart from their wives but cooked for themselves. Even plots of garden land were divided into male and female portions!

In their late teens, many male youths (about half of all youths) voluntarily joined a "bachelor society" in their parish. Here they remained for a couple of years while observing strict avoidance of women. If one member failed in this avoidance, the act was believed to bring misfortune to the whole group. As a safeguard against any inadvertent exposure to women, the bachelors performed monthly purificatory rituals such as "washing their eyes under a waterfall to remove the stigma of the female image" (Glasse 1965: 43).

After learning all about the dangers of women and sex, young men eventually married. On average, they married at age twenty-five to women of about age fifteen. Understandably, the young male approached sexual relations with some trepidation, but fortunately the Huli made available to married men a magical preparation that would help fight off the dangers of sexual intercourse. Even so, another practice no doubt dampened sexual enthusiasm in a young male: "Before copulating for this first time, the husband pours foul-smelling tree oil on his wife's vulva, for the genitals of a virgin are 'hot' and may damage his penis" (Glasse 1968: 59).

Eventually, of course, life went on and men and women reproduced. Many men later took additional wives; Glasse (1968: 48) estimated that married Huli men had an average of 1.5 wives. An opportunity for acquiring secondary wives was available to married men through "courting parties," which involved the sacrifice of pigs to ghosts. Married women and unmarried men were rigorously excluded from these parties, but older, married men were provided an opportunity to meet unmarried women and widows (Glasse 1968: 53).

Sexual intercourse between husband and wife was carefully timed around the wife's menstrual cycle. During her period, of course, a woman kept great distance from her husband. Afterward, however, "a wife sends a leaf to her husband to signify that she is no longer dangerous. The next day she emerges from seclusion, but still must avoid her husband. The following day she may speak to him from a distance, but they should not look at each other. As each day passes, more intimate relations are permitted, until they resume copulating. As the wife's period approaches again, the couple once more restrict their action" (Glasse 1968: 60). Thus, husband and wife may not have been having intercourse frequently, but they were free to indulge around the time of the wife's ovulation. And, indeed, a wife was desired for the children she would produce. A husband's rights in children were superior to those of the mother; and in cases of divorce, children would normally remain with the husband.

To a certain extent, childbirth lessened a woman's dangerousness. Before a child was born she was considered an especially potent menstrual polluter, but afterward she was regarded as safer (Glasse 1968: 60). Another reward for fertility was that a woman who had borne many children was believed to have won the favor of certain deities (Glasse 1965: 47).

Husbands were considered to have exclusive sexual access to wives. In cases of adultery, the male offender, and the natal kin of the wife, paid compensation (in pigs) to the husband. A wife could be punished for adultery by having stinging insects placed up her vagina, or "her husband may tie her to a tree and light a fire under her genitals. He may shoot an arrow into her buttocks, or he may merely beat her severely" (Glasse 1968: 72).

According to Glasse (1965: 48), Huli "women are inherently evil owing to their menstrual role, and their wickedness persists in the afterlife." Male ancestral ghosts were protective, whereas female ancestral ghosts (except for the ghosts of one's own mother) were harmful and dangerous. In particular, they were believed to cause barrenness in women and pigs.

Nevertheless, Glasse (1968: 76) noted, "by comparison with women from other [New Guinea] Highland societies, Huli women enjoy a fairly high status." He pointed out that Huli women could own pigs and that they could initiate marriages and divorces on their own. Yet another factor accounting for the relatively better position of Huli women was the Huli form of cognatic descent. In the same way that warring men could seek refuge in other parishes through their cognatic connections, women could abandon unhappy marriages and turn to other groups in which they had cognatic ties. Thus, according to Glasse, although the Huli system of cognatic descent stirred up trouble between men, it also provided an escape from difficulty for both men and women.

It must be pointed out that more recent investigation of highland New Guinea societies has challenged the older descriptions of menstrual pollution and exclusions of women among peoples such as the Huli. Researchers have observed that in certain groups, men express hostility to women in some contexts but envy of female reproductive powers in others. They have also found that the "pollution" of women, though negative and harmful in some settings, was positive and health-enhancing in other settings.[1]

Clearly, then, the earlier reports provided only a partial picture. One of the best accounts to balance this limited view was Anna Meigs' (1984) study of the Hua, whose concerns about women, pollution, and sex are similar to those reported for the Huli. Meigs shows that alongside these ideas are others that express a completely different gender ideology. One idea concerns the Hua concept of *nu*, a "vital essence" located especially in the fluids of the body. To the Hua, women by nature have greater nu than men, allowing them to grow faster and to stay healthier longer. Also, in sex, men deplete their nu through loss of semen, whereas women gain nu by the same process. Hua men acknowledge that women's greater nu accounts for their superiority, which is all for the good since women need this greater nu in order to carry out their life-giving functions of reproduction.

To be sure, female nu is polluting to men; but in the larger scheme of things, many individuals, both men and women, must avoid contact with the nu of another. Thus males, as well as females, can be sources of pollution. Over their lives, men and women fluctuate in terms of their pollution and their vulnerability to pollution. Children start out fairly high in pollution due to their recent contact with the mother in childbirth. Male children increasingly shed this pollution; then, when they become young men, they strive for a height of "purity" attained by avoiding contact with women and observing a number of taboos. Later in life, through marriage and contact with women, men increasingly absorb pollution from women; yet they also become less vulnerable to pollution in the process. By the time they are old, they no longer need to observe the many taboos designed to keep males "pure." At this point, the Hua say, they become "like women." For women the process is different. Their maximum pollution period occurs between menarche and menopause, but over time they lose some of this pollution, expelling it through menstruation and childbirth. Eventually, a woman past menopause, who has borne three or more children, becomes largely free of her own pollution, is allowed into the men's house, and can participate in otherwise secret male knowledge and rituals. At this point, however, she is most vulnerable to pollution by others and must submit to many of the same restrictions that young men observe to keep themselves "pure." The Hua say such a woman has become "like a man."

---

[1] An example of the latter has been found among the Huli (Glasse 1965: 43). In the bachelors' cult, each member cultivated a bog iris, which, according to Glasse, originated in ground saturated with menstrual blood. These irises, along with a tube containing a female ancestor's blood kept by the cult, were believed by the Huli to protect the health of the young men.

Descent, Residence, and Female Pollution

We may never find a fully satisfactory explanation of all the ideas about female pollution and general aversion to women that are expressed, at least in some contexts and by some men at a certain stage of their lives, in so many societies of Melanesia. But several ideas are both interesting and pertinent to our discussion of gender, descent, and reproduction. One very tempting theory is that all the ways and means by which women and sex with women are culturally denigrated are really mechanisms of population control, or cultural birth-control devices (Lindenbaum 1972). Males are taught to fear and avoid women, and sex is surrounded with restrictions in order to reduce actual rates of intercourse, pregnancy, and, ultimately, fertility. Some evidence supports this theory, but it is also weakened on many grounds. For one thing, we saw in the Huli case that despite all the fears and restrictions directed at sex, it is most permitted within marriage during the period of a wife's ovulation. Moreover, throughout the New Guinea highlands, it is young, unmarried males who are exhorted to fear and avoid women; older, married men evidently experience far less concern over the "dangers" of women and themselves show interest in procreation (Gelber 1986: 117). As we also saw among the Huli, married men attend "courting parties" from which unmarried men and married women are excluded.

Another theory is one we might call the "gerontocracy argument." It suggests that in many areas of Melanesia, older males have and vigorously seek to maintain dominance over women and junior males (Gelber 1986). These older males compete with one another to become socially prominent members of society or "big men" (informal leaders). Their success depends on the prestige they gain through displays of lavish feasting and the ability to participate in trade and ritual exchanges of pigs and other valued commodities. Since women raise pigs, men's control over women and their labor is thus a vital resource in the competition with other men. In many Melanesian societies men also gain from bridewealth transactions and, hence, seek to maintain control over the marriages of females. In addition, according to this argument, older men want sexual access to women and so reduce competition from younger men by training them to fear and avoid women. Thus older men seem to have considerably eased their own fears of women and sex at the same time that they are socializing younger males to fear and dread intercourse.

Keesing (1982) supports the gerontocracy argument in his analysis of gender in Kwaio society. According to him, the Kwaio beliefs and rituals associated with the powerful ancestors serve to strengthen the privileged societal status of adult males, who control the ancestral cult: "The physical strength of mature adulthood sustained the power of adult men. . . . But so, too, did power of the *adalo* [ancestors]. . . . This control of ancestral knowledge and power gave seniors a political power in the community far beyond their sheer physical strength" (Keesing 1982: 227).

As for female pollution, Keesing (1982: 227–228) suggests that "it is the dominance of men over women that is most directly sustained by the ideology of pollution, and the myriad rules that bind women's lives." Keesing (1982: 141) also notes that women, not men, do the labor of raising the pigs for human consumption and sacrifice to the ancestors. But after ritual sacrifice, the pork is almost exclusively consumed by men.

Keesing offers an interesting argument that ties in Kwaio gender relationships with its system of descent. In speculating that the Kwaio descent system grew out of an earlier matrilineal base, he notes that the closest linguistic relatives of the Kwaio all had matrilineal systems and, significantly, "none, apparently, had similar ideologies about isolating the dangers of menstruation and childbirth" (Keesing 1982: 228). In his view, the emergence of patrilineal and cognatic principles in Kwaio society "and the emergence of the polluting powers of women were probably closely connected" (Keesing 1982: 229).

According to Marilyn Gelber (1986), another factor helps account for the antagonism directed against women in the New Guinea highlands, and this one, too, relates to the issues of descent and residence. In her view, New Guinea highland corporate kin groups, the cores of social organization, are highly unstable given their fluid, shifting memberships. This, she says, is true both of societies with cognatic descent (e.g., the Huli) and of the patrilineal societies in New Guinea. The latter are ideologically patrilineal: Their members say that rights to membership in the group are transmitted patrilineally. But in fact many cognatic kin join these groups, and, after a few generations, their descendants are similar to real, patrilineally related members. Thus these New Guinea groups function very much like the cognatic societies we have reviewed. As corporate groups they may have benefited ecologically from shifting, fluid memberships, but one problem is that they were engaged in active warfare. For purposes of defense, the males of these groups needed to come together and cooperate; yet fluid group membership divided their loyalties. To reunite for purposes of defense, males deflected their antagonism onto women and sought cohesion in opposition to women.[2] As Gelber (1986: 55–56) puts it:

---

[2] L. L. Langness (1967) expressed a similar idea about males opposing women in order to promote the male solidarity needed in highland New Guinea warfare. And M. J. Meggitt (1964) suggested that male antagonism toward women would tend to be found in those New Guinea societies where marriage took place between hostile, warring groups. In such cases, affinal women would presumably have been associated with the "enemy."

I would suggest that the exclusion of women from ritual, the explicit devaluation of women's worth and the concomitant emphasis on the value of being a man . . . and the view of women as a mysterious and dangerous unknown quantity, may be explained in part by the significant contribution of these attitudes to a feeling of sameness, cohesiveness, and fellowship among men. . . . [B]y seeing women as outsiders, the men of a local group make themselves "insiders" with respect to one another.

Bilateral Societies

As discussed in Chapter 1, a bilateral society is one that traces kin connections over the generations through both males and females, but without the formation of corporate descent groups. Thus the descent idea is the same in bilateral societies as in cognatic ones; but the latter use this idea to form descent groups, whereas bilateral societies do not.[3]

Euro-American societies are bilateral, but there are also many other bilateral groups elsewhere in the world. One example is the Rungus of Malaysia (G. Appell 1976; L. Appell, 1988). These people cultivate rice, maize, and other crops and raise chickens, pigs, and water buffalo. They live in longhouses, and their postmarital residence is normally matrilocal. A husband moves to the bride's house, and bride and groom live with her parents for about one agricultural season. Then the husband builds a separate family apartment attached to the longhouse and the couple resides there. Longhouses may contain anywhere from two to thirty-two separate apartments, each accommodating a married couple along with any children they may have (G. Appell 1976: 79). The longhouse is not a corporate group; it does not hold common property. Rather, it is best seen as an aggregate of separate nuclear families. Each family constitutes a separate unit of production and consumption.

Each Rungus village, which comprises between one and five longhouses, is led by a headman. Villages can be seen as corporate units since they control land-use rights. But rights to village membership are not based on descent. A person has a right to reside in a village and use its land if he or she was born in the village or married someone there or, failing these connec-

---

[3] Anthropologists use the terms *cognatic* and *bilateral* in different ways. Some refer to them interchangeably. Others consider *bilateral* to be a subtype of *cognatic*, saying that bilateral societies form kin groups on the basis of kindred rather than descent. Keesing (1975) distinguished cognatic societies from societies with "bilateral kinship" and reserved the term *descent* for specifically those societies that form descent groups on the basis of descent from a common ancestor. Finally, Fox (1989) categorized societies according to both their method of recruitment to groups and their system of "focus" (i.e., whether the system was ego-focused or ancestor-focused).

tions, can make an application for membership to the headman, which can be accepted or rejected. Once in, each family farms a piece of land separately, using the surplus to acquire other goods from the market.

Inheritance of family property (excluding land, which is not privately owned by families) is essentially bilateral. For the marriage of their son, parents provide the bridewealth, consisting of brassware, ceramicware, and other items, and this becomes the joint property of the bride's parents and their unmarried children. Some of it may be used to pay the bridewealth for sons. When a daughter marries, her parents may give her and her husband some movable property. Any items not given by the time a couple is old and unable to farm usually go to the youngest child who stays with the couple.

The most important unit in Rungus society is the nuclear family. Although families aggregate in longhouses and cooperate with one another, there are no corporate descent groups among the Rungus. In other words, married couples (with children, if they exist) and villages are corporate units, but there are no groupings of descendants of a common ancestor that are corporate.

Laura Appell (1988) describes the Rungus as a case of "gender symmetry." The generally egalitarian relationships between the sexes appear unrelated to the fact that the society is bilateral. Instead, the relative gender symmetry might be related to matrilocality, to the economic roles of males and females, and to certain Rungus religious beliefs. Males are involved in the political sphere and act as informal heads of families, but in the domestic sphere female contributions are valued and considered complementary to those of males. Women also have specialized roles as spirit mediums. Another striking feature is the central Rungus premise that illicit sexual relations (defined as any sexual relations outside marriage) are dangerous to the whole society: "Any illicit sexual relationship causes 'heat' to radiate outward from the offending couple. This heat angers the spirits, who then cause illness and crop failure. Thus the act of fornication or adultery will affect the health of the offending couple, the families, the longhouse members, the village, and the world at large" (L. Appell 1988: 100). Not only are males and females equally trained and cautioned to avoid illicit sex, but the consequences of failing to do so are the same for both sexes. Interestingly, this society is also one in which there are no menstrual restrictions whatever.

Double and Cognatic Concerns

Recall that among the Beng, the group that recognizes double descent, it is *heterosexuality* and not *female* sexuality that is regarded as potentially dangerous and thus must be regulated. Female fertility is clearly valued in this society. Both the matriclan and the patriclan have interests in each new birth; but the two groups, each with their separate activities and functions, are not threatened by each other and do not compete over the fertility of women. The Beng require that different types of clans be kept separate; yet they view heterosexual intercourse as, metaphorically, a mixing of these clans. Hence sex is potentially dangerous and regulated by certain taboos. As noted, any improper sexual activity (especially sex in the forest) threatens both female fertility and crop fertility. Moreover, the dangerousness of sex applies as much to males as to females; after violating sexual taboos, men are as polluted, and as subject to punishment, as women.

The Beng case is thus quite different from the cognatic societies considered here, in which *female* sexuality is expressed as dangerous and polluting to men. Of course, cognatic descent and beliefs about female pollution are not invariably linked. There are cognatic societies in the world that do not express these beliefs, and, as we saw above, there are patrilineal societies in New Guinea that do express them. Still, following the lead of others, I suggest that a connection *does* exist between cognatic descent and cultural visions of women as dangerous and polluting. This contention, at least as it applies to the groups covered here, is supported by evidence indicating that cognatic descent and flexible rules of residence give kin groups uncertain control over female fertility, or over their own reproduction.

Melanesian beliefs and practices concerning female pollution may seem extreme, and, indeed, we may find it difficult to view them as anything other than forms of female subordination. Yet this is not the whole picture. For one thing, the other side of dangerous pollution is power. Recall Keesing's (1982: 221) observation that the Kwaio belief in women's menstrual pollution gives women "dangerous weapons" and "establishes a separate base for women's power." Also note Meigs' (1984) caution with respect to the interpretation of female pollution beliefs. According to her study, in the Hua society both men and women are sources of pollution, and relationships among men, women, and pollution change over the life course.

With this chapter we end our discussion of gender in relation to different modes of descent. The next chapter covers marriage, the institution through which new kin relationships are formed and perpetuated.

References

Appell, G. N. 1976. The Rungus: Social Structure in a Cognatic Society and Its Ritual Symbolization. In G. N. Appell, ed., *The Societies of Borneo: Explorations in the Theory of Cognatic Social Structure*, No. 6. A Special Publication of the American Anthropological Association.

Appell, Laura W. R. 1988. Menstruation Among the Rungus of Borneo: An Unmarked Category. In Thomas Buckley and Alma Gottlieb, eds., *Blood Magic: The Anthropology of Menstruation*, pp. 94–112. Berkeley: University of California Press.

Buckley, Thomas, and Alma Gottlieb. 1988. A Critical Appraisal of Theories of Menstrual Symbolism. In Thomas Buckley and Alma Gottlieb, eds., *Blood Magic: The Anthropology of Menstruation*, pp. 1–50. Berkeley: University of California Press.

Fox, Robin. 1989 [orig. 1967]. *Kinship and Marriage: An Anthropological Perspective*. Cambridge: Cambridge University Press.

Gelber, Marilyn G. 1986. *Gender and Society in the New Guinea Highlands: An Anthropological Perspective on Antagonism Toward Women*. Boulder: Westview Press.

Glasse, Robert M. 1965. The Huli of the Southern Highlands. In P. Lawrence and M. J. Meggitt, eds., *Gods, Ghosts and Men in Melanesia: Some Religions of Australian New Guinea and the New Hebrides*, pp. 27–49. London: Oxford University Press.

———. 1968. *Huli of Papua: A Cognatic Descent System*. Paris/The Hague: Mouton and Co.

Gottlieb, Alma. 1986. Cousin Marriage, Birth Order and Gender: Alliance Models Among the Beng of Ivory Coast. *Man* 21: 697–722.

———. 1988. Menstrual Cosmology Among the Beng of Ivory Coast. In Thomas Buckley and Alma Gottlieb, eds., *Blood Magic: The Anthropology of Menstruation*, pp. 55–74.Berkeley: University of California Press.

———. 1989a. Rethinking Female Pollution: The Beng of Côte d'Ivoire. *Dialectical Anthropology* 14: 65–79.

———. 1989b. Witches, Kings, and the Sacrifice of Identity, or The Power of Paradox and the Paradox of Power Among the Beng of Ivory Coast. In W. Arens and Ivan Karp, eds., *Creativity of Power: Cosmology and Action in African Societies*, pp. 245–272. Washington, D.C.: Smithsonian Institution Press.

———. 1992. *Under the Kapok Tree: Identity and Difference in Beng Thought*. Bloomington: Indiana University Press.

Keesing, Roger M. 1970. Shrines, Ancestors, and Cognatic Descent: The Kwaio and Tallensi. *American Anthropologist* 72: 755–75.

———. 1975. *Kin Groups and Social Structure*. Fort Worth, Tex.: Holt, Rinehart and Winston.

———. 1982. *Kwaio Religion: The Living and the Dead in Solomon Island Society*. New York: Columbia University Press.

———. 1987. Ta'a Geni: Women's Perspectives on Kwaio Society. In Marilyn Strathern, ed., *Dealing with Inequality: Analysing Gender Relations in Melanesia and Beyond*, pp. 33–62. Cambridge: Cambridge University Press.

Langness, L. L. 1967. Sexual Antagonism in the New Guinea Highlands: A Bena Bena Example. *Oceania* 37: 161–177.

Lindenbaum, Shirley. 1972. Sorcerers, Ghosts, and Polluting Women: An Analysis of Religious Belief and Population Control. *Ethnology* 11: 241–253.

Meggitt, M. J. 1964. Male-Female Relationships in the Highlands of Australian New Guinea. *American Anthropologist* 66: 204–224.

Meigs, Anna S. 1984. *Food, Sex and Pollution: A New Guinea Religion*. New Brunswick: Rutgers University Press.

Sinclair, Karen. 1986. Mischief on the Margins. Paper presented at the meeting of the Association of Social Anthropology in Oceania, New Harmony, Indiana.

6

Marriage

Every society in the world has something we might roughly recognize as "marriage." But beyond this, little can be said of marriage that holds cross-culturally. We may think of marriages as uniting males and females; yet we have already seen that Nuer woman-woman marriage is an exception to this, as are modern marriages of homosexual couples. We might expect that sex is universally permitted within marriage, only to discover that certain early Christian cults practiced, or tried to practice, celibate marriage. Usually marriage is enacted with some kind of ceremony, often religious in nature; but there are plenty of cases where this is not done or, at least, is not obligatory. Often marriage is associated with the legitimizing of children, or the allocation of rights over children. But this would not apply to the Navajo, for whom a child born out of wedlock still acquires full rights in his or her mother's clan, suffering no disadvantages. And we have already seen that marriage does not always involve participants in a common domestic unit or common residence. In short, perhaps the only generalization one can make about marriage is that everywhere it entails intimate, if not emotionally charged, relationships between spouses, and everywhere it creates in-laws.

In this chapter we explore two dimensions of marriage: first, relationships between spouses in terms of differences in marriage forms (monogamy, polygyny, and polyandry) and, second, the creation of in-laws, or the nature of marriage as a mechanism for alliance. This investigation will return us to the questions raised in Chapter 2 concerning the origin of gender inequality.

Monogamy, Polygyny, and Polyandry

Human societies feature three types of heterosexual marital unions: monogamy, or the union of one man and one woman; polygyny, a union between one man and two or more women; and polyandry, the marriage of one woman with two or more men. Societies characterized as "monogamous," such as Euro-American societies, do not legally permit the other types of union. "Polygynous" societies are those that permit polygyny. Monogamous unions also occur in the latter, but polygyny is allowed and possibly preferred by some people. A great many cultural groups in the world are polygynous in this sense; but within these groups most of the marital unions are monogamous. The religion of Islam permits a man to take up to four wives, but the incidence of polygyny is low in many Islamic areas. Some African societies show relatively high rates of polygyny (up to or even exceeding 30 percent of all marital unions). Many groups in Asia also permit polygyny, but here, in contrast to Africa, it occurs at significantly lower rates. Finally, polyandry is very rare. In the few societies where it is permitted, polygyny and monogamy are usually also practiced (Levine and Sangree 1980).

We have already seen examples of polygyny and polyandry in previous case studies—for example, polygyny among the Nuer and, more rarely, the Nepalese Brahmans, and polyandry-polygyny among the Nayar. From these case studies it should now be clear that even the same types of unions work differently in different societies. Among the Nepalese Brahmans, polygyny is permitted but rare; for the most part it is arranged when a first wife is childless. Women usually view it negatively, as a kind of punishment for their childlessness. Among the Nuer, polygyny was not only more common but also apparently preferred by men as a sign of wealth or prestige. (What women thought about it is less clear.) It was also used by Nuer men as a strategy to acquire children or increase the number of their children. By contrast, among the matrilineal Nayar a man's ability to have and visit several wives was not considered a strategy to increase the number of his legal children.

Plural unions inevitably raise questions about sexual jealousy. Most Euro-American women simply could not imagine, let alone tolerate, taking on a co-wife. Of course, Euro-American marriages are not arranged by kin and are ideologically rooted in the tradition of romantic love. But ethnographic studies show that, among societies with relatively high rates of polygynous unions, there is considerable individual and group variation in women's responses to these unions. Co-wife jealousy and mutual accusations of witchcraft occur alongside reports of peaceful cooperation among co-wives, or even of co-wives happily ganging up on a husband to secure their own ends. And of course in some polygynous societies, women cooperate with husbands for reproduction and domestic concerns but then have their own lovers on the side.

The effects of a predominant or prevalent type of marriage union on gender must be considered separately for each society and within the particular cultural context of each group. Euro-American women may feel that a co-wife would be most unsatisfactory, but not so many years ago many women of this culture felt it was perfectly appropriate for wives to be economically dependent on their husbands and for a double sexual standard to exist in their society. In some West African polygynous societies, women are and always have been economically independent, a circumstance that gives them considerable freedom to develop their own social lives and pursue their own interests apart from their marriages.

And what about polyandry? This form of marriage has fascinated anthropologists and other outside observers perhaps more than any other. For one thing, as noted, polyandry is rare. As we have seen, the Nayar of South India practiced it, but it also occurs (or occurred) among some Tibetan peoples, some groups in northern Nepal, some hill tribes in India, and the Shoshoni Indians of Nevada, as well as on the Marquesas Islands (Polynesia) and in a few other places in South Asia, Africa, and the Americas. Polyandry can take a variety of forms, one of which is **fraternal polyandry,** whereby a set of brothers shares a wife. Another, as exemplified by the Nayar, is **nonfraternal polyandry,** whereby the husbands are not brothers; indeed, among the Nayar, brothers could not be the visiting husbands of the same woman. There are many other variations in terms of residence patterns, property rights, and sexual arrangements in polyandrous societies.

In earlier years the study of polyandry was clouded by male biases. Some (male) observers were so upset about these unions that they branded them as perverted or decided they didn't constitute marriage at all. Only recently have we had access to more serious and objective studies of polyandry (e.g., Aziz 1978; Goldstein 1976; Schuler 1987; Levine 1988). Nancy Levine (1988: 4), whose work constitutes the next case study, pinpoints the problem behind these previous male biases in the study of polyandry: Some observers found it simply inconceivable that males would willingly give up their exclusive sexual and reproductive rights to their wives. And when they did not find sexual jealousy among polyandrous husbands, they (e.g., Aiyappan 1937) simply assumed that the jealousy was being "repressed." Levine (1988: 170) raises a good question: "Why do we assume that sharing a spouse is impossible for men, but not for polygynous women?" As Levine notes, these reactions to polyandry tell us more about our own culture's ideas about gender than about how polyandry actually works.

The following study is a case of fraternal polyandry. But, first, I should mention one important effect that fraternal polyandry may have—namely, low population growth. It's easy to see how this consequence comes about. Let's say a set of three brothers acquires one wife. She can produce only so many children in one lifetime; let's say she produces three. If the three brothers had each taken equally fertile wives, they would have produced a total of nine children. By the same reckoning, polyandry can function with fewer women than men in the population. Indeed, some anthropologists (e.g., Goldstein 1976) have argued that polyandry develops in part as a device for population control, given that it often exists in areas with scarce or precarious environmental resources. It keeps the population down and so maintains a balance between humans and the natural environment. Although Levine's study of the polyandrous Nyinba describes this phenomenon, it also suggests that population control by itself is insufficient to account for polyandry.

CASE 8: NYINBA POLYANDRY

When anthropologist Nancy Levine first entered a Nyinba village, she was struck with its relative wealth:

> I will never forget my first journey there and the impoverished villages I passed along the way. . . . [I]t was springtime, people were hungry and, lacking food for themselves, had none for sale. . . . When I finally reached . . . the first Nyinba village on the main road, there was a dramatic change of scene. The road suddenly widened; it was better maintained, lined by fruit trees in bloom, and bordered by broad, carefully terraced fields. . . . [T]he houses seemed large and the village well planned. . . . This extraordinary wealth in a difficult environment owes much to the system of polyandry, as I was to find out. (Levine 1988: xiv)

The polyandrous Nyinba are a small group of Tibetan people, numbering just over 1,300 persons. Their ancestors came from Tibet, but, like the Brahmans discussed in an earlier chapter (Case 2), the Nyinba now live in the country of Nepal. Culturally, however, they are quite different from the Nepalese Brahmans. The Nyinba speak a dialect of Western Tibetan, follow the religion of Buddhism, and have their own distinctive way of life based on herding and long-distance trade as well as agriculture.

The Nyinba reside in four villages in the far northwest of Nepal, a particularly remote and rugged region. This environmental factor is important: Since resources here are limited and difficult to manage, population expansion would put considerable pressure on these resources, resulting in increased poverty and environmental degradation (as has happened elsewhere in the country). But as noted, polyandry can support low population growth, and this is partly why the polyandrous Nyinba have been successful in the region and, indeed, why their relatively wealthy villages so impressed Levine. In addition, polyandry is central to a particular domestic economy that the Nyinba have developed and that has helped them sustain relative prosperity.

Many Nyinba males are away from their villages for long periods of time. Following particular routes, they simultaneously herd their goats and sheep and trade in salt, grain, and other items, moving all the way from

Tibet to northern India. When in their villages, men also engage in agricultural activities; but the routine tasks of agriculture are largely women's work. Women clear fields, apply compost, weed, and do the husking, drying, winnowing, and storing of grain. They also weave, fetch water, wash clothes, cook and serve food, and take care of children—all tasks that keep them close to home inside their villages. The Nyinba highly value male labor, especially trading. But women's work is relatively devalued, even though its contribution to subsistence is substantial. Women's work is seen as dull and simple, whereas men's work is seen as more diverse and requiring skill.

In times past, Nyinba society was divided into slaves and masters. Slaves lived in small houses adjacent to large master households and performed agricultural and domestic labor. They could be bought, sold, and inherited by masters. Slavery was abolished in Nepal in 1929; but after emancipation most of the former Nyinba slaves remained in their villages. Some stayed on as dependent freedmen of their former masters, continuing to labor for the large household in exchange for food, shelter, and the right to grow crops on small plots of land. Others broke away, acquired land of their own, and became economically independent and wealthier than the dependent freedmen group.

There remains a sharp status distinction between the descendants of former slaves and the descendants of former masters. The latter are the larger group, constituting about 87 percent of the population. In slave times, the two groups did not intermarry. More recently, the freedmen group that acquired land and became economically independent has gradually sought to raise its status over the generations through intermarriage with the former master group.

The Nyinba are patrilineal and largely patrilocal. It sometimes happens that parents have a daughter but no sons, and in this case they may bring in a husband to live matrilocally with them and inherit their estate. But this arrangement is not the ideal. The parents-in-law tend to distrust the incoming husband as an outsider. Although they need the new husband, they are also suspicious of him because he is a person willing to leave his own father and brothers.

The Nyinba are organized into patrilineal clans, which are descent categories, not corporate groups. The clans are exogamous, and sexual relations are also forbidden and considered incestuous between clan members. Clans do have religious significance inasmuch as members of one clan worship a set of common clan gods.

In slave times, the slaves themselves were, of course, a group apart and had no connection with the patrilineal clans of the master group. Interestingly, whereas the master group was polyandrous and patrilocal, the slaves were monogamous and matrilocal. It was the slave owners "who decided to keep slave women at home and bring them husbands from other slave households" (Levine 1988: 73). One result of this arrangement was that slave households became female-centered and slave women played a dominant role within them. At the same time, the master group considered monogamy and matrilocality to be signs of slave inferiority. Today, dependent freedmen continue these domestic patterns; the independent, landholding group, meanwhile, has been adopting polyandry and patrilocality.

Along with patrilineal descent, the Nyinba recognize important relationships traced through women. These are best seen in relation to Nyinba notions of heredity. The Nyinba say that fathers contribute their "bone" to a child, passing it on through their sperm, and that mothers contribute "blood." But the father's contribution is more important in the sense that males are believed to contribute more to a child's character and physical appearance. Also, when a woman produces a child, she passes on something of the "bone" of her father, which within her has become transformed into "blood." In this way a child has an hereditary link to his or her mother's patrilineal clan. Note, too, that the children of two sisters are considered closely related by "blood" through their mothers. Being so related, the children of sisters, though of different clans, cannot marry.

Kinship based on patrilineal descent as well as on relationships through women is very important to the Nyinba, who say that one can only really trust one's kin. This sentiment is expressed clearly, as we shall see, in their polyandrous marriages.

For Nyinba, an important group is the *trongba*. Trongbas are corporate, landholding households. Each trongba has a special name that, along with a personal name, is used to identify individuals. Trongba members own land, houses, domestic animals, and other property in common. Each trongba also has a shrine to its own gods who protect the household. The shrine consists of arrows (a symbol of male continuity), with one arrow added every New Year. When a bride moves into a trongba, her hand is tied to the arrows with a thread that remains a part of the shrine.

Sons of the trongba will jointly inherit the estate and are to remain together for life. Ideally, the trongba should not split up or partition its property. But sometimes a trongba grows too large or its members come into conflict, in which case a partition takes place. Thus, although partition is generally discouraged in a village, it is occasionally seen as necessary. The Nyinba prefer to maintain a stable village size, which for them means a stable number of village households. If at times a number of households die out, then village growth by partition of other trongba is needed.

At the core of Nyinba culture, interwoven with many aspects of daily life, is polyandry. The Nyinba practice fraternal polyandry, the marriage of a set of brothers to one common wife. Virtually all males who have brothers marry polyandrously. All brothers are equally husbands to their wife;

they all have sexual and procreative rights to this woman. Even if another brother is born *after* the marriage of his older brothers, he will, when mature, automatically acquire sexual and procreative rights to her. Ideally, a woman is expected to treat all her husbands equally, without sexually excluding any of them. It is all right if she feels or shows more affection for one over others so long as she does not deny any brother roughly equal sexual time and equal chance to father her children. In real life, of course, not all marriages conform to this ideal; yet sexual jealousy among brothers is rare.

Regarding the actual arranging of sex, Levine (1988: 164) writes that "for most couples, the problem of sexual equity is handled by having the wife spend an entire night with one husband at a time and with all husbands in more or less equal measure." The planning of sex is open and flexible, and the wife participates in the process along with her husbands: "Plans may be made early in the day, through glances, an exchange of words, and so on. At night, some women go to their husband's beds; others think this is too forward and let their husbands come to them" (Levine 1988: 164).

When the brothers and their wife are still quite young and under the authority of their parents, it may be the parents who decide the matter, "literally assigning people to various beds in the house" (Levine 1988: 164). With parental regulation, a precedent for sexual equity can be set early in the marriage. In addition, decisions about sex may occasionally be simplified when some brothers are away trading. And there is a general rule that when a brother returns from a long trading trip, he should have precedence to spend the night with the wife.

Sexual relations are not confined to marriage for either men or women. Indeed, Levine (1988: 148) reports that "virtually all women engage in extra-marital affairs, most frequently in the early years of their marriage." Men accept this situation, without necessarily approving of it; but if the affair becomes public, the woman's lover can be fined and a man might beat his wife for adultery. There is little that wives can do to prevent or stop the affairs of husbands; a woman may be motivated, however, to try to curtail the adulterous behavior of a favorite among her husbands.

Other forms of marriage are also permitted and practiced by the Nyinba, as is generally true of all polyandrous societies. Among the Nyinba, monogamy may come about naturally—for example, with the marriage of a man who has no brothers. Or it may result when a woman marries two brothers and one of them dies. But such outcomes are related to particular circumstances and changes over time; they do not represent options or preferences. In fact, among the Nyinba "there is no notion of monogamy as opposed to polyandry" (Levine 1988: 157). Marriage is simply perceived polyandrously: Brothers have rights in a common wife. But given all the fluctuations in individual cases, only slightly more than half of all Nyinba marriages turn out to be polyandrous.

Polygyny, though not common, is also practiced. It is acceptable when a first wife is childless. In this event, the brothers will add another wife to the marriage but still maintain the first one. Childless women are pitied, but childlessness by itself is not considered a sufficient reason for divorce. Levine (1988: 144) reports that in 1983, 1.3 percent of Nyinba marriages were cases of "polygynous polyandry." Nonpolyandrous polygyny can also occur. For example, a sonless couple may bring in a single husband for a daughter, in which case this man will inherit the estate. Although the arrangement starts out as simple monogamy, the bride's sisters may later join the marriage.

Yet another possibility is what Levine calls "conjoint marriage." Here, one or more brothers in a polyandrous union becomes dissatisfied in the marriage and then seeks to bring in another wife. This may happen for any number of reasons. Perhaps there are many brothers involved (say, four or more) and it becomes too difficult for one woman to cook, serve, do laundry for, and have sex with all of them. Or it may be that one or more brothers is much younger than the common wife, originally brought in by an older brother. Levine (1988: 166) writes of one youngest brother who, "in his early teens, felt that the wife treated him like a small boy or ignored him."

When a new woman joins a household in conjoint marriage, theoretically all the brothers will have sexual and procreative rights to her as well as to their first wife. But in these cases of multiple husbands and wives, distinct "subcouples" may end up forming more exclusive sexual relationships. Partition is often the result, with the groups later splitting along the lines of the subcouples into separate households. Conjoint marriages are discouraged because they so readily establish lines for partition.

Another potential cause of disharmony in the group is the presence of two childbearing women in a marriage. The two (or more) wives may not get along, and they may compete with one another to advance the interests of their own separate children. Since any sons they produce either are not brothers or are just paternal half-brothers, close brotherhood, the mainstay of the Nyinba household, is lost in the next generation. Conjoint marriages are rare, accounting for only 5 percent of all polyandrous marriages.

Reproduction, especially of sons, is important to the Nyinba. Sons will jointly inherit and carry on the management of the trongba estate; and they will patrilineally carry on the name of the ancestors. They are also expected to care for parents in old age. Daughters may be valued for the alliances with other households that their marriages will bring, but female children are not otherwise seen as long-term assets; as adults they will leave the household, contributing their labor and reproduction to another.

Wives, not husbands, are blamed for childlessness. As Levine (1988: 148) writes: "Discovering this, I asked several people if there were no sterile men. The response was that there might be, but no one knew of any cases." Of course, given polyandry and the fact that many women have extramarital affairs, any fertile woman is likely to become pregnant (Levine 1988: 149).

One might suppose that with polyandry there would be little interest among brothers in identifying individual paternity. Interestingly, just the opposite is the case. Nyinba men are very concerned about siring their own biological children, and about determining which of a woman's children are theirs. In some cases the latter is easy to do, since women keep track of their periods and sexual activity over each month, and it may be that not all brothers are home at the same time. Or, for a few years during a marriage, the eldest husband's brothers may be too young for sexual activity. But "inevitably there are pregnancies where the father could be any of several husbands. Then the parents wait for the birth of the child and compare its appearance to the men to make an assignment of paternity" (Levine 1988: 167).

The fact that wives are primarily responsible for paternity assignments gives them some power in the household: "Women may use paternity designations for political purposes: to please a husband who feels himself neglected, to insure that all her children are fathered by the man or men with whom she is likely to partition, and for other pragmatic reasons. . . . [B]oth men and women say that wives can use their rights of paternity designation to mask illegitimacies" (Levine 1988: 167). Once designated, the relation between a father and his child becomes a close one; and children are told who their "real" father is. A son must have a designated father in order to gain full membership in the trongba and rights of inheritance in it; and a daughter must have a designated father in order to receive a dowry upon marriage. Men seek to have their own sons in part because these offspring are considered a more secure source of support in old age.

The key to Nyinba polyandry and inseparable from it is the corporate household, or trongba, and its management. The ideal trongba is a large group consisting mostly of males, spanning a few generations. It is considered best to have only one fertile wife for each set of brothers in each generation, and best for each woman to have sons. Brothers should stay together in strong solidarity and keep the trongba land and other property undivided. The Nyinba point out that polyandry supports fraternal solidarity and keeps brothers together: If they all had separate wives, their interests would be divided and the brothers would split.

As mentioned, the Nyinba value the labor of males and especially their economic contributions from trade. They seek to have many men in a household, an outcome that is fostered by polyandry. Women also say that they prefer polyandry because having more than one husband brings them greater economic security (Levine 1981: 113). But this arrangement may also bring about a shortage of female labor in a household. Although female labor is not highly valued, it is recognized as essential to agriculture and, hence, to subsistence. In the past, slavery filled the gap caused by this labor shortage, since slaves did "women's work"—routine agricultural tasks and domestic labor. Thus slavery facilitated polyandry. In the process it carried implications for gender, too. Slaves were associated with "females" and female roles, masters with "males" and male roles. Both slaves and women were economically and politically dependent on nonslave males. Today, since slavery is no longer practiced, the same labor need is filled by a trongba's dependent freedmen or hired laborers.[1]

An important consequence of polyandry is that it fosters low population growth: The marriage of one woman to multiple brothers produces fewer children per household than there would be if each brother took a separate wife. In addition, marriageable women are not a scarce commodity, since only one is needed for each set of brothers rather than one for each adult male. Given the strong favoring of sons over daughters, sons are better treated and cared for. As a result, more sons than daughters live to adulthood. The sex ratio among adult Nyinba living in trongba households is 118 men to 100 women.[2]

Nyinba polyandry is also interwoven with important kinship concepts and values. One is the emphasis placed on fraternal solidarity, as already discussed. Another is the Nyinba idea that only close kin can really be trusted, or that people who are close kin will have a smoother relationship in a household. This idea is manifested in a number of ways. First, the marriage of certain cousins is permitted. The Nyinba say that this arrangement is advantageous inasmuch as a new woman entering a household as a wife will already be related to her husbands and especially to her parents-in-law (i.e., her father-in-law will be her uncle or her mother-in-law will be her aunt). It may be especially advantageous for the mother-in-law and daughter-in-law to be aunt and niece since, otherwise, this relationship can be tense. For instance, a mother-in-law may assign a daughter-in-law the heaviest and hardest work. But then later, when the mother-in-law is old and the daughter-in-law is running the household, "she can be equally difficult and make her mother-in-law's retirement miserable by withholding food and pushing her parents-in-law out of the warm hearth where the rest of the family sleeps" (Levine 1988: 119). Second, Nyinba point out that when a

---

[1] The trongba generally hires as laborers either poor freedmen or poor people from other ethnic groups in the region.

[2] Worldwide, the average sex ratio among adults is 95 men to 102 women (Levine 1988: 74).

first wife is infertile and a new wife must be brought in, it is best to choose a sister of the first wife (a case of sororal polygyny). Sisters are more likely to cooperate as co-wives, whereas unrelated women may not get along. Third, as we have already seen, conjoint marriage is discouraged in part because two or more childbearing women in a house may produce sons who are not brothers by the same woman and so are not as closely related. And males with differing maternity, living in one household, may come to distrust one another.

The Nyinba have a proverb: "As you change the sole of your shoe, so can you change your daughter-in-law or wife." The women of the household, as opposed to the men, are seen as substitutable. Each household needs adult women for labor and reproduction, but the males, related to one another as fathers, sons, and brothers, are really the core. Indeed, the Nyinba system, of which polyandry is a central part, supports a large, solid group of closely related males who jointly own, control, and pass on property. Women do not share in the inheritance of this property. At marriage a woman takes a dowry, but this consists of household utensils and jewelry and is not considered to be particularly valuable. In her husband's home, a woman has rights of maintenance, for as long as she lives or until divorce; and her sons will be coparceners of this family property.

A woman may initiate divorce, but if she leaves her husband or husbands and returns to her natal family, she may soon wear out her welcome. Her position there is also somewhat disadvantaged since she lacks the right to inherit natal family property. If she has children, they remain with or eventually return to her ex-husband(s). And other women will be suspicious that she is after their husbands.

Among the Nyinba, female sexuality is subject to little constraint. In many situations married women not only have multiple husbands but engage in extramarital affairs. The main concern is that a married woman must give equal time and reproductive opportunity to her husbands. If she has other affairs, she should be discreet. At the same time, care is taken that her children are allocated to individual husbands. In this connection, Levine and Sangree (1980: 406) note that "it appears to be virtually universal for polyandry to entail a jural separation of a woman's sexual and procreative attributes." In other words, her sexuality can be shared by many men, but each of her children is allocated to a particular husband. This separation between the sexual and reproductive attributes of women recalls the situation of the Nuer (Case 1), in which female sexuality is effectively given free reign but legal paternity is secured through bridewealth cattle payments.

As discussed, Nyinba women are needed for their fertility. However, if a woman is infertile or bears only daughters, the trongba secures heirship through other means—for example, by taking in another wife or finding a husband for a daughter. In terms of both their labor and their fertility, then, women appear to be appreciated but are also seen as easily substitutable.

Nyinba women do have some sources of power. As we have seen, they can use the right to designate the paternity of their children to their own advantage. In addition, each household includes the position of head-woman as a counterpart to the male household head. Still, the male head has formal authority in the household and receives deference from others. This authority is shown by the fact that he "has first rights to occupy the seat directly beneath the main beam and pillar of the hearth room" (Levine 1988: 119). The position of male household head normally passes from father to eldest son, whereas the position of headwoman is generally filled by the senior woman of the household (usually the wife of the household head) and passes at her old age or death to her daughter-in-law. The head-woman supervises women's work. She also has a special seating place above the hearth. It is here that she cooks "with household members surrounding her, and this facilitates her domination over mealtime conversations. Since she serves the meals as well, she can regulate the portions to reward her allies with better or more food" (Levine 1988: 120).

The Nyinba seek sons for a set of brothers through one wife. As noted earlier, the result is low population growth.[3] Many anthropologists have tried to explain the existence of polyandry, in Nepal, Tibet, and elsewhere, in terms of its role in population control. They point out that polyandry tends to occur in areas, such as that inhabited by the Nyinba, where population growth would place considerable stress on already scarce environmental resources. In Levine's (1988) view, however, population control—though clearly related to polyandry—cannot be given as its sole cause or foundation. She points out that many ethnic groups other than the Nyinba live in the same hilly, rugged Nepalese environment but do not practice polyandry. Rather, her work has shown that polyandry among the Nyinba has complex and pervasive connections with the domestic economy, kinship values, household structure, gender, and other cultural traditions of these people.

Marriage and Alliance

The use of marriage as a mechanism for alliance between groups may have been a brilliant human invention, but arranging a marriage between groups is no easy task. In the last three chapters, and in Case 8 especially, we have seen how notions of common descent are frequently associated with kin group solidarity and members' mutual feelings of "oneness." Getting two

---

[3] Population growth among the Nyinba occurs at a rate of 1 to 1.5 percent per year, compared to more than 2.6 percent per year in Nepal overall (Levine 1988: 241–242).

such kin groups to come together and agree to entrust their members in marriage to each other is another matter. In fact, in-law individuals and groups often *mistrust* one another. Possibly this is why many societies practice various forms of in-law avoidance—as we saw, for example, among the Navajo. The mother-in-law jokes told in Euro-American society may similarly both reflect and defuse in-law tensions. In many societies a great deal of time, energy, negotiating, and bickering goes into the arranging of a marriage. And in many societies divorce is frequent enough to indicate a relative fragility of affinal ties.

Euro-American society remains somewhat distinctive in regarding marriage as a means of securing happiness for individuals and in imbuing marriage with notions of romantic love and sexual exclusivity. Throughout most of the rest of the world, especially in the past, marriages have been arranged by kin groups with a view toward their own social, economic, and political interests. Yet in all cultures, Euro-American and otherwise, there is, I think, a basic tension between marriage as a social, political, or economic strategy and marriage as an institution involving individuals in intimate interpersonal relations.

The issue under discussion in this section, marriage as alliance, returns us to the concept of exogamy (marriage outside a certain category or group). Later, we will also examine endogamy as a political and economic marriage strategy. But for now, in the context of marriage as alliance, let us concentrate on descent group exogamy, with special attention to a new piece of kinship jargon: the distinction between **cross cousins** and **parallel cousins.**

Exogamy

Exogamy and Cross-Cousin Marriage

Cross cousins are the children of two opposite-sex siblings. Parallel cousins are the children of two same-sex siblings. Figure 6.1 illustrates both in relation to one ego. The importance of this distinction will be more easily grasped if I confine the discussion to unilineal descent groups (i.e., groups that are either matrilineal or patrilineal). Accordingly, Figure 6.2 shows an ego's cross and parallel cousins in relation to the broader picture of unilineal descent. To clearly illustrate both the matrilineal and patrilineal cases in this diagram, I have darkly shaded the symbols representing ego's patrilineal kin and lightly shaded those representing ego's matrilineal kin. The diagram shows that, for either mode of unilineal descent, ego's cross cousins are always excluded as members of his own unilineal descent group. But his parallel cousins may be members; his MZC will be members of his group if the group is matrilineal and his FBC will be members of his group if the group is patrilineal.

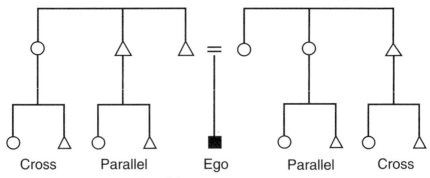

Cross   Parallel   Ego   Parallel   Cross

FIGURE 6.1   Ego's Cross and Parallel Cousins

In some societies, only one type of cross cousin (an FSC or MBC) is permitted as a spouse; in others, both types are permitted. Cross-cousin marriage does not necessarily mean that ego is marrying a first cousin, or that the people involved are systematically practicing first-cousin marriage. It may be that ego is marrying, say, a second or third cross cousin, or, for that matter, any person who is linguistically classified as a cross cousin.

Thus it is easy to see that cross cousins might be permissible spouses in societies that have exogamous descent groups. But why would some societies prescribe or generally prefer cross-cousin marriage? In the next section we will see how cross-cousin marriage has been related to certain types of marital exchanges between groups.

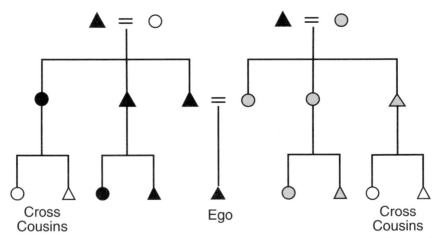

Cross   Ego   Cross
Cousins   Cousins

FIGURE 6.2   Cross Cousins and Unilineal Descent. Ego's patrilineal kin are darkly shaded and the matrilineal kin are lightly shaded. Cross cousins will always be excluded as members of Ego's unilineal descent groups.

Exogamy and Exchange:
Manipulating Women?

In Chapter 1 we examined the idea that rules of exogamy would force groups to look beyond themselves for spouses and develop alliances with other groups. Exogamy would thus help promote peaceful relations, or at least prevent groups from forming only hostile relationships and killing each other off.

Anthropologist Claude Lévi-Strauss (1969) took this line of thinking one step further. First, for societies practicing descent group exogamy, he distinguished between those with "complex" marriage systems and those with "elementary" marriage systems. In the former, there is just a rule that one must marry outside the descent group. Most societies that practice descent group exogamy are of this type. In the latter, there is not only a rule of descent group exogamy specifying whom one *cannot* marry but also rules specifying whom, or into what groups, one *should* marry. Lévi-Strauss then said that early human groups were of this "elementary" type. These groups were not just marrying out, they were systematically *intermarrying* with other groups; they were not just practicing descent group exogamy, they were *exchanging women*. By exchanging women over the generations, these early groups were essentially setting up forms of enduring and perpetual alliances with one another.

The gender implications of this view will be discussed later, but first we need to look at how systematic exchange of spouses works on paper. The simplest place to start is to imagine two sets of brother-sister pairs who intermarry. As illustrated in Figure 6.3, these pairs represent two descent groups, A and B. Let's also assume that the two groups are patrilineal. To clarify who belongs to which descent group, I have shaded in the circle and

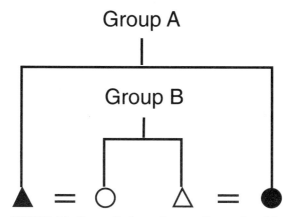

FIGURE 6.3   Spouse Exchange Between Groups A and B. Members of Group A are shaded.

triangle symbolizing the members of patrilineal descent group A. Here, a man of A is marrying a woman of B and a man of B is marrying a woman of A. This exchange may be kept up over the generations, such that the children of these first two unions intermarry, their children also intermarry, and so on. Figure 6.4 shows what happens. In short, every male ego is marrying a FZD who is also a MBD—in other words, a double cross cousin. Likewise, every female ego is marrying a MBS who is also a FZS. Thus cross-cousin marriage (or in this case, double cross-cousin marriage) is a systematic way of perpetuating the alliance between groups A and B over the generations. Another way to put this is to say that if A and B decide to systematically exchange spouses in each generation, the result will be a case of systematic double cross-cousin marriage.

Figure 6.4 is highly idealized. What it shows, in the simplest way possible, is that two unilineal descent groups could practice exogamy, link up through marriage, and perpetuate their alliance over and over. Real societies, of course, deal with much larger numbers of people and greater numbers of descent groups. It may help to look again at this diagram and imagine that the triangles and circles represent not individuals but whole

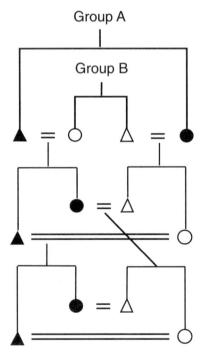

FIGURE 6.4 Systematic Spouse Exchange Between Groups A and B over the Generations. Members of Group A are shaded.

lineages or clans. It is sometimes the case that a group of people is divided up into clans, which in turn are clustered into two moieties, or halves; the marriage rule is then that one must marry into a clan of the moiety opposite one's own.

These types of exchange marriages are no longer common on a world scale, but they have been found, with many variations, among some hunting and gathering peoples. For example, Australian aborigines developed highly complex forms of spouse exchange (sometimes called "section systems") that are variations of the idealized model in Figure 6.4. Lévi-Strauss (1969) interpreted all these versions of spouse exchange among remote hunter-gatherers as evidence of similar kinds of marriage exchange among early humans.

Other ways of arranging marital exchanges between groups are also possible. For example, Group A could give women systematically and in each generation to Group B, which in turn could give its women to Group C, which could then give its women to Group A. A simplified version of this type of exchange is illustrated in Figure 6.5; in real life, of course, many more groups would be involved, and the situation would be far more complex. The diagram focuses on the circulation of women, but a circulation of men could just as easily be represented. Note that the broken circles represent the women of C who are marrying the men of A.

In this type of system, every ego winds up marrying only one type of cross-cousin. A male ego marries his MBD and a female ego marries a FZS.

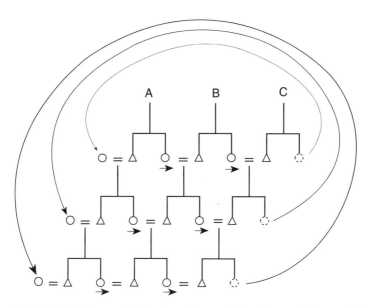

FIGURE 6.5 Systematic Marriages Among Three Groups. Women of A marry men of B; women of B marry men of C; and the women of C (shown in broken circles) marry men of A. Arrows indicate the circulation of the women.

An example of a society that practices this form of marriage is the Purum, a tribal group in India (see Keesing 1975: 85–88).

I could go much further in this vein, showing all sorts of spouse-exchange marriages that entail different kinds of cross-cousin marriage. These systems have preoccupied anthropologists and provoked many arguments. Thus far, in fact, there is no consensus as to exactly how these systems work or what precisely they mean to the groups who practice them or what they should mean to the outsiders who study them. Some theorists who attempt to account for cross-cousin marriage focus on social structure and discuss the implications of this type of marriage in terms of the maintenance of marital alliances between groups of people. Against this approach, however, Margaret Trawick (1990) has offered a novel interpretation of cross-cousin marriage among the Tamil people of South India. She suggests that cross-cousin marriage in this society is in part related to the culturally patterned emotional dynamics between certain kin. In particular, she points out the highly affective bond between brothers and sisters in Tamil culture. A sibling, then, "may become like a desired but forbidden mate" (Trawick 1990: 183). A kind of "longing" between brother and sister cannot be directly fulfilled, but it can be indirectly expressed through the marriages of their children to one another. What makes Trawick's approach all the more interesting is that she discusses marriage practices not as abstractions of social structure but in terms of the emotional lives and cultural experiences of real people.

This having been said, we can now return to Lévi-Strauss' ideas about exogamy and the origin of spouse-exchange. Even more important than what Lévi-Strauss said about marital exchanges is the *way* in which he phrased his original proposition: Early human groups exchanged *women*. Needless to say, for those interested in exploring the origins of female subordination, this was a very powerful idea, the implications of which were drawn out by Gale Rubin (1975). It suggested that very early in human adaptation, women became subordinated to men because they were, in a sense, the first items of trade between men of different groups. In other words, males were playing a political game with women as the pawns; they were in control of allocating female sexuality and reproductive capacity, whereas women were merely the allocated. This idea concurs with Fox's (1980) view, discussed in Chapter 2, that older males maintained power over the allocation of females to others and used it to recruit other males as allies and build up their followings. Fox (1989: 179) has also suggested that the custom of bridewealth emerged when men, in order to acquire wives, started offering goods instead of their own sisters and daughters as exchange.

If women appear somewhat passive in Lévi-Strauss' scheme, it is certainly not because he intended that they be seen as lacking in value. On the contrary, he saw a woman as the "total gift" between men. At some point, he said, human men emerged from a state of primitive promiscuity and incest. They renounced sexual access to their own women in order to trade with one another and so become allies. They bonded together precisely because their items of exchange, live women, *were* valuable. Thus was alliance born between men—and thus was marriage born, too. But according to Lévi-Strauss, marriage was primarily a relationship between men and only secondarily involved a union between a man and a woman. Women were valuable, but valuable in the world of men as items of exchange between them.

Is any of this true? It's hard to say, because so little is known about the actual behavior of Paleolithic hunter-gatherers. As for modern groups, some anthropologists have criticized the idea that males exchanged women (in elementary systems), or merely farmed them out to form alliances (in complex systems), in order to play their own political games. Karen Sacks (1979: 114–115) wrote that marriage exchanges in hunting-gathering societies do not involve exchanges of women, who in these societies are economically and socially equal to men. And Diane Bell (1980) showed that, among one group of Australian aborigines, although spouse exchange was ceremonially in the hands of men, women had also directly participated in the selections before the ceremony. We have seen, too, that among the Beng (Case 5), a group with double descent, husbands arrange the marriages of the odd-numbered daughters, and wives, the marriages of their even-numbered daughters. Finally, my own study has shown that, among Nepalese Brahmans (Case 2), women actively work to set up their children's marriages. For their daughters, women maneuver to arrange marriages to men from the villages of their own brothers in order to secure some source of support for the new brides. In all these cases, marriages are definitely "political" in that they establish alliances between groups, but matchmaking appears to be a game that both women and men can play.

Marriage alliances may have helped early humans to develop cooperative intergroup relationships, but they did not (and still do not) always work to maintain peace between groups. It is probably true that if two descent groups systematically intermarried over the generations (as illustrated in Figure 6.5), they would be unlikely to attack one another, since each group would encompass one another's sisters, daughters, and grandchildren. But in any looser arrangement, marriage bonds are not enough to prevent war. In some groups, such as the Huli (Case 7), much warfare took place between male affines, and there was the saying that "we fight where we marry." In addition, alliances can be terminated through acts of divorce when need be.

Endogamy

Now, what about descent group endogamy or, more specifically, endogamy within a unilineal lineage? We presume that few Paleolithic hunter-gatherer groups practiced descent group endogamy, inasmuch as we know that few, if any, modern hunter-gatherers have done so. But descent group endogamy *is* found among some other groups. Arab societies with patrilineal lineages are one example. Here, a man is permitted to marry his parallel cousin, an FBD (though she need not be a first cousin). In some areas of the Arab world (or in regions that have converted to Islam and adopted many Arabic customs), a man's marriage to an FBD is preferred and widely practiced, though not mandatory. In the case of lineage endogamy, the descent group cannot use marriage to forge or maintain alliances with other descent groups, but it acquires other advantages. One is that the descent group retains its rights in the reproduction of its female members; it does not need to rely on cooperation with other descent groups to reproduce itself. Another advantage is that, in situations where females as well as males inherit lineage property, this property will stay in the lineage. Otherwise, with lineage exogamy, women at marriage might take property out of the lineage (say, in the form of dowry). The latter advantage is the one most frequently mentioned by people practicing this form of endogamy. Along with material property, valued but more abstract assets such as power, prestige, and social status can be kept within a group through endogamy. A third advantage falls to women. Since a woman is marrying into her own descent group, she is not moving into a new group where her natal kin have no influence and where she will be left to fend for herself. If she has trouble in her married life, she can rely on her F, Bs, and many others to exert influence on her husband, who is their own (and her) lineage kinsman.

Probably no group has made better use of marriage to forge and break political alliances than the ancient Romans, the subject of the next case study, which traces the marital history of the Julio-Claudian dynasty. (Recall that early Roman kinship was briefly introduced in Chapter 3.) By the time of the Julio-Claudians, much had changed; most notably, the Romans were by then well along the path of their long-term shift away from patrilineal descent and toward becoming a bilateral society. On the one hand, the marital history of the Julio-Claudians is complicated; and in some respects it may seem that they got a bit carried away with their blatantly political marriages, divorces, and remarriages, to say nothing of their innumerable adulterous affairs. On the other hand, their marital behavior is already familiar to us in that it closely parallels that of modern-day Hollywood stars and American soap opera characters. Their scandals aside, what the Julio-Claudians did politically—within, through, and sometimes despite their marriages—was to establish the Roman Empire and influence the course of Western civilization for many centuries. But Roman history, long studied for its lessons in warfare, law, politics, architecture, and technology, has only recently been appreciated as an arena for the study of gender.

CASE 9: THE JULIO-CLAUDIANS

As noted, we already glimpsed at the life of the ancient Romans in Chapter 3. Here we will probe the institution of marriage in the Roman upper class, with a particular focus on the great house of the Julio-Claudians. The Julio-Claudians were two gens (clans), intertwined by several marriages, that gave Rome its first emperors. The historical period in question encompasses the Late Republic and the Early Empire, roughly the period from 100 B.C. to A.D. 100.

We saw in Chapter 3 that during an earlier time of the Roman Republic, the male head of a family, the *paterfamilias*, held great authority over all his dependents, including his children, slaves, and any others attached to his household. The paterfamilias was the eldest male of a family line; and his control over his patrilineal descendants lasted until his death, so that if a man lived long enough he could be the paterfamilias not only of his children but of his grandsons and great-grandsons as well. When the paterfamilias died, his sons or other male descendants, if mature, were now independent, able to become paterfamilias themselves. His unmarried daughters, by contrast, would have a legal guardian appointed to them.

In this early period, most upper-class marriages were marriages with *manus*, meaning that the power (*potestas*) a father held over a daughter was transferred, at marriage, to her husband. At this point a woman became rather strongly (though never completely) incorporated into her husband's descent group. She took up worship at her husband's family altar and ceased worship at the altar of her father (Pomeroy 1975: 152). A woman married with manus brought a dowry to her marriage (this became the property of her husband or his paterfamilias) and lost rights to her father's property. She did, however, acquire rights of inheritance to her husband's property. Legally speaking, a woman in this type of marriage was in many respects like a daughter to her husband.[4]

A woman married with manus could not initiate divorce. But her husband could divorce her or, in consultation with her consanguineal relatives, put her to death for particular offenses such as adultery or drinking wine. (Wine was believed, at least by men, to inflame women's passions and induce "sexual aberration" [Baldson 1963: 213].) He could also divorce her for counterfeiting his keys, some of which might unlock the wine cellar. This exercise of male control over female sexuality, played out in reference to wine, also involved a woman's male consanguineal kin: "Women were customarily kissed on the mouth by their male blood relations in order to determine if they had alcohol on their breath" (Pomeroy 1975: 153).

---

[4] Not known, however, is whether the husband had the power of life and death over his wife, as he would have had over his daughter (Pomeroy 1975: 154).

Marriages were strictly monogamous. Most, especially first marriages, were arranged by families, but the law required the consent of bride and groom (Rawson 1986: 21).[5] Marriage was explicitly believed to serve the purpose of providing legitimate children for the husband in whose legal power they would be placed (or in that of the husband's father or grandfather, if alive) and with whom they would stay in the event of divorce. As the Roman Republic advanced, marriages also became increasingly important in creating political alliances between aristocratic families.

In this earlier period we find the expression of certain ideals regarding women. Women were to be hard-working, modest, deferential to men, and, as mothers, very dedicated; but above all they were to be chaste and virtuous. Brides were to be virgin (women were married young, often at the legal minimum age of twelve [Rawson 1986: 21]), and wives were to be absolutely faithful to husbands. Husbands, by contrast, had automatic sexual rights not only to their wives but also to their female slaves; and their relations with prostitutes or lower-class women were their own affair.

There was great emphasis on the sexual purity of women. Culturally, this emphasis was expressed in the cult of the Vestal Virgins, which survived for more than a thousand years, until A.D. 394. These virgins (always a total of six) were selected before their first menstruation from upper-class families. For a period of thirty years they were to tend the sacred fire in the temple to the Goddess Vesta (Goddess of the Hearth), making sure it never went out. They took a vow of virginity for the period of their service; and if this vow was violated, which fortunately happened only very infrequently, they were punished by being buried alive. In times of great national strife, the chastity of the Vestal Virgins was surrounded with suspicion (Beard 1980: 16). On another social plane, ordinary women tended the household hearth, and it was likewise on their virtue that the honor of the family rested (Cohen 1991).

The Vestal Virgins and the fire of Vesta were symbols of the unity, continuity, and honor of the Roman State. The cult itself also symbolized fertility; the virgins' rituals were carried out to promote the fertility of the Roman people, a cause for which their own fertility was sacrificed (Fantham et al. 1994: 235).

Human fertility was of concern throughout the long history of ancient Rome. Men needed heirs to their property and descendants to continue the worship of ancestors. Great importance was attached to continuing the name of the patrilineal gens. And as marriages became politically useful, "the more children a man had, the greater the number of potential connec-

---

[5] However, if the woman refused the groom, she had to give evidence of his bad moral character (Rawson 1986: 21).

PHOTO 6.1 Statue of a Vestal Virgin in the Roman Forum (Rome). Photo courtesy of J. Thomas Bradley.

tions with other families" (Pomeroy 1975: 155). Women were apparently blamed for a couple's infertility (Rawson 1986: 32). In the event of childlessness, divorce and remarriage were possible; legal adoption was another, more widely used option. Nevertheless, during certain periods, human fertility was deemed by some to have reached dangerously low levels among the upper classes, and, as we shall see, legal steps were taken to promote fertility.

Upper-class Romans were well aware that alternative modes of gender existed. They had many close neighbors, whom they conquered rather early; and they were in contact with the cultures of the Greeks and Egyptians, whom they conquered later. Near at hand and in clear contrast to the Romans were the Etruscans, who, having once been rulers in Rome, were overthrown to found the Republic. Not much is known about gender relations among the Etruscans, but from their tombs historians have derived a picture of relative gender equality and an elevated position of women. The famous sarcophagus of a husband and wife (reproduced on the cover of this book) shows a tender, loving couple with serene, yet mysterious, smiles. But the Romans found the Etruscans rather disgusting and immoral (Fantham et al. 1994: 245).

Upper-class Roman women of the early Republican period were not in every sense subordinated to men, and history has left a record of some women who achieved great public respect and honor. But most descriptions of women's lives, marriages, and legal status readily bring the word *patriarchy* to mind. This situation had largely changed, however, by the time of the Late Republic, the period to which we will now turn. One difference had to do with shifts in property relationships. The gens had lost its corporate control of property long ago, though rights to property remained the corporate concern of a family group, a paterfamilias, and those descendants under his power. These rights, too, were gradually eroded as males exercised the authority to make individual wills, starting as long ago as the fifth century B.C.; meanwhile, women were leaving valid wills by the second century B.C. (Saller 1991: 32). In the larger picture, Rome was becoming a bilateral society. By the Late Republic, the gens was still a descent category but no longer an exogamous one. Marriages were permitted with first cousins, either cross or parallel. There was still some concern with the name of the gens, and with passing it on patrilineally. But gradually the concept of "ancestry" and all it implied in terms of prestige and claims to status came to depend as much on the mother, and links through the mother, as on the father and a patriline (Treggiari 1991: 100).

A second difference concerned the rise of new relationships between property and marriage transactions. Whereas earlier most marriages had been with manus, by now, in the Late Republic, most were "free" marriages whereby a woman remained under the legal power of her father after marriage and retained his gens name. In such cases a woman took a dowry to her marriage, but it remained her legal property. Her husband could use or invest this property for the duration of the marriage; but, upon divorce, the dowry had to be returned to the woman's paterfamilias, or, if he were dead, it became her property. Some portion of it could be kept by the husband to help support the woman's children, who would remain with him; and the returned dowry could be reduced in the event that the woman had committed a particularly grievous sin such as adultery. But by the Late Republic, husbands did not have great power over wives. Divorce, undoubtedly rare before, was now both frequent and easy to obtain. Wives (or their fathers who had legal power over them) could initiate divorce as easily as men. This shift to "free" marriages may have been related to the fact that upper-class Romans were becoming wealthier and more concerned with wealth (Pomeroy 1975: 155). Large dowries could be used to attract good husbands for one's daughters (and, thereby, to secure political alliances), but, at the same time, a paterfamilias did not wish to see all that wealth pass out of his family and into another. "Free" marriage allowed him much greater control over this wealth.

For women these changes were very significant and led to their increasing autonomy and independence. A woman in a "free" marriage was still under the authority of her father (or eldest male ascendant of that family). If her father died, she was then given a legal guardian (usually a brother of the father or someone appointed by the father before his death), but the powers of guardians were weak compared to those of the paterfamilias. Guardians were appointed primarily to ensure that women did not foolishly lose property that devolved upon them. Even though these guardians officially had authority over a woman's property, many ways and means were found around them, and by the Late Republic, women's legal guardians were largely a formality (Crook 1986: 85).

A third, and perhaps most impressive, difference between the earlier Republican period and the Late Republic was that adultery seemed to be breaking out all over. Previously, as we saw, men could have relations with women outside marriage; but they were not to have sex with married, upper-class women. Yet this is what was happening now: Men were having affairs with elite married women, and upper-class married women were taking lovers. Some historians have referred to this occurrence as a kind of sexual "liberation" of women, and have described the Late Republic as seeing the emergence of a "new woman" (Fantham et al. 1994), one now assertive, willful, and in command, if not of the official rules and values of her society, then of her own sexuality and its consequences.

For the practitioners, adultery was surrounded by thrill and romance but not by guilt. As Morton Hunt (1994: 67) has noted, among sexual unions outside marriage "up-to-date Romans favored . . . [adultery] above all others, regarding it much as modern man regards cheating on his income-tax return—a zestful wrongdoing that involves no sense of wrong or sin, but only apprehension lest he be caught." Adultery probably contributed to the rise in divorce and remarriage as well.

In accounting for the rise of the "new woman" of this period, historians have referred to the impact of warfare (e.g., Pomeroy 1975: 181). Previous centuries had seen the expansion of Roman rule through conquest. As the Roman state expanded, it bumped into that of the Carthaginians, a people of Middle Eastern origin who, after overtaking North Africa and Spain, were now attempting to take control of Sicily. This confrontation led to the Punic Wars (218–146 B.C.) and the ultimate victory of Rome. During this time many Roman men died or were away for long periods on military campaigns, leaving wives and widows on their own for many years. Wives of military men had to learn to fend for themselves and to manage estates in their husbands' absence. These wars also brought back new wealth; and as women were by now more financially autonomous and adept, some of this wealth found its way into their hands.

It was not the case that all the old ideals regarding women and sex had changed, or that all women were committing adultery. Female virtue was still praised; and sexual indiscretion, though more common during this period, was occasionally still frowned upon. But now, "the Roman woman had choices" (Pomeroy 1975: 188); she could select from among a greater variety of socially tolerated lifestyles.

Matchmaking and the Rise of Julius Caesar

It is in this historical context that we will explore marriage among the Julio-Claudians, taking a look at the lives of some individual men and women from the time of Julius Caesar to the Emperor Nero. Beginning with Caesar, this is a time when Rome was not only expanding and feeling its glory but also painfully passing from its status as a Republic to that of an Empire.

The Roman Republic adhered to some democratic ideals and looked back with pride to its overthrow of the Etruscan monarchs; but in fact it was an oligarchy, with real rule by members of a few aristocratic families. These families dominated the Roman Senate, which had become more powerful over the centuries and fought desperately to keep its power during the years of the Late Republic. The Senate had imbued the leading position of the *consul* with great powers; but these were limited since consuls were elected to serve for only one year and there were to be two of them at all times. Retired consuls then became members of the Senate.

Economic changes gradually took place as a result of Rome's expansion. Though the wars had enriched many people in Rome, some had become poor and dispossessed of their land. These bottom layers of society began to challenge senatorial power. Their voice was heard through a political faction know as the *Populares*. Populares were politicians, themselves often aristocrats, who sided with the people against aristocratic power. Opposed to this faction were the *Optimates*, politicians who promoted the status quo and sought to keep power with the aristocratic families. Aside from battling with the Populares, the Optimates had something to fear, from any and all sides: the rise of a single powerful ruler, which would spell the end of the Republic. This end, of course, is exactly what occurred with the emergence of the Empire. It was probably inevitable since Rome had grown too big and too complex to securely remain under a republic as then organized.

In the 80s B.C., power shifted between the Populares and the Optimates, until one man, Sulla, allied with the latter, seized control. Ironically, in the name of preserving the Republic and fighting off others who were becoming too powerful for Republican comfort, he himself became a dictator for life. He later retired from rule, but he had shown that it could be done— that a single ruler could rise to power. Another important figure at the time was Pompey, a great military leader who was becoming very powerful himself as a result of his impressive military victories for Rome. But his own political affiliations wavered.

Julius Caesar (actually Gaius Julius Caesar)[6] rose to prominence during this fervent political period. In tracing his ascension, we will see that one of the central roles of Roman upper-class marriage, aside from legitimate reproduction, was the making of political alliances. But we will also see that this strategy did not necessarily work on more than a short-term basis.

Julius Caesar was himself betrothed or married four times, and he played important roles in arranging the marriages of others. Indeed, the history of his making and unmaking of marriages is inseparable from that of his political career. His first engagement, to a woman named Cossutia, was, however, of relatively minor importance. His father had arranged this union when Caesar was quite young and had just "assumed the toga of manhood" (Deutsch 1918: 505). The match brought little in the way of political connections, though evidently Cossutia and her family were thought to have been advantageous in-laws because of their wealth. In any event, at the still young age of sixteen, and after his father had died, Caesar broke his engagement to Cossutia and maneuvered a politically brilliant marriage with a second wife, Cornelia. Cornelia was the daughter of a powerful political leader (Cinna) among the Populares. In 83 B.C., after one year of marriage, Cornelia gave birth to Julia, Caesar's only legitimate child.

This marriage lasted sixteen years until Cornelia's death in 68 B.C. Through it, Caesar's alliance with the Populares was developed, thus pitting him against Sulla and his faction. It was also through this marriage that Caesar made his political statement even clearer. In 82 B.C. (when Caesar was eighteen years old), Sulla became dictator and determined that the time was ripe for a number of political realignments. He therefore commanded several prominent men, including Caesar, to divorce their current wives and marry women closely related to him. All but one of these men complied—among them Pompey, who divorced his wife to marry a stepdaughter of Sulla. It was Caesar who refused. For this affront, Sulla sent henchmen to murder Caesar. Caesar escaped, and assorted relatives eventually intervened to dissuade Sulla from attempting to get rid of Caesar.

Much later, ten years after Sulla's death and a year after Cornelia's death, Caesar, now thirty-two, married Pompeia, a granddaughter of Sulla. By this time the two political factions were engaged in a temporary truce. But this

---

[6] Roman names can be confusing. It helps to know that the first name was the personal name; the second name was the gens, or clan, name; and the third name referred to a branch of the gens (Massie 1963: 5). Thus "Caesar," which came to have other meanings, was originally just a kinship group. And the man we now know as Julius Caesar was probably called "Gaius" by his friends.

spirit of reconciliation did not last long, and neither did Caesar's marriage to Pompeia. The divorce, in 62 B.C., may have been related to shifts in the political wind and/or to the fact that the union was childless; but it also followed upon a curious scandal. Pompeia was evidently being pursued by Publius Clodius, a debauched playboy. (He, incidentally, was the first husband of a famous woman, Fulvia, who later became the wife of Mark Antony.) The scandal had its onset at Caesar's house, where an all-female religious ceremony, the Festival of Bona Dea, was taking place. Clodius attended the festival by dressing up as a woman, in order to gain entrance to the house and make love with Pompeia. The deception was found out and the event enraged Caesar's mother, a woman well known for her great virtue.

By the time of this divorce, Caesar's own political career was well under way. He had waged some successful military campaigns, had held important administrative posts, and had become popular in at least some corners of the public. He now sought the consulship, but desperately needed more support. He was fiercely opposed by the Optimates, and even in his own circle there was already a more powerful and notable man, namely Pompey, who had achieved great overseas military glories. At this point Caesar, in a stroke of genius, brought about an alliance with Pompey and another powerful (and wealthy) man, Crassus. This informal alliance, known as the First Triumvirate, represented a forging of forces between three men who deeply mistrusted one another but saw that, united for now, they each had a lot to gain. And gain they all did. The alliance between Caesar and Pompey was swiftly solidified with Caesar's arranging of the marriage of Pompey to his only daughter, Julia, in 59 B.C. Julia was at the time engaged to another man, a relatively minor political figure but one who nevertheless strongly supported Caesar for the consulship. Still, this was nothing compared to what Caesar could achieve with Pompey as a son-in-law, so he broke off the betrothal. The political payoffs were great. Caesar did become consul, establishing him as a serious political figure at Rome.

It was also in 59 B.C., at age forty-one and three years after he had divorced Pompeia, that Caesar married his last wife, Calpurnia. She was the daughter of an important man, Piso. With Piso's help, along with that of Pompey, Caesar secured his next aim, the command of the province of Gaul. This would enable him to achieve stunning military victories and add substantial territory to the Roman state, all of which would be decisive in his political rise to the top. Caesar's military glories in Gaul were so great that he now equaled Pompey in status.

Meanwhile, the First Triumvirate was falling apart. Pompey, realizing among other things that Caesar was soon to overshadow him, began to show signs of breaking with Caesar. The rift between them was greatly facilitated by the death in 55 B.C. of Julia, Pompey's wife and Caesar's daughter. She died in childbirth and her child died soon thereafter. Before her death, Julia had played a strong role in mediating between these two men and preventing their differences from upsetting the First Triumvirate. When she died, many Romans feared the inevitable. At one point, Caesar actually tried to smooth things over with Pompey and so, in 54 B.C., he proposed to divorce Calpurnia and marry Pompey's daughter by an earlier marriage. But this was not to take place, and the rupture between Caesar and Pompey, along with the death of Crassus in 53 B.C., brought about civil war. The war ended when Caesar's forces defeated those of Pompey in 45 B.C. Caesar then became dictator for life, but not for long since he was murdered in 44 B.C.

Caesar's life was not entirely taken up with wars, marital alliances, and becoming dictator, for he also found time for innumerable romantic affairs. Many years before the First Triumvirate, he had an affair with Mucia, Pompey's own wife. In fact, Pompey divorced Mucia for this adultery. A long-term mistress of Caesar was Servilia, herself married and mother of Brutus, one of the men who murdered Caesar. And then there was Cleopatra, Queen of Egypt, who lived in Rome as Caesar's mistress during the last years of Caesar's life, along with her son, Caesar's child. We do not know how any of Caesar's wives felt about these and other of his philanderings, or what his daughter, Julia, thought about the sudden change in her wedding plans. Did even Calpurnia know that in 54 B.C. Caesar was coolly plotting to divorce her to marry Pompey's daughter? History does record that the marriage of Julia and Pompey was a very happy one, and that Calpurnia, despite the presence of Cleopatra more or less next door, was affectionately concerned about Caesar on the eve of his death.

Augustus.   This glimpse into Julius Caesar's life has shown us how marriages were manipulated to form political alliances and secure advantageous positions. In the next segment of Julio-Claudian history we will see that this use of marriage continued, but with some new developments. First, we will see the use of clan endogamous marriage strategies as well as exogamous ones. As mentioned at the beginning of this chapter, exogamous marriages reach outward; they have the advantage of connecting individuals and families to new groups. This was the pattern for all of Caesar's marriages. Endogamous marriages lose this advantage but gain another: consolidation of power and wealth inward, within the family group. Indeed, Augustus, Rome's first emperor, made great and repeated use of this strategy. Another advantage of endogamous marriages for emperors and royal families generally is that royal blood does not, as it were, seep out of the family, allowing others to use it as a claim to power. Second, we will see that although males dominated marriage manipulations, women were active in promoting particular marriages for their own ends and in influencing events through their selection of lovers. And finally we will see the tension that existed between the institution of marriage as a sheer political ploy and the institution as a locus of intimacy and, occasionally, affection. We can follow the Julio-Claudians' acts of marriage and reproduction by consulting Figure 6.6, which illustrates the main kinship connections between the emperors.

The man who was to become the Emperor Augustus[7] had one thing going for him: His MF had married Julius Caesar's sister. As Caesar had no

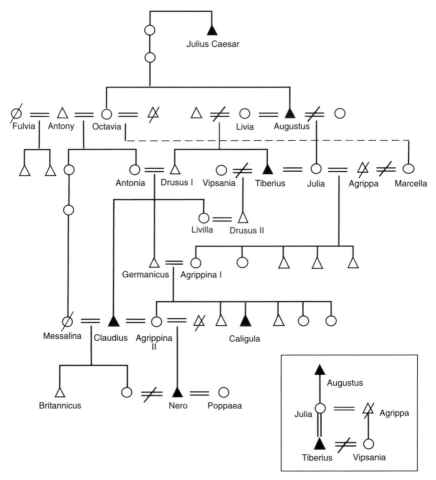

FIGURE 6.6   A Genealogy of the Julio-Claudians. Julius Caesar and the emperors are shaded. Some deaths and divorces are shown to indicate the sequence of marriages. The box at the lower right shows the complex relationships between Julia, Agrippa, Tiberius, and Vipsania.

---

[7] For simplicity, I consistently refer to this man as Augustus, even though his original name was Gaius Octavius Thurinus. In the historical literature he is sometimes referred to as Octavian, and the Senate gave him the honorific name of Augustus in 27 B.C.

legitimate son and his only daughter died childless, he selected his heir among his next closest consanguineal kin. Except for this kinship connection, Augustus, given his relatively humble origins, had little reason to expect particular prominence in life. But Caesar had named him as his heir, and in 44 B.C. the young Augustus, now nineteen years old, headed off to Rome to claim his inheritance. Needless to say, he became enmeshed in the chaotic politics of Rome, where several factions were now fighting for power in the vacuum left by Caesar. One faction was led by Mark Antony, Caesar's lieutenant. Augustus temporarily allied with him in the Second Triumvirate (an alliance that also included a relatively minor figure, Lepidus). Augustus and Antony, each seeking supreme power, were uneasy allies and quickly fell into dispute. In 40 B.C. they tried to patch things up with a new agreement called the Treaty of Brindisi, and this renewed alliance they sealed with a marriage: Antony, whose wife, Fulvia, had conveniently died, married Augustus' sister, Octavia. This marriage was to have far-reaching effects, though it did not last long and failed to keep the Second Triumvirate together. One problem was that earlier, while off on military campaigns, Antony (like Caesar before him) had begun an affair with Cleopatra in Egypt. Though temporarily set aside while Antony formed the Second Triumvirate, the affair was definitely not over.

Further cementing the alliance, meanwhile, was Augustus' betrothal to Mark Antony's step-daughter. This was Clodia, a very young girl who, in fact, was the daughter of Fulvia and her first husband, Publius Clodius. (As we saw earlier, Clodius was the degenerate playboy who drew Julius Caesar's second wife into scandal.) But Augustus broke this engagement when he determined that he could secure even more advantageous political connections by marrying another woman, Scribonia. Scribonia was much older than Augustus but very well connected politically (she was a relative of the Pompeys). Even so, the marriage did not last long. Augustus divorced Scribonia on the day that she bore him a daughter, Julia—his only child.

One reason Augustus divorced Scribonia was to free himself up for marriage to yet another woman, Livia, in 38 B.C. Livia was nineteen years old; and Augustus, now twenty-five. Livia might have seemed an odd choice since she was married, the mother of one child, and pregnant. In fact, the union was scandalous, even by the looser Roman standards of the time; and some historians have written it off as a case of desperate love (e.g., Massie 1983: 54). Yet this marriage brought Augustus enormous political advantages, for Livia's natal family was among the most influential of the old Roman aristocracy, precisely the group with which Augustus now needed a connection. Both Livia and her husband were Claudians.

For whatever reasons of his own, Livia's husband, Nero, agreed to this match. He attended the wedding, gave the bride away, and provided Livia with a dowry for her new marriage. Her two sons by him (one born after the wedding to Augustus) remained with Nero; but Nero willed that upon his death Augustus should adopt them. Nero died five years later.

However this marriage came about, it proved successful and affectionate. Augustus and Livia showed respect and devotion to one another and worked together as a team. True, Augustus indulged in infidelities on the side, but such behavior was hardly unusual in his day.

In the years after Augustus and Livia were married, the Second Triumvirate fell apart. Antony sent his wife Octavia away and married Cleopatra, an action that considerably widened the gulf between him and Augustus. By 32 B.C. Antony had divorced Octavia. Earlier, Augustus had ordered Octavia to divorce Antony, but she refused; her motives are not known.

While Antony was off for long periods in Egypt with Cleopatra, Augustus' influence and power grew in Rome. Eventually a naval battle (at Actium, Greece, in 31 B.C.) ended the rivalry, with Antony's forces defeated and Antony and Cleopatra having committed suicide. Little did Antony know, on his deathbed, that his own descendants would one day be rulers of Rome.

PHOTO 6.2   Bronze statue of the Emperor Augustus on Via dei Fori Imperiali (Rome), a copy of the marble original in the Vatican Museum. Photo courtesy of J. Thomas Bradley.

Augustus was now supreme, and four years later the Senate bestowed on him the honorific name "Augustus" (venerable one). He was subsequently proclaimed a god. Somewhat like Sulla before him, Augustus advertised his rule in the name of "restoring" the Republic, but in fact the Roman Republic was dead. On the bright side, Augustus brought peace and prosperity to the Roman world and founded the Empire that was to endure for more than four hundred years in the West.

There was one thing Augustus, a man of many achievements, could not do and that was to reform the sexual behavior of the Roman upper class. This was not for lack of trying. Once secure in power, Augustus launched a strong campaign for what we would now call "family values." He sought a return to the Rome of the Early Republic, when women were virtuous and men were valiant protectors of that virtue. He also focused new attention on children and sought to promote female fertility and motherhood. His famous Altar of Peace in Rome shows an early representation of children in Western art. Possibly for the first time in Roman art, the Altar depicts women not as goddesses but as ordinary mortals (Fantham et al. 1994: 295).

Augustus' own family came to epitomize the new moral order, with his wife, Livia, and his sister, Octavia, serving as exemplary models of virtuous women. Fantham et al. (1994: 313) describe what this family meant to the Roman people:

> First, the Imperial family *was* a family and its continuity under a dignified and protective father and a noble and fertile mother guaranteed the health and happiness of the Roman people, its children. Second, this notion of family was disseminated throughout the empire on works of art, coins, and domestic shrines, in the patronage of buildings and the inscriptions that marked them, and the ceremonies and choreographed public appearances of members of the court.

In addition to this, Augustus enacted laws on marriage and adultery in 18 B.C., later amending them in A.D. 9. These laws made adultery illegal, but the implications were different for men and women. For a married woman, sexual relations with any man other than her husband constituted adultery. For a man, however, adultery meant sexual relations with a married upper-class woman; sexual relations between a married man and a prostitute, a lower-class women, and so on, were not considered adultery. If caught in the act, a woman could be killed by her father; and her husband, under certain conditions, could kill her lover though he could not kill his wife (Cohen 1991: 111). These laws of Augustus also attempted to promote fertility. Divorced or widowed women were required to remarry within a specified time. Adults who were unmarried could not claim their inheritances; those who were married but childless had to forfeit some of their inheritance. And there were rewards for high fertility: If a freeborn woman had borne three children (for a freedwoman, or ex-slave, the number was four children), she no longer had to have a legal guardian. Aside from their attempts to promote fertility and discourage adultery, these laws represented a new encroachment of the state into the private lives of citizens (Cohen 1991: 124).

In fact, the laws did not succeed either in curbing adultery or promoting fertility. Regarding the former, a severe blow came to Augustus' quest for Roman moral reform with the case of his own daughter, Julia. Augustus had arranged marriages for her a few times, as we shall see, and she had pleased Augustus by bearing many children. But then, in 2 B.C., Augustus was notified that Julia had not only committed adultery but was leading a rather sexually licentious life. Augustus was told that she had had dozens of lovers, roamed about at night having sexual adventures in the Forum, and was, indeed, a prostitute. Mortified, Augustus banished her to an island where she was expressly forbidden both men and wine. One of her recent lovers (who was, incidentally, a son of Mark Antony and Fulvia) was ordered to kill himself, and others were exiled.

Augustus' efforts to promote fertility were also ineffective. The Roman upper class, like the lower classes, lived in a context of low life expectancy (at birth, it was only about twenty-five years), high infant mortality (about half of all children born died before age ten [Garnsey 1991: 52]), and frequent deaths of women in childbirth. Still, it appears that fertility among upper-class people decreased with time and was significantly lower than that among other groups. It is likely that these people, concerned with wealth and the status it maintained, sought to limit the number of their children in order to limit the divisions of their property (Saller 1991: 26). Some historians (e.g., Hunt 1994: 88–89) have speculated that a voluntary low fertility or infertility of the upper classes came about as family life disintegrated—that is, as sex moved outside marriage and into adultery where it became entwined with romantic love. Certainly Roman society was familiar with techniques to reduce fertility, such as infanticide, abortion, and contraception. Augustus' wayward daughter, Julia, though quite fertile herself, may have claimed that, in order to ensure that her children belonged to her husband, she took lovers only when she was already pregnant. One Roman writer, Macrobius, satirizes Roman morality of this period by attributing to Julia this remark: "I never take on a passenger unless the boat is full" (Macrobius 2.5.9, cited in Richlin 1992: 72). Some contraceptive techniques may have been effective, such as the use of goat bladders for condoms or oils and wool as blocking agents. But other Roman techniques, as when a woman held her breath during the man's ejaculation, or wore amulets containing cat liver (Pomeroy 1975: 167), were no doubt disappointing.

With regard to the new morality, "family values," and the issue of lowered fertility, Augustus had one other serious problem: no male descendant and thus no obvious successor. He and Livia were childless, but most assuredly not by choice. Thus Julia, by his previous marriage, remained his only child, a fact that affected the whole of his reign and the lives of many people. Sonless, Augustus manipulated marriages and ties through women to find a successor. As for his use of such ties, a precedent had been set since he himself was consanguineally related to Julius Caesar only through women.

Augustus pursued several strategies at once, keeping his options open. One strategy was to ally potential successors more closely to his own consanguineal line; another was to count on the fertility of his own single descendant, Julia. In his search for a successor, he vacillated over the years between certain choices. Figure 6.7 shows what he had to work with in the last few decades B.C.

Tiberius. One choice for a successor was Tiberius, a Claudian, Augustus' eldest stepson through Livia. Apparently Augustus did not much like Tiberius, whose case was promoted by his mother, but at times there seemed no other option. Another choice was a man named Agrippa, who earlier had no kinship connection with the imperial family but had been a loyal supporter of Augustus and was still a close aid. In Agrippa's favor, Augustus had made some previous matches. One was the marriage of Agrippa to Augustus' ZD, Marcella, a daughter of Octavia from her first marriage, before her marriage to Mark Antony. Another was the marriage of Tiberius to Agrippa's daughter, Vipsania, from his earlier marriage. These unions gave Agrippa at least some link to the family; and the marriage of Tiberius and Vipsania was reportedly a very happy one.

Later, believing even more strongly that Agrippa and/or his potential descendants might succeed him, Augustus in 21 B.C. married Agrippa to his daughter, Julia. Of course, this event took place long before Julia's scandalous sex life had become a problem. At this point Julia was only about

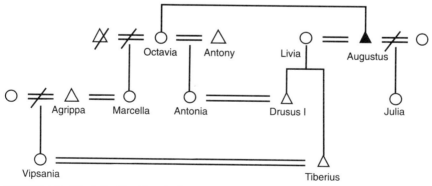

FIGURE 6.7 The Julio-Claudians in the Last Decades B.C.

sixteen years old; and Agrippa, about forty. Now, in order to marry Julia, Agrippa first had to divorce Marcella (who was of course Julia's own cousin, an FZD). This was a serious move on Agrippa's part,[8] but it placed Agrippa in a very promising position. Much to the delight of both Augustus and Agrippa, the marriage was fruitful and Julia gave birth to five children. (It was around this time, unknown to her father, that Julia allegedly was having affairs while pregnant to ensure that Agrippa was the father of her children.) The first two children, Gaius and Lucius, were especially important since they were sons. Seeing these two grandsons as possible heirs at some point, and wishing to secure their future, Augustus legally adopted them himself.

Then in 12 B.C. Agrippa died. His sons, Gaius and Lucius, were still very young boys, but Augustus himself was now over fifty. Determining that he might not live much longer, he renewed his search for a more immediate successor. At this point he turned toward his stepson, Tiberius. It is possible that he chose Tiberius over his brother, Drusus I,[9] because Tiberius was older. In any case, Drusus I had been married to Antonia, daughter of Augustus' sister, Octavia (and Drusus I's MHZD), so at least the descendants of Drusus would be drawn into Augustus' own line if they were ever needed.

Tiberius was already married to Vipsania, Agrippa's daughter, and she was pregnant as well; but Augustus ordered Tiberius to divorce her (now that her father, Agrippa, was dead, she had no political value at all) and marry Julia. With reluctance, Tiberius agreed, and the two were married. One historian commented on Tiberius' probable feelings: "That he [Tiberius] regretted it is certain. He only once saw Vipsania after the divorce; his eyes filled with tears and his gaze followed her about the room. Measures were taken to prevent a repetition of this distressing scene. Vipsania was married off to Asinius Gallus, a senator of high repute" (Massie 1983: 94). Needless to say, Vipsania's son, Drusus II, remained with Tiberius. Meanwhile, Tiberius and Julia most decidedly did not hit it off.

It was nine years later that Julia's scandalous sexual life came out and she was banished. Augustus promptly took the necessary legal measures to divorce Tiberius and Julia. The death of Augustus' two grandsons, Gaius and Lucius, occurred a few years after this, dashing Augustus' hopes for any future direct male descendant to succeed him. In A.D. 14 Augustus himself died. Tiberius immediately arranged for Julia's one last son by Agrippa to be murdered. Then Tiberius became emperor.

---

[8] Augustus had actually married his daughter Julia once before, to Marcellus, a son of Octavia from her first marriage (before her marriage to Mark Antony). This first marriage took place in 25 B.C. But Marcellus died two years later.

[9] For convenience, I use numerals to distinguish among the several Julio-Claudians who have the same personal name. This was not a convention among the Julio-Claudians themselves.

The Later Julio-Claudians

The Emperor Tiberius is probably best remembered for the wild sexual fantasies he allegedly acted out as a recluse on the island of Capri during the last years of his rule. But long before all that, his reign, too, was beset by the problem of succession. Tiberius had one son, Drusus II, a logical heir. But another branch of the Julio-Claudians had been growing in the meantime, and these people could claim an illustrious ancestry, one going back consanguineally to Augustus. Years before, Tiberius' own brother (Drusus I) had been married to Antonia, daughter of Octavia and Mark Antony. Figure 6.8 shows how this side of the Julio-Claudians was shaping up by around A.D. 20.

At this point the Julio-Claudians turned altogether rather nasty. Two kinship factions were solidifying. One consisted of Livia and Tiberius, who wanted to see power continue in their direct line, devolving now on Drusus II. The other centered on Germanicus and his wife, Agrippina I. The latter faction had every reason to hope to eventually assume power since Augustus himself had designated that Germanicus be Tiberius' heir and successor. In addition, Germanicus was popular with the people whereas Tiberius was not. Germanicus' line had high prospects for continuity since his wife, Agrippina I, eventually bore nine children, though some died in infancy. (None of those who died in infancy are shown on the diagrams.)

In A.D. 19 Germanicus fell ill, claiming he had been poisoned. He soon died. Agrippina I believed that Tiberius had sent an agent to poison him, and this she persuaded many others to believe as well. Then, Tiberius' son,

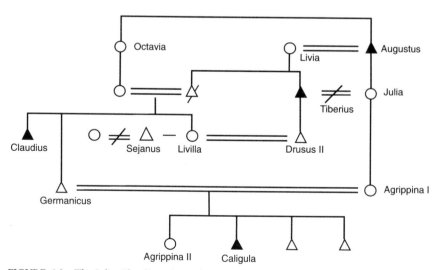

FIGURE 6.8   The Julio-Claudians Around A.D. 20

Drusus II, died in A.D. 23. His death was brought on by yet another political and romantic entanglement. This one involved Livilla, Drusus II's wife and the sister of Germanicus. Livilla had been having an affair with another man, Sejanus, who, though politically ambitious and lacking solid connections, had won the trust of Tiberius. Sejanus wished to rise in power by marrying Livilla, and Livilla was apparently in love with him. These two murdered Drusus II. To further increase his chances of marriage to Livilla, Sejanus divorced his own wife. Sejanus possibly represents every royal family's worst nightmare. He was the very thing that endogamous marriages were arranged to guard against, the sneaking in of an outsider. But it was only later that Tiberius became aware of any accusations that Sejanus and Livilla had killed his son, and for many years he continued to trust Sejanus and support him in his rise to power. A few years after the death of his son, Tiberius moved to Capri and lived in seclusion.

Things got worse. Believing that Agrippina I and her sons were planning treason as well as his death, Tiberius had them exiled or imprisoned. Sejanus himself, wishing them all out of his way, had led Tiberius to believe in the treason. But one male child of Agrippina I, Caligula, was spared, along with his sisters—partly owing to Caligula's youth but also because his FM, Antonia, intervened with Tiberius on his behalf. In addition, Antonia told Tiberius what Sejanus had done; and Sejanus' ex-wife claimed that Sejanus had murdered Tiberius' son. As a result, Sejanus was executed for treason (and Livilla was forced by Antonia to starve to death for her role in the murder). Then, when Tiberius died in A.D. 37, Caligula became the next emperor.[10] Germanicus was long gone and Agrippina I died of starvation in exile; but power had passed to this faction of the family.

The Julio-Claudian line continued, after Caligula, through two more emperors, Claudius and Nero. The manipulation of marriages, intrigues, and murders also continued. Figure 6.9 shows the kinship connections of these last rulers.

Caligula had reigned for only four years when he was murdered by his Palace Guard, after which his uncle, Claudius, took power. (At the time, Claudius was the only surviving adult male of the Julio-Claudian line.) Claudius married a disastrous woman, Messalina, who was a cousin (a MZDD). Messalina was somewhat like the scandalous Julia of earlier days, in that she engaged openly in innumerable affairs. Once her behavior went a bit too far: While Claudius was away, she carried out a public marriage ceremony with her lover, thinking it fun to parade about the palace as man

---

[10] Before Drusus II's death, he and Livilla had had a son, Tiberius Gemellus, who was a grandson of Tiberius. This grandson could have succeeded Tiberius. However, he was only eighteen when Tiberius died, and he himself died (was killed?) in the same year.

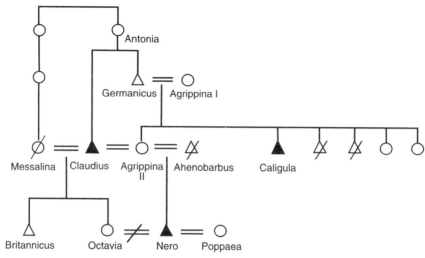

FIGURE 6.9   The Last Julio-Claudians

and wife. Soon after, she was murdered by officials close to Claudius, who figured this would be best for everyone, especially Claudius himself. Later Claudius married his own niece, Agrippina II, the daughter of Germanicus and Agrippina I and the sister of Caligula. Claudius had to enact a new Roman law in order to marry Agrippina II since at that time marriage to a brother's daughter was considered incestuous.

Agrippina II had borne a son, Nero, by a previous marriage (her former husband, Ahenobarbus, was in fact a DS to Mark Antony); and to advance Nero's status she brought about his marriage to Claudius' daughter, Octavia, by Messalina. When Claudius died (and he may have been murdered by Nero or Agrippina II or both), Nero became emperor.

Initially very close to his mother and in political league with her, Nero eventually moved against her. This he did largely because of his growing attachment to a woman, Poppaea, who would later become his wife. Agrippina II had disapproved of this association, fearing it might lead Nero to divorce Octavia, thereby lessening his chances to succeed Claudius. At one point Nero attempted to kill his mother by sending her out to sea in a collapsible boat. When this attempt failed, others killed her for him. He also poisoned Britannicus, Claudius' son, a possible future rival for the throne. Indeed, he committed many other despicable deeds as well, and in the end he was declared by the Senate to be a public enemy; hearing that the punishment for this was death, he had himself killed. Earlier, in a drunken rage, he had kicked Poppaea, then pregnant, to death. Unfortunate as this incident was for her, it did have the virtue of ending the Julio-Claudian line.

Perhaps the Julio-Claudians got a bit carried away, but their case certainly shows how upper-class Roman marriage was interwoven with the making and breaking of alliances. Sometimes, the individuals involved seemed to be merely pawns of more powerful actors. Yet there were also signs of individual resistance as well as variations in the affective quality of unions. For example, Octavia refused to obey her brother and divorce Mark Antony, but why? Pomeroy (1975: 156) raises these questions: Was she resisting her brother's use of her for his own political ends? Or, despite everything, did she feel affection for Antony? Recall, too, that Tiberius agreed to divorce his beloved Vipsania in order to marry Julia, but not without great emotional cost. Many of these marriages were undoubtedly miserable ones; but some, especially that between Augustus and Livia, were warm and affectionate. We have also seen that although men were the political leaders and directed marriages to their own ends, women were active as well. Certainly Julia with her sexuality threw a wrench into Augustus' public campaign for "family values." Some historians have also speculated that she was, perhaps unwittingly, involved in political plots against Augustus. Livilla, in her affair with Sejanus, supported his cause and so played a role in the whole drama of the imperial succession. And finally, Agrippina II, through matchmaking, promoted her own son's chance to become emperor. In fact, much of Julio-Claudian history could be written as an account of how the female descendants of Octavia and Livia helped direct the course of the Roman Empire for more than a hundred years.

From this history we have seen that, as in all societies, there are cultural rules and meanings surrounding marriage, but no standard model fits all real marriages, consisting as they do of very human actors. We have also seen that the Julio-Claudian women were nothing if not varied, some virtuous, some licentious, some murderous.

In the next chapter we will trace certain historical developments in the patterns of Western European and American kinship and gender—developments in which, to this day, we can hear the echoes of ancient Rome. But before leaving the Romans, we should note that they, along with the other society examined in this chapter, the Nyinba, exhibit a trait we have not encountered before: human interest in *limiting* fertility. Individuals in any society may wish to limit their own fertility, but among the Romans and the Nyinba we see a broader expression of this theme. Possibly these two cases are based on similar motivations to regulate fertility according to available resources. The Nyinba seek to control village and household size in an effort to adapt to their rugged, precarious environment; the upper-class Romans possibly sought to limit the number of their heirs in order to prevent a wide dispersion of their wealth. But the two methods of limiting fertility are quite different. The Nyinba use polyandry, whereas the Romans used birth control and infanticide. And, as is not true of the Nyinba, for the Romans the issue of low fertility was apparently controversial, given that people like Augustus became alarmed at the low fertility of the upper class and tried (albeit unsuccessfully) to alter the trend. Later on in Europe, fertility rates remained relatively low, again because of birth control, but also because of something quite new: a relatively late age of marriage for women.

As for the relationship between female sexuality and fertility, the Nyinba and Roman cases appear in some ways to mirror a contrast we saw in Chapter 3 between the Nuer and the Nepalese Brahmans. Like the Nuer, the Nyinba effect a separation between a woman's sexuality and her fertility. A woman may have many sexual partners (husbands and lovers), but each child is allocated to a particular husband. Female sexuality is not constrained, and husbands acquire children whether or not they are the biological fathers. The Romans, in turn, shared a number of features with the Nepalese Brahmans, especially during the earlier period discussed here. Roman culture emphasized female sexual "purity," premarital virginity for women, and a man's exclusive sexual rights to his wife (despite all the adultery of the later period). A woman's sexuality was, ideally, directly linked to the provision of heirs for one man, her husband. If a woman sexually transgressed (e.g., by committing adultery), her future fertility was not necessarily devalued; but the woman herself sometimes was, as we saw in the case of Julia. Europe, and later America, continued to express some of these Roman ideas, although a lot happened between the fall of Rome and modern times to change both kinship and gender in the Western world.

References

Aiyappan, A. 1937. Polyandry and Sexual Jealousy. *Man* 37: 104.

Aziz, Barbara Nimri. 1978. *Tibetan Frontier Families: Reflections of Three Generations from D'ing-ri.* Durham: Carolina Academic Press.

Baldson, J.P.V.D. 1963. *Roman Women: Their History and Habits.* New York: The John Day Company.

Beard, Mary. 1980. The Sexual Status of Vestal Virgins. *Journal of Roman Studies* 70: 12–27.

Bell, Diane. 1980. Desert Politics: Choices in the Marriage Market. In Mona Etienne and Eleanor Leacock, eds., *Women and Colonization: Anthropological Perspectives*, pp. 239–269. New York: Praeger.

Cohen, David. 1991. The Augustan Law on Adultery: The Social and Cultural Context. In David I. Kertzer and Richard P. Saller, eds., *The Family in Italy from Antiquity to the Present*, pp. 109–126. New Haven: Yale University Press.

Crook, J. A. 1986. Feminine Inadequacy and the *Senatusconsultum Velleianum*. In Beryl Rawson, ed., *The Family in Ancient Rome: New Perspectives*, pp. 83–92. Ithaca: Cornell University Press.

Deutsch, Monroe E. 1918. The Women of Caesar's Family. *Classical Journal* 13: 502–514

Fantham, Elaine, Helene Peet Foley, Natalie Boymel Kampen, Sarah B. Pomeroy, and H. Alan Shapiro. 1994. *Women in the Classical World.* New York: Oxford University Press.

Fox, Robin. 1980. *The Red Lamp of Incest*. New York: E. P. Dutton.

_____. 1989 [orig. 1967]. *Kinship and Marriage: An Anthropological Perspective*. Cambridge: Cambridge University Press.

Garnsey, Peter. 1991. Child Rearing in Ancient Italy. In David I. Kertzer and Richard P. Saller, eds., *The Family in Italy from Antiquity to the Present*, pp. 48–65. New Haven: Yale University Press.

Goldstein, Melvyn C. 1976. Fraternal Polyandry and Fertility in a High Himalayan Valley in Northwest Nepal. *Human Ecology* 4: 223–233.

Hunt, Morton. 1994. *The Natural History of Love*. New York: Anchor Books/ Doubleday.

Keesing, Roger M. 1975. *Kin Groups and Social Structure*. Fort Worth, Tex.: Holt, Rinehart and Winston.

Levine, Nancy. 1981. Perspectives on Love: Morality and Affect in Nyinba Interpersonal Relationships. In Adrian C. Mayer, ed., *Culture and Morality*, pp. 106–125. Oxford: Oxford University Press.

_____. 1988. *The Dynamics of Polyandry: Kinship, Domesticity, and Population on the Tibetan Border*. Chicago: University of Chicago Press.

Levine, Nancy, and Walter H. Sangree. 1980. Asian and African Systems of Polyandry. *Journal of Comparative Family Studies* 11(3): 385–410.

Lévi-Strauss, Claude. 1969 [orig. 1949]. *The Elementary Structures of Kinship*. Translated by James Harle Bell, John Richard von Strurmer, and Rodney Needham; edited by Rodney Needham. Boston: Beacon Press.

Massie, Allan. 1983. *The Caesars*. London: Secker and Warburg.

Pomeroy, Sarah B. 1975. *Goddesses, Whores, Wives and Slaves: Women in Classical Antiquity*. New York: Schocken Books.

Rawson, Beryl. 1986. The Roman Family. In Beryl Rawson, ed., *The Family in Ancient Rome: New Perspectives*, pp. 1–57. Ithaca: Cornell University Press.

Richlin, A. 1992. Julia's Jokes: Galla Placida and the Roman Use of Women as Political Icons. In Barbara Garlick, Susanne Dixon, and Pauline Allen, eds., *Stereotypes of Women in Power: Historical Perspectives and Revisionist Views*, pp. 65–191. New York: Greenwood Press.

Rubin, Gayle. 1975. The Traffic in Women: Notes on the "Political Economy" of Sex. In Rayna Reiter, ed., *Toward an Anthropology of Women*, pp. 157–210. New York: Monthly Review Press.

Sacks, Karen. 1979. *Sisters and Wives: The Past and Future of Sexual Equality*. Westport, Conn.: Greenwood Press.

Saller, Richard P. 1991. Roman Heirship Strategies in Principle and in Practice. In David I. Kertzer and Richard P. Saller, eds., *The Family in Italy from Antiquity to the Present*, pp. 26–47. New Haven: Yale University Press.

Schuler, Sidney Ruth. 1987. *The Other Side of Polyandry*. Boulder: Westview Press.

Trawick, Margaret. 1990. *Notes on Love in a Tamil Family*. Berkeley: University of California Press.

Treggiari, Susan. 1991. Ideals and Practicalities in Matchmaking in Ancient Rome. In David I. Kertzer and Richard P. Saller, eds., *The Family in Italy from Antiquity to the Present*, pp. 91–108. New Haven: Yale University Press.

Weiner, Annette B. 1976. *Women of Value, Men of Renown*. Austin: University of Texas Press.

7

A History of Euro-American Kinship and Gender

What characterizes our own Euro-American traditions in terms of kinship and gender? One central feature, first found in Northwest Europe far back in time, is the idea that each marriage will establish a new independent economic unit. People felt that one had to be able to *afford* marriage and reproduction. Regarding Northwest Europe in the period from 1350 to 1800, Beatrice Gottlieb (1993: 14) writes: "Every marriage there was regarded as an occasion for establishing a new household. It was assumed that nobody would get married until there was a place for the couple to live and a way for them to have a livelihood." This is quite different from the many other societies we have examined, where new wives or husbands are simply brought into larger economic units in which their labor is considered an asset. Possibly this pattern is related to another distinctive feature of Europe, as compared to the rest of the world—namely, a relatively late age at marriage, especially for women (Hajnal 1965). Between 1350 and 1800 the average age of marriage was around twenty-five, though women were often a little younger and men usually a little older (Gottlieb 1993: 60). In Europe, dowries needed to be secured for daughters and land or a livelihood needed to be arranged for sons before a new viable economic unit could be set up. Age at marriage varied in time, by region, and by social class. Aristocrats tended to marry at younger ages; in Eastern and Southern Europe and in the colonial New World, age at marriage was lower than in Northwest Europe; and in America it remained lower until the twentieth century (Gottlieb 1993: 59). But for Northwest Europe the later age had some important consequences: Women had fewer children, and couples entered marriage as mature adults.

Another frequently mentioned distinction, possibly related to these others, is that in the Western tradition, "love" becomes a fundamental part of marriage. Today, Euro-American marriages are not arranged by parents or elders, and they are supposed to be based on mutual attraction, affection, and emotional commitment. Normally, the purpose of these marriages is not to create political or social alliances, nor to continue lines of descent, but to make individuals happy and fulfilled. If children are part of the picture, their purpose, too, is to make parents happy and fulfilled. My own opinion is that this distinction has been somewhat overemphasized, not in terms of the importance of love in Euro-American marriages but, rather, in terms of its alleged lack in other parts of the world. To be sure, in most of the cases we have seen so far, the inclinations of brides and grooms are subordinated to the interests of larger kin groups. But this is not to say that sexual attraction plays no role in marriage initiation, since it clearly did so among the Nuer and the Navajo, or that some kind of affection and compatibility is not expected or at least hoped for in arranged marriage, as it is among the Nepalese Brahmans. What I have found is that in many cultural traditions there is some tension between the practical or sociopolitical dimensions of marriage and its emotional dimensions. One problem with this issue—having specifically to do with the question of deciding just when love entered marriage in Europe—is that no one is quite sure what "love" should mean. Are we talking about "consensual union," as opposed to arranged marriage? Or are we referring to what some have called "companionate marriage"? Or does "love" necessarily imply passion and romance, exclusiveness and sexual jealousy? As we will see in this chapter, the Euro-American tradition has developed a strong ideal of marital "love," but the nature and meaning of that love is not always easy to interpret.

Other features covered in this chapter concern the relatively restricted ties of kinship and lack of corporate descent groups in Euro-American societies. Historians and anthropologists have offered varying ideas about the origins and implications of this Euro-American pattern.

Finally, the chapter will show that, in some respects, the Euro-American tradition of kinship and gender is not unique; in fact, it has shared many important features with the Asian tradition (Goody 1993). One such feature is the differential evaluation of male and female sexual behavior, which I refer to simply as the "double sexual standard." Why in so many areas of Europe and Asia has there been such a concern with female premarital virginity (which must have been a particular challenge in Europe, given the late age at marriage for women)? Why in so many of these areas has the sexual behavior of women reflected on the honor of male kin? Why has female sexuality, and not male sexuality, been seen in so many contexts as negative? Because the double sexual standard has been such a vital part of gender in Euro-American history and lingers on to the present day, this chapter begins with a discussion of ideas about how and why it may have developed. Specifically, we will start with the work of anthropologist Jack

Goody, who draws several links between European and Asian patterns of marriage.

Dowry and the Double Standard

Goody (1973, 1976, 1993) has noted some general contrasts between the societies of sub-Saharan Africa and those of Europe and Asia (referred to collectively as "Eurasia"). In both cases he is talking about older, preindustrial societies, rather than about practices in the late twentieth century, although many of these traditions remain in some areas. Prominent among these contrasts was the widespread use of bridewealth in Africa and dowry in Eurasia. Recall that bridewealth is a marriage payment that passes from the kin of the groom to the kin of the bride. Eurasian dowry, according to Goody, is wealth that parents bestow upon a daughter at her marriage. It is wealth that "devolves" (to use Goody's term) upon the bride, but its ultimate purpose is to serve as an economic resource for the new couple and, beyond that, to support and be inherited by the couple's children. Dowry, together with the property that a groom will bring into the marriage in the form of his inheritance, becomes what Goody calls a "conjugal fund." Seen in this way, bridewealth and dowry are not mirror opposites of one another. The former ends up with the kin of the bride, and the latter ends up in a conjugal fund. However, the whole of a dowry need not be a conjugal fund. In some Eurasian societies, for example, certain dowry items (e.g., clothing, jewelry) are regarded as the bride's personal property, and other parts of a dowry may enrich not the bride or the couple but the kin of the groom.

Other Eurasian societies practice a form of marriage payment whereby the groom's family gives goods or property to the bride (or it gives goods to her father, who then gives most of these to the bride). Some writers have referred to these goods as bridewealth or "brideprice," but Goody calls them "indirect dowry," since, like the type of dowry discussed above (which Goody calls "direct dowry"), the goods come to the marriage with the bride and become a part of the conjugal fund.

Goody then links this contrast between African bridewealth and Eurasian dowry (direct or indirect) to broad differences in agricultural practices and inheritance patterns between Africa and Eurasia. In Africa (at least before the economic changes caused by colonialism in the nineteenth century), agriculture was largely a matter of shifting cultivation, carried out with a hoe or digging stick. Women were active in this type of agricultural production, which was oriented toward subsistence (Boserup 1970). Land was relatively plentiful, and was corporately controlled and used by kinship groups. Perpetuating this economy over time was an African pattern of inheritance that Goody calls "homogeneous": Males inherited from males and females from females. Productive property was generally held by and transmitted between males. It may help at this point to think in terms of a patrilineal-patrilocal society where males of a patriline inherit corporate rights to land, which they prepare for cultivation. Females marry into these units and plant, weed, and so on. From their mothers, these women will inherit personal possessions. Productive property is in the hands of males, who are organized into corporate kin groups; but women play essential roles in production.

This kind of production and inheritance system has been found in, and is compatible with, societies that are not stratified into socioeconomic classes. Imagine a society like the Nuer (Case 1) that pays bridewealth in cattle. If one family or kin group produces a lot of daughters, it may become temporarily wealthy because it will receive cattle upon the marriages of the daughters. But, who knows, in the next generation there may be a lot of sons, such that all this wealth moves out upon their marriages. With bridewealth, the cattle circulate, but they do not accumulate in one group. Hence bridewealth, tied as it is to the vagaries of the production of male and female children, works against the formation of true socioeconomic classes.

Goody sees the systems of production and bridewealth in the African situation as closely intertwined with African marriage forms. For one thing, he said, bridewealth facilitates polygyny. In cases where it takes some time for a family to amass enough wealth to pay out upon their sons' marriage, the males will marry relatively late. But the same family will be eager to marry its daughters, because doing so will bring in wealth that can then be used to pay the bridewealth of the sons. Thus, the females will marry relatively early. It also follows that husbands will tend to be older than wives. In short, the "surplus" of marriageable women is built in: There will always be more females of marriage age than males, allowing at least some males to have multiple wives without depriving other males of a wife.

Goody thus links up such African features as hoe agriculture, lack of socioeconomic classes, bridewealth, and polygyny. Before going further in this context, however, let's take a look at the Eurasian dowry situation along similar dimensions. Here the economy was quite different, in that it was predominantly based on plow agriculture. This form of agriculture increased productivity; fostered population growth; made land a more important but, with greater population density, a less abundant commodity; and ultimately promoted the rise of the state and the formation of socioeconomic classes. Some groups grew powerful and leisured while others became dependent workers. Thus, as plow agriculture was adopted in different regions, Eurasian societies became class stratified. Control of land (now a scarce resource) became a primary basis of status. Differences between families or status groups were rooted in differences in landholding. "Consequently it became a strategy of utmost importance to preserve those differences for one's offspring, lest the family and its fortunes decline over time" (Goody 1973: 25). The upper classes now had property and wealth to protect and pass on. These class divisions and the wealth within the upper classes were maintained by the practice of **class endogamy,** or what Goody calls "status group endogamy." The wealthy and privileged carefully arranged marriages within their own ranks to ensure that their children would enjoy the same or better status and wealth in the next generation.

How did this system work? Goody claims that it worked through the development of what he calls "diverging devolution," an inheritance pattern whereby property or wealth goes to both males and females—say, from one estate to both daughters and sons. Sons receive their portions (usually land) by becoming direct heirs; daughters receive their portions (usually movable property and cash) in the form of dowries at marriage. To maintain class endogamy, parents need only look for a *match* between a prospective bride's dowry and a prospective groom's inheritance. Indeed, according to Goody (1976: 14), it is this match of property or wealth that lies behind the English expression of marriage "as a 'match,' a word that implies the pairing of like to like."

Class endogamy does not mean that everyone marries an exact equal. In Europe, for example, parents were only too pleased to marry a son or daughter into a slightly wealthier or higher-status family, seeing this achievement as enhancing their own status. Here, "marriage into another social group was, in fact, the recognized path of social mobility in this rigidly stratified world" (Gottlieb 1993: 58). Moreover, in areas of India, hypergamy, or marriage of a woman upward into a higher group, was the norm. Hypergamous marriages have also been a theme of European myth and folklore, as in the story of Cinderella. But throughout Eurasia a general class endogamy was maintained, and wide gaps in the status of husband and wife were rare and usually denounced.

Thus dowry marriage became an instrument of class endogamy. And further, according to Goody, just as bridewealth promoted polygyny, so dowry promoted monogamy. Today, monogamy is the primary form of marriage throughout Eurasia. Even though some Asian societies permit polygyny, it is generally rare, for the most part used only in cases of a couple's infertility. Dowry promotes monogamy because, along with the groom's inheritance, it establishes a "conjugal fund" that will ultimately go to the children of the couple. It would be difficult and complicated to merge additional wives' dowries into the fund and to sort out the inheritance rights of the separate sets of children of these women. But when the conjugal fund is combined with monogamy, according to Goody, the husband-wife bond becomes strengthened and the relationship more solid and intimate. This arrangement contrasts with the African bridewealth-polygyny pattern whereby husbands and wives are more independent of one another.

The Eurasian type of economy, based on plow agriculture, also brought a profound change in sexual divisions of labor. Essentially, women's roles in production decreased whereas male labor became vital to agriculture. Boserup (1970: 51) makes the point that under hoe agriculture women were valued as workers and as child bearers, whereas in systems of plow agriculture they were valued only as mothers. Of course, in the upper classes, everyone was withdrawn from production since agricultural labor, depending on the period in question, was performed by slaves, serfs, or hired laborers. But upper-class men had important economic roles as land owners and managers, whereas upper-class women, with some exceptions in certain times and places, did not.

With this understanding of plow agriculture, social classes, and Eurasian marriages, Goody's analysis moves us deeper into the issue of gender. A key point, following Goody's thinking, is that perpetuation of the class system through class endogamy requires that property *devolve upon women*. Specifically, dowry must be given to a daughter to attract a husband of appropriate rank; the dowry is used to "match" what the prospective groom stands to inherit from his family. With a dowry, then, a woman is not merely inheriting personal items from her mother; she is now dowered, and can take a chunk of family wealth with her to her marriage. One might suppose that this arrangement was advantageous to women, or that it was gender equalizing, since both males and females would have been bringers of wealth to a marriage. But in fact women were not benefited.

Since family property was at stake in Eurasian dowry marriages, parents carefully arranged the unions of their offspring. We may presume that, since males were usually a little older at marriage than females and were seen as more responsible, they had more say in the arrangement of their own marriages. But regarding Eurasian women in this system, Goody (1973: 21) wrote that "it is a commentary on their lot that where they are more propertied they are initially less free as far as marital arrangements go." This statement, which sounds a bit indifferent to the plight of women, covers only a part of the difference between men and women in dowry systems. Later, however, Goody hints at what I think is really at stake— namely, a difference between men and women in terms of not only marital but also sexual freedom.

Goody writes that, just as it became important to control marriages to perpetuate status group endogamy, so it became important to control the premarital activities of offspring as well—hence the use of chaperones and the many restrictions on the behavior of young people to ensure that marriageable children did not form inappropriate attachments on their own. As Goody (1976: 17) further notes, one way to prevent the formation of inappropriate attachments was to "place a high positive value on premarital virginity, for sex before marriage could diminish a girl's honor, and reduce her marriage chances." But why was just the *girl's* honor diminished and *her* marriage chances reduced ? Alice Schlegel (1991: 345) has raised similar questions about Goody's statement, saying that we can accept it at face value only if we assume an innate male preference for virgins; otherwise, the statement takes for granted precisely what we need to explain. Schlegel then goes on to posit her own answer to the question of why it is *female* premarital virginity that is guarded, valued, or insisted upon, at least among the upper classes in Eurasian dowry systems. She argues that a girl's virginity had to be protected in order to prevent her from being impregnated by a lower-class man, a man who, claiming to be the father of her child, might demand a right to her (and hence her property) in marriage. Premarital sex for males, then, for the obvious reason that males do not get pregnant or give birth, was not nearly as great a threat to the system. It is interesting to note that, in Schlegel's argument, the social concern is not that a daughter will produce children out-of-wedlock, or that she will produce illegitimate children as such, but rather that her premarital sexuality could open a way for an undesirable (lower-class) male to stake a claim to her family's property.

The work of both Goody and Schlegel provides an insight into that most important element of Eurasian gender, one very familiar to all of us as it lingers on in Euro-American society: the double sexual standard. It's a little grim to think that, throughout all these centuries, Eurasian women themselves complied with, or even enforced, the double standard, only to wind up as the tools by which the privileged perpetuated the class system and socioeconomic inequality!

Possibly the whole complex of Eurasian cultural values centering on female "purity," including the notion that the honor of kin groups rests on the sexual purity of its women, is related to the institution of dowry as an instrument for preserving and perpetuating socioeconomic classes. Indeed, Schlegel (1991) holds that the value placed on female premarital virginity acquired "secondary meanings" in Eurasia, culminating in an emphasis on female marital chastity, discouragement of widow remarriage, and the view that celibacy is spiritually higher than marital sex—all factors we will encounter in the next section as we look at European traditions.

Others, too, have criticized Goody's work on Eurasian dowry. Some point out that in certain cases (e.g., in India) dowry is not considered female property, or property devolving on women, since women have no control over the use and distribution of their dowries (Stone and James 1995). And Diane Hughes (1978) sees dowry in southern Europe in a way that entirely differs from Goody's interpretation. She claims that although dowry was important in asserting family status, it was not so important in terms of inheritance. In fact, she says, dowry was a way to disinherit a daughter since it usually cut off any claim on her part to the truly valuable portion of her father's estate, namely the land. Meanwhile, Caroline Brettell (1991) has shown the great variation in actual marriage payments and inheritance practices in Mediterranean Europe, challenging the broad pattern that Goody tries to draw. She also observes that dowry may be determined not by inheritance interests but by cultural ideas about gender, such as the cultural notion that men are under obligation to provide for women.

Other explanations of the double sexual standard have also been offered. Sherry Ortner (1978), for example, discusses what she terms the "female purity ethic," the cultural idea that the honor of a social group rests on the purity of its women—that is, on female virginity and chastity. Unlike Goody, she emphasizes not changes in agricultural production but the rise of the state, which she says was based on those changes. The rise of the state was interwoven with class stratification and led to changes in the division of labor, religious thought, family structure, and marriage patterns. Ortner outlines the ways in which all these developments may have contributed to the female purity ethic; but she gives most weight to changes in marriage patterns, focusing in particular on the factor of hypergamy, or marriage of a woman into a higher-status group. She bases her argument on the assumption that hypergamy is an ideal, if not an actuality, in premodern state societies.

Ortner notes that families in class-stratified societies seek to marry their daughters "up" in order to enhance their own status through this link by marriage with higher-status families. Even when, and where, hypergamy was not easily achieved or at all common, it was a social ideal—an ideal for families that had a daughter to give in marriage. But in order for daughters to be married upward, their value needed to be enhanced. This, Ortner writes, is why dowry developed: to enhance the value of daughters so as to make them worthy of marriage to higher-status spouses. Similarly, a daughter's *virginity* enhanced her value "because virginity is a symbol of exclusiveness and inaccessibility. . . . A virgin is an elite female among females, withheld, untouched, exclusive" (Ortner 1978: 32). Women themselves are drawn into the whole hypergamy ideal. They want to marry up as Cinderella did; their culture encourages them to fantasize that "someday my prince will come" (Ortner 1978: 32).

In Ortner's view, it is not just that a daughter's virginity guards the honor of the kin group; indeed, females in this system also come to represent the higher classes. They represent what everyone wants and at the same time hates others for having: higher status. This, Ortner (1978: 32) says, may account for the "anger toward women expressed in these purity patterns."

Ortner's ideas are compelling; and a relation among hypergamy, status aspirations, and female virginity is easy to see. However, her argument breaks down precisely where, according to Schlegel, Goody's analysis falters. The idea that a daughter's virginity *enhances* her value is considered a given by both Ortner and Goody; it once again assumes some "innate preference" for virgins. (As noted, Schlegel argues that it takes for granted exactly what we want to explain.) In saying that a virgin is "withheld, untouched, exclusive," Ortner merely restates the issue. Why would males necessarily prefer brides who are "withheld, untouched, exclusive"? Why doesn't a little sexual experience enhance the value of brides instead? And, ultimately, why is it that virgin brides are seen as "enhanced" in some cultures but not in others?[1]

At least in Ortner's scheme, female compliance with the double standard is a little more understandable. Goody holds that dowry promotes status group endogamy and so maintains the class system; Schlegel's idea is that female virginity protects the family estate from seductive lower-class fortune hunters. In these models, women—who themselves uphold and cater to the double standard, or the female purity ethic—emerge as mere tools by which the upper classes maintain and transmit their hegemony. But in Ortner's analysis, women uphold the purity ethic for another reason: *They* want to marry hypergamously; after all, it is by this means that they and their children will rise in status and enjoy a higher standard of living. In Ortner's model, women may be crass materialists and status seekers, but at least it is *their own* motives and interests that play a role in maintaining the status quo.

Despite their different approaches and the occasional flaws in their arguments, Goody, Schlegel, and Ortner have all drawn a connection between the widespread double sexual standard and the equally widespread concern with social status. The emphasis on female premarital chastity (at least among the upper ranks) and the notion that the honor of a family or kin group depends on the sexual purity of its women are, according to these three authors, interrelated with issues of maintaining and transmitting status and wealth. Their work, especially that of Goody (1993), has drawn attention to what Euro-American cultures share with those of Asia in terms of kinship and gender. Whether we assume an "innate preference for virgins" or agree with Schlegel that the female purity ethic was connected to

---

[1] In a later publication Ortner (1981) addressed this question, but by this time she had modified her views on female virginity. Here she claims that the female purity ethic arises not in state societies but in "hierarchical" societies, regardless of whether they are also part of state systems. This observation was intended to accommodate her finding that female premarital chastity was emphasized in Polynesia before the advent of the state. Ortner also claims that the status of women is higher in hierarchical societies because here they are classed with men at various levels (castes, rank, etc.) in the hierarchy. She then suggests that a concern with female virginity and chastity is an expression of this higher status.

avoidance of lower-class fortune hunters, the fact remains that Eurasian societies placed new burdens on men and women to monitor and control the sexual behavior of women. Eurasian women had important connections to property, but they lost sexual autonomy and their behavior was subjected to a different standard than that applied to men. Thus the work of Goody and Schlegel addresses a question raised in Chapter 3 relating to a comparison between the Nuer and the Nepalese Brahmans—namely, Why do some societies develop concerns for female sexual purity? The ideas expressed by Goody and Schlegel place this issue in a broad regional and historical perspective and draw out the important interrelationships between gender and class inequalities.

From its Eurasian roots, the Euro-American system took some new turns of its own. In the following sections we will trace these changes as they occurred, first, in Europe and, then, in America.

From the Middle Ages to Modern Times

We saw in the last chapter that Roman society had become largely bilateral by the fall of the Roman Empire. So, too, had many Germanic tribes that invaded Rome; and some groups were already Christian as well. However, some of the Germanic tribes may have been patrilineal. As we know, these groups settled in the former Western Empire and developed a new culture that drew from Roman, Christian, and Germanic influences. Later in some parts of Europe, and among the aristocracy, patrilineal descent groups developed and persisted for a time; but the vast majority of Europe's people experienced a weakening of kinship groups altogether.

In Europe, certain marriage practices of the Germanic peoples persisted into the early Middle Ages. Some historians claim that earlier there had been a form of bridewealth marriage payment involving a transfer of wealth from the kin of the groom to the kin of the bride (McNamara and Wemple 1988: 84; Hughes 1978: 242). And later there emerged what Goody terms "indirect dowry"—as noted, the bestowing of property on the bride herself by the groom's kin. In some regions and during some periods, there were also various combinations of marriage payments, but gradually a shift to full direct dowry took place throughout Europe (Hughes 1978).

Another Germanic practice was polygyny, which in the early Middle Ages occurred among peoples such as the Anglo-Saxons and, at least at the level of the ruling classes, the Franks (Wemple 1981). For example, Merovingian and Carolingian kings were polygynous. And even after the Christian Church managed to impose monogamy on Europe's monarchs, the keeping of mistresses and concubines continued, often quite openly, among royalty and nobility. Among the Germanic peoples, husbands, but not wives, also had relatively easy access to divorce (Herlihy 1985: 51)—a situation that persisted until the eleventh century, when, once again, the church managed to make marriage indissoluble.

Bilateral societies, strict monogamy, and dowry characterized Europe, and later the European New World, for many centuries. Only in the last two centuries has one of these features, dowry, declined in importance and practice. But what was kinship like for these European peoples? How were their views and practices regarding kinship interrelated with gender? And in what ways did kinship and gender change over time?

Some readers may be surprised to learn that in certain respects, and for most classes of people, there has been very little change at all. During much of the Middle Ages and up to the 1800s, most men and women of Europe married in their middle to late twenties, had marriages that lasted only one or two decades at best, raised only a few children, and lived in small nuclear families (though their households may have contained servants and other nonkin). The variation in family forms in Europe has occurred not so much over time as between classes and regions. For example, it was only among the small, upper classes that large extended families lived in one household.

It is a myth that the small, nuclear family either helped to precipitate or was itself fostered by the Industrial Revolution; in fact, it was a well-established norm long before the 1800s.[2] Moreover, as Gottlieb (1993: 13) notes, "The outstanding fact about the nuclear family households is that all through the past in the Western world, no matter where we look or how far back we go in time, they were extremely common."

It is also a mistake to assume that marriages in the European past were of long duration, in contrast to the impermanence of modern marriages. Granted, in the period between 1000 and 1800 divorce was virtually impossible; but couples were instead commonly separated by death. As a result of low life expectancy, most marriages lasted only about ten or twenty years. In comparing modern marriages with those of earlier times, Gottlieb (1993: 105) comments that "it almost looks like a balancing act: a high rate of separation by death goes along with a low rate of separation by legal action, and vice versa. In the past when a couple got married they could not help but have ambivalent expectations about the durability of their relationship."

Yet, other aspects of family life and gender did undergo transformations in Europe. Undoubtedly an important force in shaping European kinship

---

[2] It may be another popular misconception that the small, nuclear family is unique to Western civilization. Indeed, Goody (1972) has demonstrated that, throughout the world, the rural "farm family" (a single unit of production, reproduction, and consumption) is typically nuclear and small-sized and varies only within very narrow limits, even in areas where joint or extended households mark a temporary phase in household development.

and gender was the Christian Church. For one thing, Christianity presented a revolutionary new message: Sex, for both men and women, is equally unspiritual and, outside marriage, equally sinful. The view of the early church was that lifelong celibacy among both men and women was the highest state. Marital sex was accepted, but only because it helped to avoid fornication. Many early Christians responded to this message by entering celibate religious orders; others attempted "continent marriage," whereby man and wife would live together but resist the temptations of the flesh. Of course, such an arrangement, if successfully practiced, would deny them children; but this was an age of religious fervor in which St. Augustine had proclaimed that the Second Coming of Christ would not be served by procreation, and in which it was popularly felt that the world was already worn out, overcrowded, and straining its resources (Herlihy 1985: 24).

Another interesting response to the Christian glorification of celibacy was "spiritual marriage," whereby unmarried virgins (called *agapetae*) lived with male clergy as the spiritual wives of these men. Not surprisingly, this arrangement, widely practiced between 100 and 500 A.D., came under suspicion of church leaders and was later pronounced heretical. The official Christian ideas about sexuality ultimately held firm. Celibacy, praised for all, was mandatory of clergy, and marital sex was permissible (indeed, sex came to be defined as a marital duty); but human lust was bad, both for men and women, and both outside and inside marriage.

Christian theology may have downgraded sex, but at least it did so equally for men and women. And yet the double standard lived on. In fact, as far as the law was concerned, it grew, reaching a peak around 1800 (Gottlieb 1993: 100). Throughout the Middle Ages and into the modern period, a wife could be repudiated by her husband for adultery or punished in court. But confronted with her husband's infidelities, she was expected to look the other way and had no legal recourse against him. Thus Christian Europe retained the attitudes of pagan Rome regarding adultery (Clark 1993: 39); and it likewise retained the association between the honor of a family and the chastity of its daughters and wives (Gottlieb 1993: 100). But there were other ideas at work here, too—ideas that bolstered the double sexual standard. These concern the ambivalent male images of women that have come down to us in the art and literature of the period. On the one hand, women were feared and blamed as sexual temptresses. Because the unholy but powerful force of human sexuality was believed to reside in women, they were seen as sexually charged and out of control. This comes very close to the view of women as inherently more sexual than men, and as having very little control over their own impulses, that we saw among the Nepalese Brahmans discussed in Chapter 3. In Europe, this image of women was attached to the biblical Eve, who tempted Adam away from God's command. On the other hand, women were idolized as good and pure and so were identified with the Virgin Mary. Mary was the ideal woman. But of course no mortal woman could actually be like Mary, who encompassed both virginity and motherhood. A married, and thus nonvirgin, woman was particularly vulnerable to these ambivalent male views. As Gottlieb (1993: 100–101) comments, "The awful thing about married women was that, once they had sexual experience, the floodgates might open and the potential Eve in every woman might emerge. Men seem to have been both repelled and fascinated by this possibility."

Although Christianity opposed the double sexual standard, Christian teaching affirmed the subordination of wives to husbands. We may recall what the Apostle Paul had written:

> Wives, be subject to your husbands, as to the Lord. For the husband is the head of the wife as Christ is head of the church. . . . As the church is subject to Christ, so let wives also be subject in everything to their husbands. . . . [A] man shall leave his father and mother, and shall be joined to his wife, and the two shall become one. . . . Let each one of you love his wife as himself, and let the wife see that she respects her husband. (Ephesians 5:22–33)

Thus husbands were to love wives and spouses were to be "one," but within this unity the divinely sanctioned authority of the husband is clear. Gottlieb (1993: 91) refers to the proper attitude of European husbands as one of "loving despotism." This attitude was supported by the social and legal fact that "when a woman married, her identity was swallowed up in her husband's." Disobedient wives were disparaged as "shrews," whereas "there were laws all over Europe giving men the right to beat their wives" (Gottlieb 1993: 92).

In short, the prominence and general position of women may have been relatively high in the early Middle Ages; but just as official Christian teaching lost out to a double sexual standard as it filtered through real society, medieval women apparently lost ground on other fronts as well. In the early and high Middle Ages, the absence of males (who had gone off to wars and the Crusades) left upper-class women to manage estates on their own, perhaps giving them an independence similar to that of Roman women during the Punic Wars. Also in the early Middle Ages, women were prominent as land managers and landowners (Herlihy 1962). But later, in most of Europe, changes in law and inheritance practice considerably restricted women's ability to accumulate property (Herlihy 1985: 100).

Their role in medicine was likewise restricted. Women had been active in healing, particularly in mid-wivery, but this potential could not develop because medical training moved into the universities, from which women were excluded (Williams and Echols 1944: 43). Moreover, in the medieval towns where a class of rich merchants grew, women initially played active economic roles. But later the merchant guilds excluded women, and by the

1400s they predominated in the lower-paying, less prestigious jobs, much as they do today.

Herlihy (1971) notes the effects on women of the Gregorian reform (1073–1085) that banned marriage of the Catholic clergy. Before this reform was enacted, marriage of the clergy was common, though long officially discouraged by the church. Also common were monasteries containing both men and women; and, as noted earlier, the virgin *agapetae* were "spiritually married" to clergy. But all of these practices disappeared after the reform. Men continued in their religious roles, albeit more celibately; but what effect did the reform have on women? As Herlihy (1971: 9–10) describes it:

> The Gregorian reform of the medieval Church . . . seems to have lowered the status of women, by virtually excluding them from one of the most powerful elite groups in society. . . . In the battle for clerical celibacy, the leaders of the reformed Church nurtured an exaggerated fear of women. . . . This hostility towards women went on to influence other institutions of society, most notably the schools and the new universities. With some notable exceptions, the world of formal scholarship in the Middle Ages was a bastion of male chauvinism, and this particular tradition has been slow in dying.

Although European society was bilateral, there was a patrilineal twist in the system that emerged in several contexts. When the use of last names became common (around the mid-1300s), they were transmitted from fathers to children, and wives adopted the last names of husbands. Women received dowries, but inheritance otherwise favored sons. (In the absence of sons, however, a daughter might have inherited property.) In most regions the dowry was under the husband's control for the duration of the marriage. A woman could not ordinarily sell or alienate either this dowry or property she inherited from a deceased husband, as both were destined to be inherited by her children.

Above all, at least in the upper classes, there was a "patrilineal ideology"— a widely expressed feeling that sons, and not daughters, carried on the "line" by continuing the family name and serving as its heirs. For this reason the birth of sons was often favored over that of daughters. Indeed, this was always the case where royal succession was concerned. Daughters may have been particularly unwelcome during the period of dowry inflation, in the thirteenth century. According to Herlihy (1985: 98), the transition from indirect dowry to direct dowry shifted the "burden of matrimony" from the groom's family to the bride's family. But the burden grew until "poets and preachers protested the rising costs of marriage, which the bride and her family were forced to meet. In the early fourteenth century Dante remarked in *The Divine Comedy* that the size of dowries was exceeding all reasonable measure, and he harkened back to better days, in the eleventh and twelfth centuries, when the birth of a daughter did not strike terror in her father's heart" (Herlihy 1985: 99).

This situation became a major social problem. Many females were unable to marry at all for lack of adequate dowry. Convents were able to absorb some of them, but even this remedy had its limits; and in any case, convents also required dowries (albeit lesser ones) from the girls they took. Providing dowries for otherwise unmarriageable girls became a major focus of Christian charity during this period (Herlihy 1985: 99).

Part of the problem behind dowry inflation was precisely the fact that dowries were used to express the social status of the brides' families. In short, the momentum was driven by the status-seeking of the brides' families, not by the quest of the grooms' families to enrich themselves. As Gottlieb (1993: 222) writes: "A woman's dowry was as much an expression of her family's status as were abstract notions of blood and honor. To obtain a wife with a large dowry did not necessarily make a man richer. In fact it could be a zero sum game. The constant preoccupation with dowries would probably cause him to turn his wife's dowry into a dowry for a sister or daughter, thus constantly recirculating the money for the same purpose."

Along with preserving or enhancing their status through the marriage of daughters, Europeans of the propertied classes were, as we have seen, concerned with transmitting their property and status over the generations. There were many different patterns of inheritance, but the central issue was: How can estates be transmitted intact over time, given that each generation may produce a number of sons? One solution was **primogeniture,** or inheritance by only the eldest son. This arrangement was used in parts of northern Europe and was particularly favored by England. Primogeniture preserved an estate intact, but it did not address the problem of what to do with younger sons. Not being heirs, they were obviously poor marriage prospects. Some went off to religious orders or to fight in the Crusades; others went off to become fortune hunters in search of an heiress with no brothers. Still others simply remained behind to work on their older brother's estate.

In the southern part of Europe it was more common to divide estates equally among sons, but a drawback, of course, was that estates would be fragmented. One way to guard against this outcome, or to lessen its effects over time, was to adopt a practice we encountered in the last chapter: kin group endogamy. In this case, two brothers, as equal heirs, could split an estate in one generation; but if the daughter of one married the son of the other, the property would come back to the original estate in the next generation. In a similar way, occasional marriages between second cousins, third cousins, and so on, could help keep property consolidated within a kin group.

In parts of Italy, where property was usually divided equally among sons, yet another development occurred. Brothers sometimes kept their property together in a system of communal ownership. Over time, this system encompassed true corporate patrilineal descent groups. Some of these Italian *consorteria*, as they were called, developed a solid patrilineal solidarity, expressed through the adoption of a lineage name and a coat of arms, as well as through the offering of prayers for their ancestors in the groups' own corporately owned family chapels. Others became powerful merchant groups in cities. By legal contract they admitted some nondescent members into their corporations and went on to found banks and commercial companies that ultimately played a great role in the economic transformation of Italy during the Middle Ages.

Elsewhere in Europe, nobility formed patrilineal descent groups that likewise developed names and coats of arms. But none of these latter groups persisted for very long or set the pace for the modern age. Europe embarked instead on another path, leading away from descent groups or large kin groups of any kind. Indeed, the overall thrust of European history was toward a breaking down of the wider ties of kinship, a paring back until only egocentric kindreds and restricted sets of relatives remained. This was a distinct trend, one that clearly established the first patterns of kinship and gender among Europeans in North America. But how and why did such patterns come about?

A few anthropologists have tried to answer this question in different ways. Robin Fox (1993: 143–144) suggests that the wider ties of European kinship were broken down with the rise of the modern state. The state, in turn, works through bureaucracy and binding contracts, not through ties of "blood" or alliances made through marriage. And since it requires the loyalty of its citizens, it would be threatened by a people's higher loyalties to powerful kin groups. According to Fox, the state can and does tolerate small families, but this is as far as it will go.

A more intriguing, though also more controversial, answer to the same question has come from Goody (1983), whose earlier work on dowry we have already reviewed. Goody claims that the real force behind the breakdown of wider ties of kinship in Europe was the Christian Church. As Christianity rose in Europe, moving from its status as a minor sect to that of a fully organized and eventually very powerful church, kinship groups declined, having failed to develop and flourish as corporate units. The reason, according to Goody, is that the church sought to acquire property and wealth. The success of its quest is, of course, well documented. But in the beginning the church had no wealth and, according to Goody (1983: 91), needed funds to establish itself and to conduct its ecclesiastical and charitable activities. How did it achieve this end, and what connection was there between church wealth and European kinship? Goody argues that in order to facilitate bequests and other donations from its followers, the church sought to sever the hold that kin groups had on property. Toward this end it instituted "reforms" in marriage and other practices that ultimately broke down kin groups and ties between kin in Europe.

Starting in the fourth century, the church explicitly introduced a number of changes in the lives of its members. Specifically, it attempted to ban such practices as polygyny, clerical marriage, cousin marriage, adoption, the levirate, divorce, and concubinage, to name just the major ones covered by Goody. (We have already examined the early church's position on some of these practices, such as polygyny, clerical marriage, and divorce.) A ban on close cousin marriage began in the fourth century; and by the eleventh century, the prohibition had been extended to cover all persons related consanguineally within seven generations.[3] The church successfully discouraged adoption until the Reformation. It also banned the levirate in the fourth century; indeed, it banned marriage to the widow or widower of any close kin, as well as marriage to a dead spouse's sibling. Finally, the church strongly discouraged men from taking concubines.

All of these practices, says Goody, had one thing in common: They were *strategies of heirship*. All of them involved the passing of property from one generation to the next, and some of them involved ways of doing this *within the kinship group*. In earlier chapters we saw how polygyny, for example, can be a used by a man to increase the number of his heirs or, if a first wife is infertile, to produce an heir. We also saw that divorce, with remarriage, can be used by childless married men and women to test their fertility in other unions and so potentially acquire children and heirs. The Nuer, as noted in Chapter 3, made use of both of these strategies. And the levirate, another option among the Nuer, can be used to keep a woman's fertility (her ability to produce heirs) in her husband's kinship group. In this chapter and the last one, we also saw how parallel cousin marriage, or endogamy within a kin group, works to keep property intact and in the control of the kin group as it moves between the generations.

What the church did, then, was to ban or discourage such practices in order to lessen the use of these handy means of promoting the production of heirs. Thus, in situations where people had property but no heir, they could be persuaded to give the property to the church. If a married man found his union to be childless, well, instead of trying polygyny, adoption, or divorce and remarriage, he could stay childless and bequeath his property to the church upon his death.

---

[3] Following Germanic custom, the generations were counted as "degrees." The number of degrees between ego and another relative covered the number of generations between their common ancestor and the person furthest removed from the common ancestor. Thus, for example, ego's FBSS would be a relative in the third degree. The church's restrictions on marriage were gradually reduced to relatives in the fourth degree.

Similarly, the church not only banned the levirate but discouraged the remarriage of widows to anyone. Widows reclaimed control of their dowries; and if they were childless, they could also gain control of their husband's property. If they remarried, their property would go into another marriage. But if they did not, it could be given to the church. Indeed, the church readily took widows (with their property) into nunneries, cared for them, and made them caretakers of others, such as orphans. It is also true that a significant proportion of the early converts to Christianity were women and that women were the largest donors of property to the church (Herlihy 1962).

When viewed in this way, many of the church's policies make a new kind of sense, one in keeping with the "motive" of property acquisition. Goody claims, for example, that the ban on clerical marriage, though it did not bring property in, nevertheless prevented church property from seeping out, since the celibate clergy would not have been tempted to use church wealth to provision their own wives and children.

According to Goody, some of the church's moves, such as its ban on polygyny and divorce, were aimed at increasing heirlessness—by reducing the number of people who had claims, by kinship, to property. The church's policies on concubines would have had this effect, too. Earlier a man could name his children by a concubine as his heirs; but now, as decreed by the church, these claims were taken away. In Goody's (1983:77) words, "under Christianity, the concubine became the mistress and her children bastards."

Other of the church's moves appear to have been aimed not at increasing heirlessness as such but at loosening the hold of kin groups on property—that is, by finding ways to prevent property from staying within kin groups over the generations. Of course, whatever the church could do to place a wedge between kin groups and property, it did to its own material advantage since any such loosened property could more easily wind up in church coffers. Goody (1983: 45) puts it best: "If they [the church's prohibitions] inhibited the possibilities of a family retaining its property, then they would also facilitate its alienation." In essence, the church wanted persuadable *individuals*, not powerful *corporate kin groups,* to have control over property and to make uncontested decisions about its ultimate destination. Marriage between cousins or between certain degrees of consanguineal kin was banned, then, precisely because such marriages promoted the consolidation of estates and their undivided inheritance within kinship groups.

With the ban on cousin marriage, the church seemed to win out on two fronts. First, the ban gradually helped break up property. Second, for centuries to come, people (especially those in the upper classes) were able to marry their cousins anyway, simply by paying for dispensations from the church; and the payments for these dispensations increased church wealth (Goody 1983:146).

The church fought for and eventually gained control over marriages in general. It won its battles against endogamy and divorce, and increasingly influenced the marriage ceremony. More and more it came to define not only who could or could not marry whom but what marriage itself should mean. In 1439, marriage became the seventh Sacrament.

In this process the church came to define marriage as based on the consent of the partners rather than on the arrangement of the parents. Thus a consensual union made in defiance of parents was still valid in the eyes of the church.[4] Again, according to Goody, this position was in the interests of the church since it eroded kin groups' control over property transmission, as exercised by the older generation through its arrangement of the younger generation's marriages. This point is significant because it suggests how a particular Western idea—that love should be *a basis for* marriage—may have been promoted. Goody claims that another distinctive feature of the modern Western family—its "child-oriented" nature—was also linked to the church (1983: 153). The church did encourage a strong mother-child bond—for example, by discouraging wet-nursing and glorifying the Madonna and Child in art.

Regarding love matches and child-oriented families, Goody (1983: 155) concludes that "these features, sometimes seen as definitive of the 'Western Family' (and sometimes only of the English variety), are surely intrinsic to the whole process whereby the church established its position as a power in the land, a spiritual power certainly, but also a worldly one, the owner of property, the largest landowner, a position it obtained by gaining control of the system of marriage, gift and inheritance." In addition to love within marriage and child-oriented families, the autonomous nuclear family began in Europe with church policies. All of these developments, moreover, owe little to "mercantile capitalism, industrial society, Hollywood or the Germanic tradition" (Goody 1983: 155).

According to Goody, all of the "strategies of heirship" that the church fought against, and conquered, mark the very set of traits (such as monogamy, love matches, and lack of corporate kin groups) that came to distinguish the European pattern of kinship and marriage from the pattern that remained in Asia. Indeed, Goody groups these traits within a single frame, and it is a frame grounded in a single cause: the material acquisitiveness of the Catholic Church. In support of this claim, he presents a wealth of historical evidence. He also demonstrates that other forces were not behind these "reforms," that the church in fact had to fight hard for them, and that several levels of European society strongly resisted them.

---

[4] This ruling was made official by the Council of Trent in the mid-sixteenth century.

Some critics, uncomfortable with this image of the church as a single-minded pursuer of property (Verdery 1988; Herlihy 1985: 13), question whether the church leaders could have been so consistently far-sighted and cunning over so many centuries or, for that matter, so materialistic and manipulative in the first place. Goody (1983: 57) does point out that the church leaders never couched their policies in such terms; instead, they gave moral or practical explanations for their position. For example, marriage within a range of consanguineal kin was prohibited not in the name of breaking up property but for the moral reason that consanguineal kin should be respectful of one another and not intimate, or for the practical reason that marrying more distantly would widen the social net of alliances.

But then we must ask, Did the church leaders even know what they were up to? On this point, Goody (1983: 215) himself seems not entirely sure:

> It may seem that I have allocated the Church a rather calculating role in the development of kinship. But when I refer to the Church acting in its own interest, I do not necessarily mean that the whole Church was monolithically engaged in consciously promoting those interests. . . . [Rather] . . . I am talking about the means by which ends are achieved, whether or not those means are aspects of the actor's intention. . . . But in the long run I do assume some kind of relationship between actions and interests.

However the church's rulings on marriage came about, Goody also points out how the church fostered notions of a new "spiritual kinship," almost as though it realized that it needed to give back to its people something of what it had ripped away from them. God was the Father, and priests became "fathers"; members became "brothers" and "sisters" to one another; and so on. On top of this, it created a new, special category of fictive kin—godparents—that created new ties between people. These ties did not involve property, and, in the absence of adoption, which was discouraged, they provided some security to children in the event that they were orphaned.

Another critic of Goody's ideas is historian Richard Saller (1991), who points out that some of what Goody considers to have been new marriage practices urged by the Catholic Church were not really new at all; for example, Roman society also was strictly monogamous and did not practice the levirate.

An even more challenging criticism has come from Michel Verdon (1988), who essentially turns Goody's argument on its head. His thesis is that European kinship, far from being the result of church acquisitiveness, came about as "a strategy of female emancipation!" (1988: 488). He notes, as did Goody, that many of the early Christian converts were women and that many of the bequests to the church over the early centuries were made by women. But Verdon (1988: 500) then charges that Goody's thesis characterizes women as powerless victims, as "people who are acted upon instead of people who are capable of deciding for themselves, capable of understanding their own interests and acting accordingly." Next, from a perspective opposite that of Goody, Verdon takes up the question of the development of European kinship. He asks not why and how the church pursued women's property but, rather, why women wanted to give their property to the church. His answer is that what women saw in Christianity, and what they wanted, was *freedom*—namely, freedom from marriage and reproduction. This, according to Verdon, was what the new religion of Christianity offered, and what no other major religion had offered before: the freedom to choose to marry or not. Some religions, he notes, prescribed celibacy for a priesthood, "but no church openly stated that the ideal life was a *life outside marriage*, not for a chosen few, but for everyone" (1988: 493; original emphasis).

The church freed women through its praise of lifelong celibacy as the highest state and, for weaker people, through its praise of chastity; in other words, it took the core position that, where possible, "the less sex the better" (1988: 496). As we saw before, the early church deemed sex to be decidedly unspiritual: It was best to choose lifelong celibacy, but since many ordinary people could not, they should at least marry to avoid fornication. Indeed, as the Apostle Paul had written: "But if they cannot exercise self-control they should marry. For it is better to marry than to be aflame with passion" (1 Corinthians 7:9). Even within marriage, sex was excusable only as a means for reproduction. Carnal desire—again, even within marriage— was bad. And celibacy and chastity, like conversion to Christianity itself, were matters that had to be freely chosen by individuals. In effect, Christianity promoted individual free choice over both religion and sex.

From this core position on sex followed many of the church's new policies on marriage. For example, as noted, the church came to define marriage as based on the consent of the partners rather than on the arrangement or permission of the parents. And the free choice of partners, Verdon argues, logically followed from the free choice to marry or not. In the same way, both the ban on marriages between close kin and the ban on the levirate can be interpreted as means of freeing women from social pressure *to* marry—that is, as means of freeing them from being pressured by their kin into unions they did not want.

Why did women find liberation in the choice to marry or not? Verdon (1988: 503) provides an answer:

> In circumstances where reproduction is not controlled and women do not have equal access to labour opportunities, to wealth and means of production, women remain above all child-bearers and child-carers. This is precisely where Christianity struck, and why it had such appeal for women. It offered women an ideal life free of child-bearing and child-caring, and free of their subordination

to reproduction and, indirectly, to men. . . . Freedom from men could only come from freedom from reproduction; and freedom from reproduction, from freedom from sex. . . . If the Church saw its profit in women's property, women saw their own profit in virginity and church-assisted widowhood.

Thus, women, or at least many women, saw in Christianity a sanctioned alternative to the reproductive roles that were otherwise imposed upon them and immersed them in subordination to men. In this way, Verdon draws close ties among European kinship, gender, and religion. These ties are strengthened in his discussion of adoption, which, he points out, was not so much banned by the church as discouraged. Adoption largely disappeared as a European practice over the centuries; and the reason it did so, according to Verdon, is that, with the conversion to Christianity, the ancestral cult disappeared. In earlier Roman society, he notes, "the spiritual salvation of any man . . . depended entirely on his leaving descendants to perform this cult . . . since . . . the soul left without anyone to look after it is condemned to eternal damnation" (1988: 497). Thus men without male descendants to perform the ancestral cult adopted other men as heirs, leaving their property in return for this service. But when Christianity took hold, adoption was no longer necessary; now that salvation was a matter of the individual soul, it no longer depended on reproduction. It was this change that allowed Christianity to assert a new equality between the sexes: "Christianity established an absolute equality between the sexes from the spiritual point of view since spiritual salvation no longer rested on the ability to produce a line of sons" (1988: 498).

In valuing neither marriage nor reproduction, early Christianity was liberating to women, but what about men? What was in it for them? Verdon writes that the church offered men, as husbands, domination over wives: "Once women chose marriage, the Church then advocated submission to their husbands. There was thus enough in it for men" (1988: 504).

Historians and anthropologists may disagree about how the European pattern of kinship and gender emerged, but many, including both Goody and Verdon, trace it to and through the Christian Church. Goody holds that material conditions (namely, the economic interests of the church) were the prime movers, whereas Verdon holds that Christian ideology and its appeal to women paved the way. In Goody's view, male clergy were in command and women remained fairly passive, perhaps guilelessly losing their money, whereas in Verdon's scheme women were assertive, self-interested actors. It is also possible that parts of both views are true. But in opposition to Verdon we should note that, if women used Christianity for their own liberation, it was a strategy that ultimately did not work. Most women ended up married, with children and dominating husbands, in a society that stressed the double standard. Those who opted for a life of celibacy were secluded from society.

In the end, what did emerge was a European pattern that saw the break-down of kin groups and stressed monogamy, marital permanence, and marital love. Concomitant developments included class endogamy, dowry, and a relatively late age of marriage for women. Our next question must then be: What happened when this pattern was transferred to the shores of America?

The American Experience

Just as Gottlieb (1993) and others assert that families of the European past were in some ways not so different from modern ones, Stephanie Coontz (1992) makes a similar point regarding the families of the American past. Coontz argues that Americans nostalgically look back to a past that never was, that we have created an image of stable, happy families of the past that is largely mythical. In doing so, she says, we blur our vision of the troubled present, rife with family "breakdown," domestic violence, teenage pregnancies, and alienated youth. Today 20 percent of American children live in poverty; but in 1900 the same percentage lived in orphanages because their parents could not afford to raise them (Coontz 1992: 4). And marriages of the past did not last longer than modern ones because they were likely to be terminated by the death of a partner. Thus, about the same proportion of children were raised in single-parent households in 1900 as at present. Divorce rates have continually risen since the 1960s, but some studies have shown that marital satisfaction was greater in the late 1970s than in the late 1950s (Coontz 1992: 16). As for teenage pregnancy rates, they reached a peak in 1957, not during the 1990s (Coontz 1992: 39). All these comparisons with the past, and many others, suggest extreme caution in interpreting the country's problems as stemming from a breakdown of "family values" or the movement away from the "traditional" American family.

But what did happen in America? And how did our organization of kinship and family, whatever it was, affect ideas about gender and relations between the sexes? Of course, these questions are complicated by the fact that America has long been a land of ethnic and class diversity. The history of working-class families has been quite different from that of the middle class. The experience of black families has contrasted with those of white families (see Gutman 1984; Stack 1974). And immigrant groups have had varying experiences in this country (see Yanagisako 1987 on Japanese Americans and di Leonardo 1984 on Italian Americans). Moreover, even within one ethnic group, peoples' experiences with kinship and gender relationships vary by region and by class (di Leonardo 1987). Bearing all this diversity in mind, we will briefly explore some major shifts in American kinship and gender from the colonial period to the present with a focus on the white middle class.

The early European settlers in the New World brought with them some key features of their European tradition that I have just discussed—namely, attachment to the state and notions of private property and socioeconomic class stratification. But one thing the colonists did not bring with them were large descent groups; nor, with few individual exceptions, did these ever develop among their descendants or the new European immigrants.

The colonists lived in households, each typically consisting of a nuclear family; wealthier households contained servants as well. In addition, many less wealthy families sent their children to wealthier households to work as servants or to learn a trade, a practice also common in Europe. Some people had come to the New World as indentured servants, agreeing to serve a master's household in return for the cost of passage out of Europe. Thus many households contained large numbers of people who were not kin to one another. It was these households, rather than their own "biological" families as such, that were important in people's daily lives (Coontz 1988: 83–85). Biological children were treated much like servants, especially if they were of the same or similar age.

The households themselves did not contain separate, private spaces for married couples or for parents and their children. As Coontz (1988: 85) writes: "The central room or hall was where work, meals, play, religious instruction, and often sleep took place. . . . Even genteel families put several people to a room and several people to a bed. Most household members sat together on benches for meals and prayers, rather than in separate chairs. There was thus little concept of a private family set apart from the world of work, servants, and neighbors." Households were closely linked to one another, and highly interdependent on one another for cooperation and economic exchanges. People freely intruded into one another's households, and the affairs of all were carefully monitored and regulated by village and church officials. What we would consider very private business today was then considered the business of neighbors and the whole community. This point is strikingly illustrated by Coontz (1988: 85–86), who cites a study by Cott (1976):

> The assumption that household affairs were the business of all community members is seen in Nancy Cott's study of divorce records, which show that neighbors nonchalantly entered what modern people would consider the most private areas of life. Mary Angel and Abagail Galloway, for example, testified that they had caught sight through an open window of Adam Air "in the Act of Copulation" with Pamela Brichford. They walked into the house "and after observing them some time . . . asked him if he was not Ashamed to act so when he had a Wife at home."

The contrast to the private, bounded nuclear family of later American life is obvious. The family of colonial times was not separated out, nor was "the home" seen as a retreat from the strain of the outside world. Indeed, since the colonial household was a center of economic production (in terms of, for example, agriculture and farm management, cloth production and trade), there was little division between the public and domestic spheres of life. In the household, both women and men played active roles in production. Aside from food processing and preparation, wives wove cloth, traded with neighbors, managed servants, and helped to keep accounts (Coontz 1988: 93).

Each household was under the authority of its male property owner. Wives were under the authority of husbands, but so were children, servants, apprentices, and anyone else attached to the man's household. In fact, colonial society itself was altogether hierarchical, such that lower males were subservient to higher ones to the same extent that wives were to husbands. Women "did not need to grapple with reasons for their lack of equal status, since equal status was not even a social value for men" (Coontz 1988: 97). This was a society that viewed its parts as interdependent and so required a hierarchy for its organization. Women were clearly subordinate, but "a colonial woman's subordination was viewed as a social necessity—one of many unequal relations required by society—not as a unique female condition caused by her biology" (Coontz 1988: 97).

Many of us associate colonial society with rather strict rules governing sex. And, indeed, there were laws against fornication and adultery in all the colonies (though these laws seem to have reverted to the Roman definition of adultery as involving sex between a man and a married women, excluding sex between a married man and an unmarried woman). Adultery was often severely punished, with public flogging or even death. Dancing and certain forms of dress were also widely forbidden. Still, sex was openly and frankly discussed, offenses were openly described and punished, and sexual matters were not hidden away from children (Coontz 1988: 89). Moreover, wives were expected to be affective companions to husbands (Hunt 1994: 236).

Initially, marriages followed the general European pattern of dowry (both direct and indirect) and parental control. In some places, such as the South (U.S.) and New France (Quebec) (Molloy 1990: 8), cousin marriage was practiced in order to consolidate land and transmit wealth in family lines; and thus, as in Europe, the dowry and endogamy promoted the solidification of classes.

The patriarchal colonial family faded away as population expansion, migration, new waves of immigrants, urbanization, and other economic and political changes occurred in America. In general terms there was a trend toward increasing *privacy* of the nuclear family. However, this trend took hold much more slowly in rural and working-class families (Hareven 1977), and its effects were gradual among all classes. Nevertheless, families maintained important ties with wider kin for support and help, especially during periods of war, economic disruption, and urbanization over the next few centuries.

Important changes in family life and gender correlated with industrialization in the late eighteenth and early nineteenth centuries. New industries needed workers and managers, often at work sites away from the home. Whereas the household had formerly been a unit of production and consumption, it was now a unit of consumption only. Hence the split between the home (private, domestic) and the workplace (public, productive) was born. Among poor and working-class people, both women and men went out to work, though women were pushed into lower-paying jobs with less hope of advancement—as is still generally true for American women today. Among the middle and upper classes, industrialization meant the withdrawal of women from production. Their roles became confined to the home, to childrearing, to domesticity. Indeed, among the middle classes, a nonworking wife was important for the social image and self-esteem of males, who believed it was their duty to provide for and protect wives and children. It was with a sense of shame that a middle-class married woman went to work because she *had* to, owing to widowhood, sudden unemployment in the husband, or some other financial difficulty.

This shift of production from the home to the workplace had an impact on American family life and gender that cannot be overstated. Many writers have drawn attention to the links between the industrial capitalist economy that prevailed at the time and the perpetuation of patriarchal social relations in America and Europe. Removed from production, wives become economically dependent on husbands and in this condition are easily subordinated to them. Males, now expected to support wives and children, "become bound to their work and often endure difficult conditions out of fear of losing their jobs and falling short of their society's and their own expectations" (Bonvillain 1995: 171). Thus in the "capitalist patriarchy," workers are subordinate to employers, and women are subordinate to men. Women are also useful to capitalism because in their domestic roles they sustain and reproduce the workers. In addition, when and where women have to work, their labor is available at less cost to the capitalists.

Between the period of early industrialization and the present, important shifts have occurred in men's and women's roles, masculine and feminine ideals, and the ideals and realities of family life and kinship. A cornerstone on which these changes have turned, and one that may be unique to the American experience, is that notions of female sexuality appear to have been perpetually at odds with ideas about female fertility. Sheila Rothman (1978) discusses the transitions in American ideas about "woman's proper place" that have taken place between the end of the 1800s and the 1960s. These ideas have passed sequentially through stages she labels "virtuous womanhood," "educated motherhood," "wife-companion," and, finally, "woman as person." These terms refer to ideals of womanhood, and they apply largely to middle-class women; but they are ideals that have shaped the lives of real women and have permeated American popular culture. We will take a look at these stages and examine the tension in each between female sexuality and fertility.

"Virtuous womanhood" appeared after the Civil War in the closing decades of the nineteenth century. At that time, women considered themselves and were considered by men to be innately more pure, more virtuous, than men. Of course, bad, unvirtuous women existed as well, but the idea was that women had a natural capacity for higher virtue and that this higher virtue could benefit men and society. Women were supposed to encompass and foster this "inherently feminine kind of morality, chastity, and sensibility in their families and throughout the society" (Rothman 1978: 5). The virtuous woman was also perceived to be frail and, indeed, quite vulnerable to periodic mental breakdowns. Doctors and others urged that great care be taken to ensure her well-being, which entailed restrictions on all kinds of physical and mental activities.

The virtuous woman was particularly needed in the home, especially in her role as mother. Children were now seen as creatures in great need of the care and love that only a mother could give. Wives were supposed to be caregiving "mothers" to their husbands as well. With their virtue, they were to tame their husbands who, after all, were "savage beasts" (Rothman 1978: 82). These nurturing and caretaking aspects of women, which rested on their child-bearing capacities (i.e., fertility) were opposed to women's other dimension, their sexuality. This dichotomy was seen not only in ideas about proper female chastity and sexual restraint but, even more so, in attitudes toward contraception. The virtuous women condemned contraception. It was believed to draw attention to female sexuality and thus to work against the taming of men through virtue: "Contraceptive practices were so reprehensible precisely because they separated sexual activity from procreation, thus enabling the male to indulge all his lusts while free of the responsibility of rearing children. . . . Contraception would turn woman into a 'slave to her husband's desires'" (Rothman 1978: 82). In short, the sexual dimension of woman was at odds with her fertility dimension; and, indeed, female sexuality could be justified only in terms of motherhood. We can trace this antagonism between female sexuality and fertility back to the Christian Mary/Eve problem, in which, as we saw earlier, Eve was depicted as the sexual temptress in contrast to Mary, the *Virgin* Mother.

The idea of the virtuous woman encompasses what has elsewhere been referred to as the "cult of domesticity" for this period (Bonvillain 1995: 154). According to this "cult," men and women are innately different and so properly perform very different activities in different spheres, with men outside at work and women inside at home. Women as nurturing caretakers are needed to balance the competitive, aggressive, stressful world of male providers. Husbands need the home, with a wife inside it, as a retreat from this stressful outside world (Bonvillain 1995: 155). These two separate worlds—one male, individualistic, and competitive, the other female, caring, and altruistic—are to be "bridged by love" (Coontz 1992: 59). Yet Coontz sees this love as tainted, given that wives in the late nineteenth century were, after all, economically dependent on husbands. Thus, she says, a wife's "giving" nature was suspect, which had a rather dismal impact on husband-wife relationships: "Men were uneasily aware of the material considerations that contaminated a wife's gift giving and altruism; that is why men's greatest veneration of female self-sacrifice was often reserved for mothers and why deference to mothers has historically been compatible with contempt for other women" (Coontz 1992: 55).

While women's proper place was in the home, the virtuous woman was not actually confined to it. On the contrary, she was expected to take her virtue outside to society and so reform it (Rothman 1978: 63). Indeed, middle-class women of this period were active in reform-minded social clubs and temperance movements. And within these they built strong female friendships and solidarities.

Gradually, according to Rothman (1978), the ideal of the virtuous woman shifted to include a notion of "educated motherhood." Benevolent childrearing came to be seen as too important to be left to a woman untrained for it. Thus the way was opened not only to innumerable books and manuals on childrearing but also to something truly new and potentially transformative: the value of a college education for women. Women's colleges opened and were justified on the basis not of freeing women from domesticity or preparing them for careers but of enhancing their capabilities as mothers. Needless to say, though women in 1900 may have been studying art, music, and home economics in these colleges, the seeds of more fundamental change were planted.

Later, around the 1920s, there was another and more radical shift to the "wife-companion." According to this ideal, a woman's tie to her husband was her most important relationship. But instead of the virtuous nurturer she had been in the past, she was now to be a romantic, sexual partner. As Rothman (1978: 177) puts it, women "moved from the nursery to the bedroom." As for premarital sex, a minor sexual revolution was involved since women were now encouraged to loosen their sexual restraints (without going all the way to sexual intercourse) in order to attract a husband. Rothman notes that these new ideas and ideals grew among young people on college campuses, many of which had become co-educational. Moreover, according to Rothman, sociologists were encouraging the shift toward the wife-companion ideal, claiming that the American family was in crisis because it had lost its solidarity with the demise of home-based production and the rise of industrialization. The way to bring the family back together was romantic love and marital sexuality. This solution was considerably advanced by campus sororities, which became training grounds for wife-companions and offered courtship opportunities as well.

Women were now supposed to be beautiful and exciting and to maintain these characteristics not only in courtship but throughout marriage. The cosmetics industry boomed, and the advertising industry put out a new message: "Advertisements that once had presented full-bosomed mothers holding their babies and proclaiming the sanitary marvels of a particular soap gave way to pictures of slim and attractive young girls praising deodorizing qualities of the product" (Rothman 1978: 185).

As women's sexual dimension came to the fore, their fertility dimension receded, as seen not only in advertisements but also in the dramatic shift in attitudes toward birth control. Birth control was embraced as a device to liberate marital sexuality and to prevent pregnancy and children from interfering in the romantic love of the husband and wife. Women were now focused on securing and keeping *the* man in their lives, and their concerns with both motherhood and their female friendships were sacrificed to this end.

The wife-companion ideal was set aside in the emergencies of the Depression and World War II, only to reemerge and flourish in the 1950s. During the war many women had entered the work force while men were away on military duty. But upon the men's return, women left or were pushed out of the workplace and the ideal of the wife-companion began anew.

As noted earlier, restrictions on the premarital sexual behavior of women were somewhat relaxed in the 1920s. This was true of the postwar period as well. Romantic love was now the basis for marriage, and parental control over spouse selection had become a thing of the past. Young people found one another, engaged in courtship, and got married.

It was also during these postwar years that a curious and distinctively American precourtship ritual developed (or, more precisely, was revived from the 1920s). This phenomenon, best seen from an outsider's perspective, was described by British anthropologist Geoffrey Gorer. Upon visiting the United States, he reported on an odd media program:

> Pairs of young service men, chosen from the audience, had to compete . . . for the favors of invisible models, the model making her choice on the basis of a couple minutes' . . . conversation, herself saying just enough to keep the conversation going. The winners spent an evening together at the Stork Club at the sponsor's expense. . . . The exhibitionist fervor with which the competitors put over their "lines," with a considerable part of the United States listening in, was extremely revealing. (Gorer 1948: 118)

This was not the televised *Dating Game* of later decades; the year was 1943, and Gorer was listening to a radio program called *Blind Date*. He had discovered the peculiar American institution of dating, about which he made a number of interesting observations. For openers, he was quite correct in observing that "no other society has been recorded which has developed a similar institutionalized type of behavior for its young people" (1948: 110).

The point of American dating, as Gorer noted, is not to provide opportunities for premarital sexual experimentation. Rather, in American dating, "sensual and sexual satisfactions may play a part (though this is by no means necessary) as counters in the game, but they are not the object of the exercise; the object of the exercise is enhanced self-esteem, assurance that one is lovable and therefore a success" (1948: 110). Indeed, Gorer saw American dating as comparable to a game. Usually the male initiates the "date" by inviting the female to some public place of food or entertainment. As the two converse, he gives out "lines."

> The object of the "line" is to entertain, amuse, and captivate the girl, but there is no deep emotional involvement. . . . [T]he girl's skill consists in parrying the "line" without discouraging her partner or becoming emotionally involved herself. To the extent that she falls for the "line" she is a loser in this intricate game; but if she discourages her partner so much that he doesn't request a subsequent "date" in the near future she is equally a loser. (Gorer 1948: 116)

In this game, a male "scores" when "he is able to get more favors from the girl than his rivals, real or supposed, would be able to do" (Gorer 1948: 116). But it is not his intention to attempt seduction; an "easy lay" would be disappointing, "too easy a victory," and definitely not a good date.

Both males and females reaped their real rewards not so much during the date as after it, in intense discussions about the date with their respective same-sex peers. Here their self-esteem was truly on the line. The male sought to prove to his peers that he was able to secure a date with a popular girl and to extract more favors from her than others had managed. The female wished to show her peers that she was popular and worthy of attention from males (as measured, for example, by the number of requests for dates she received and the amount of money males spent on her), but without being an "easy lay."

The American dating game seems to have been harmless enough. Yet one has to wonder about the "lines" and the parries, the bantering, frivolous, deceptive male-female communication into which the participants poured so much time and energy between adolescence and marriage. What male-female hostilities and mistrusts were being built up in the minds of these participants? Did the youth of the postwar generation gradually outgrow this way of relating, or did aspects of these gendered dating discourses spill over into marital life? For that matter, why, as Gorer might have asked, were American youth in such desperate need of self-esteem in the first place? Why were they reduced to seeking it in the form of female popularity with males and male scoring with females?

Gorer himself located many American peculiarities in childrearing practices. Americans, he felt, tried to raise a child to be independent and self-reliant in order to set the child on the ideal American path, "to go further and fare better than his parents" (1948: 71). From birth, children were pushed to demonstrate their independent achievements, their "success." And, indeed, success brought signs of love, particularly in the form of attention. But then the child came to confuse love with success and, at the same time, to crave attention as a sign of worth: "By adolescence most Americans have inextricably confused the two ideas: to be successful is to be loved, to be loved is to be successful. . . . [T]he child becomes insatiable for signs of love, reassuring it that it is worthy of love, and therefore a success" (1948: 106–107). This insatiability was then carried over into the heterosexual interactions of adolescence and beyond. Attention from the opposite sex and recognition of this attention by same-sex peers were all wrapped up in the dating game, becoming ploys by which to enhance and maintain self-esteem.

There is another important question: To what extent is this dating game still going on? No doubt its rituals have changed, and sexual restrictions are, if anything, more relaxed. Nevertheless, as Dorothy Holland and Margaret Eisenhart's (1990) recent study of women on two U.S. college campuses suggests, many women college students, whatever their previous ambitions, still quickly fall into a consuming "culture of romance." On the campuses of their study, the prestige of men comes from their attractiveness to women *and* their success in other areas of life; but "women's prestige and correlated attractiveness comes *only* from the attention they receive from men" (Holland and Eisenhart 1990: 104; original emphasis).

In Gorer's time, participants in the dating game went on to marriages based on romantic love, within which women strove to become the ideal wife-companions discussed by Rothman. Some look back to this postwar period as the Golden Age of the American family, a time when what Coontz (1992) refers to as the 1950s "Leave It to Beaver" family prevailed. A thoroughly middle-class phenomenon, this was a nuclear family that had moved to the suburbs, where it eventually owned its own home. The father-husband went off to work and functioned as the "breadwinner." The full-time wife-mother stayed at home, absorbed in domestic efficiency, wife-companionship, and childrearing. According to this particular ideal, the father, though busy at work, had an active family life too. The family was very private, and its members spent quality time together; all were happy and had a lot of good, clean middle-class fun.

256   *A History of Euro-American Kinship and Gender*

But Coontz suggests that this 1950s family is largely a myth; it represents American nostalgia for a recreated past, not a solid American tradition. For one thing, she contends, this ideal family was never a reality for the majority of Americans and certainly not for groups such as blacks and the poor. Some families maintained a facade of this ideal on the outside, but inside were wracked by alcoholic parents and abusive relationships. And women of this time were excluded from so many fields and suffered so many financial restrictions (e.g., not being allowed to take out credit cards in their own names) that "there were not many permissible alternatives to baking brownies [or] experimenting with new canned soups" (Coontz 1992: 32).

Many women were not happy with their isolated, domestic roles or their full economic dependence on their husbands. Of the same period Rothman (1978) writes that the wife-companion became lonely in suburbia and saw that her identity was encompassed by that of her husband and children. Everything she did was for others, not herself.

Even for those few Americans who had anything like the ideal 1950s family, this outcome, according to Coontz, was a historical fluke. It is true that, with the end of the war and relief at its end, the age of marriage dropped, fertility rose, divorce declined, and the middle class moved to the suburbs. But the 1950s family with its nonworking wives and affordable homes emerged only because of America's brief postwar prosperity. Within a short span of time the American dream was no longer affordable and middle-class women went out to work.

Indeed, women's participation in the labor force increased then and has been increasing ever since. Today, a majority of working-age women and of women with young children are in the work force. This increase among working women was as much a function of economic necessity as a response to the doldrums of housework. But once begun it may have played a role in inciting the feminist movements of the 1960s and 1970s. Rothman (1978: 231) describes this development in terms of the shift from the wife-companion ideal to that of the "woman as person":

> This was a view of woman as autonomous, energetic, and competent. Woman was not to be defined by her household role, by her responsibilities as wife or mother; she was in no way to be limited by any special gender characteristics. This new definition of womanhood emphasized the similarities between the sexes, not the differences. It rendered the notion of special protection outmoded and irrelevant. In brief, woman as person was fully capable of defining and acting in her own best interest.

But no sooner had the "woman as person" emerged to lead another sexual revolution and to battle sexual discrimination of all kinds than a new problem developed. Whereas female fertility (motherhood) had previously been at odds with female sexuality, it was now at odds with female personhood.

This dichotomy has been expressed in innumerable debates and discussions about the conflict between the perception of women as autonomous *persons* in the work force and the perception of women as mothers. Once again, the different dimensions of American womanhood are split up and at war with one another, leaving many women at war with themselves.

Where are we now? The last few decades in America have seen much turmoil over gender and the family. This turmoil springs not merely from nostalgia for the past, however mythical, nor merely from a rising concern over family "breakdown" and wife abuse; rather, it has to do with contested and sometimes sharply conflicting attempts to define gender identities in relation to issues of kinship and reproduction. Delving to the heart of this issue, Faye Ginsburg (1989) analyzes the current dynamics of kinship, family, and gender in American culture by focusing on the abortion debate. She shows how this debate and its connections with gender identity have grown out of the current challenges facing women as mothers, as domestic caregivers, and as female participants in the work force.

Ginsburg studied women activists, pro-choice as well as pro-life, in the midwestern town of Fargo, North Dakota. Here she found that both groups, through their activism and debate with one another, are trying to define what it means to be a woman in America. Individual women in these movements are formulating and asserting their own feminine identity within those meanings.

By the media, and especially by national-level debates on abortion, we are led to imagine that pro-life women activists are ultraconservative, New Right, religious fundamentalists. Not so in Fargo, or in many other towns across the country. In Fargo, pro-life activists, like the pro-choice ones, span a diversity of political and religious views, though most are white and middle class. What holds the pro-lifers together is not conservatism but rather a concern that abortion is anti-woman. Their position is that "woman" should represent those very values that American culture has so dangerously let go—namely, nurturance, unselfishness, a caring concern for dependents, and meaningful ties between kin and community members. To advance these values, they wish to *preserve* the one thing that differentiates women from men: the fact that for women sexual behavior may result in pregnancy and birth. In their view, legalized abortion simply severs sex from reproduction and so makes women more like men. In the process, legalized abortion devalues motherhood. It feeds right into the dominant "male" trends in our troubled society—materialism, selfishness, and the dehumanizing aspects of our market-value, capitalist society. In essence, then, these pro-life activists are criticizing America for its irresponsible sexual behavior, its devaluation of dependent people (e.g., the sick, the elderly), and its "instrumentality in human relations" (Ginsburg 1989: 9). In addition, they believe that legal abortion only weakens women's position because it encourages men to be even more irresponsible in their sexual behavior and less willing to support the potential consequences. These pro-lifers in some ways resemble the late-nineteenth-century reformist women who argued against birth control. They, too, see reproductive issues as bound up with larger social problems and, by taking a stand on reproduction, seek to reform the larger society. Indeed, like their precursors they see women as essentially different from men and men (though not quite the "savage beasts" of the nineteenth century) as in need of the civilizing influence of women.

Like the pro-lifers, the pro-choice advocates of Fargo feel that their position helps women and is best for the larger society. Many of these pro-choice women also support kin ties, family values, and nurturing, though they do not necessarily see these domains as intrinsically female in nature. Instead, they promote gender equality in all domains and believe that women's interests are best served when sex can be severed from reproduction. Legal abortion, they argue, is "an essential safeguard against the differential effects of pregnancy on men and women;" it gives women "the power to control whether, when, and with whom they will have children" (Ginsburg 1989: 7). For them, abortion is part of a larger struggle for gender equality in America.

Thus the two groups are radically opposed on the question of abortion and hold different perspectives on the essential nature of men and women. Yet they share a concern for helping women and improving society. Ginsburg found that women became activists in one group rather than the other largely due to their own personal experiences with reproductive and other crises in their lives. The way that these crises were resolved in the particular social, generational, and life-history context of each woman led her to adopt one or another position on abortion. But the significant point is that it is through abortion activism (whether pro or con) that the women of Fargo are seeking to define the nature of womanhood and their own identity as women. One group considers it beneficial for women to be more like men and sees abortion as one of several ways to give women equal chances with men, or to prevent discrimination against women. The other seeks to preserve the differences between the sexes and to save both men and women from the dehumanizing consequences of fully severing sex and reproduction. It is a debate that clearly reflects the conflicting perception of women as autonomous persons (like men) versus women as mothers and guardians of domestic caregiving and nurturance. It is as though American womanhood, throughout a long span of history, has been continually split up into incompatible parts.

While the abortion debate continues in Fargo and across the country, yet another reproductive challenge has emerged. This one even more deeply rattles our cultural constructions of gender, kinship, and the family. It not only severs sex from reproduction in novel ways, but also severs biological or genetic reproduction from gestation and birth. The challenge I refer to concerns the New Reproductive Technologies and their implications for kinship and gender, the topic to which we now turn.

References

Bonvillain, Nancy. 1995. *Women and Men: Cultural Constructions of Gender*. Englewood Cliffs: Prentice Hall.

Boserup, Ester. 1970. *Women's Role in Economic Development*. New York: St. Martin's.

Brettell, Caroline B. 1991. Property, Kinship and Gender: A Mediterranean Perspective. In David I. Kertzer and Richard P. Saller, eds., *The Family in Italy from Antiquity to the Present*, pp. 340–353. New Haven: Yale University Press.

Clark, Gillian. 1993. *Women in Late Antiquity: Pagan and Christian Lifestyles*. Oxford: Clarendon Press.

Coontz, Stephanie. 1988. *The Social Origins of Private Life: A History of American Families 1600–1900*. New York: Verso.

_____. 1992. *The Way We Never Were: American Families and the Nostalgia Trap*. New York: Basic Books.

Cott, Nancy F. 1976. Eighteenth-Century Family and Social Life Revealed in Massachusetts Divorce Records. *Journal of Social History* 10(1): 20–43.

di Leonardo, Micaela. 1984. *The Varieties of Ethnic Experience: Kinship, Class, and Gender Among California Italian-Americans*. Ithaca: Cornell University Press.

Fox, Robin. 1993. *Reproduction and Succession: Studies in Anthropology, Law and Society*. New Brunswick: Transaction Publishers.

Ginsburg, Faye D. 1989. *Contested Lives: The Abortion Debate in an American Community*. Berkeley: University of California Press.

Goody, Jack. 1972. The Evolution of the Family. In Peter Laslett and Richard Wall, eds., *Household and Family in Past Time*, pp. 103–124. Cambridge: Cambridge University Press.

_____. 1973. Bridewealth and Dowry in Africa and Eurasia. In Jack Goody and S. J. Tambiah, *Bridewealth and Dowry*, pp. 1–58. Cambridge: Cambridge University Press.

_____. 1976. *Production and Reproduction: A Comparative Study of the Domestic Domain*. Cambridge: Cambridge University Press.

_____. 1983. *The Development of the Family and Marriage in Europe*. Cambridge: Cambridge University Press.

_____. 1993. *The Oriental, the Ancient and the Primitive: Systems of Marriage and the Family in the Pre-industrial Societies of Eurasia*. Cambridge: Cambridge University Press.

Gorer, Geoffrey. 1948. *The American People: A Study in National Character*. New York: W. W. Norton.

Gottlieb, Beatrice. 1993. *The Family in the Western World from the Black Death to the Industrial Age*. New York: Oxford University Press.

Gutman, Herbert G. 1984. Afro-American Kinship Before and After Emancipation in North America. In Hans Medick and David Warren Sabean, eds., *Interest and Emotion*. Cambridge: Cambridge University Press.

Hajnal, J. 1965. European Marriage Patterns in Perspective. In D. V. Glass and D.E.C. Eversley, eds., *Population in History: Essays in Historical Demography*, pp. 101–143. London: Edward Arnold Publishers.

Hareven, Tamara K. 1977. Introduction. In Tamara K. Harevan, ed., *Family and Kin in Urban Communities, 1700–1930*, pp. 1–15. New York: New Viewpoints.

Herlihy, David. 1962. Land, Family and Women in Continental Europe, 710–1200. *Traditio* 18: 89–120.

_____. 1971. Women in Medieval Society. The Smith History Lecture, University of St. Thomas, Houston, Texas.

_____. 1985. *Medieval Households*. Cambridge: Harvard University Press.

Holland, Dorothy C., and Margaret A. Eisenhart. 1990. *Educated in Romance: Women, Achievement and College Culture*. Chicago: University of Chicago Press.

Hughes, Diane Owen. 1978. From Brideprice to Dowry in Mediterranean Europe. *Journal of Family History* 3: 262–296.

Hunt, Morton. 1994. *The Natural History of Love*. New York: Anchor Books/ Doubleday.

McNamara, Jo Ann, and Suzanne Wemple. 1988. The Power of Women Through the Family in Medieval Europe, 500–1100. In Mary Erler and Maryanne Kowaleski, eds., *Women and Power in the Middle Ages*, pp. 83–101. Athens: University of Georgia Press.

Molloy, Maureen. 1990. Considered Affinity: Kinship, Marriage and Social Class in New France, 1640–1729. *Social Science History* 14(1): 2–26.

Ortner, Sherry B. 1978. The Virgin and the State. *Feminist Studies* 4(3): 19–35.

_____. 1981. Gender and Sexuality in Hierarchical Societies: The Case of Polynesia and Some Comparative Implications. In Sherry B. Ortner and Harriett Whitehead, eds., *Sexual Meanings: The Cultural Construction of Gender and Sexuality*. Cambridge: Cambridge University Press.

Rothman, Sheila M. 1978. *Woman's Proper Place: A History of Changing Ideas and Practices, 1870 to the Present*. New York: Basic Books.

Saller, Richard P. 1991. European Family History and Roman Law. *Continuity and Change* 6(3): 335–346.

Schlegel, Alice. 1991. Status, Property and the Value on Virginity. *American Ethnologist* 18(4): 735–750.

Stack, Carol B. 1974. *All Our Kin: Strategies for Survival in a Black Community*. New York: Harper and Row.

Stone, Linda, and Caroline James. 1995. Dowry, Bride-Burning and Female Power in India. *Women's Studies International Forum* 18(2): 125–134.

Verdery, Katherine. 1988. A Comment on Goody's Development of the Family and Marriage in Europe. *Journal of Family History* 13(2): 265–270.

Verdon, Michel. 1988. Virgins and Widows: European Kinship and Early Christianity. *Man* 23: 488–505.

Wemple, Suzanne Fonay. 1981. *Women in Frankish Society: Marriage and the Cloister*. Philadelphia: University of Pennsylvania Press.

Williams, Marty Newman, and Anne Echols. 1994. *Between Pit and Pedestal: Women in the Middle Ages*. Princeton: Markus Wiener Publishers.

Yanagisako, Sylvia Junko. 1987. Mixed Metaphors: Native and Anthropological Models of Gender and Kinship Domains. In Jane Fishburne Collier and Sylvia Junko Yanagisako, eds., *Gender and Kinship: Essays Toward a Unified Analysis*, pp. 86–118. Stanford: Stanford University Press.

8

Kinship, Gender, and the New Reproductive Technologies: The Beginning of the End?

"Home, home—a few small rooms, stiflingly overinhabited by a man, by a periodically teeming woman, by a rabble of boys and girls of all ages. No air, no space; an understerilized prison. . . . Psychically, it was a rabbit hole, a midden, hot with the frictions of tightly packed life. . . . What suffocating intimacies, what dangerous, insane, obscene relationships between the members of the family group! Maniacally, the mother brooded over her children . . . brooded over them like a cat over its kittens; but a cat that could talk, a cat that could say, 'My baby, my baby' over and over again" (Huxley 1946 [orig. 1932]: 24). This passage from Huxley's science fiction novel, *Brave New World,* gives a society's comment on its past, a despicable past when humans reproduced their own offspring and lived in families. In this brave new world reproduction is entirely state-controlled and carried out in test tubes and incubators. There is no kinship whatsoever in this new society. There is also no marriage. Women and men are equally expected to be sexually promiscuous, and sex is solely for pleasure. But apart from this, rather amazingly, there are few changes in gender. Women of the brave new world appear passive and fluffy-headed. Men apparently run the new society and hold all the prestigious or powerful jobs. In real life, meanwhile, new modes of reproduction are very definitely challenging conventions of both gender and kinship, as this chapter will show.

In 1978 the first "test-tube" baby, Louise Brown, was produced in England. Human conception had taken place inside a petri dish, outside the womb, and without sexual intercourse. By now, thousands of babies have been created in this way. About a decade after Louise Brown was born, we began to see cases of "surrogate" mothers and complex legal battles over the fate of their children. In 1987 Mary Beth Whitehead sought custody of a child, the famous Baby M, whom she had borne through a surrogacy contract. She had agreed to bear a child for William Stern, using his "donor" sperm. Stern's wife, Elizabeth, felt that because she had a mild case of multiple sclerosis, a pregnancy would be too great a risk to her health. The case went through two New Jersey courts. Both awarded custody of Baby M to Stern, although the higher court ruled that the surrogacy contract was invalid.

Surrounded by controversy, these and other New Reproductive Technologies (NRTs) have raised thorny legal and moral issues. They also present a challenge to our deepest ideas and values concerning kinship, and carry profound implications for gender. What are these NRTs, how do they work, and what implications do they have? In this chapter I discuss the new technologies and trace their overall impact.

The New Reproductive Technologies

Reproductive technologies, as such, are not new. Various forms of contraception, abortion, fertility-enhancing concoctions, cesarean surgery, and so on have existed for a long time. As far as I know, every human culture in the world offers local techniques for assisting conception as well as some methods of contraception, effective or not. But the NRTs go beyond promoting or preventing conception, or inducing or ending pregnancy. Some, for instance, provide knowledge about particular reproductive acts, knowledge that humans have never had before. Other NRTs open up new reproductive roles that humans have never played before. What follows is a listing of the new technologies along with explanations of how they work. The first two are technologies that give us new—and, in some contexts, problematic—knowledge.

Determining Biological Fatherhood

Throughout most of human history biological motherhood was taken for granted, but an equivalent "paternal certainty" did not exist. Then, around 1900, some techniques were developed that were capable of specifying, with certainty, who could *not* have fathered a particular child. Thus these tests could *exclude* individuals from a group of potential fathers but could not determine which particular individual was the actual father. The most common test performed back then was based on the well-known ABO blood group system. All humans are phenotypically either A, B, AB, or O. The A phenotype corresponds to an $I^A I^A$ or $I^A I^O$ genotype; B corresponds to an $I^B I^B$ or $I^B I^O$ genotype; AB is always $I^A I^B$; and O is always $I^O I^O$. Let us assume that a child belongs to the A blood group and that its mother is in the O group. This means that the mother is $I^O I^O$ and the child is either $I^A I^A$

or $I^A I^O$. We know that this child could not possibly have inherited the I^A gene from the mother and, therefore, that the I^A gene had to have come from the father. Let us then assume that a particular man is thought to be the father and that the mother is suing him for child support. The ABO blood test is performed and the man is found to belong to the B group. In other words, the man's genotype is $I^B I^B$ or $I^B I^O$, meaning that he could not have contributed the I^A gene. This man could not possibly be the father, and he is *excluded*.

But even if the suspected man turns out to belong to the A blood group (making it possible for him to have contributed an I^A gene), he is not proven to be the biological father. Indeed, since the whole human population is subdivided into only four blood groups, hundreds of millions of men can be found in each category. But obviously not all A-type men should be suspected, as it would be impossible for the mother to have had sexual intercourse with hundreds of millions of men from all over the planet.

The new so-called DNA fingerprinting technique has considerably altered this situation. The technique relies on amplifying portions of human DNA in a test tube using the polymerase chain reaction (PCR) and identifying DNA fragments based on restriction fragment length polymorphism (RFLP). DNA can be isolated easily from a small quantity of blood taken from the individual in question. The general principle here is that human individuals differ in their DNA in many subtle ways and that no two individuals (except identical twins) have exactly the same DNA patterns. The PCR and RFLP techniques are capable of discerning these subtle variations and thus can provide a genetic (DNA-based) "fingerprint" of an individual that *corresponds to that individual only*, to the exclusion of all others. Genetic fingerprinting is now widely used to determine paternity with a very high degree of certainty, up to 99.99 percent or better. It has also been used to trace the parentage of orphans whose parents were killed and buried in known locales during wars. Under proper conditions, DNA can survive, even in bones, for thousands of years. Had DNA fingerprinting existed during the life of Anastasia, who claimed to be the sole surviving daughter of Tzar Nicholas II, her bluff would have been uncovered at the time. Recently, DNA analysis applied to bone material showed that Anastasia was indeed an impostor.

Determining biological fatherhood may be of great interest or advantage to many individuals in a variety of situations. But what are the broader implications of the fact that this determination can now be made so easily, and so "scientifically"? Many people have argued that paternity *un*certainty in many ways shaped human culture around the globe. They suggest that a whole host of practices in different regions of the world—having to do with female seclusion, restrictions on female behavior, medieval chastity belts, and so on—were all predicated on the principle of paternity uncertainty.

But such uncertainty is now a thing of the past. We do not yet know what the long-term consequences of this may be for women or men.

As noted in Chapter 6, the polyandrous Nyinba are very concerned with biological fatherhood. But culturally they have constructed a rather efficient and normally satisfying way of designating paternity to husbands. Wives simply announce which husband is the father of a given child, even though in some cases this could not have been "scientifically" known; or husbands and wives together determine which brother the child most closely resembles. The process of designating paternity gives women a lot of power and, in cases of successful marriages, serves to equitably distribute children to husbands. But what will happen to this system when "real" paternity can be easily and quickly determined through a simple blood test? Will it bring discord between brothers? Will it result in the loss of power and influence for women? And what will happen to women in societies where the accepted punishment for proven infidelity is severe beating or death?

Determining the Sex of the Unborn Child

Sex determination techniques are by-products of a technology first developed to screen for genetic defects. These defects are detectable at the chromosomal level. The basic procedure involves harvesting fetal cells *in utero* (from inside the uterus), preparing their chromosomes, and looking at them under a microscope. The resulting chromosome spread is called a **karyotype,** and the process of characterizing chromosomes from an individual is called karyotyping. It turned out to be the case that, while karyotyping chromosomes to detect for genetic defects, technicians found it also very easy to see what sex the fetus was going to be. Karyotyping readily identifies the sex of the fetus since the Y chromosome (unique to males) is very small whereas X is large.

Two techniques are used to sample fetal cells. One is **amniocentesis,** the process of inserting a needle into the uterus (through the abdomen) and harvesting fluid from the amniotic sac that surrounds the fetus. Fetal skin cells are normally shed into this fluid. Usually only a few cells are present in the fluid, so it has to be cultured *in vitro* (i.e., in an artificial environment outside the living organism) to allow for cell manipulation. These cells are then karyotyped. Amniocentesis cannot be applied before the twelfth week of pregnancy since sufficient amniotic fluid is not present until that time.

The other technique, **chorionic villus sampling,** is less invasive because the abdomen is not punctured. In this case, a sample of **chorion** is taken by introducing a tube through the vagina into the uterus. The chorion is fetal tissue that lines the uterine cavity and surrounds the amniotic sac. Since this tissue is abundant, no cell culture is necessary and karyotyping can be done right away. There is enough chorion to allow the procedure as early as the eighth week of pregnancy.

In societies that do not express a cultural preference for male or female children, a couple's knowledge of the sex of a fetus is without much consequence. But, as we have seen, there are some societies that strongly prefer male children. In India, for example, amniocentesis is a major social issue. When the test became available, female fetuses were aborted at a very high rate. Many women underwent amniocentesis, either voluntarily or at the insistence of husbands and in-laws, with the idea that their pregnancy would be terminated unless the fetus was male. Many Indian women's organizations have fought to protect women and unborn females from this abuse. In some Indian states amniocentesis is now illegal (except in cases where genetic defects are an issue), but the test is still widely used illegally.

In the United States amniocentesis is a common procedure used to detect genetic defects. Rayna Rapp's (1990) study of amniocentesis in New York City showed that this test carries cultural meanings that vary among the people involved in it. Biomedical personnel discuss amniocentesis using an abstract, authoritative, impersonal language that contrasts sharply with the personal, emotional discourse of many women undergoing, or refusing to undergo, the test. Rapp also found that women talked about amniocentesis in ways that varied according to their class and ethnic backgrounds. For example, compared with others, white middle-class women spoke about amniocentesis in much the same way that biomedical personnel did, supporting a positive image of science assisting reproduction. Yet the same women spoke about their experiences with great ambivalence and self-criticism, especially when tests indicated a genetic defect and thus brought up the issue of abortion. Rapp's study relates these and other findings to the changing constructions of womanhood and motherhood among the diverse groups of women who consider technological reproductive interventions.

Artificial Insemination and In Vitro Fertilization

Certain NRTs are used in cases of infertility of an individual or a couple. In males, infertility is usually caused by either sperm defect (low count or immotile sperm cells) or impotence (physiological or psychological). In females, the situation is more complicated. A woman may be sterile, meaning that she is unable to conceive a child, due to absence of ovulation (either no eggs are produced or the egg cannot travel through fallopian tubes that are blocked). However, a sterile woman may still be able to carry and bear a child. Another problem is that a woman may be fertile (i.e., able to conceive a child), but the fertilized egg fails to become implanted in her uterus. Some reproductive problems can be corrected by surgery, drugs, or, in some cases of male impotence, psychotherapy. But if these treatments do not work, there are two other procedures that can allow an individual or couple to have a child. These procedures are **artificial insemination (AI)** and **in vitro fertilization (IVF)**.

Artificial insemination can be used when a couple seeks to have a child but the male is infertile. In this case the biological father may be an anonymous sperm donor whose sperm is stored in a sperm bank. The sperm bank categorizes sperm according to the physical characteristics of the donors (skin, eye and hair color, height and general body features) so that the future parents can roughly determine the looks of their offspring. For example, the parents may seek a child who will look something like its legal father.

Artificial insemination is a simple technique. Donor sperm is simply placed into the uterus of the female at the proper stage of her menstrual cycle. Nature does the rest. Artificial insemination has long been routinely used in animal husbandry to ensure production of animals with desired characteristics. Its average cost ranges from $200 to $400, and its success rate is about 30 percent if fresh sperm is used and about 15 percent if frozen sperm is used.

Artificial insemination can also be used by women who seek pregnancy without sexual intercourse. For example, a single woman may wish to have a child without involvement of the biological father beyond anonymous sperm donation. Or a woman may wish to serve as a "surrogate" mother for a married couple who cannot have a child of its own due to the wife's infertility. In this case the surrogate is artificially inseminated with the husband's sperm. The sperm donor is obviously not anonymous, but sexual intercourse between the husband and the surrogate is unnecessary.

The technique of in vitro fertilization (IVF) is much more complicated and expensive (about $25,000); it also has a lower success rate than AI with fresh sperm (about 14 percent). It was developed for humans in the late 1970s. In this case, **oocytes** (immature eggs) are surgically removed from the ovaries of a woman and incubated with sperm in a sterile petri dish in the presence of a nutrient medium. After fertilization occurs, the embryo is allowed to undergo cell division for a few days. The embryo is then removed from the dish and implanted into the uterus of a woman, where, if all goes well, it will grow to term.

Usually, several oocytes are removed, fertilized in vitro at the same time, and implanted together. Often only one embryo, or none, will continue to develop. However, cases of multiple birth have occurred. Excess embryos resulting from IVF and not implanted can be frozen and used at a subsequent time, even many years later. One current problem concerns the fate of all the frozen embryos now in existence and the question of who has rights over them. In the United States alone there are tens of thousands of frozen embryos; and throughout the world, hundreds of thousands.

With both IVF and AI, the biological father can also be the would-be legal father of the child, or the biological father may be a sperm donor. With AI, too, one woman may be the legal mother while another woman is the biological mother. But with IVF, something altogether new happens to "motherhood." The woman who contributes the oocytes *may or may not be* the woman who carries the child and gives birth. Once the eggs of one woman are fertilized outside the womb, they may be implanted back either into her or into another woman. This is an important point to which we will return later.

Table 8.1 summarizes the different forms of AI and IVF, and shows what options are available depending on the reproductive problem involved. Note that the "father" (F) is designated as either fertile or sterile, whereas the "mother" (M) may exhibit different combinations of sterility (unable to conceive) or fertility, and be either able or unable to bear a child. The table indicates the circumstances under which a couple would need a "donor" egg, sperm, or womb. It also shows what genetic connection the child will have with either or both parents, given the various options. In preparing this table I have assumed that it is a couple, rather than an individual, who is seeking a child; that to the extent possible the couple seeks to have a child genetically related to at least one of its members; and that, if possible, the mother seeks to give birth. In real life, some alternative possibilities may also exist. For example, in case 1 of the table, the mother cannot conceive

TABLE 8.1   NRTs: Contributions of Egg, Sperm, and Womb, with Genetic Outcomes

| | Donation Needed | | | | |
Problem	Egg	Sperm	Womb	Technique	Genetic Result
1. F fertile, M sterile but can bear child	X			IVF	child = 1/2 F
2. F fertile, M sterile and cannot bear child	X		X	AI	child = 1/2 F
3. F fertile, M fertile but cannot bear child			X	IVF	child = 1/2 F + 1/2 M
4. F sterile, M sterile but can bear child	X	X		IVF	child = 0% parents
5. F sterile, M fertile and can bear child		X		AI	child = 1/2 M
6. F sterile, M fertile but cannot bear child		X	X	IVF	child = 1/2 M

Note: F stands for Father; and M, for Mother.

but can bear a child. Although the table specifies the use of IVF, an actual couple in this situation might elect to avoid the expense and trouble of IVF and use AI instead (as in case 5).

The table also shows three different circumstances under which a so-called surrogate mother might be used, along with the different outcomes involved. In case 2 the surrogate not only carries the child but is the genetic mother, whereas the father is also genetically contributing to the child. In case 3 the surrogate has no genetic relation to the child, and the child is the genetic product of both of the parents. Finally, in case 6, the surrogate has no genetic connection to the child, and the child is genetically related to only one parent, the mother.

As this table clearly shows, IVF can be used to assist reproduction in a greater variety of situations than AI. At the same time, however, it is more problematic than AI. For one thing it is not always safe for women. Depending on her particular role in the process, a participating woman may have to take fertility drugs, some with possible side effects. If she is using or donating her eggs, these must be removed from her through invasive laparoscopy; and if the IVF procedure fails to result in fertilized eggs, it must be performed again. Some women argue that the real beneficiaries of IVF are the highly paid medical professionals who exploit the desperation of childless couples and offer them false hope (Raymond 1993). Based on her own experience, one woman asserted that IVF programs encourage couples to seek their identity in genetic reproduction rather than considering other options for their lives. As she put it: "I look back in amazement at the person I was, traversing the country from one IVF program to another, in search of an infertility 'fix.' . . . I found IVF an extremely arduous, life-dominating experience, involving some eight unsuccessful attempts" (Bartholet 1992: 254).

Some Additional NRTs

Among the NRTs available, a few are not widely used as yet but may become more prevalent in the future. One, called **embryo adoption**, would apply to the situation of case 1 in Table 8.1. Here, the mother cannot conceive but can bear a child. Instead of using IVF with donor eggs, the husband could artificially inseminate another woman who serves as a very temporary surrogate. After a week, the embryo is flushed out of the surrogate's uterus and inserted into the uterus of the mother. Another type of reproductive technology is called **oocyte freezing**, a procedure in which oocytes, or eggs, are taken from a woman and frozen for later use. So far this procedure has not proven very successful; but if perfected, it could open a whole range of reproductive options. For example, a woman could freeze her oocytes when she is young and healthy and use them later in life when her fertility would otherwise be lower. Technically, she could use them even past menopause. Alternatively, a much older woman could take oocytes donated by a young women. These could be thawed, fertilized in IVF, and then implanted in the older woman. Already one woman aged fifty-nine has given birth through oocyte donation. Some people are repulsed by the image of very old women giving birth or becoming mothers. Others point out that men have all along been able to reproduce at any age.

Social, Legal, and Moral Implications

NRTs are becoming available just when other options for reproduction seem to be diminishing. Fewer children are now available for adoption both because effective contraception has decreased unwanted births and because a more accepting social climate has allowed more single women to keep their children. At the same time, natural fertility has been decreasing—at least in the United States, where about one in six couples suffers some fertility problem. The sperm count of the American male has fallen by 30 percent over the last fifty years and continues to decline (Blank 1990: 13–14), possibly due to environmental pollution. Female fertility is also decreasing.

Although NRTs clearly assist the infertile, they are also bringing about some new kinds of social relationships. Some ramifications of these technologies are easy to imagine—and many of these have already occurred. For example, through the use of frozen embryos, two genetic twins could be—and, indeed, have been—born years apart. By means of the same technology, a woman could give birth to her own genetic twin, or to her own genetic aunt or uncle. In 1991, a forty-two-year-old woman in South Dakota, Arlette, gave birth to twins who are her genetic grandchildren. Her own daughter could not bear a child, but she and her husband desperately wanted children. Through IVF, the daughter's eggs were fertilized with the husband's sperm, and later the pre-embryos were implanted into Arlette's uterus. Another woman, Bonny, donated an egg for her infertile sister, Vicki. Bonny's egg was fertilized with the sperm of Vicki's husband and implanted into Vicki's uterus. A male child, Anthony, was born. In this case the genetic mother, Bonny, is a social aunt; her sister, Vicki, gave birth to Anthony who is her social son but her genetic nephew. Even more disconcerting, through the use of frozen embryos it is also possible for dead people to reproduce.

As confusing as these and other cases may be, they have had some happy results, at least for those couples blessed with children they desperately desired. Usually all of the participants in the making of a baby fully agree about its social and legal status. But as we know from the many cases covered in the media, this does not always happen. Baby M was just one such case. Other problems have emerged with the use of frozen embryos. In a famous case of 1989, *Davis v. Davis,* a Tennessee couple attempted IVF because Mrs. Davis was able to conceive but could not bear a child. Nine eggs were fertilized. Two were implanted, unsuccessfully, in Mrs. Davis' uterus, and the remaining seven were frozen for a later try. But then the couple divorced. They went to court over the fate of these embryos. Mrs. Davis wanted to have them implanted, but Mr. Davis wanted them destroyed. He argued that he had a right *not* to be a father. In the end, Mrs. Davis remarried and requested that the embryos be donated to some other infertile couple. Thus the case was resolved; but it opened the difficult question: Who should have rights over frozen embryos? Or, for that matter, should frozen embryos have any rights, protected by the law? In another interesting case from Australia, a woman's eggs were fertilized in IVF by an anonymous donor. One of these was unsuccessfully implanted in the woman and the other two were frozen. This woman and her husband then died in a plane crash. It turned out that the couple left a sizable fortune. Should the embryos have rights of inheritance? This was a question that troubled the couple's adult children. Even more pressing, morally speaking, are the larger questions of whether frozen embryos should have rights to be born, or who should decide if, when, and under what circumstances human embryos are to be donated to medical research. Should frozen embryos even be produced in the first place? Certainly, embryo freezing is a useful NRT for infertile couples; and in the case of IVF, a woman is spared repeated laparoscopies through the option of freezing the extra embryos produced the first time. But is embryo freezing a form of irresponsible reproduction? What kind of society, with what views of human life, are we constructing? How should we even think about frozen embryos? Sarah Franklyn (1995: 337) argues that the frozen embryo straddles the boundary between science and nature, giving it an ambivalent status such that its identity and meaning will be contested:

> The embryo is a cyborg entity; its coming into being is both organic and technological. Though it is fully human (for what else can it be?) it is born of science, inhabits the timeless ice land of liquid-nitrogen storage tanks. . . . At once potential research material (scientific object), quasi-citizen (it has legal rights) and potential person (human subject), the embryo has a cyborg liminality in its contested location between science and nature.

Moral and legal difficulties also surround the practice of surrogacy, particularly "contract" or "commercial" surrogacy. This form of surrogacy, though permitted in the United States, is illegal in most countries that have laws regulating the NRTs (Blank 1990: 157). Some people have severely censured surrogates, calling them "baby sellers." Others have merely wondered what sort of woman would contract to carry a baby for another woman or couple. Surrogates typically receive a fee of about $10,000 for their service. Yet most surrogates insist that they do it not for the money but because they're genuinely motivated to provide a child to an infertile couple. Apparently some women also enjoy the experience of pregnancy and seek to experience it again after they have had all the children they want for themselves. Helena Ragoné's (1994) study of surrogate motherhood in America shows how the surrogate role gives women confidence and a sense of self-importance and worth. These women, she says, are adding meaning to their lives by going beyond the confines of their own domestic situations or their unrewarding jobs to do something vital for others.

Other studies have shown that surrogates are usually not poor women in desperate need of cash but, rather, working-class women. According to Ragoné's (1994: 54) study, the personal income of unmarried surrogates ranged from $16,000 to $24,000, and the average household income of married surrogates was $38,000. Still, in the context of surrogacy the issue of social class and economic inequality is easily raised. The couple seeking a surrogate is generally wealthy, at least wealthy enough to be able to afford a surrogate plus the other expenses ($20,000 or more) that they will pay to doctors and a fertility clinic. But surrogates, though not poor, are not of this privileged social class. They may feel rewarded by the attention, care, gifts, and positive social treatment they receive from the couples they are assisting (Ragoné 1994: 64–66). Is this all well and good, or is contract surrogacy enmeshed in a new type of class exploitation?

In a discussion of surrogacy, Sarah Boone (1994) invokes both racial and class inequality by drawing some disturbing cultural parallels between contemporary surrogate motherhood and the former practice of slavery in America. Boone describes black slave women as "bottom women" in the gender and racial hierarchy of earlier American society, a hierarchy that placed white males on top, followed by white females and black males. One measure of the "bottom" status of black slave women was wide sexual access to them, for in their position in slave society white male slaveholders could easily exploit them sexually. In addition, black women were themselves considered property and had no legal rights to their children. Meanwhile, "the white woman as top woman became the physically delicate asexual mother/wife, subordinate helpmate" (Boone 1994: 355). Boone asks whether the surrogate mother is another kind of "bottom woman," one whose status is measured not by sexual access to her but by reproductive access to her body: After all, "CCM [commercialized contract motherhood] allows men and privileged women to purchase or rent the gestational capacities of other women in order to produce a genetic heir" (Boone 1994: 358).

A new "top woman" thus emerges here too, but she is still a wife and the member of a privileged class. Yet this is a "top woman" with a new twist:

"Now a career woman in her own right but naturally drawn to mother-hood, she is fully appropriate for the more refined roles of genetic contributor and rearer of children," whereas the "bottom woman" surrogate is given "the 'unrefined' work of gestation and childbearing for men and more privileged women who are incapable or unwilling to do this work" (Boone 1994: 358). We may argue that, unlike slave women, surrogates choose their "work" and, as we have seen, are not poor or disadvantaged persons. Still, Boone's observations suggest that surrogacy occurs not in a vacuum but in a sociocultural context where it is inseparable from issues of gender and social inequality.

Moral concerns, debates, and controversies rage on over the NRTs. But it is on kinship and gender that these new technologies may yet have their greatest impact.

Kinship and Gender

We have already seen how the use of frozen embryos confounds some conventional notions of kinship relation. Is the woman who gives birth to her genetic uncle his niece or his mother? What happens to our kinship system when the boundaries of our core concepts of "kin," set long ago by our ancestors and taken for granted for so many centuries, are blurred? Even more jolting, perhaps, is the fragmentation of motherhood that results from the technological ability to separate conception from birth and eggs from wombs. Robert Snowden and his colleagues (1983: 34) claim that, with the advent of NRTs, we now need a total of ten different terms to cover the concepts of "mother" and "father." The terms they propose are as follows:

1. Genetic mother
2. Carrying mother
3. Nurturing mother
4. Complete mother
5. Genetic/carrying mother
6. Genetic/nurturing mother
7. Carrying/nurturing mother
8. Genetic father
9. Nurturing father
10. Complete father

The first three terms cover the distinct stages of conception, gestation, and care for a child. These three aspects of motherhood can be carried out by one, two, or three different women. If one woman does all three, she is the "complete" mother. Note that a child could conceivably have five different persons as "parents" in this system (1–3 as mothers and 8 and 9 as fathers), even without including stepparents (Blank 1990: 10). But it is really only motherhood that has fragmented as a result of the NRTs, since we have long been accustomed to the idea that a child can have one man as its "genetic" or "biological" father and another as its "nurturing" (or perhaps a better word here might be "legal") father. Similarly, we are familiar with the idea that "legal" or "nurturing" mothers can be different from "natural" or "biological" mothers. What is new is the division of biological motherhood into two parts: conception and gestation.

In comparison to our society, a people like the Nuer (Case 1) would perhaps have had different conceptual problems with kinship in relation to the NRTs. For them, legal rights to children were held by fathers (and their patrilineal kin groups), not by mothers. Also, these rights were clearly established by cattle payments, not by concerns with biological fatherhood. Recall that Nuer culture constructed kinship such that children belonged to fathers, defined as the men who paid bridewealth for the mothers.

In American society, however, ideas about kinship have been based on cultural notions of biology (Schneider 1968). Americans have strongly defined "real" parenthood as biologically based. And they have taken for granted that this way of thinking about kinship is in line with "science." But now science itself has thrown a wrench into the American system of kinship by showing that unitary "natural" motherhood is actually divisible. In the courts and in our own minds we thus face the challenge of reconstructing motherhood and, hence, reconstructing kinship. Will we need to devise a nonbiologically based definition of the *mater* as the Nuer have done for the *pater?* Marilyn Strathern (1995) discusses how the NRTs challenge Euro-American notions of "nature" itself as well as fundamental ideas about what constitutes personal "identity."

We do not know what the future may bring. But what seems to be happening at present is that those involved with the NRTs are not discarding the old American ideas about kinship but, on the contrary, are making every effort to preserve the cultural notions of "real" biological parenthood. Toward this end, they are reinterpreting the NRTs and their tricky implications so as to reconcile them with these core cultural notions of biological parenthood and the resulting American family ideal. This process has played out in two very interesting contexts.

One context concerns lesbian couples. Those seeking to have children and to become a family in the conventional sense have of course benefited by the NRTs. At a minimum, one member of the couple may become impregnated with donor sperm. Corinne Hayden's (1995) study of American lesbian couples shows that some lesbian couples with children are constructing something truly new in kinship: double motherhood. They are raising their children to perceive that they have two mothers. One way to support this perception is to have the children call both of them "mother."

Another way is to hyphenate the co-mothers' names to form the children's surname. In short, these couples seek to raise their children in an environment of parental equality—a process that, in their view, constitutes a true challenge and alternative to the conventional husband-dominant household of broader American society. Of course, the creation of equal, dual motherhood is confounded by the fact that only one woman can be the biological mother. Even if the lesbian couple themselves perceive their motherhood to be equal, the surrounding society, and courts of law, may not.

In trying to create new forms of kinship and family, lesbian couples are not so much rejecting biology as a basis for kinship as making use of the NRTs to bring their situation into line with biologically based kinship. For example, they may strive for a more equitable double motherhood by getting pregnant by the same donor. In this way, each partner becomes a mother, their children are born genetically related to one another, and they all more closely resemble a family in the conventional American sense. Another possibility is for one woman to be artificially inseminated using the sperm of the other woman's brother. Each woman would then have some genetic relation, as well as a conventional kinship relation, to the child. Even more creative is what Hayden (1995: 55) refers to as the "obvious and 'perfect' option for lesbian families: one woman could contribute the genetic material, and her partner could become the gestational/birth mother." Thus even the idea that homosexual unions are "inherently non-procreative" (Hayden 1995: 56) is challenged, now that a woman can give birth to the genetic child of her female partner. Going a step further, a lesbian couple could combine the last two options: One woman could contribute an egg to be fertilized by the brother (or, for that matter, son) of her lesbian partner, after which the egg would be implanted in her partner.

The other context in which efforts are being made to reconcile the NRTs with core cultural notions, especially American ideas about kinship, concerns surrogate motherhood. As Ragoné (1994: 109) concluded from her study of surrogate mothers in America, "Programs, surrogates and couples highlight those aspects of surrogacy that are most consistent with American kinship ideology, deemphasizing those aspects that are not congruent with this ideology. Thus, although the means of achieving relatedness may have changed, the rigorous emphasis on the family and on the biogenetic basis of American kinship remains essentially unchanged." One way in which surrogates and their couples maintain this emphasis is to downplay the relationship between the husband and the surrogate in cases where the surrogate has been impregnated with the husband's sperm. Indeed, since the surrogate is carrying the husband's (and her) child, there are disturbing parallels with adultery. In some surrogate programs the relationship that is given priority and becomes strong is that between the surrogate and the wife. This arrangement is obviously more comfortable for the surrogate; it also allows the wife to feel that she is participating in the process of creating the child. In addition, the wife, or the adoptive mother, in such cases may emphasize her role in the creation of the child as one of intention, choice, and love: "One adoptive mother . . . described it as conception in the heart, that is, the belief that in the final analysis it was her desire to have a child that brought the surrogate arrangement into being and therefore produced a child" (Ragoné 1994: 126).

The NRTs have spurred debates among women in general and feminists in particular over how these technologies are affecting women and relations between the sexes. Some feminists approve of the NRTs precisely because they fragment motherhood and in many ways distance women from "nature" and "natural" reproduction. Their argument is that women have been trapped by their reproductive roles, that their lower status has been due all along to their entrenchment in reproduction and motherhood. According to this view, the NRTs not only expand reproductive choices for individual women and men but can help to liberate women from the inferior status that their biological roles have given them. Other feminists have argued that the legal use of NRTs supports women's right to control their own bodies. They also approve of contract surrogacy because it allows a surrogate to use her body as she wishes for her own economic benefit.

Yet another argument is that the NRTs are potentially good for women but need to be subjected to proper controls and approached with caution (Purdy 1994). Thus, for example, regulations should be implemented to ensure that surrogate mothers retain control of their pregnancies and, by extension, that contracting fathers not be given rights to say how a surrogate should behave while pregnant, to decide whether she should have a cesarean, to sue her for miscarriage, and so on. With such controls in place, according to this argument, contract pregnancy can considerably benefit infertile women or women with high-risk pregnancies. As for accusations of "baby selling" by surrogate mothers, those taking this position raise an important question: Why are there no parallel objections against the payments made to men who donate their sperm? Laura Purdy (1994: 316) also questions the view that "women can be respected for altruistic and socially useful actions only when they receive no monetary compensation, whereas men—physicians, scientists, politicians—can be both honored and well paid."

Perhaps the strongest feminist criticism of the NRTs has come from Janice Raymond (1993). In her book, *Women As Wombs*, Raymond describes the NRTs as a form of "violence against women": Since a male-dominant "medical fundamentalism" defines both the problem (infertility) and the cure (the NRTs), application of the new techniques entails "appropriation of the female body by male scientific experts" (1993: xx). Raymond argues directly against the position that NRTs liberate women by freeing them from their previous reproductive roles. On the contrary, she says, the fragmentation of motherhood, the conceptual wedge that the NRTs place between a woman and a fetus, results in the loss of women's control over reproduction. When the fetus is seen as so separable from a woman, the fetus itself becomes the focus of attention, and, in the process, male rights over reproduction are increased: "Reproductive technologies and contracts augment the rights of fetuses and would-be fathers while challenging the one right that women have historically retained some vestige of—mother-right" (Raymond 1993: xi).

Raymond notes that in the case of Baby M, even though William Stern and Mary Beth Whitehead were equally the genetic parents and Whitehead was also the birth mother, Stern was continually referred to in the media as "the father" whereas Whitehead was always "the surrogate." The courts also awarded custody to Stern. About this situation Raymond (1993: 34) wrote: "A woman who gestates the fetus, experiences a nine-month pregnancy, and gives birth to the child is rendered a 'substitute' mother. On the other hand, popping sperm into a jar is 'real' fatherhood, legally equivalent, if not superior, to the contribution of egg, gestation, labor, and birth that is part of any woman's pregnancy."

Of course, one could retort that the genetic/birth mother in the Baby M case did sign a surrogacy contract, thus bringing about the whole trouble in the first place. But Raymond's point is that the NRTs are changing our society's perceptions of motherhood and fatherhood, conceptually and legally, and that women may be losing out in the process. Legally speaking, what Raymond (1993: 30) calls "ejaculatory fatherhood" does appear to be gaining ground—in part, perhaps, because ideas about biological fatherhood have not been fundamentally changed by the NRTs whereas ideas about motherhood most definitely have been. In the American biogenetic ideology of kinship, fatherhood is still simple, but motherhood is no longer so.

And what of future reproductive technologies? Cloning and the growing of a fetus outside a uterus may be a long way off. Much closer, and possibly far more radical in terms of the implications for gender, is male pregnancy. As Blank (1990: 29) notes, "There is increasing evidence that the embryo might be transferred to the abdominal cavity of a male, thus enabling male pregnancy. The birth of a baby from a New Zealand woman who had no uterus, and successful male procreation in other species, contribute to the expectation that IVF will soon permit human male pregnancies."

Continuities

In this book we have examined a variety of ways in which kinship and gender are culturally constructed and interrelated. This analysis has involved us in discussions of sexuality and reproduction, and of the interests of many people and groups in exercising control over women's reproductive capacities. We have seen cases, specifically among the Nuer and the Nyinba, in which female sexuality is largely unrestricted but cultural rules allocate a woman's children to her legal husband or husbands and their kinship groups. And among the matrilineal Nayar, female sexuality is unrestrained (except for sexual intercourse before the tali-tying ceremony and at any time with a lower-class man) but children are allocated to a woman's own kinship corporation under the leadership of her senior matrilineal kinsmen. In all three societies, female sexuality and female fertility are separate social concerns.

We have also seen cases in which a woman's sexuality is, or was, ideally restricted to one man, her husband: Examples include the Nepalese Brahmans, the ancient Romans, and early Europeans and Americans. In these societies, a woman's "inappropriate" sexual behavior (premarital sex or adultery) could result in devaluation of her person, dishonor to her family, and, among the Nepalese Brahmans, devaluation of the woman's future fertility. The Nayar, sharing some of the Hindu caste ideas related to female purity and pollution, also showed this connection between female sexuality and fertility, inasmuch as sex with a lower-caste man would expel a woman and her future children from her caste and kin group. In all of these Eurasian cases we have seen that the concern with female sexual "purity" is interwoven with concerns over property and its transmission, as well as with the maintenance of class and caste divisions; in other words, they are bound up with larger issues of socioeconomic inequality.

Many of the cases discussed in this book have dealt with male-led kin groups seeking control over women's reproduction. We have also seen a few cases where a woman's reproduction was not of much concern to larger groups of kin. Among the Navajo, for instance, although a woman reproduces for her own and her husband's matriclans, clan continuity is not a strong concern. Navajo culture venerates women for their reproductive powers, but it does not punish women for childlessness. Another group, the early Christians in Europe, valued celibacy over reproduction and held that sexuality was equally unspiritual for women and men. As noted, one historian argued that early Christian women found in Christianity a welcome liberation from both marriage and reproduction.

By and large, white, middle-class Euro-American women have not had to contend with the interests of kin groups in their reproduction, nor have they been under pressure to reproduce for anyone but themselves and their partners. Furthermore, over the centuries, restrictions on their sexuality have relaxed. Yet, paradoxically, these Euro-American women have expressed problems and tensions of their own in the process of trying to reconcile their sexuality, fertility, and personhood in a meaningful and satisfying way.

With the emergence of the NRTs, we cannot fail to ask ourselves who we will become, as women, as men, as persons, and as kin. But this is not a new question. All human groups throughout history have continually constructed kinship and gender, seeking meaning and identity within these cultural constructions. And along the way, the constructions themselves have been contested between men and women, young and old, powerful and powerless. Now, as we face the development of new (and newer) reproductive technologies, the struggle continues. In this way, perhaps the NRTs are not taking us into a brave new world so much as dealing out new cards in an older dynamic human game of self, kin, and gender definition.

References

Bartholet, Elizabeth. 1994. In Vitro Fertilization: The Construction of Infertility and of Parenting. In Helen Bequaert Holmes, ed., *Issues in Reproductive Technology*, pp. 253–260. New York: New York University Press.

Blank, Robert H. 1990. *Regulating Reproduction*. New York: Columbia University Press.

Boone, Sarah S. 1994. Slavery and Contract Motherhood: A "Racialized" Objection to the Autonomy Argument. In Helen Bequaert Holmes, ed., *Issues in Reproductive Technology*, pp. 349–366. New York: New York University Press.

Franklyn, Sarah. 1995. Postmodern Procreation: A Cultural Account of Assisted Reproduction. In Faye D. Ginsburg and Rayna Rapp, eds., *Conceiving the New World Order: The Global Politics of Reproduction*, pp. 323–345. Berkeley: University of California Press.

Hayden, Corinne P. 1995. Gender, Genetics, and Generation: Reformulating Biology in Lesbian Kinship. *Cultural Anthropology* 10(1): 41–63.

Huxley, Aldous. 1946 [orig. 1932]. *Brave New World*. New York: Bantam Books

Purdy, Laura M. 1994. Another Look at Contract Pregnancy. In Helen Bequaert Holmes, ed., *Issues in Reproductive Technology*, pp. 303–320. New York: New York University Press.

Ragoné, Helena. 1994. *Surrogate Motherhood: Conception in the Heart*. Boulder: Westview Press.

Raymond, Janice G. 1993. Women As Wombs: *Reproductive Technologies and the Battle over Women's Freedom*. San Francisco: Harper San Francisco.

Schneider, David M. 1968. *American Kinship: A Cultural Account*. Englewood Cliffs: Prentice-Hall.

Snowden, Robert, G. D. Mitchell, and E. M. Snowden. 1983. *Artificial Reproduction*. London: Allen and Unwin.

Strathern, Marilyn. 1995. Displacing Knowledge: Technology and the Consequences for Kinship. In Faye D. Ginsburg and Rayna Rapp, eds., *Conceiving the New World Order: The Global Politics of Reproduction*, pp. 346–363. Berkeley: University of California Press.

Glossary

affinal related through marriage.

age-set a lifelong affiliation of similar-aged persons who pass through various life stages together as a unit; age-sets are characteristic of East African pastoral societies.

altruistic acts individual behaviors that enhance others' reproductive success while simultaneously reducing one's own.

ambilocal referring to a postmarital residence pattern in which a married couple can choose to live with or near the kin of either the groom or the bride.

amniocentesis a procedure for drawing a sample of amniotic fluid from a pregnant woman by inserting a needle into the uterus; the results provide genetic information about the fetus.

artificial insemination (AI) a process of placing donor sperm into the vaginal cavity of a female at the proper stage of her menstrual cycle in an attempt to achieve pregnancy.

avunculocal referring to a postmarital residence pattern in which a married couple moves to or near the household of the groom's mother's brother(s).

bilateral kinship the recognition of kin connections through both parents; virtually all societies exhibit bilateral kinship.

bilateral society a society that traces kin connections over the generations through both males and females, but without the formation of descent groups.

bridewealth the transfer of wealth from the kin of the groom to the kin of the bride at marriage.

chorion fetal tissue that lines the uterine cavity and surrounds the amniotic sac.

chorionic villus sampling a technique for retrieving chorionic cells from the uterine cavity by introducing a tube into the uterus through the vagina.

clan a group or category of people who claim to share descent through a common ancestor, but whose genealogical links with one another are obscured and no longer traceable; the common ancestor of the group is often a mythical figure.

class endogamy marriage within a given social class.

cognatic descent descent based on any combination of male or female links.

consanguineal related through descent (or "blood" ties).

corporate group a group of people who collectively share rights, privileges, and liabilities.

cross cousins the children of two opposite-sex siblings.

descent group a kin group based on descent (patrilineal, matrilineal, or cognatic).

domestic group people who live together and share resources for their subsistence.

double descent the existence in one society of both matrilineal and patrilineal descent groups; each person simultaneously belongs to two descent groups.

dowry wealth that accompanies a bride to her marriage.

embryo adoption the result of artificial insemination achieved by using the uterus of a surrogate, from which the embryo is then flushed and inserted into the uterus of the mother-to-be.

endogamy marriage inside a certain social group or category.

exogamy marriage outside a certain social group or category.

fitness reproductive success; the more fertile offspring a person has, the greater his or her fitness is considered to be.

fraternal polyandry a marriage union in which two or more brothers share one wife.

genitor the biological father of a child.

ghost marriage the practice whereby a patrilineal kinsman takes a wife in the name of a deceased man in order to have children by the woman in that man's name.

hominid a Family-level classification that includes modern humans and their extinct ancestors.

hominoid a Superfamily-level classification of primates that includes apes and humans.

hypergamy marriage of a woman upward into a higher-status group.

inclusive fitness the process whereby an individual enhances his or her reproductive success through altruistic acts that favor the fitness of others who share some genes in common with that individual, as in the case of close relatives.

in vitro fertilization (IVF) the process of incubating oocytes with sperm in a petri dish to produce a fertilized embryo.

karyotype a chromosome spread prepared for microscopic examination.

kindred a set of relatives traced to a particular ego.

kin selection the process whereby natural selection acts on inclusive fitness.

levirate the practice whereby a man marries the widow of his deceased brother.

lineage a group of people who trace their descent to a common ancestor through known links.

matrilineage a group of people who can trace descent from a common ancestor through female links and who can trace the links among themselves.

matrilineal descent descent based on links through females only.

matrilocal referring to a postmarital residence pattern in which a married couple lives in the household or place of the bride's kin; also called *uxorilocal*.

monogamy marriage between two persons, generally a man and a woman.

mother-in-law avoidance an interaction between a man and his wife's mother characterized by respectful restraint.

multimale, multifemale units groupings of primates that consist of numerous males living and mating with numerous females.

natolocal referring to a postmarital residence pattern in which husbands and wives reside with their own respective natal groups and so do not live together.

neolocal referring to a postmarital residence pattern in which a married couple moves to a new location, living with the kin of neither the groom nor the bride.

nonfraternal polyandry a marriage union in which one woman has two or more husbands who are not brothers.

one-male units primate units in which one adult male lives and mates with several females.

oocytes immature eggs.

oocyte freezing the process of taking oocytes from a woman's uterus and then freezing them for later use.

parallel cousins the children of two same-sex siblings.

parental investment the contributions of parents to the fitness of their offspring.

pater the legal father of a child.

patrilineage a group of people who can trace descent from a common ancestor through male links and who can trace the links among themselves.

patrilineal descent descent traced through males only.

patrilocal referring to a postmarital residence pattern in which a married couple lives in the household or place of the groom's kin; also called *virilocal*.

phratries groupings of two or more clans.

polyandry marriage of one woman to two or more men at the same time.

polygyny marriage of a man to two or more women at the same time.

postmarital residence the location in which a newly married couple will reside.

primogeniture a pattern of inheritance in which only the eldest son receives a patrimony.

sexual dimorphism the external physical differences between males and females.

sexual selection the process by which one sex (usually male) competes for sexual access to the other sex.

sororal polygyny a marriage of two or more sisters to one man.

sororate the practice whereby a man marries the sister of his deceased wife.

totemism the symbolic identification of a group of people with a particular plant, animal, or object.

unilineal descent descent traced through only one sex, as in the case of matrilineal or patrilineal descent.

woman-woman marriage the marriage of a barren woman (who counts as a "husband") to another woman; a genitor is arranged for the "wife," and the barren woman becomes the legal father of the children.

About the Book and Author

This undergraduate textbook uses anthropological kinship as a framework for the cross-cultural study of gender. Connecting kinship with gender, Linda Stone focuses on human reproduction and the social and cultural implications of male and female reproductive roles. Her insightful narrative introduces new ways of approaching and understanding cross-cultural variations.

Stone provides coverage of the field of kinship at the introductory level, but she also explores the major issues and debates in the study of the interrelation of gender and culture. The book reviews studies of primate kinship, considers ideas about the evolution of human kinship, and looks at kinship and gender in relation to different modes of descent, as illustrated by seven in-depth ethnographic case studies. Stone examines marriage through case studies of marriage in ancient Rome and Himalayan polyandry and offers a history of Euro-American kinship and gender, as well as an examination of the repercussions of the New Reproductive Technologies on both kinship and gender.

Linda Stone is associate professor of anthropology at Washington State University.

Index